Praise for David W. Cameron

'David Cameron not only leads the way for books on Australia in World War I he sets a standard for authors to emulate . . . A fine work of military and social history.' *The Australian* on *The Battle for Lone Pine*

'We now have a powerfully written and well-illustrated book that focuses on this tragic action.' *Sydney Morning Herald* on *The Battle for Lone Pine*

'A riveting read.' *Daily Telegraph* on *The Battle for Lone Pine*

'A vivid picture of the hair-raising charge.' *The Age* on *The Charge*

'Brings the archives alive to tell the soldiers' stories in ways that do not sacrifice accuracy for accessibility.' *Weekend Australian* on *Gallipoli: The Final Battles and the Evacuation of Anzac*

'Cameron has honoured the veterans by telling their stories.' *Australian Defence Magazine* on *The Battle of Long Tan*

Also by David W. Cameron

Convict Era Port Arthur: 'Misery of the deepest dye'

Australians on the Western Front 1918 Volume II: Spearheading the Great British Offensive

Australians on the Western Front 1918 Volume I: Resisting the Great German Offensive

The Charge: The Australian Light Horse Victory at Beersheba

The Battle of Long Tan: Australia's Four Hours of Hell in Vietnam

Our Friend the Enemy: Anzac from Both Sides of the Wire

Shadows of Anzac: An Intimate History of Gallipoli

The Battle for Lone Pine: Four Days of Hell in the Heart of Gallipoli

Gallipoli: The Final Battles and the Evacuation of Anzac

'Sorry lads the order is to go': The August Offensive at Gallipoli

25 April 1915: The Day the Anzac Legend Was Born

Hominid Adaptations and Extinctions

Bones, Stones and Molecules: Out of Africa and Human Origins (with Colin Groves)

THE BATTLES FOR
KOKODA PLATEAU

Three weeks of hell defending the gateway
to the Owen Stanleys

DAVID W. CAMERON

ALLEN&UNWIN
SYDNEY · MELBOURNE · AUCKLAND · LONDON

First published in 2020

Copyright © David W. Cameron 2020

Allen & Unwin
83 Alexander Street
Crows Nest NSW 2065
Australia
Phone: (61 2) 8425 0100
Email: info@allenandunwin.com
Web: www.allenandunwin.com

A catalogue record for this book is available from the National Library of Australia

ISBN 978 1 76052 955 0

Internal design by Lisa White
Maps by MAPgraphics
Index by Garry Cousins
Set in 11.5/16 pt Minion by Post Pre-press Group, Australia
Printed and bound in Australia by SOS Print + Media

10 9 8 7 6 5 4 3 2

This book is dedicated to Emma, Anita, Lloyd
and little Naomi—love you

Contents

Part Three: The First Battle for Kokoda

Part Four: The Second Battle for Kokoda

Part Five: Lines of Escape

Maps

Prologue

The devastating Japanese bombing of the United States Pacific Fleet at Pearl Harbor on 7 December 1941 brought America and Japan into the Second World War, within days Nazi Germany foolishly declared war on the United States. It was now truly a world war. The Japanese invaded and conquered Malaya, the Philippines and Singapore. They were soon heading south towards Australia, but with no real intentions of invading the continent; they were, however, keen to occupy the island of New Guinea to its north to help isolate Australia and New Zealand from the United States. Not long after, additional Australian troops were sent to Port Moresby to help defend the island from any Japanese invasion.

Few if any seriously considered Port Moresby was in danger of attack from a Japanese force from its northern coast. This would require them to push south over the dense jungle of the Owen Stanley Range. All agreed this was an impossible task—even for the Japanese. Any enemy force landing to the north would likely have the objective of building airstrips for operations against Port Moresby and other targets within the region, like the operations they were now conducting at Lae and Salamaua in North-east New Guinea. The tortuous nature of the terrain separating the north and south coast—representing some of the most appalling terrain on earth—was considered an impossible obstacle even for small-scale military operations. That said, over the previous six months, the Japanese had shown repeatedly that they were capable of attacking an objective from an 'impossible' approach. Even so, few believed that the Japanese would attempt to capture Port

Moresby from the north using the only route available to them—the Kokoda Track.

Indeed, Major General Basil Morris commanding all Australian forces in New Guinea stated perceptively 'let us meet them on ground of our own choosing and as close as possible to our own base. Let us merely help their own supply problems to strangle them while reducing our supply difficulties to a minimum.'[1] However, on 21 July 1942 a large Japanese reconnaissance force landed in the vicinity of Gona along the north-eastern coastline of Papua at Basabua. Their objective was to capture the inland village of Kokoda and provide recommendations for future operations against Port Moresby via the 'road' that was thought to cut through the mountains. Within weeks this reconnaissance mission would turn into a full-blown attempt by the Japanese to take Port Moresby using the narrow and treacherous Kokoda Track, and the first critical objective after landing was to take Kokoda Plateau and its airstrip, which would provide a forward base for the operations against Port Moresby.

A small Australian militia force consisting of just one company of the 39th Battalion, supported by a small number of Papuans from the 1st Papuan Infantry Battalion (PIB) and the Royal Papuan Constabulary, defended the coast in the Gona–Buna area at the time of the Japanese invasion on 21 July 1942. After a week of intense fighting they were forced to retreat from the coastal lowlands towards the Kokoda Plateau. During the fighting these men were usually outnumbered by at least three to one, sometimes more. The Kokoda Plateau was the last significant defensive position on the northern lowlands, before entering the cloud-covered Owen Stanley Range. The Kokoda Plateau was the gateway to the mountains, and all agreed it had to be held at all costs, if only to deny the Japanese the use of its airstrip. With each passing day the Australians—now desperately short of ammunition and food, and stranded in the northern lowlands' fetid swamps and jungles—looked south for reinforcements. Could they hold the plateau and its airstrip, and if so, for how long?

•

As the battles raged, two Anglican missionary groups had managed to evade the Japanese since the day of the invasion. Both groups increased in size as lost Australian soldiers and downed American airmen joined them; all were trapped behind Japanese lines and for the next three weeks they attempted to break through to reach the Australians thought to be digging in on the Kokoda Plateau.

PART ONE

PREPARATIONS

1

'Lower, Sport'

In early 1942, the Japanese, having captured Singapore, were heading south towards Papua New Guinea. Just north of Papua is the island of New Britain and its deep-water harbour at Rabaul. This island was held by a single Australian battalion. Before the Japanese could launch an invasion against Papua, they needed to capture New Britain, and critically, its harbour.

The Australians garrisoning New Britain designated 'Lark Force' were part of the 8th Division, Second Australian Imperial Force (2nd AIF). These men had in 1940 signed up to fight the Germans and were by 1941 expecting to join their mates of the Australian 6th, 7th and 9th divisions fighting so gallantly in Greece, the Middle East and North Africa. However, they soon found themselves stationed in South-east Asia to help protect the region from an expected Japanese attack—they did not have long to wait. The 8th Division's brigades and battalions were soon fighting desperate battles to save Malaya, Singapore, New Britain, Ambon and Timor. Most of these men were either killed or forced to surrender to the Japanese. By February 1942 the 8th Division ceased to exist as a fighting force and was essentially struck from the Australian Army Order of Battle.[1]

Among the last to fall were the men of Lark Force. This force consisted of the 2/22nd Battalion from the 23rd Brigade.[i] These men were effectively forgotten—allowed to be slaughtered and captured by

---

i The 2/ indicates the 2/22nd was a battalion of the 2nd AIF (serving in the Second World War) differentiating it from its parent unit the original 22nd Battalion of the 1st AIF (serving in the Great War)—militia battalions such as the 39th Battalion were not part of the 2nd AIF and were not allocated this distinction.

the Japanese, with no real effort to support them in their struggle against overwhelming numbers. Of the 1400 men attached to Lark Force, fewer than 400 would escape to mainland New Guinea or Australia.[2]

Just before the inevitable Japanese invasion—numbering around 5500 troops—an enemy reconnaissance aircraft slammed into a mountain close to Rabaul while flying in low cloud cover, killing both airmen. The Japanese noted, after occupying the town, that these men had been buried with full military honours. As a result, Japanese soldier Nishimura Kokichi remembered an order being issued that all Australian prisoners were to be treated with similar respect. It was not to be. During the fighting for New Britain around 160 men of the 2/22nd Battalion—including several Australians with the New Guinea Volunteer Rifles (NGVR)—were captured about 80 kilometres south of Rabaul. They were soon after massacred at the neighbouring Tol and Waitavalo plantations—some tied to trees and used for bayonet practice, while others were taken away in small groups and bayoneted with their arms tied behind their backs. The 'lucky' few were shot. The victims of the massacre were simply covered with palm fronds and when Australian troops recaptured the area in April 1945, they discovered the exposed bones of 158 victims.[3]

•

One of the seven survivors of the massacre was Private William 'Billy' Cook of the 2/10 Field Ambulance who was bayoneted eleven times. He and seven of his mates were forced to surrender on 4 February 1942 after being surprised by the Japanese. It was not long before Cook noticed 'two Japs grinning, and one gave the impression of shooting the other. They looked at us and laughed and I realised that this meant that we were to be killed.'[4] It was not long before a Japanese officer came up and tore off their Red Cross armbands and cut off their identity discs. Cook turned to one of his mates, Raffles,[ii] and asked, 'What's on?'

---

ii   In telling his story, Cook provides no further details that might help identify Raffles. The author could find no records of anyone with the surname or given name 'Raffles' attached to the 2/22 Battalion or the 2/10 Field Ambulance; it is likely this was a nickname and the identity of this soldier unfortunately remains unknown.

'Don't know, pal,' was his reply, 'but I've got a fair idea.'

Cook then noticed that Raffles was about to spit at the Japanese officer as he was 'moving his mouth, developing spittle, but I nudged him, and he swallowed it'.[5]

They were marched to a plantation about 2 kilometres beyond Tol in the direction of Rabaul, where they were ordered, by signs, to sit down on a slight rise on the track which led from the road to the plantation. Cook recalled that one of his mates took a chance to escape but 'they smacked him with the butt of a rifle, breaking his jaw. I dropped my head between my knees and felt like vomiting. Raffles nudged me. "Head up, pal." I lifted my head'.[6] Cook saw Raffles moving his mouth again, but then 'I saw him swallow it. Sitting down as we were he couldn't have reached the Jap's face'.[7] The Japanese then began to take the men down the track in twos and threes. Cook recalled that the face of the first man to get up was 'very white and the muscles at the side of his mouth were quivering. But he just said, "See you in hell, fellers," and though his voice was high it didn't break. He went out of sight behind us down the rise into the plantation, followed by two of the Japs. "Christ, oh Christ." That was Raffles, muttering through tight lips, and further along two men were praying, distinctly and unashamedly'.[8]

The Japanese took more men down the track. The only ones to return were the guards. It was soon Raffles' turn and he turned to Cook: '"So long, boy. I'll see you at the bottom of the hill" . . . With my thumbs tied I couldn't shake hands with him. I just nodded. He winked at me, moving his mouth, then swung quickly and let the lot go straight into the face of the officer. He turned on his heel and the three of them walked down the hill behind me. The officer wiped his face with a handkerchief, cursing in a high shrill voice, then he ran down the slope and, in a moment, I heard three shots'.[9]

Cook recalled at this point, 'by two's and three's [sic] the rest were taken away—no noises, just the English word spoken by the Japs "Next", and the next group would stand up, say "Cheerio, fellows" and walk to their death—head erect and without a falter, truly a grim indication of these boys' guts'.[10] Soon Richard Buck and his brother Cecil, who had signed up together in Sydney with the 2/10 Field Ambulance, were taken away—they died together. It was now the turn of Billy Cook and two of his mates.[11]

The Japanese officer pointed to his revolver and then to the bayonet, seemingly to ask us what method we preferred to be killed—shot or stabbed. Needless-to-say, we wanted to be shot . . . we stood up and one of them said 'Well, Cookie, now we will know what the next world is like'.

We walked down a slight slope and could see to our left three Japs converging on us until we were about 50 yards from the water when they immediately lunged at us from behind with their bayonets. During the walk down, I could see the Nips plainly and could recognise the one who stabbed me even now—a big fellow, easily six feet tall, built in proportion and at least four gold teeth in the front of his upper jaw.

The first stab knocked us down. In my case the wound was in the back about level with the lower ribs. The Japs stood over us stabbing, each stab being accompanied by a snarling grunt. In all I received six wounds in the back—two just missing the spine, two more breaking ribs and the last two, one under the shoulder blades and the other sliding across the shoulder blade . . . my companions had not uttered a sound. I think that one of them must have died very quickly and the other lingered a short time because, when the Japs started to leave us, he groaned a little and one of the Japs returned and stabbed him again. I had been holding my breath and feigning death but could not hold it any longer. When I breathed again, I either made a noise or moved. Whether this made the Jap start on me again or whether it was a parting measure, I do not know but he stabbed me another four times in the neck and another through the ear which entered my face at the temple, severing the temporal artery, and the point of the blade finished in my mouth.

Each of the wounds which I received had not hurt a great deal except the last which grated across the cheek bone and, when he withdrew the bayonet, it lifted my head. Blood spurted from my mouth, he then covered the three of us with palm leaves and bushes, then left us.

I just lay there waiting to die and I heard two distant shots followed by a scattered volley of rifle shots which meant that the last two had been shot.

For a space of time I lay there—I don't know how long. Flies attracted by the pools of blood started to worry me and I heard a voice call to me. Although it was a voice in my imagination, this saved my life and I decided that I would die trying to get away rather than stay as I was. The idea of living to tell the tale did not enter my head.

The native loin cloth which tied me to my companions was my first obstacle but, after a little manoeuvring, I got the knot between my hands and managed to get it undone. This freed me from the others, but my thumbs were still tied.

I spoke to see if either of my mates had survived although I do not think I could have helped them much if they had and started walking towards the water. My legs were rubbery and could just support me and my head seemed a long way from my body. In the first few yards I had to step past the body of the first of the party to be killed. There was no bleeding evident and he was lying on his side. Several times I fell down and realised that I would have to free my hands to save myself from further injury. I collapsed and lost consciousness—for how long I do not know. When I came to, I tried to saw the cord binding my thumbs on the iron 'horseshoe' of my boot. I had often read about this method, but it failed in my case as my swollen thumbs got in the way.

Finally, after a lot of bending, I managed to work my hands down over one leg and so get them within reach of my teeth. I then chewed the cord until I was free. All this had started my wounds bleeding again and, when I started walking again, I suffered another 'black-out'.

After another unknown period, I walked to the water and waded out waist deep and let the saltwater wash my wounds. This caused a lot of pain, but it just had to be done. I realised my position—the Japs were between me and freedom ... Walking in the water to avoid leaving footprints and blood stains in the sand, I staggered along until I reached a patch of rocks where I could move without leaving marks and I crawled under a tree trunk and went to sleep.[12]

Bill Cook did not sleep long, and soon made his way into the jungle; coming across a path, he followed it reaching a small party of Australians. Among them was 52-year-old Lieutenant Colonel John Scanlan, who as a young lieutenant with the 7th Battalion on 25 April 1915 was lucky to survive the Gallipoli landings, stranded north of the main invasion force along North Beach. He survived Gallipoli to later command the 59th Battalion on the Western Front, playing a significant part in the Battle for Villers-Bretonneux on the night of 24–25 April 1918 and later at Mont St Quentin on 2 September, and then the attacks against the Hindenburg Outpost Line and the Hindenburg Line itself in late September and early October 1918.[13] He was now the commander of Lark Force. As Cook approached his CO, he asked if they 'had any dressings or antiseptics. Scanlan took my shirt which was caked with blood and gave me one of his.'[14]

Lance Corporal Clifford Marshall, a 31-year-old from Prahran in Victoria with the 2/22nd Battalion, was another of the survivors from the massacre: 'When my turn came, I was motioned to move off into the bush. There was a Japanese soldier walking behind me. I sort of turned, my hands being tied behind my back, to see what he was doing. I saw that he was making a rush at me with the bayonet. I received three wounds: one in the back just under the shoulder blade, not very deep, another through the arm into the side, and another into the side lower down. It came to me naturally to lie and sham dead. I could hear cries from the other men for a while and then a lot of shooting.'[15] Marshall later crawled into some undergrowth and worked his hands free. After dark he moved through the plantation and came across several of his mates—all dead. He staggered on alone in a state of shock. Within hours he came across a couple of other survivors in a similar traumatised state.[16]

Another who escaped was 38-year-old Private Alfred Robinson, a resident of Rabaul with the NGVR. He recalled, like Billy Cook, the Japanese took his pay book, papers and identity discs; he and his mates were then marched towards the plantation, guarded by soldiers with fixed bayonets, some carrying shovels: 'I decided this was a shooting party and if I was going to be shot, I might as well be shot trying to escape,' recalled Robinson. 'The line I was with happened not to be linked together and I was number two in the line. We made our own way through the plantation cover crop and came out on a track going through the plantation ... (at an 'S' bend in the track) ... I'd ducked out of the line and hid under a bush.'[17] While the vegetation here was lush, the man behind him noticed he could be seen and said as he passed 'Lower, Sport'.[18] With this, Robinson pushed deeper into the scrub and was not seen by the Japanese guards. With his hands still tied behind his back, he wandered through the jungle for the next three days before being found by civilians.[19]

•

After a month of additional hardships and further tragedies in trying to escape the Japanese, Bill Cook, Clifford Marshall, Alf Robinson, and the other four survivors of the massacre managed to escape from the island by ship and made their way back to mainland New Guinea and Australia. Their accounts would be used in war crimes trials conducted during and after the war.[20] Colonel John Scanlan, on hearing of the massacre from Cook, decided to stay and defend his men from any future Japanese atrocities as a prisoner of war. He would not return to Australia until 1946 after suffering four years of brutal Japanese captivity.

•

Major Bill Owen, a 37-year-old bank clerk from Kew in Victoria with movie-star good looks, who had commanded 'A' Company of the 2/22nd Battalion, was among the lucky few to escape from New Britain. His battalion confronted the Japanese landings at Rabaul against Vulcan Beach. After fighting for several hours, Owen, whose men faced the bulk of the Japanese during the initial landings, at odds of fifteen to one, ordered his men to fall back as they were about to be surrounded. He led his men around the coast and, along with other troops and civilians, was eventually rescued by the government steamer *Laurabada,* which two weeks later arrived in Port Moresby with 156 escapees. On returning to Australia, he was promoted to lieutenant colonel and quickly found himself on his way back to New Guinea to command the 39th Battalion. He would soon again be fighting Major General Horii Tomitarô and his men of the 144th Regiment, who were responsible for the murder of prisoners and civilians in New Britain, but this time he would not be so lucky.[21]

2

'The best of the local bunch'

The Japanese high command, having captured Rabaul and its harbour, were under no illusions that they needed a buffer to protect this key tactical asset in the South Pacific. The Australians still held Papua and, from there, they and the Americans could launch aerial strikes against the harbour, which was fast becoming a major strategic hub. Not only that, New Guinea provided a jumping-off point for any future Allied invasion of New Britain. If New Britain fell, then the Philippines would be vulnerable—the consequences did not bear thinking about. Indeed, New Guinea along with the Solomon Islands, Samoa, New Caledonia and Fiji were to be incorporated into a forward defence 'line' defining the Japanese Southern Resource Zone, which was to isolate Australia and New Zealand from the United States.[1]

The Japanese invasion force that was to capture Port Moresby along its southern coast was repulsed with the Allied naval victory at the battle of the Coral Sea in early May 1942. American general Douglas MacArthur, on arriving in Australia, having been ordered earlier by President Roosevelt to escape from the Philippines, was promoted to Supreme Commander of Allied Forces in the South West Pacific Area (SWPA). MacArthur made much of the so-called 'Brisbane-line' which was said to be an Australian plan to cede parts of northern Australia to the Japanese; however, the Japanese never seriously considered invading Australia and such talk of evacuating the north of the country was quickly howled down long before MacArthur arrived. However,

MacArthur and his acolytes did much to portray the false impression that it was MacArthur who turned the situation around from an Australian passive defence to an all-out American offensive strategy against the Japanese.[2] As succinctly stated by American historian Walter Borneman in his study of MacArthur and the war in the South Pacific:

> The concept of a Brisbane Line was relatively short-lived and never implemented. Frederick Shedden, Prime Minister Curtin's key civilian advisor on defence matters, asserted that MacArthur's reference to it 'was a flamboyant utterance' and that 'no such plan existed.' By the time MacArthur arrived in Australia, far from hunkering down in the southeast behind an imaginary line stretching southwestward from Brisbane, the Australian chiefs had begun to increase troops at Darwin from two brigades to a full division, at Perth and points along the western coast from one brigade to a division, and in and around Townsville, in [northern] Queensland, from one brigade to a division . . . the general movement was definitely northward.[3]

On 14 May 1942, MacArthur wrote to Australian Lieutenant General Thomas Blamey, a 58-year-old professional soldier from Victoria, that he wanted to establish several airfields in Papua to be used against Japanese forces that had recently captured Lae and Salamaua in Northeast New Guinea. Blamey, with MacArthur's promotion, had been appointed the commander of Allied Land Forces, SWPA. However, with the increasing number of American troops being fed into the SWPA, especially by early 1943, 'Blamey's command of the Allied Land Forces was to be more in name than fact' with MacArthur and his staff calling the shots, although Blamey would remain Commander-in-Chief of Australian Military Forces.[4]

The 62-year-old American warlord wanted to know whether Blamey had enough troops to protect the proposed airfields and bases in Papua. In early May Blamey had ordered the Australian 14th Brigade to Port Moresby to reinforce the Australian 30th Brigade that was already based there—both brigades consisted of militia battalions. Meanwhile, the Australian 6th and 7th Infantry divisions of the 2nd AIF who had fought so gallantly in Greece, the Middle East and North Africa were now returning to Australia with Japan's entry into the war. Blamey replied to MacArthur that he had enough troops to defend the township and the proposed airfields. MacArthur ordered the Allied squadrons at Port Moresby to be brought up to full strength as quickly as possible.[5]

•

Blamey remains a controversial figure in Australian history. The Great War veteran became infamous in the 1920s when, as the Victorian Commissioner of Police, he left his badge behind after visiting a brothel. During his time in Egypt and Palestine during the Second World War he was known to frequent similar establishments—he was apparently attracted to one belly-dancer in particular. He was known to hit the whisky bottle and was strongly criticised by many for evacuating Greece with his son in 1941, leaving behind many of his men. Officers and men of the 2nd AIF generally disliked him with news broadcaster for the Australian Broadcasting Commission (ABC) Chester Wilmot commenting of his performance during the Middle East Campaign: 'Widespread lack of faith in Blamey . . . In two years, I have heard him denounced in the strongest possible terms . . . in private conversations by senior officers, who had no interest in supplanting him, by junior officers and by the ordinary Digger.'[6] The men's dislike for him would only intensify when he turned his criticism towards his men fighting and dying along the Kokoda Track while he was comfortably ensconced in Australia.

MacArthur said Blamey was 'sensual, slothful and of doubtful moral character . . . [but] a tough commander likely to shine like a power light in an emergency. The best of the local bunch.' This was not saying much, and Blamey didn't think much of MacArthur either stating: 'The best and the worst of the things you hear about him are both true.'[7]

MacArthur was famous for his distaste for all things Australian; he considered the Australian military establishment a nuisance to his grand vision. While the American Army Chief of Staff, General George Marshall, back in Washington strongly advised MacArthur to take advantage of Australian staff offices, when MacArthur announced his staff, they were all American—no Australian need apply.[8] The all-American general wanted this to be an all-American war and an all-American victory. United States Major General George Brett, commanding the Allied Air Forces (AAF) in the SWPA in 1942, said MacArthur was a 'brilliant, temperamental egotist; a handsome man, who can be charming as anyone who ever lived, or harshly indifferent to the needs and desires of those around him ... Everything about MacArthur is on the grand scale; his virtues and triumphs and shortcomings.'[9]

•

With the outbreak of war, Australia had two military systems in place—the militia and the AIF. By law the militia could not serve outside Australia, its territories or protectorates; only members of the AIF could serve overseas. The south-eastern part of New Guinea—Papua—became an Australian protectorate in 1906; and with the defeat of Germany in the Great War, North-east New Guinea and the islands of New Britain, New Ireland and Bougainville, which had been German colonies, were ceded by the League of Nations to be administered by Australia in 1920. By international law they were not to be fortified. The initial defence of these protectorates would fall upon the men of the Australian militia. While Australia complied with the League of Nation's dictate, this did not stop the Japanese from extensively fortifying the former German colonies now designated the South Pacific Mandate, consisting of the Marianas, Carolines, Marshall Islands and Palau groups. They had been ceded to Japan by the League of Nations after the Great War as Japan had sided with the Allies.[10]

Twenty-two-year-old Sergeant Victor Austin, from Prahran in Victoria with the 39th Battalion, would later go on to write the battalion's history: 'Since the men of the AIF had enlisted for overseas service and were thus fairly assured of seeing active service in one or other theatres of the war, they understandably felt "martially superior" to the men serving in the militia, referring to them disparagingly as "chockos"'. This was a derisive term implying they were chocolate soldiers who would likely melt in the heat of battle. It was also suggested by some that the militiamen should 'get some weight on their shoulders', referring to the brass 'AUSTRALIA' shoulder flashes worn by the men of the 2nd AIF. Some of those with the 2nd AIF soon to be assigned to the militia battalion even refused for a time to wear the 39th Battalion's 'Mud over Blood' (brown over red) colour patch, keeping the 2nd AIF 'grey background' colour on the inside of their hatbands.[11]

The Australian 14th Brigade, 2nd Division, commanded by Great War veteran Brigadier Walter Smith, a 47-year-old engineer from Sydney, consisted of the poorly trained 3rd (regional New South Wales and Canberra), 36th (Sydney area) and 55th (New South Wales) militia battalions, who had arrived in Port Moresby in May 1942. They were the first substantial infantry reinforcements to reach Port Moresby since early January 1942 when the 39th (Victoria) and 53rd (Sydney area) militia battalions arrived to reinforce the 49th Battalion (Queensland); collectively these three battalions formed the independent 30th Brigade.[12]

With Japan's entry into the war and with most of Australia's front-line troops of the 2nd AIF fighting in Greece, the Middle East and North Africa, and the 8th Division stationed in Malaya and Singapore, the Australian government was greatly concerned about home defence. It was decided to halt recruitment into the 2nd AIF with all new recruits now assigned to militia battalions to bring them up to strength.[13] Lieutenant Douglas McClean, a 27-year-old furrier from Melbourne, was then a member of the 6th Battalion in Australia and volunteered to join the 39th Battalion—as part of this battalion he would be among the first Australians to confront the Japanese in what was to become known as the Kokoda Campaign. 'One day in October the battalion officers were informed that volunteers were required for the formation of a garrison battalion to protect Port Moresby. I seized the chance to volunteer, as some half a dozen applications in triplicate to enlist in the AIF had remained unanswered.'[14]

The 49th Battalion had been the first Australian unit to be sent to Port Moresby, arriving in March 1941. These men had spent most of their time as 'pressed wharfies', loading and unloading ships, rather than conducting combat training and establishing defensive positions— not surprisingly the morale of these men was rock bottom. Chief of the Australian General Staff, Lieutenant General Vernon Sturdee, a 52-year-old professional soldier from Victoria, stated at the time that the 49th was the 'worst battalion in Australia'.[15] However, Australian Air Commodore Frank Lukis, a 46-year-old veteran of Gallipoli and later airman with the Australian Flying Corps during the Great War, recalled that the low morale of these militiamen did not mean they would 'not fight but they cannot overlook the lack of naval, air and political support. An impression is growing rapidly that the policy of the government is to let the garrison at Moresby, and Thursday Island go, in the same way as that at Rabaul and that no serious assistance will be given.'[16] Assigning the men to combat training and providing them with effective officers may have gone some way to resolving this unsatisfactory situation—this was a problem of the senior command's making, not due to the men themselves.[17]

The men of the 53rd Battalion had been treated even more harshly— if that was possible—leaving many of them angry and bitter not only towards their officers, but the army in general. The battalion was formed by issuing orders to the commanders of the existing eighteen militia battalions to each provide 62 men so that a new battalion could be formed for duties in Darwin. As such, some took the chance to off-load their more troublesome men to the commander of the 53rd Battalion. A member of the battalion, 22-year-old Private Clarence James, from Canberra, recalled on hearing of their intended move to Darwin: 'Most of us were excited at the prospect of the coming adventure and settled down to prepare ourselves for departure.' However, far from all were happy about the assignment as he admitted, 'unfortunately, more than a hundred of our battalion members applied for exemption from military service. A great deal of the CO's time and the time of others was taken up hearing the applications with the consequent disruption of training.'[18] To make matters worse, 275 of the battalion's 800 men failed to answer roll call the day before embarkation to Darwin. To help make up the numbers, around 100 young single men were press-ganged from the streets of Sydney and quickly sent to Ingleburn army camp.[19] Private James recalled the many questions raised by these youngsters on Boxing Day 1941, as they stood in their civilian clothes: 'That night, the new recruits gathered around the Orderly Room, most of them distressed, many of them crying and asking me, "Where are we going?" "Is there a telephone I can use?" "Can you get a message to my mother?" In the half-light filtering through the windows, I tried to talk to them—to console them. There was nowhere for them to go. There was no poss-ibility of breaking camp—the provosts were there to see to that.'[20]

The next day—27 December—these young recruits and the rest of the battalion were herded onto the transport ships HMT *Aquitania* and SS *Sarpedon*. Sydney-sider, Sergeant Keith Irwin, a 19-year-old former copy boy with the Sydney *Sun* newspaper with 'A' Company, 53rd Battalion, was onboard the *Aquitania* and concerned as most of these 'reinforcements' were mere teenagers (like himself!).

We received a draft of soldiers, mostly eighteen years of age. These poor devils had no idea what was happening to them. They had not been told where they were going, what unit they were destined for, or any information at all. They had received no final leave, were given no chance to let their families know what was happening to them. They were just taken down to the *Aquitania* and put on board. Most of them had never seen or handled a rifle. This was a disgrace and many of these youngsters, who had literally been shanghaied, later paid the supreme sacrifice during the battles in the mountains and at Sanananda. Once the *Aquitania* put to sea, we were told that we would be heading for Port Moresby, not Darwin. A training programme was implemented so that we NCOs [non-commissioned officers] could give the new recruits some elementary training in the use and handling of the .303 rifle.[21]

The padre of the battalion, 29-year-old Captain Roy Wotton, was busy writing letters to the parents of these teenagers telling them that their missing sons were off to war in New Guinea.

•

By mid-1942, the six brigades of the battle-hardened veterans of the Australian 6th and 7th divisions were in Queensland undergoing training for 'jungle warfare'. They had returned from conducting large-scale war in the open terrain in North Africa—the jungles of the South Pacific called for a whole new paradigm in tactical fighting. The men of the Australian 9th Division would remain in North Africa until they completed their pivotal role in the battle for El Alamein—they would not leave for Australia until February 1943 and from there they would head to the jungles of the South Pacific. Why one of the AIF brigades training in Queensland was not sent to confront the very real and growing threat of a Japanese attack against Port Moresby is still debated. Senior military and political figures likely assessed it better to keep the integrity of the division in place for a later decisive battle against the Japanese. Splitting up a division had serious logistical implications—none of them good. Indeed, no one seriously considered at this point that the Japanese would attack Port Moresby from its northern coastline.[22]

•

Allied intelligence had broken the Japanese naval signals code in May, and assessed the next major Japanese thrust after the Battle of the Coral Sea would be against Midway atoll. The Americans took the risk of concentrating their naval force to launch a strike against the Japanese, including all three of their remaining aircraft carriers—the *Enterprise*, *Hornet* and *Yorktown*. On the morning of 3 June 1942, the Japanese force was sighted several hundred kilometres south-west of Midway and several strikes were launched against it by American airmen based on the small island. The next morning, while Japanese pilots were bombing the defences of Midway, American carrier pilots launched multiple sorties against the Japanese strike force of four aircraft carriers. During the next two days the battle raged, primarily an engagement of naval aircraft seeking out and destroying enemy carriers. When the smoke cleared, the Japanese had suffered the worst of it, losing a cruiser and critically all four strike carriers along with around 250 aircraft; the Americans lost one carrier—the *Yorktown*—and about 150 aircraft. The Americans could replace their losses, the Japanese couldn't. This decisive battle, along with the Japanese defeat during the battle for the

Coral Sea, helped significantly in redressing the balance of naval power in the Pacific. Indeed, with this defeat the Japanese Imperial General Headquarters was forced to cancel its operations to capture Fiji, Samoa and New Caledonia. The much-vaunted Japanese Southern Resource Zone was now to be defined by just New Guinea and the Solomons. What chance remained of the Japanese holding off the Americans in the vast Pacific largely sank with their burning carriers. However, another three years of land, sea and air battles would rage in the Pacific and Asia before the Japanese finally bowed to the inevitable.[23]

3

'Four cases of whisky'

A few days after the battle of Midway, Allied intelligence indicated a renewed threat to Port Moresby. On 9 June 1942, MacArthur wrote to Blamey that the Japanese were likely planning to launch an operation to capture Buna, just east of Gona on the northern Papuan coast. Intelligence indicated their intent was to capture the airfield at Kokoda: 'There is increasing evidence that the Japanese are displaying interest in the development of a route from Buna on the north coast of . . . New Guinea through Kokoda to Port Moresby. From studies made in this headquarters it appears that minor forces may attempt to utilize this route for either attack on Port Moresby or for supply of forces [attacking] by sea route through the Louisiade Archipelago. Whatever the Japanese plan may be, it is of vital importance that the route from Kokoda westward be controlled by Allied Forces, particularly the Kokoda area.'[1]

MacArthur asked Blamey what he was doing to protect Kokoda. His reply was that Major General Basil Morris, a 56-year-old professional soldier from Victoria, commanding Australian forces in New Guinea, had in February ordered a small force of soldiers from the 1st PIB, commanded by Australian officers and NCOs, to cross the mountains from Port Moresby. They were currently conducting patrols in the Yodda Valley area along the northern coast of Papua, which incorporated the Buna and Kokoda areas. Blamey now ordered Morris to 'take all necessary steps to prevent a Japanese surprise landing along the coast, north and south of Buna, to deny the enemy the grasslands in that area for an airdrome, and to assure that we command the pass at Kokoda'. Morris replied with: 'Re. the Japs, I don't think you need to worry about them. It is not likely they will want to commit suicide just yet.'[2]

That said, it was not long before additional intelligence came in of Japanese intentions for Papua. A daring raid by Australian commandos of the 2/5th Independent Company conducted against the Japanese garrison at Salamaua on 29 June 1942 resulted in the death of over 60 Japanese and the capture of several documents.[3] This crucial intelligence was soon back in Australia and quickly assessed by intelligence officers—the documents confirmed Japanese radio traffic picked up from Rabaul throughout June.[4] MacArthur's headquarters reported on the collection of intelligence:

> Jap interest in the area not incidental—has background of history.
>
> I link BUNA reconnaissance with general Jap movement now in progress; captured document shows dates of future arrival, etc., of engineer or A/me construction units at KAVIENG, GUADALCANAL, LAE, and EAST NEW GUINEA—units for latter are part of No. 14 Construction Unit and part of No. 5 Sasebo Special Naval Landing Party scheduled to land 16 July. East New Guinea interpreted as BUNA and possibly MILNE [BAY]. I recommend concentrated reconnaissance of these points and the formation of an immediately available striking force to intercept the expected landing and take enemy vessels out.[5]

Morris considered the Kokoda Track—the only way of reaching Port Moresby on foot from the Buna–Kokoda district—an impossible place to conduct large-scale military operations: defensive or offensive. He sensibly judged that the force with the longest supply line would suffer the worse of any adventure through the mountains. He considered it wise to maintain the bulk of his force in and around Port Moresby and if the Japanese were foolish enough to attack from the north, through the Owen Stanley Range, let them wither and die from a lack of logistical support in terms of food, ammunition and medical supplies. At the end of the track they would be in no condition to successfully attack Port Moresby. Morris argued fighting the Japanese well forward of a tenuous supply line was a recipe for disaster; he had no transport aircraft and he would have to depend on local native carriers, and it was doubtful they alone could keep his military force supplied, even one consisting of just a few battalions. Any force sent forward would be fighting a delaying action, helping to sap the strength of the Japanese as the Australians fell back towards Port Moresby, where the main battle would be fought in the nearby mountains which offered a strong defensive position, just north of the relatively flat and open terrain of Moresby. The terrain at and around Ioribaiwa or Imita ridges would provide strong defensive terrain with little opportunity for Japanese flanking manoeuvres—which they had perfected. Critically, it was also close to the Australian main centre of supply at Port Moresby and conversely well forward of the Japanese supply bases.[6]

Even so, on 24 June 1942 Blamey ordered Morris to form an independent force to protect the northern coastal approach to Port Moresby. Kokoda, just below the Owen Stanleys' northern slopes where the track climbs into the mountains, was to be held at all costs. Morris instructed Brigadier Selwyn 'Bill' Porter, a 37-year-old bank clerk from Wangaratta in Victoria, who had just arrived, to take over command of the 30th Brigade to form 'Maroubra Force'. At its core was the 39th Battalion with the 1st PIB in support. It was also to include the Royal Papuan Constabulary (RPC), which was already based in the Buna area, but the RPC there numbered fewer than 50 men.[7]

Brigadier Porter was highly regarded, being a veteran of the fighting in the Middle East, having the year before been wounded while commanding the 2/31st Battalion, 25th Brigade, 7th Division. On arriving at Port Moresby, Porter was unhappy, writing of his new command in July 1942, 'bad discipline, sloppy office work, slipshod methods'.[8] He called his officers together and laid down the law: 'The Brigade is not in a fit state to fight a battle. Officers and men are so obviously backward that the training programme will go on around the clock. I will make no allowance for the weather.'[9] He replaced several officers he considered too old—including several First World War veterans—and others he considered unfit for command. These were replaced with around 30 officers from the 2nd AIF and others promoted from the ranks.[10] However, Porter would later recognise the fighting spirit of his militiamen, stating: 'My choco's [sic] earned fame in the scrap over here.'[11]

•

By July 1942, MacArthur and Blamey were focusing on constructing airbases at Buna and at Milne Bay to support future Allied operations against New Britain, as well as those soon to be launched against the Japanese in the Solomons at Guadalcanal. In mid-June an Australian and American engineering team flew into Buna on a Catalina flying boat to assess its suitability for a major airbase. Buna already had a rudimentary small runway, which was overgrown, but it was not suitable due to significant problems of drainage so they conducted a survey in the surrounding area and identified an excellent site near Dobodura— here they would build their airbase.

It would be a race between the Allies and the Japanese to see who could occupy the northern coast of Papua. The Allies planned to begin construction at Dobodura in mid-August (code name Operation Providence) and the first stage of this operation was for the Australian 39th Battalion to secure the Kokoda–Buna area. However, MacArthur would lose to the Japanese, who would invade the beaches around Buna in late July, planning to have their own airfield operational by mid-August.[12]

•

Since the arrival of the 39th Battalion in Port Moresby in January 1942, several changes had occurred to help bring the battalion up to battle readiness. Several officers and men arrived in March to reinforce the battalion, but these men had originally volunteered to join the 2nd AIF and were resentful at being assigned to a militia unit, which they considered to be second rate. Indeed, after the reshuffle the only First World War veteran remaining as an officer in the battalion was Captain Samuel 'Sam' Templeton commanding 'B' Company—it would turn out to be a wise decision to retain him, although several NCOs were still represented by battle-hardened Great War veterans who would come to the fore in the fighting around the Kokoda Plateau.[13]

It was not only officers and men from the 2nd AIF who were assigned to the 39th Battalion. Nobby Earl, a 31-year-old Catholic chaplain from Kensington in Sydney, was based in Port Moresby at the time and there joined the battalion. He approached his commanding officer, almost certainly the militia battalion's first CO, 53-year-old Lieutenant Colonel Hugh Conran from Red Cliffs in Victoria, who had served with the 23rd Battalion in the Great War. On seeing Nobby, the senior officer was initially skeptical.

Nobby: 'I am Father Earl. I have just been appointed chaplain of the 39th Battalion.'

CO: 'That's news to me. I haven't been informed' (pause). 'Where's your uniform?'

Nobby: 'They didn't have any uniform to give me.'

CO: 'Do you mean to tell me you haven't a uniform! What clothes have you got?'

Nobby: 'All I stand up in—a shirt, a singlet, pair of shorts, pair of long socks, a pair of shoes.'

CO: 'Where did you join the Army?'

Nobby: 'In Port Moresby, half an hour ago.'

CO: 'Have you a pay book?'

Nobby: 'Oh yes! I have a pay book!'

CO: 'That means all you have is a pay book and the clothes you stand up in?'

Nobby: 'No! I have something else.'

CO: 'Well man, tell me what that is.'

Nobby: 'Four cases of whisky.'

CO: 'Come in, Padre. What are you standing out there for?'[14]

Father Nobby Earl would follow the 39th Battalion into battle against the Japanese, tending to the dead, dying and wounded directly in the front lines during the heat of battle and would be a much-admired member of the battalion.

•

Japanese Lieutenant General Hyakutake Harukichi commanded the Japanese XVII Army. At 54, he was a small slender man, his overall appearance giving perhaps an impression of frailty, but he was anything but, he was tenacious and totally dedicated to the bushido warrior creed and his emperor. His army consisted of the 5th, 18th and 56th divisions and was now concentrated around Davao after the end of the fighting in the Philippines. He was intent that Major General Horii Tomitarô's South Seas Force, built around the battle-hardened 144th Regiment, which had recently captured and occupied New Britain and its deep-water harbour at Rabaul, should now capture Port Moresby. It was vital that the Allies be denied airfields in eastern New Guinea, otherwise this would leave Rabaul and its harbour exposed to air attacks. The 144th Regiment had already seen action in Northeast New Guinea when its II Battalion, under the command of Major Horie Masao, captured Lae and Salamaua in March 1942—around 200 kilometres west of Buna. Even so, most men of the regiment could not be considered experienced jungle fighters, but since arriving in New Britain they had conducted extensive around-the-clock jungle training.[15]

The Japanese, Australians and Americans were all about to be introduced to the grim realities of combat in the South Pacific. The fighting here would be in a class all its own in terms of brutality and primitiveness. Combat on these jungle-covered islands reverted to the very basics—close-quarter killing—which in other theatres of the Second World War was quite rare. The fighting on these islands often involved small parties of men, numbering fewer than 30 on each side, rather than great land battles involving countless infantry divisions, tanks, aircraft and massed artillery support. The strategic campaigns fought in the South Pacific at the tactical level were dominated by decisions made at the company and platoon level.[16] In these jungles and mountains, the rifle, bayonet, sub-machine gun and grenade were king. Historian Eric Bergerud wrote succinctly:

Land combat in the South Pacific was harsh, crude, and from a military viewpoint, technically primitive. The situation was unique in time and place. None of the combatants initially possessed the knowledge or equipment to overcome the challenge raised by the brutal and distant terrain with technology and appropriate weaponry. The secondary status given to the Pacific by the Allies slowed the introduction of more appropriate tools of war for American and Australian soldiers. Japan lacked the economic resources to equip its army with more complex weaponry and supporting services. In addition, ethnic arrogance and racism were common to all combatants. This, combined with a fanatical and wasteful battle ethos on the part of the Japanese, created a horrifying battle psychology that transformed what would have been a cruel struggle into a battle to the death.[17]

While combat was up close and personal, it has been estimated that of all Australian troops who fought the Japanese throughout the war, around 75 per cent never saw the enemy during their attacks, with one Australian saying for many: 'You can't see the little bastards.'[18] Many within the 39th Battalion later admitted that while fighting and killing the enemy, they never saw them. This was not just because of the skill of the Japanese, but also down to the appalling terrain, climate and vegetation which often brought visibility down to metres.

The Japanese troops' complete disregard towards civilians, non-combatants and prisoners is partly explained in a captured document taken from a dead Japanese officer of the 3rd Special Landing Party by Australians after the fighting at Milne Bay. It was entitled 'Notes for Unit Commanders' and reads in part that their duty as officers was to: 'Eradicate the sense of fear in raw soldiers' carnivals of bloodshed (or) human sacrifice to the war god are most effective. Killings with the bayonet should be carried out whenever an opportunity occurs. Raw troops, being unused to fighting, suffer relatively heavy casualties, and attention should be paid to this point.'[19] Japanese troops were to take the 'opportunity' of killing civilians and prisoners with the bayonet in order to toughen them up and improve their fighting abilities and chances of survival.

The intense hatred of the Japanese by many Australians during, and often after, the war was strongly tainted by this ethos which was clearly demonstrated not just by the massacres at the Tol and Waitavalo plantations, but by other well-documented atrocities such as those conducted in China, particularly what became known internationally as the 'Rape of Nanking'. The killing of Australian prisoners was not isolated to the Tol and Waitavalo plantations, as demonstrated by the execution of 150 men of the Australian 2/13th General Hospital during the fighting in Singapore; and the massacre of over 100 Australian and 35 Indian wounded at Parit Sulong during the Malay campaign.[20]

Perhaps the best known—although the story would only emerge after the war—was the massacre of Australian nurses on Radji Beach on Banka Island in 1942. They had been assigned to the Australian 2/13th General Hospital and, along with the wounded, had been evacuated from Singapore by ship, but two days out the ship was sunk, and some of the survivors made their way to Banka Island. Of the 22 nurses who made their way to the island there would be only one survivor to tell the story of the massacre that soon followed. With them were about 100 British soldiers, many of them wounded. After the war, Lieutenant Vivian Bullwinkel, a 26-year-old nursing sister from South Australia, vividly recalled how the soldiers were killed on the beach and then the nurses were ordered to wade out into the water from Radji Beach before a Japanese machine gun opened fire. Two weeks later, a wounded Bullwinkel surrendered to the Japanese—she spent the rest of the war as a POW. Of the 65 nurses who left Singapore in 1942, only 24 would ever return to Australia.[21]

The war against the Japanese was seen by many Australians as being far more sinister and horrific than the war experienced in Greece, the Middle East and North Africa. Japanese callousness and brutality towards helpless men, women and children—fuelled by the racist elements of the times—caused a great animosity towards the Japanese not witnessed against the Germans and Italians. That said, it is difficult to disagree with one historian who wrote: 'The special character of Australian soldiers' hatred of the Japanese derived from the reality of the fighting rather than the prejudices of civilian life.'[22]

4

'. . . if he went into action against the Japs, he wouldn't come back'

In early July 1942, the 39th Battalion received its new commanding officer, Lieutenant Colonel William 'Bill' Owen, who had commanded 'A' Company of the 2/22nd Battalion, which confronted the Japanese landings at Rabaul. Owen was one of fewer than 400 men who escaped from New Britain.[1] In mid-July Owen was ordered to send one of his companies across the Owen Stanley Range to support elements of the 1st PIB and the RPC that were already operating in the area. One of his first decisions as battalion commander was to pick his most trusted unit—'B' Company led by 44-year-old Captain Sam Templeton—to make the crossing. Templeton and his men would be the first Australian force to cross the Owen Stanley Range, however, they were not the first troops to cross the mountains, this honour belonged to the Papuan troops of the 1st PIB.[2]

•

The 1st PIB had been raised in June 1940 and by July 1942 it numbered six Australian officers and a similar number of NCOs leading 105 Papuans. These men were paid 10 shillings a month in their first year, which would rise to £1 per month in their third year.[3] Major William Watson, a 55-year-old gold miner, commanded the battalion; he was described as 'bluff outspoken, quick on the uptake and quick in speech. A man with the highest standard of personal courage, and utterly intolerant of those who lack resolution and coolness in danger. As a subaltern in the 1st AIF he had probably won more decorations than any other artillery officer of his rank. His officers say he made the PIB.'⁴ Lieutenant Douglas McClean recalled: 'We had there a Major Watson— known as "Stand and Fight" Watson—who was an Australian who lived in America, married an American girl . . . every time we had a council of war Watson would take his pipe out of his mouth and we'd say, "What do you think, Watson?" He'd say, "Stand and fight!"⁵ His actions during the first month of the fighting in and around Kokoda further added to his fighting reputation and command abilities. To this day, he remains a largely unknown hero of the Kokoda Campaign.

In February 1942 the men of 'A' Company, 1st PIB, led by Captain Harold Jesser, a 28-year-old railway employee from Brisbane, accompanied by fellow Queenslanders, lieutenants John Chalk, a 26-year-old warehouse assistant from Eagle Junction, and William Wort, a 23-year-old farmer from Wynnum, crossed the Owen Stanley Range using the Kokoda Track. They were to patrol the northern coast from Buna Station to the Waria River mouth. These men were the first of the battalion to confront the Japanese when on 10 March, while patrolling close to Buna, they saw a Japanese seaplane target the schooner *Maclaren-King*, which belonged to the Anglican mission. Just moments before, the visiting Bishop of New Guinea, Philip Strong, had left the schooner on a small launch heading for the beach. The Japanese airmen targeted the larger schooner and then the launch. When Bishop Strong reached the shore, he flung himself into the scrub. The Japanese plane was seen to land on the water and the Japanese airmen, using sub-machine guns, continued to fire on the bishop, but Captain Jesser and his men came to the rescue. Reverend James Benson, a 57-year-old Yorkshireman, who had headed the Gona mission station since 1937, recalled: 'By now rifles were firing from the shore at the plane . . . John Duffill thought the plane was hit, and fearing a bullet in a vital spot, the Japs . . . took off; and so ended the first battle of Buna.'⁶ Indeed, Australian mission Sister May Hayman, based at Gona, stated at the time: 'My Word do you realise that history has been made today? Probably this battle of Buna will go down in the records as the first battle on Australian Soil.'⁷

Soon after, back onboard the *Maclaren-King*, Bishop Strong was on his way back to his main residence at Dogura, a few hundred kilometres east of Gona along the northern coastline; he recorded the incident in his diary:

As we drew near at Buna about 9.45 am [we] saw an aeroplane, looking as if it was coming down on the sea. Duffill said it was one of ours. I had my doubts. Did not come down but flew round and round and was going over the MK [*Maclaren-King*], from which we were about half a mile away. Then it made a dive towards us and came very low over us and I saw the rising sun mark and knew that it was a Jap plane. Fortunately, it did not attack us, otherwise we should have been help-less and probably doomed in the small launch.

It made another circle and then went over the MK and to my horror I saw a bomb falling, aimed at the MK but it seemed that it diverted and fell wide of its mark and fell between the boat and the beach. It circled again and dropped another bomb and I feared it was going to go on doing so until it succeeded in hitting the MK, prayed earnestly that our boat might be spared. Anxious about our boys, wondering if they were still on board or not. We were too far away to see. Second bomb also seemed diverted and fell wide. Directed Duffill to steer our launch straight for the nearest shore. Put on speed and ran it straight up on the beach, jumped out quickly as we could and ran into the scrub for cover. Only just in time, for evidently having no more bombs, the Jap plane then made for our launch, coming into the water. As we lay in the scrub heard machine-gunning. They were machine-gunning the launch and us in the scrub. I could not see them, but it sounded so near I feared they were landing and said to Duffill that I thought we had better get further back. He said: 'Stay where you are'. However, I moved back a few inches and then found that if I went any further, I should come into the open with no cover overhead and would have had to get across a creek.

Just after I moved, a bullet whizzed past where my head had been lying before I moved. The machine-gunning seemed then to become more distant and we learnt afterwards that the sea plane had gone over to machine-gun the radio station and the MK at close quarters. We heard the crack of rifle fire and guessed that some of the Government people and soldiers of the station had opened fire. Soon after that the plane went away, having difficulty, they said, in rising. Afterwards we learnt that it had machine-gunned the MK before it bombed it, when our boys were still on board. Most of the boys then had jumped overboard and swam to the shore and the plane passed over again and machine-gunned them while they were swimming in close formation to the shore, but though the bullets had rained down upon them not one of them had been touched.

Edward [Guise] and Ruben had got ashore in the dingy and had just landed when the first bomb fell, bursting just behind them . . . Went on board the MK to inspect it. Found to my great relief that it had suffered no harm—a few bullet holes only and none in vital parts— one through the St George Flag, two or three in the upper parapet of the boat and one through a pair of my shorts which were hanging out to dry after the inland trip yesterday.[8]

Not long after, another 'battle' took place at Ambasi, about 50 kilometres west of Gona. Benson recalled that a Japanese fighter was 'forced down on the beach a few miles from Ambasi. Cpl. John Hannay [*sic* Sergeant Robert Hanna], in charge of the signal station at Ambasi went off to capture the pilot, who, from the verandah of a native house, put up a brave fight with a small pistol, refusing to surrender, though wounded in several places. Finally, Hannay [*sic*] said: "I had to kill him." The body was reverently buried by Vincent Moi, teacher in charge of Ambasi, and the three Australian soldier lads.'[9]

•

Things were heating up in the Buna–Ambasi districts. Two weeks before Templeton and his men made the crossing to reach Kokoda, Major Watson led 'C' Company of the 1st PIB over the mountains to join his men of 'A' Company, while his 'B' Company, commanded by Lieutenant Arthur Smith (a 21-year-old truck driver from Balmoral in Queensland), had already crossed the Owen Stanleys and was now patrolling the Ambasi district. With the establishment of Maroubra

Force, the rest of the 39th Battalion would soon be following behind Watson and Templeton. They would blaze the way forward for the rest of the men who would be forced to slog across the Owen Stanley Range along the Kokoda Track to halt or at least slow the Japanese advance.[10]

•

Sam Templeton will forever be linked to the early fighting of the Kokoda Campaign. He was born in Belfast in 1901, the eldest of six children, and after leaving school at an early age, he worked for a short time in the Belfast shipyards as a carpenter.[i] Towards the end of the Great War, he was serving with the naval reserves. After the war he joined the Royal Irish Constabulary which was tasked with putting down the Irish Republican Army. He left for Australia in 1923 and took up a position on the Victorian railway, later becoming a manager at Corns Pastrycooks. He soon met and married the love of his life, Doris Allen, and together they had four children, three boys and a girl. Thomas, who tragically died when just three years old, Malcolm, Reginald (known to all as Reggie) and Margarette. In 1928 Sam joined the Australian Militia, and quickly rose through the ranks; by 1942 he was a captain in the 39th Battalion which was about to be sent to New Guinea.[11]

Among his men he was known affectionately as 'Uncle Sam' and was one of the battalion's most revered officers. That said, by all accounts he was a loner, as recalled by 22-year-old Lieutenant Alan Moore from Melbourne who served with him as a platoon commander in Australia, and later in Port Moresby as his Second-in-Command (2i/c).

> I first met Sam Templeton in company with a couple of other young
> officers and quite a few troops at the Bacchus Marsh railway station
> when we were on our way to form the 39th Battalion. He called a roll,
> instructed us to all 'fall in' and marched us to Darley Camp. I marched

---

i   There has been much nonsense written about the early life of Sam Templeton (none of it orig-
     inating from Sam himself), including that he joined up as a submariner at the beginning of
     the Great War (he was then just 13 years old!); that he had fought in the Spanish Civil War (his
     militia records indicate otherwise); and that he tried to join the 2nd AIF at the outbreak of the
     Second World War. Research conducted by Historian and former Secretary of the 39th Battalion
     Association, David Howell, refutes these assertions, which almost all historians of the campaign
     have uncritically regurgitated.

close to him and tried to converse at the two 'smoke-ohs'. All I found out was that he spoke quietly with a slight North of Ireland accent but preferred not to talk. At Darley I was posted to his B Company where I remained during all of the training there for a short time after arrival at Port Moresby. Later, in mid-March 1942, following my return from hospital and until sometime prior to B Company's move to the Owen Stanleys, I replaced Captain Alex Eager as Sam Templeton's Acting Second-in-Command. During those weeks as his Acting 2i/c we shared a tent and I got to know him somewhat better. He never talked when I could observe him, but often, after the hurricane lamp was doused at night, he used the darkness to talk about his life, frequently about what he considered his problems and failures, but just as often about his determination to excel at leading and protecting his troops in action.

Nevertheless, he remained something of an enigma. He was remote, at times almost aloof, but fervently wanted to be friendly. He was reserved and shy but used his rank and seniority in his efforts to indicate otherwise. To combat his uncertainty he drove himself incessantly, seeking personal perfection. He sought to become involved in solving the personal problems of his troops and was possibly better at that then [sic] in solving his own. Finality seemed to be an integral part of his thinking and I am sure he knew that he would die in battle.[12]

With the appointment of several battle-hardened veterans of the 2nd AIF to the battalion, the young and relatively inexperienced 2i/c Lieutenant Alan Moore was replaced by Captain Cathcart Stevenson, a 24-year-old bank clerk from Armadale in Victoria and veteran of the Middle East Campaign having served with the 2/14th Battalion. However, it would not be long before Lieutenant Moore would find himself in the thick of the fighting.[13]

Lieutenant Arthur 'Judy' Garland, a 22-year-old salesman from Parkdale in Victoria who had signed up with the 39th Battalion, led Templeton's 10 Platoon and recalled how his CO 'set an example to the whole of his company, in other words, I think he realised that we were a lot of young blokes ... A man that you couldn't get to know very well, but he always said that if he went into action against the Japs, he wouldn't come back and that's exactly what happened.'[14] Similarly, Lieutenant Arthur Seekamp, a 26-year-old labourer from Berri in South Australia, who led 11 Platoon and was a veteran of the Middle East Campaign having served with the 2/10th Battalion, recalled: 'The amount of time that we had Sam Templeton with us, he always was going somewhere by himself; he never took any runners or anything with him . . . He always seemed to be by himself—he never seemed to delegate or didn't want to. He was a funny bugger!'[15] One of his men—only identified as JWB[ii]—recalled how his OC (Officer Commanding) caught him with two scavenged bottles of whisky: 'The usual—AWL [absent without leave]; failing to attend parade; looting when Burns Philip [*sic*] was bombed at Port Moresby—two bottles of whisky, taken off me by Sam Templeton.' That was his only punishment.[16]

•

Captain Sam Templeton and his men were now preparing to push over the Owen Stanley Range, which was still an unknown element to the Australians. The range was named after a Royal Navy captain who documented their existence in 1849. Templeton had no maps to guide him and was to just follow the path across the mountains. However, the Kokoda Track is not really a track per se, but several interwoven and evolving networks that all connect by accident—not design—to form a passage over the Owen Stanley Range. The track across the mountains adapted over hundreds of years by villagers slogging along the ridge-lines and down into the deep dark ravines either side as part of their local trade network and slash-and-burn agriculture. Each of these local village networks connect to form the tortuous 100-kilometre Kokoda Track through the mountains—each village maintaining their section according to local requirements. Just as the course of the 'track' evolves by necessity, so do the location of villages. If parts of the main track wash away or large trees fall blocking its path, or the associated villages need to relocate to rejuvenate local gardens, a new track is formed, and

---

ii   This could possibly be one of the four privates identified by the author as being attached to the battalion with these initials—James W. Billings; Jack W. Boland; Jeffrey W. Burton; or John W. Butler.

the old path disappears into the encroaching jungle. Associated with the main track are numerous parallel and subsidiary paths that may later become the main track. Then, as now, the track remains a system of local works very much in progress. Indeed, those who cross the track today in many parts are not following the path taken by the soldiers of 1942—they are following more recent branches of the track.[17]

•

The Australian advance across the Owen Stanleys would be dependent on the knowledge and experience of Herbert 'Bert' Kienzle, a 37-year-old miner and planter of Yodda Valley who was serving as an officer with the Australian New Guinea Administrative Unit (ANGAU).[iii] Earlier in June, General Morris had invoked the National Security (Emergency Control) Regulations to terminate all existing contracts of service in Papua enabling the conscription of local labour required by the services.[18]

With the creation of ANGAU, all Papuan workers were to enter into a contract of employment for a period not exceeding three years with the government. ANGAU was staffed by civil service officers based at Port Moresby and beyond—usually pre-war district officers—tasked with maintaining law and order as well as being responsible for the medical services and recruiting, organising and the supervision of labour for the war effort. By mid-1942 around 35,000 Papuans had been recruited.[19] The military operational orders for ANGAU headed by individual district officers were stated as:

a. Maintaining control of the native population.
b. Locating and eradicating fifth column activities and enemy agents.
c. Providing early information of enemy activity and movement in the respective areas of responsibility.
d. Capturing crashed Japanese airmen etc. and giving every assistance to our own airmen forced down, in their Districts.[20]

---

iii With the establishment of ANGAU the distinction between Papua and North-east New Guinea for the Australian military ceased in administrative terms at least, with the Australian forces in both regions collectively known as New Guinea Force (NGF).

However, orders were originally issued that district officers were not
to recruit more than 25 per cent of the male population from a village
to ensure the social fabric of the villages was maintained. Orders also
stated: 'Labourers are to be employed in their home districts' although
it also recognised that 'exceptions will have to be made to provide for
Port Moresby labour pool, rubber tappers and other skilled labour,
but the majority of the Labourers should be indentured in their own
districts, though they can be employed in a district adjacent to their
own if they are in easy walking distance of the villages'.[21] Indeed, with
the emerging crisis of the Japanese invasion of Papua in late July and
throughout the ongoing associated crisis during August and September
1942, further exceptions were adopted with additional orders issued
to all district officers: 'You are required to recruit for Kokoda Road all
available able-bodied natives living in the villages under your control.
Visiting natives, and natives of the District not employed are to be
recruited and signed-on for one year in accordance with Native Labour
Ordinance No. 6 of 1942 . . . Kokoda Road has priority over all labour
demanded. The need for carriers is urgent, therefore recruiting must be
carried out forthwith.'[22]

5

'Some twit in headquarters . . .'

As a child, Bert Kienzle bore witness to the death of his mother as she gave birth to his brother, Wallace. Bert's German-born father worked for the German firm Hedemann & Evers, based in Fiji, as well as having stakes in a plantation there. With Britain at war with Germany, Bert's father was interned in Australia in 1916 as an enemy alien, even though he was a naturalised British citizen. A year later, twelve-year-old Bert, along with three-year-old Wallace and his sisters, ten-year-old Laura and seven-year-old Elsa, and their stepmother were also interned as enemy aliens. Rather than this and other hardships making Bert cynical, it brought out a strong humanitarian stance in him, which later showed in the way he treated his workers and the villagers when he arrived in New Guinea. His concern for them would come to the fore as he was charged with organising and caring for the carriers who would become so crucial in the logistical battle during the fighting along the Kokoda Track in 1942.[1]

Arriving in New Guinea in 1927 as part of a gold rush, Bert soon became fluent in pidgin English and the local dialect—Matu. He quickly established a successful plantation at Kokoda and built an all-weather airstrip to help service the plantation and surrounding gold-mining operations. It was not long before Kokoda consisted of a magistrate's house, native hospital, station gardens, police station, officers' house and the rubber plantation. While Bert was visiting Sydney in 1935, his sister Laura organised a blind date, and within a week of meeting Meryl Holiday he was engaged to her, but it would be another year before they were married with Meryl accompanying Bert back to Kokoda. It was not long before their children, Carl and Katherine, were born.[2]

Soon joining Bert and Meryl at Kokoda was Bert's brother, Wallace, who worked on the plantation. However, in 1940 he left for Australia telling Bert and Meryl that he was going for a holiday—his real reason was to join the 2nd AIF as Australia was at war with Germany. Wallace, who at age three had been branded a German enemy alien by the Australian government during the Great War, joined the 2/2nd Australian Machine Gun Battalion and within a year would be fighting Rommel's Afrika Korps and later serving in the Pacific, rising to the rank of major.[3]

Prior to the war with Japan, both Bert and Meryl were surprised one day to be confronted by two well-dressed gentlemen from Japan who claimed to be anthropologists. They said they wanted to cross the Owen Stanleys to get to Port Moresby to study the indigenous people of the region. At this point Australia was already at war with Germany and while Bert and Meryl showed their usual hospitality towards guests, they were very circumspect in providing them with any information. For months now, rumours were thick on the ground that war with Japan—now an ally of Nazi Germany—was not only inevitable, but imminent. Meryl insisted these men must be spies. Bert later recalled if they were spies, they 'must never have got back to Japan with their information [as it] was poor reconnaissance and in particular a lack of understanding of the difficulties in crossing the mountains separating north from south that ultimately led to Japan's defeat in Papua in 1942–43'.[4]

In October 1941, Bert and Meryl, along with their two children, left for Sydney for an overdue holiday. They were enjoying lunch in a King Street restaurant in Sydney on 8 December (7 December United States time) when they heard of the Japanese attack against the American Pacific fleet at Pearl Harbor. Due to the fear of Japanese invasion in New Guinea, the Australian government refused women and children to travel there and Bert was soon heading back to Kokoda alone. Seeing him disappear around the corner, Meryl said to herself: 'I shall never see him again.'[5]

•

Six months later, and the now Lieutenant Bert Kienzle of ANGAU was to play a prominent part in the battle along the Kokoda Track. Captain Noel Symington, a 25-year-old clerk from Perth, who had fought with the 2/16th Battalion in Syria and was now commanding 'A' Company, 39th Battalion, recalled Kienzle during the early phase of the campaign: 'A second generation planter, a bloke of six feet two. He was big, eighteen stone of muscle. He had a good brain and successfully ran a plantation. He was very highly regarded in the civil community up there, a very good operator. I do not consider that sufficient recognition was made to this gallant officer by the army commander or his country. They gave him an MBE [Member of the British Empire] or something; a bloody insult.'[6]

Kienzle recalled his recruitment into ANGAU when he was awoken during the early hours of March 1942 with a message sent to him from Port Moresby. He was then on business away from Kokoda Station, but still in the Yodda Valley. 'About midnight on the 31st of March 1942, I was awakened by a loud knocking to be confronted by a native constable of police, who handed me an important message from Kokoda. It was a message from H.Q. Port Moresby to the effect, I was to "close down mines and plantations, and report to H.Q., immediately".' He got word that he was to report to Kokoda straight away to receive instructions from Lieutenant Peter Brewer, a 37-year-old Australian patrol officer of Port Moresby. Kienzle was told he was to 'take a number of "deserters"; these were natives who had deserted their employ, during the earlier air raids on Port Moresby, back to their villages, and I was to escort them back to Port Moresby. It was my first crossing of the now famous "Kokoda Trail", and it took me 7 days to reach Koitaki with my line of about 64 "deserters".'[7]

Indeed, until then, Bert had made his way to Port Moresby from Kokoda (and back) either by boat or aircraft. For the first time he made the exhausting trip along the track across the mountain, but he did not stay long, making his way back over the northern side of the Owen Stanleys. However, it was not long before he got another message, as recorded in his report of ANGAU operations from July 1942 to February 1943; he was to go by boat to Port Moresby: 'I was ordered to report to ANGAU HQ N.G.F. [New Guinea Force] as quickly as possible end of June and left Kanosia district, where I had been employed by the Army to open up rubber estates DOA and LOLOUA, on 2nd July at 0700 hrs. in RAAF crash launch, Commander Hunt in charge. Arrived Port Moresby 0945 hrs'.[8]

On his arrival, he noticed that pack animals were at work with about 600 local labourers who he described as being 'very sullen and unhappy. Conditions in the labour camp were bad and many cases of illness were noted. Desertions were frequently being reported ... I commenced reorganising and allotting labour to various jobs.' One of his first jobs was to build clean and dry buildings to house the carriers. There was plenty of native material close by enabling him to complete this task relatively quickly. He also noted the 'consideration shown and an address to the natives had the effect of bringing about a better understanding and appreciation of the task ahead.'[9]

Kienzle must have been dumbfounded by the complete ignorance of those in command at Port Moresby and beyond who now ordered him not only to build a *road* across the Owen Stanley Range to Kokoda— but to do so within two months! He was ordered to use ANGAU personnel and carriers 'on the construction of a road from ILOLO to KOKODA; the completion of which was ordered for end of August 1942'.[10] He also added diplomatically in his official report: 'A colossal engineering job and one not to be taken lightly.' He later vented his true reaction: 'Some twit in headquarters looked at a map and said "we'll put a road in there"' also adding his own thoughts on the matter: 'It is asking too much to organise (A): a line of communication with suitable stages/depots/camps en route, all equipped and manned with sufficient carriers; and (B): to build a road over this mountainous terrain within a time limit. I have heard of superman but have yet to see him in action.'[11] Some sense prevailed as shortly after he was instructed to assess the feasibility of constructing such a road—undoubtedly, he could have given his answer then and there.

Added to this, he kept hearing from those apparently in the 'know' about the 'Kokoda Gap', which was argued to be a place where just a few men could hold up any Japanese advance from the north, if they were foolish enough to attack from that direction. He heard it being described as so narrow that only one man could pass at a time and he would have to turn sideways to do so. It was knowingly stated by the ignorant, most of who had hardly been beyond Port Moresby, if in New Guinea at all, that just a few men with an endless supply of ammunition could hold off an entire army there. There was only one problem: Kienzle having crossed the mountain range knew that no such place existed. Indeed, the term 'gap' had originally been coined by airmen for the low-lying part of the mountain range which allowed them to cross the Owen Stanleys in their flights to and from Kokoda, being around ten-kilometres wide![12]

The troops had also been told about the gap but, as they crossed the mountains, reality quickly set in, as recalled by Joseph Dawson, a salesman from Footscray in Victoria, who at the age of just 21 was appointed by Captain Templeton to act as his company sergeant major: 'They had this misguided idea that the Range was like the Greek Gap; about as wide as a track.[i] But in fact, that gap, there's a big mountain there and a big mountain over there, then valleys down there and valleys down there, that was as the crow flies, about seven miles [10 kilometres], so there's no way—I think the top brass thought "Well, they can hold them at the gaps".'[13]

During the early phase of the Kokoda Campaign, Major General Richard Sutherland, MacArthur's Chief-of-Staff—who had selected the group of advisers and subordinates who accompanied MacArthur (and himself) in their escape from the Philippines—heard of the Gap in mid-August and advised Australian Lieutenant General Sydney Rowell that a: 'Reconnaissance be made of critical areas of the trail through the Owen Stanley Range for the selection of points where the pass may be readily blocked by demolition and that the necessary charges be placed in the most forward areas and assembled for ready installation in the rear areas.' Rowell, who had just replaced Morris as the commander of NGF, waited a week before replying, perhaps to temper his initial reaction. He wired back to Sutherland: 'Some parts of the track have to be negotiated on hands and knees and the use of some tons of explosive

---

i   Likely referring to the narrow mountainous pass at Florina Gap in Greece where Australians of the 19th Brigade in April 1941 under Brigadier George Vasey attempted to hold up a German advance.

would not increase these difficulties [for the Japanese]. It is respectfully suggested that such explosives as can be got forward would be better employed in facilitating our advance than for preparing to delay the enemy!'[14]

•

It was not only the Allied high command who were ignorant of the track, as indicated by the Japanese Yokoyama Advance Butai report of July 1942. As part of the preliminary invasion force, Lieutenant Colonel Tsukamoto Hatsuo temporarily commanded the combat arm of the invasion force, centred around his 1st Battalion of the 144th Regiment (I/144th Regiment). He was instructed to: 'Have the infantry . . . reconnoiter the route to Moresby in the occupied forward zone as quickly as possible. Reports of its value must be made, as well as reports on how quickly construction of roads for packhorses, light and heavy traffic . . . can be carried out. Reports also on whether or not the main force of the detachment could capture Moresby by overland route. Guard particularly against "defeat by detail" by the enemy.'[15] Indeed, the Japanese forces in July 1942 would land with trucks, bicycles, artillery and pack animals, which, while useful to varying degrees on the northern coastal plain, were of no use beyond the coast, with the exception of the small-calibre mountain guns.[16]

That said, the Japanese were not completely ignorant of the Buna–Kokoda region as Japanese intelligence officers disguised as businessmen—and likely anthropologists—had visited the area, while others in Australia had purchased maps of eastern New Guinea of varying utility. Further west in North-east New Guinea was Swiss national and Nazi sympathiser Josef Hofstetter, who had been prospecting for gold in the region for twenty years and knew the area well. He provided valuable intelligence to the Japanese. Indeed, during the Japanese attack against Wau in July 1942, he was acting as a guide for a Japanese patrol and was reportedly killed in an Australian ambush.[17]

Several air reconnaissance sorties had also been flown by Japanese airmen before the invasion at Gona–Buna, providing details of the road and track networks on the coastal lowlands, with pilots reporting that the track beyond Kokoda Station disappeared into the jungle. However, the same airmen stated bizarrely that there appeared to be a road suitable for motor transport from Isurava that led all the way to Port Moresby! The Japanese were also aware of four other routes over the Owen Stanley, but Kokoda was by far their best option.[18] Indeed, Geoffrey 'Doc' Vernon, who would become a legend of the Kokoda Campaign, recalled: 'From Kagi towards Kokoda there are many tracks. I know of three which cross the range at different places. Enemy captured maps show at least four. Where their information comes from is a mystery.'[19]

Captain Geoffrey 'Doc' Vernon was a 60-year-old physician and planter in Papua at the time of the Japanese invasion and had in June been assigned to help look after Papuan carriers who were attached to ANGAU. He had falsely lowered his age to 52 to sign up at Port Moresby with the AAMC in February 1942. Vernon had served as a medical officer with the Australian 11th Light Horse at Gallipoli and while there suffered from a shell burst which resulted in his near total deafness. Even so, he remained with his men throughout the Middle East Campaigns of 1916–18 and was awarded the Military Cross (MC) for 'conspicuous gallantry' during the fighting at Romani in the Sinai in 1916. His citation states in part: 'He showed exceptional devotion to duty, especially on 7th August 1916 during the Battle of Romani. He worked unceasingly amongst the wounded and remained out all night with a wounded man who could not be brought in; he set a fine example of courage.'[20] He was promoted to major in January 1917, but was wounded in the fighting at Tel el Sheria in late November 1917, just after the battle to take Beersheba, which saw the Australian Light Horse famously charge to take the town and its wells—one of the last successful full-scale cavalry charges in history. Even so, he stayed on until he was forced to return to Australia in August 1918.[21]

Doc Vernon himself recalled at the time the benefits of his near total deafness: 'Being very deaf from concussion deafness on Active-Service 1915, I do not gather much information from others. I therefore miss much, including all the rumours and false reports that constantly passed along the line. The absence of these may be an advantage.'[22] Undoubtedly another benefit must have been 'selective hearing' when it came to verbal orders issued to him.

Doc Vernon would later type his report to ANGAU entitled: *Diary of Field Services on the Owen Stanley–Buna Campaign, 1942* sometime in early 1943. Paper must have been scarce as on the other side of each diary page is scribbled, likely in Doc's own small flowing cursive script, his narrative of other matters of the day. Obviously, Doc was no typist as turning over the last page he typed: 'This machine is no good Imperial typewriter.' He recorded that by mid-June 1942 he was: 'acting as M.O. [medical officer] to the native hospital at Sapphire Creek.'[23]

•

Most European civilians had been evacuated from northern New Guinea in late 1941 and early 1942 due to fear of a Japanese invasion. Even so, 121 missionaries (with their 26 children) elected to stay. Major Caesar Townsend, who had been in the New Guinea Administration since 1921 and was now with ANGAU, told Bishop Philip Strong that all mission women were to be evacuated as the lives of his men would likely be lost in defending them. However, the bishop instead encouraged all to stay, writing in his pastoral letter: 'We must endeavour to carry on our work in all circumstances no matter what the cost. God . . . the Church at home which sent us out . . . the tradition and history of missions . . . require it of us . . . We could never hold up our faces again if, for our own safety, we all fled. Special circumstances may make it imperative for one or two to go. For the rest of us, we have made our resolution to stay. Let us not shrink from it. The Lord be with you.'[24] As feared by Major Townsend, stranded Australian soldiers and downed American airmen behind the lines would be killed trying to defend the missionaries and their parishioners from their Japanese pursuers.

6

'Rum turned out to be mostly metho spirits'

Lieutenant Bert Kienzle was assigned to escort 'B' Company of the 39th Battalion on their trek across the Owen Stanleys. He found Sam Templeton and his men on 7 July waiting for him at Ilolo—at the southern foothills of the range. They had just traded one of their First World War–vintage Lewis machine guns for a brand-new Bren gun still covered in packing grease; Templeton's men were trying to figure out the intricacies of its workings.[1]

Corporal Donald Daniels, a nineteen-year-old interior decorator from Caulfield in Victoria with 'A' Company, who would soon be following 'B' Company over the mountains, recalled at the time that he was the only one in his section 'who could fire a machine gun. So, I had to teach one of my men how to fire it ... We only got the [Bren] guns halfway over the track, they were still in grease.'[2] He also considered the .303 Lee-Enfield rifle a hindrance in the jungle fighting: 'My section had a Bren gun [and] I had a Thompson sub-machine gun ... The rest of them had .303 rifles, huge things ... They could fire ... to seven hundred yards away. All you needed in the jungle was something you could fire ... to thirty-five yards.' He also considered the Lee-Enfield a 'darn nuisance going through the jungle because you put it over your shoulder, and it stuck up in the air eighteen inches. It got caught in vines. It was a problem. Whereas the Thompson sub-machine gun you'd just tuck it under your arm ... Short bursts with sub-machine guns ... You can just spray the area.'[3]

Lance Corporal Alexander Lochhead, a twenty-year-old clerk from Essendon in Victoria also with 'A' Company, recalled many years later that they were not well clothed or equipped: 'The clothes we were in were not suitable—we just had shirts and shorts—and our normal webbing, old-fashioned equipment . . . We still had our .303 rifles, which were First World War . . . We had a Thompson sub-machine gun—one per section.' He and his men carried the Lewis guns half-way across the mountains before carriers caught up with them bringing forward brand new Bren guns. He membered with some frustration, 'Unfortunately, no-one knew anything about them at all . . . We didn't have any heavy equipment—our mortars were left behind; our heavy machine guns were left behind—there was nothing at all that was it.'[4]

Lance Corporal William Mahoney, a 22-year-old labourer from Balranald in New South Wales with 'C' Company, also recalled getting their Bren guns as they crossed the mountains: 'While we were . . . on the Kokoda Track we were brought a few Bren guns which we didn't know how to operate and we asked how to operate them and they said, "You will find out when you are in battle how to use them", and that was what happened.'[5]

With their new Bren gun and several vintage Lewis guns, and with most carrying rifles, the men of 'B' Company were ready to move out. There was no way they could carry all the supplies over the Owen Stanleys, so arrangements were made for the lugger *Gili Gili* to be loaded at Port Moresby and unloaded at Buna. By the time it arrived, Templeton and his men would be on the other side of the mountains. Bert Kienzle, with his large party of native carriers, would lead the advance across the mountains and establish camps for the exhausted troops who would be many hours behind. Accompanying the troops were another 120 Papuan carriers who would assist in carrying supplies that were needed in the crossing of the mountains. Within days they would also be carrying many of the men's packs as the soldiers succumbed to exhaustion in trying to negotiate the unforgiving, wet, stinking mountainous jungle terrain.[6]

Doc Vernon knew the pending departure of 'B' Company from Ilolo—south of Ower's Corner—would add new demands on his carriers. He recorded many carriers were sick and all were exhausted as they arrived back from the line, there were constant demands for more men. He noted it was hard to find 'sufficient fit men to undertake all the work that was called for. The situation became acute when I had to rest a large convoy just returned from Kage [*sic* Kagi] for two days. I told Capt. Kelly LOC [Lines of Communications], that carrying would have to be held up for that period [two days]. He realised the exhausted state of our reserves and delayed operations to assist it.'[7] It was then that Doc Vernon undertook his first trek along the Kokoda Track, later writing: 'Before leaving on a tour of inspection of the whole LOC I made a "trial trip" to Uberi. On the way I met two ANGAU Warrant Officers who assured me I would never get through the long arduous track to Kokoda, a mistaken opinion as events proved. Before reaching Uberi I encountered the first of the appalling Owen Stanley Hills and was duly impressed by their all-comprehensive difficulties. It proved to be [a] great deal worse than I expected.'[8]

•

At 8 a.m., 7 July, Captain Sam Templeton, his five officers and 120 men left Ilolo to start their eight-day trek through the mountainous backbone of Papua. As they moved forward, the jungle swallowed them whole from a mid-twentieth century world war into the prehistoric domain of the Owen Stanleys. Their first day's hard slog would take them to the staging post at Uberi. During the trek across the steep peaks and deep valleys, Templeton became a further inspiration to those around him, who in most cases were half his age. Many remembered how he 'would go up and down the line of men as they toiled under their equipment. He would encourage them as they went and helped those who were finding the going tough by carrying their rifles.'[9] Another vividly recalled: 'Sam at one time during the trek with at least four rifles over his shoulder. It was thought by some under his command, that given the fact he was continually going from front to rear of the column to keep the men going that he actually travelled double the distance as the rest of the company.'[10]

The track during the campaign was famously described by Colonel Frank Norris, assistant director of medical services, Australian 7th Division:

Before the campaign, this route had been considered passable only to native or trained district officers. Imagine an area of approximately 100 miles long [160 kilometres]—crumple and fold this into a series of ridges, each rising higher and higher until 7,000 feet [2100 metres] is reached, then declining in ridges to 3,000 feet [around 900 metres]— cover this thickly with jungle, short trees and tall tangled with great entwining savage vines—through the oppression of this density cut a little native track two or three feet [around a metre] wide, up the ridges, over the spurs, around gorges and down across swiftly flowing happy mountain streams. Where the track clambers up the mountain sides, cut steps—big steps, little steps, steep steps—or clear the soil from the tree roots. Every few miles bring the track through a small patch of sunlit [razor sharp] kunai grass, or an old deserted native garden, and every seven or ten miles [11 or 16 kilometres] build a group of dilapi- dated grass huts—as staging shelters—generally set in a foul offensive clearing. Every now and then leave beside the track dumps of discarded putrefying food, occasional dead bodies, and human fouling. In the morning flicker the sunlight through the tall trees, flutter green and blue and purple and white butterflies lazily through the air and hide birds of deep throated song or harsh cockatoos in the foliage. About midday and through the night pour water over the forest, so that the steps become broken and continual yellow stream flows downwards, and the few level areas become pools and puddles of putrid mud. In the high ridges . . . drip this water day and night over the track through a fetid forest grotesque with moss and glowing phosphorescent fungi.[11]

The men must have marvelled at the speed and agility of the bare- footed carriers who were laden with three times the weight they were carrying. These men, along with Bert Kienzle in the lead, quickly

The Kokoda Track

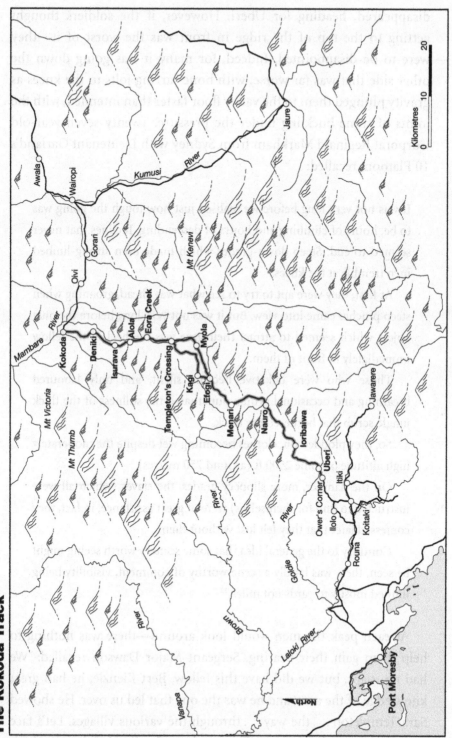

disappeared, heading for Uberi. However, if the soldiers thought getting to the top of the ridge in front was the worst of it—they were to be disappointed. Indeed, for many it was going down the other side that was far worse, with bone-jarring jolts to the knees as gravity plunged them to the valley floor faster than intended, with the joints of some buckling under the pressure. Twenty-seven-year-old Corporal Reginald Markham from Sydney with Lieutenant Garland's 10 Platoon, recalled:

It was not very long before we realised just how tough the going was to be, hours of climbing and hours of descending. Inclines that never seemed to end. Steep down-grades which made even strong-limbed men tremble at the knees.

At first, they were apt to try to see what was ahead, groaning when steep pinches came into view. But it was not very long before the only object which seemed to attract their gaze was the heel of the fellow immediately in front of them.

Those who were talkative became silent, and only laboured breathing and occasional grunts punctuated the stillness of the thick jungle scrub that bordered the track.

So, they plodded on, clothes becoming wet despite the moderately high altitude of some 2500 ft [around 750 metres].

On the damper, more slippery grades, the staves (which all were instructed to find for themselves) were of great assistance; in fact, they confessed later that they felt lost without them.

Contrary to the general idea that some scenery worth seeing might be seen, there was hardly a scene worthy of comment, visibility being limited mostly to yards not miles.[12]

At each peak the men would look around—there was nothing to help them gain their bearing. Sergeant Major Dawson recalled: 'We had no maps, but we did have this fellow, Bert Kienzle, he had great knowledge of the area, and he was the one that led us over. He showed Sam Templeton . . . the way . . . through the various villages. Let's face it, there were tracks running off everywhere. But [he] led the way, that's the only way we knew the way . . . I don't think anybody knew where to get a map of that area.'[13]

Everywhere they looked as they reached another peak or ridge was low cloud cover, green jungle and mountain peaks and river valleys. Distance was measured in hours not kilometres—'How many more days to Kokoda?' must have been the dominant question. What they usually could not see, but were all too aware of, was the primeval life forms that thrived in the thick tropical jungle: 'Man might find it hard to long endure such conditions, but just about every other life form seemed to prosper there as nowhere else . . . Amid the vines, trees, wild orchids, palms, ferns, staghorns and all the rest, snakes, spiders and leeches slithered and sheltered together, competing for space. It was the classic Darwinian environment, where only the strongest survived, and that strength was measured either by the force of the individual organism or, failing that, by having enough numbers of weaker organisms to prevail anyway.'[14]

They would not reach the highest peak, Mount Bellamy at 2200 metres, until day seven of their march. Along the way they would have to climb and descend around a dozen significant peaks, cross any number of dark river valleys where they would plunge into freezing water. Indeed, their clothes were wet, always wet, either from river crossings or from the bucketing of rain that fell—the men went to sleep in wet clothes and woke up freezing in wet clothes. Their descent to Kokoda from Mount Bellamy would also involve climbing half-a-dozen more peaks and then plunging down into river valleys before they reached the lowlands of the northern fetid coastal swamps.[15]

Lieutenant Arthur Seekamp recalled how Bert Kienzle and his men were a godsend: 'We had about 250 carriers taking us through and half of those were going through fast; as soon as we camped in the morning they'd go through, dump their load at the next station's point and then they'd build us a shack and get the fire going. First thing next morning they'd do the same thing again.'[16]

•

Among Sam Templeton's company was Corporal Jack Wilkinson, a 35-year-old mining operator from Misima in Papua. With the outbreak of war, he signed up with the 2nd AIF and served in the Greek and Middle East campaigns. On returning to New Guinea he was assigned to ANGAU but soon after was transferred as the medic to 'D' Company, 39th Battalion. However, he volunteered to move out with 'B' Company when they got their marching orders to cross over the Owen Stanleys in early July as Templeton had no medic. Wilkinson, like Corporal Markham, kept a detailed diary and recorded their crossing of the Owen Stanleys and the ongoing fight against the Japanese in the early days of the Kokoda Campaign.[17] He recorded their trek across the mountains, leaving Uberi at 8 a.m. on 8 July and arriving at Ioribaiwa.

> Uncle Sam and Bert Kienzle in the lead. I brought up the rear ... several chaps sent back ... with fever and bad knees; hell of a strain on the knees on the downgrade ... Had busy time patching feet. Made Ioribaiwa ... Missed out on the tea as I was with last of troops. Had a job to get some of them to make it. Uncle Sam came back and helped me about half way up last hill. Was carrying four rifles and three packs and had doubts about making it myself. Uncle Sam insisted on carrying all my gear as well as that of others ... Had a busy time when reached camp. Many feet blistered and chaf from packs, haversacks and rifle slings. Camp cold and wet. Made a brew of rum and sipora and hot water, which revived some. Many non-drinkers among these kids. Rum turned out to be mostly metho spirits. Doled out by Steve (Captain Stevenson). Had a bad cold night.[18]

Corporal Markham also wrote at the end of this hard slog on reaching their destination: 'Being situated on a "Razerback", this village [Ioribaiwa] gave a considerable view of the next day's ramble. The food position was good throughout the "Trek"—there being ample and sufficient of M&V [meat and vegetable], salmon, soup, butter, cheese, jam and tinned fruits, without the fresh fruit and vegetables traded from the villagers. Night came partnered by a fairly heavy shower, but all heeded it not a bit, being very, very tired from the day's march. To get more warmth, many pooled their blankets and dossed together.'[19]

Kienzle also recorded on 8 July: 'I left UBIRI [*sic*] at 0800 hrs. with 120 carriers and troops of "B" Coy 39th Bn. Capt. Templeton in charge. The carriers stood up to the work well carrying packs belonging to the troops and rations. Arrived at IORIBAIWA at 1400 hrs. Sgt. MAGA had completed two large grass shelters and erected tents for troops and shelters for carriers.'[20] The next day—9 July—they pushed on to Nauro, which Wilkinson recorded being 'a long day but not too bad ... bothered by native bees en route crawling all over us after the salt in sweat ... Last downhill to camp very hard to take. Many falls as knees give way ... Conference with Uncle Sam and decided to stay here for one day to give troops a spell. One man shows signs of dysentery. Age about 48. Has son in company and trying to keep up. Oldest man in company—First War also. Said nothing about being sick hoping he would improve. Decided to leave him here to come on later ... He did follow later and was killed.'[i][21]

Corporal Markham and his mates were more than happy for the day off—10 July—later recalling that most took the 'opportunity to do washing. Others went for short strolls, to a very dirty native's home and about the nearby native gardens. Those who were lucky enough to have some "trade" twist did a little trading with the natives for paw paws, mandarins etc. Looking at these men after that day's rest, one would never have thought that they had gone through ... they looked more fit than when they began the journey.'[22]

The next day—11 July—they were back on the track as recorded by Wilkinson: 'Made Efogi ... A long day but not too bad ... Day's spell worked wonders ... Uncle Sam very annoyed about the rum and metho. Pity any QM blokes he can pin the blame on.'[23] Corporal Markham also recorded in his diary their arrival: 'Efogi, like most of the villages situated on high ground had limited building space. What huts there were, were built right along the ridge, which was no wider than 40 ft [12 metres]; they were however, well-made, and happily water-proof.'[24] If the men thought they had faced the worst of the trek they were wrong. Efogi was around 1350 metres above sea level, however, the

---

i   The author, using the battalion's nominal roll and casualty figures, was unfortunately unable to identify father and son.

next day—12 July—they would have to plunge into the 400-metre deep Efogi River gorge and from there climb to Kagi on the other side of the steep valley at a similar height to Efogi.

Lieutenant Peter Brewer and his carriers were coming in the opposite direction to help 'B' Company on the second half of the journey to Kokoda. Wilkinson recorded in his diary: 'Made Kagi. Only a short walk but steep. Fairly high and cold. Peter Brewer here [with] carriers from Kokoda. Long talk about track ahead. Eric Turner arrived . . . en route to Moresby. Told of his capture of Jap airman . . . Got a hell of a shock when Jap pointed a pistol at him and tried to shoot him. First Jap prisoner. Peter Brewer in good form. All our original carriers back to carry supplies.'[25]

Lieutenant Kienzle also recorded: 'We left EFOGI at 0745 hrs. and arrived at KAGI at 0930 hrs. We struck steep climbing between these two camps. A.D.O. [Assistant District Officer] Brewer from Kokoda with 186 carriers had been waiting for two days to assist in crossing the main range from KAGI to KOKODA. He sent his carriers back with instructions to start building up supplies at the various depots established so far. He found that to 'have carriers based at each stage and to carry only between two stages was the best method making the carriers feel more settled and contented.'[26] Corporal Markham recalled the parting of the carriers.

> Kagi . . . consisted of two large huts, with thin samplings for a floor, which were not so very comfortable to sleep upon . . . At this stop a large number of native carriers, whose 'time' had expired, started to go the rounds of their friends that night, bidding them farewell for in the morning they would not have time to do so. It was a strange sight to see these 'G' string clad natives shaking hands with each other, and at times even kissing. They were very sincere in their parting, giving one handshake then continuing to hold hands while they gave their final words. Losing the very efficient cook-boys was felt more than anything, for those at [Kagi] . . . knew little, or no English . . . These new carriers were a less civilised lot than the old ones . . . they certainly were a tough looking crowd, with their coloured armlets,

made of beads; punctured nostrils, thru which many had bones or pieces of polished stick.[27]

Pushing forward from Kagi—13 July—it would be a long and difficult trek to Eora Crossing. The men fell through the thin, mossy carpet, or floundered on roots concealed by the mud. Sergeant Major Dawson recalled the exhausting hard slog along the track, likely often wondering if it would ever end.

I should mention that it was a 'track'. As in a footpath—not the Yankee sanitized 'trail' nonsense we hear it called now. We were in what was termed 'battle order', i.e., haversack on back with some additives inside, plus webbing and other accoutrements and, of course, whatever weapon you happened to have been issued with. In my case it was a .303 rifle. The Lewis machine guns were moved around the sections from time to time to share the load burden . . .

What a dreadful test of pure physical strength! . . . Some of the troops were suffering from chafing, bad knees, vomiting and sheer exhaustion. Some of the fellows had to be helped. I recall carrying another bloke's rifle and equipment at some stage; he was totally exhausted and continually vomiting. I remember seeing Sam Templeton at one point carrying three or four rifles. It was a case of climb three steps, then hang onto a tree, or slide back three . . . A few of the troops had to be sent back with bad knees and other problems.

Apart from the ups and downs, there were the regular downpours of rain that mixed with your own sweat, so you were never dry. Other joys we encountered were lawyer vines, their tendrils that literally grabbed your clothes, skin, whatever, and hung on. Then there were leeches that had the ability to get through your clothing and all parts of your body, including the most delicate parts, to suck your blood. If you moved off the narrow track to dodge the mud, you would inevitably walk into a large spider web, strung between the trees with an enormous spider in the middle, usually about face high.[28]

Kienzle remained with Brewer and Templeton and accompanied them on their trek to Kokoda. From Kagi, Templeton and his men climbed to the summit of Mount Bellamy, at 2200 metres, using the pre-war mail route—perhaps the worst part of the track—this was *keru gabuna*, the 'Cold Place'.[29] It was a miserable journey, passing through the 'Moss Forest'. They marched in a heavy, continuous downpour, the track swirling with water, churning it into mud. Corporal Jack Wilkinson continued to write in his diary even though exhausted after a hard day's slog and having to tend to the men after he himself reached camp: 'To Eora Crossing No 2. Long day over range. Rain forest and lawyer vines. Deep moss and slippery track. Rain and mist. Cold and dreary. Camp not too good. Building material short. Very little flat ground. Creek roaring loudly. To bed in wet clothes after working on various small injuries. Getting used to wet clothes now. Hope my feet stand up to it for a bit longer. To flat below Deniki.'[30]

Leaving Eora Crossing on 14 July, Kienzle, Brewer, Templeton and their men began to make the long descent towards Kokoda, pushing through Isurava and making their way towards Deniki, 400 metres below this village was Kokoda Station. That afternoon, they reached Deniki, with Wilkinson recording: 'Long day but reasonable walking. Could see Kokoda from hilltop. Kienzle, unlike Sam and Brewer to Kokoda first and sent back tents for troops. Much warmer than the hills. Troops in good form.' The next day—15 July—the men reached Kokoda with Wilkinson writing: 'To Kokoda. Nice place. Glad to be here. Took over native hospital.'[31]

Corporal Markham also wrote in his diary: 'Passing from the scrub into a large clear garden area, they continued thru and on to the rubber plantation; first an area of sapling rubbers, then the main group was penetrated. The time occupied to cover the open patch was about fifteen minutes, and the rubber twenty. As the long single file of carriers neared the settlement they broke into a weird chant, which was rather eerie to listen to, beginning with something that sounded like "Aaaw" repeated perhaps a dozen times, then ending with a high pitched "Ohhh"! At last "Kokoda".'[32]

Lieutenant 'Judy' Garland briefly recalled the journey: 'On the first day out each man carried 80 lbs. [36 kilograms] of equipment. But on the second day we had to considerably reduce the load each man carried; the very difficult terrain we encountered on that first day had taken its toll. I will not go into any further details as to what happened on the days that followed during our march to Kokoda except to say this. The native carriers were a great help to us each day.'[33]

7

'Condemned latrines and ordered new ones'

The men had finally made it to the other side of the mountain barrier. The 39th Battalion War Diary records that while Templeton had set out with five officers and 120 men, by the time they got to Kokoda seventeen of his men had dropped out, leaving him with five officers and 103 men—14 per cent of his force had succumbed to the track.[1] However, compared to others who would follow in the weeks and months ahead, they had a relatively easy time of it, with plenty of carriers, time to stop and rest when necessary and they did the crossing during the 'dry' season—others would have no time to stop and rest, having to push on regardless of injuries during the wet season with its heavy tropical downpours, while at numerous points having to fight the advancing Japanese.

On taking up their position at Kokoda Station, Bert Kienzle organised for Sam Templeton's men to be fed from his plantation's stores. Wilkinson recalled: 'Kokoda suited us well while we were there. There was plenty of native fruit and vegetables and the men were in good shape. The climate was good. Mosquitoes were few. Housing was good. We had radio communications. Life looked sweet. For a full week.'[2]

Lieutenant Kienzle did not stay long and on 17 July he headed back over the mountains to Port Moresby to assess the supply situation. He had gained invaluable experience and insights regarding the logistical requirements during his first journey with a body of troops, writing: 'The trail from Uberi to Kagi is a series of steep ascents and descents, crossing six ridges en route. It is indeed a test of endurance. A steady stream of urgent rations, supplies, medical, and ammunition had to be planned and put into operation immediately and maintained on the Line of Communication from Ilolo or Ower's Corner to Kokoda, to help provision a company of men. Little did I know or was advised at this stage, that this was to be my responsibility for a full battalion, then a brigade and later a division.'[3]

His experience in his first crossing with troops clearly demonstrated to him that, even with the superhuman efforts of his carriers, they alone could not hope to keep even this small body of troops adequately supplied. As he approached Kagi on his return to Port Moresby, he checked on the supplies that had since arrived and found just 42 tins of biscuits, 42 loads of rations and 1225 kilograms of rice.[4] By now, hundreds of carriers were employed to take up supplies to various staging depots. He wrote in his report to ANGAU: 'The establishment of small food dumps for a small body of troops was now underway as far as Kagi. This ration supply was being maintained by carriers over some of the roughest country in the world.' He noted with the limited number of carriers available maintenance of supplies was going to be impossible without the aid of air drops by transport aircraft. He estimated that a carrier carrying nothing except food would eat through his load in thirteen days; half that if he was also carrying rations for a soldier. The problem was exacerbated considering many were not carrying food, but 'arms, ammunition, equipment, medical stores, ordnance, mail and dozens of other items needed to wage war, on the backs of men. The track to Kokoda takes 8 days so the maintenance of supplies is a physical impossibility without large-scale co-operation of plane droppings.'[5]

Indeed, the twenty-minute flight from Port Moresby to Kokoda airstrip by one cargo plane alone could deliver what otherwise required hundreds of porters to carry in relays over an eight-day hard slog.

●

Captain Sam Templeton and his men went about establishing their base at Kokoda and becoming familiar with the area from the station to the coast. They were expecting the rest of the battalion to follow within weeks and were waiting on the arrival of the supplies onboard the *Gili Gili*. Lieutenant Garland recalled: 'At Kokoda, Sam allotted each platoon to the defensive positions they were to occupy. My 10 Platoon's task was defence of the drome and surrounding areas including the river and bridge, which joined the plateau ... we trained, patrolled and obtained knowledge of the area where we were now stationed; Sam Templeton kept us on the move.'[6] Company Sergeant Major Dawson also recalled the men remained at Kokoda for about a week, recuperating, training and conducting patrols to familiarise themselves with the area. His job was to organise the dispersal and distribute the ammunition, which also required him to prime the boxes of hand grenades. This meant 'unscrewing the base plug of each grenade, inserting the J-shaped fuse and cap and replacing the base plug—a delicate operation.' At the time he noted that Captain Templeton had gone down to Buna to meet the coastal trader *Gili Gili*, which was 'carrying our kitbags and stores from Port Moresby with the company quartermaster, [Sergeant] Allan Collyer, in charge. These were to be transported to Kokoda by native carriers, who were later referred to as "Fuzzy Wuzzy Angels" as, apart from carrying stores, they played a major role in carrying out the badly wounded.'[7]

•

On 20 July, on the other side of the Owen Stanleys, Doc Vernon was getting ready to start a tour of inspection along the Kokoda Track. The 60-year-old Gallipoli and Light Horse veteran was easily recognised from a distance by his 'uniform' consisting of trousers which, weather permitting, would be rolled up, taking on the appearance of long shorts, a shirt with a blue army pullover, with his slouch hat crumpled up almost unrecognisable, a small dilly bag containing a basic medical kit along with some army biscuits and, most critically—tobacco. Indeed, a cigarette rolled in newspaper always seemed to be dangling from his lips. He later wrote in his diary of the campaign: [i]

---

i   A copy of Doc Vernon's personal 'diary' has been published by the 39th Battalion Association. This 'diary' was clearly written after the events as Doc refers to places by name before they were then designated as such (e.g., Templeton's Crossing) and subsequent events, it is likely a combination of records of his personal diary and additional information likely gained in early 1943—it is best considered a narrative of his experiences of the campaign as opposed to a strict diary.

Began to get accounts of many cases of illness and bad condition for native carriers along the then newly opened Owen Stanley track. Large numbers of sick were arriving at the Carriers' base at Ilolo and their state generally was said to be deplorable. Subsequent observation proved this to be substantially correct allowing for the usual amount of exaggeration. I was ordered to Ilolo and arrived there with WO [Sergeant Harold] Ferguson who was to look after hygiene.

We found a newly formed bush camp with insufficient accommodation for the 800 odd carriers there, a number of whom were ill. A bush hospital was erected in about 24 hours, and under an energetic OC the housing increased as if by magic. Ferguson, an artist in the construction of latrines, brought the sanitation to the highest pitch. At sunrise every morning the carriers detailed for duty were paraded for medical inspection and, by this method, those with sore feet and abraded shoulders, were weeded out. They seemed to be, at best, a rather sorry crew, and as at that time carried for 4 days to Efogi, half-way to Kokoda, the number really fit was limited. Urgent demands for their service necessitated sending some who were only partially fit. Towards the end of the day the inward carriers struggled in and threw down their loads, often exhausted. The sick were picked up and frequently I found it necessary to put others off for a rest.

Captain [Bartor] Falthorn [sic Faithorn] met me at Ilolo and gave me a mandate to look after the carriers and try and improve their working conditions which were none of the best. In those early days along the lines, when as yet the importance of the carriers was not appreciated, they were occasionally hard used by the LOC personnel. To remedy this loads and distances were standardized, the former being reduced to 40-pounds [18 kilograms]—10-pounds less than the previous government maximum. Before then carriers had been given 100-pound bags of rice and other heavy loads to carry. But from now on, at Ilolo at least, the new weights were faithfully adhered to.

Shortly before my arrival Lieutenant Kienzle . . . had been appointed OC Carriers on the L.O.C., his command extending to Kokoda. He asked Major [Sydney] Elliott-Smith ANGAU if my appointment to Ilolo could be extended to that of MO for the whole line. This was agreed to and I was glad to be given work of a greater scope than any previous allotted to me.[8]

This is an understatement, as the 60-year-old Gallipoli veteran would soon be responsible for the medical care not only of the Papuans but initially at least also many of the Australian troops who slogged their way across the track and then battled with the Japanese. While Doc Vernon and others tried to better the conditions for the carriers, the ordeal for many was understandably more than they bargained for, even before the Japanese landings: 'Some account of the general disinclination of the native medical orderlies [NMO] to leave Moresby and face the discomforts of the Owen Stanley Range is worth mentioning,' wrote Doc Vernon, 'it was more than disinclination, and led to all sorts of subterfuges, including some subtle examples of malingering. Natives are accustomed to producing blood at will by rubbing their gums as evidence of internal hemorrhage, and some marvelous concoctions of pounded bully beef mixed with blood from the mouth were handed in as dysenteric stools! It took me quite some time to comprehend and expose such deceptions.'[9] Indeed, it was not only the carriers, but also some of the NMOs that were loath to enter the highlands. Doc Vernon wrote in his diary at the time: 'Our orderlies were reluctant to go forward because they were given a rather too easy a time at the base, added to by the fearsome tales told by the boys who had been over the line; they had not been trained by route marches to stand fatigue of patrol over the range . . . but later they became adept at hill climbing.'[10]

He recorded leaving Ilolo to 'inspect all medical establishments for carriers along the line, taking a small supply of drugs & dressings arrangements beyond that being in the hands of the A.D.O. Kokoda with medical assistants to help him. I picked up a N.M.Ord. close to Uberi to go with me. Arrived 1300 [hours], inspected camp and found sanitary orders carried out.'[11] Just before leaving he came across the Australians of the Independent Light Horse who were operating around Port Moresby, tasked with scouting and patrolling the region, occasionally, as now, they were helping to move up supplies to the start of the Kokoda Track at Ilolo and sometimes as far as Uberi.

The Independent Light Horse were then working with us carrying pack teams between Ilolo and Uberi. These cheerful dusty lads outwardly closely resembled our Diggers of 1914–18 in Palestine; the years fell back, and I felt thoroughly at home with them. I had a packet of sweet biscuits with me, and that night at Uberi we played Whiskey Poker for them, the winner handing them round with a good night cup of cocoa.

On the next day, 21st July, we found the comparatively well stepped path ceased at the gap beyond Uberi, and for a time the going was as hard as anything on the whole track. Halfway down the next hill, however, a particularly long and steep one, we met some soldiers putting in some steps again, and from this a little tale emerged. It seems that the road gang had had to knock off their work owing to the non-arrival of certain stores and were told that they could take a rest while waiting for them. Instead of doing so they . . . had voluntarily gone on putting in steps to make the track easier for the carriers. In digger language they said they pitied the poor buggers scrambling over the slippery hillsides, so they put in their spare time to help them.[12]

It is possible that these steps were the initial construction of what would become famously (or infamously) known as 'The Golden Stairs' which was the signpost that you were truly about to ascend into the highlands of the Owen Stanleys. In all it would consist of around 1800 steps cut and reinforced up a steep slope. It reputedly got its name when 42-year-old Lieutenant Colonel Stanley Legge, who was attached to the headquarters staff, climbed the stairs in August 1942, and while stopping near the top for a breather gasped out the words 'Golden Stairs'. However, most Australian soldiers at the time had another name for them: 'Stairway to Hell'.[13] It was during the height of the Kokoda Campaign that Australian Salvation Army Major Albert Moore—who had earlier accompanied the Australians to North Africa—set up his 'coffee and comfort bar' to supply the men with a hot meal and coffee or tea before they climbed the stairs to fight the Japanese beyond. Many soldiers later recalled how the Salvos would often be close by and would bring them a hot cup of tea even as the fighting raged.[14]

Doc Vernon continued his journey, later writing: 'This day's walk took us up two steep hills each about 1000 feet [300 metres] and down a very steep one, with a long rough traverse along the ravine between them. We reached the hill station of Ioribaiwa long after midday. One of the objects of my patrol was to see that camp sanitation was kept up to the mark, and Ioribaiwa was the worst example of bad sanitation along the line.'[15] He recorded with disgust: 'Condemned latrines and ordered new ones. This order had not been carried out on my return there on 25 August when flies were breeding freely in the latrines and Dysentery had already broken out.'[16]

PART TWO

INVASION

8

'How safe we all felt—alas!'

During the morning of 21 July 1942, Captain Sam Templeton, in true character, had gone out alone to Buna to check that the 20 tons of stores on the *Gili Gili* were on their way to Kokoda. Over the last few days, Captain Thomas Grahamslaw, a 40-year-old civil servant from Port Moresby and the senior ANGAU officer in the district, had organised large groups of carriers to get all supplies to Kokoda by that afternoon.[1] Grahamslaw recalled 30 years later:

> Early in July advice was received that a company of 39th Battalion troops under the command of Captain Templeton were to march across the Owen Stanleys and that I was to meet them at Kokoda. At the same time, I received a signal advising that stores and ammunition for the Company were being shipped to Buna by the auxiliary vessel *Gili Gili*, and that I was to make the necessary arrangements to have them transported to Kokoda. At this time enemy aircraft were making daily reconnaissance visits during which they paid much attention to the Buna–Kokoda road.
>
> In view of this increasing enemy aerial activity I deemed it advisable to discharge the *Gili Gili* in the small harbour at Oro Bay, instead of the open roadstead at Buna, where she would be more conspicuous. There was such a feeling in the atmosphere, as it were, that something was about to break that I decided to transport all the *Gili Gili*'s cargo in one move. We worked it out that there would be 1500 carrier loads. [Jack] McKenna at Ioma and Brewer at Kokoda were instructed to

provide 800 carriers between them, while I assisted [Alan] Champion to obtain the remainder.

McKenna was the first to arrive with his quota. He strode into my office at Awala with blood in his eye to demand an explanation as to why I should make such a savage demand on the already denuded manpower in his sub-district. Jack readily appreciated the situation when I explained it to him, and he gave invaluable assistance in organising the three-day carrier haul from Oro Bay to Kokoda. I proceeded to Kokoda to meet Captain Templeton and his men of B Company, 39th Battalion. On arrival, I found that Lieutenant Brewer with his customary efficiency had provided adequate accommodation for the troops. I spent several days at Kokoda. During this period Templeton left for an inspection of Buna.[2]

Captain Templeton, now satisfied that all stores were on their way to the station, headed back towards Awala—halfway between Buna and Kokoda—unaware that a Japanese invasion force, including two large troop transports, was about to anchor off the coast of Gona where an Anglican mission station was located, just west of Buna.

•

At about 3 p.m., a lone Japanese navy high-speed Kawanishi E15K Shiun float-plane launched from a cruiser flew in low from the north over Holnicote Bay. At first it flew over the small village of Buna and the government station but quickly gained height and, banking, it dived towards the village with machine-gun bullets tearing into the government radio station. The plane quickly banked away and headed back out to sea. The radio post was manned by members of ANGAU and it was part of several outposts strung along the northern coast of Papua to act as an early warning system to any Japanese invasion.[3] The ANGAU war diary records for 21 July: 'Buna: Beach patrol reports the approach of an enemy aircraft (single float) seaplane which circled the Government Station at a low altitude and fired several bursts of machine-gun fire, then flew off . . . This incident may be called the opening gambit in the Japanese invasion of Buna.'[4]

Alan Champion, a 37-year-old lieutenant with ANGAU, had been the assistant magistrate at Buna and with Japan's entry into the world war had wisely evacuated his wife and young son to Australia.[5] With him now at Buna was his radio operator, 33-year-old Sergeant Barry Harper from Wangaratta in Victoria, who was with the New Guinea Air Warning Wireless Company (NGAWWC) of ANGAU. Both took cover as bullets tore into the radio station. At the time, 22-year-old George Clasby from Tunstall in Victoria, who had signed up with the 39th Battalion but had since volunteered to join NGAWWC, was also there, along with twenty-year-old Selwyn 'Scottie' Barrett from Moonee Ponds in Victoria, who was also with NGAWWC. They had arrived from further up the coast to collect mail that had arrived on the *Gili Gili*.[6] Within minutes Harper was on the radio to Port Moresby informing them that the station had been targeted by Japanese aircraft—he waited but got no acknowledgement. In his report to ANGAU, Champion wrote that soon after a beach patrol reported to him the arrival of a 'strange formation of cloud' just off Gona. He rushed to the beach:

I sent to the radio station for binoculars and found that this object was a large destroyer or light cruiser heading in the direction of Gona. I then saw the stern of another vessel well towards shore, the forward part being obscured by Cape Kellerton. On sweeping the sea with the glasses I saw two more destroyers and two merchant vessels of approximately 5,000 to 8,000 tons heading towards Buna. Visibility was rather poor owing to a haze on the sea, but I estimated the distance of the ships to be about 8 to 10 miles from Buna [13 to 16 kilometres]. I immediately instructed the Cipher Clerk [Harper] to send a clear message—there not being time to code a message—on 'X' frequency reporting the convoy off Buna. The Cipher Clerk was also instructed to stand by with native police in readiness to evacuate the radio equipment at a moment's notice.[7]

They were not the only ones to spot the ships. At the Anglican mission station at Gona, west of Buna, was Reverend James Benson.

Father Benson was highly regarded as an enlightened and tolerant missionary who went to New Guinea after suffering an overwhelming personal tragedy in Australia. While serving as the Rector of Bodalla on the New South Wales south coast, he was driving with his wife and four children heading for a ferry which would take them across the Clyde River. It was night and some workmen had left a light burning near where the ferry should have been. He mistakenly took this to be the light of the waiting ferry and drove his car into the river—he was the sole survivor. One can only imagine the intense pain and survivor guilt he had to endure.[8]

With Benson at the mission station at Gona were two Anglican Sisters. Mavis Parkinson, aged 26, was the head teacher of the mission, and May Hayman, aged 36, was the station's nurse. Mavis was from Ipswich in Queensland and was described by Benson as slim with sandy hair, fun-loving and cool and dainty; she had arrived at Gona in 1941 to do the 'Lord's Work'. May had been a nurse in Adelaide and had left for New Guinea in 1936 to also do missionary work. Described as petite, with sparkling eyes, she had recently become engaged to 37-year-old British missionary Reverend Vivian Redlich who had headed the mission station at Sangara for about a year and had the month before been sent to Dogura to recover from illness. On his way to Dogura he had stopped off at Gona—he was a man with a mission; he proposed marriage to May, who, while surprised, happily accepted.[9]

Australian soldiers liked to stop at Gona; it was considered an outpost of Australiana with well-constructed buildings, gardens and even a cricket pitch. The soldiers undoubtedly also enjoyed the female company of the two mission Sisters and the sociable priest. James Benson wrote a manuscript shortly after the war outlining the mission station and the coming of the Japanese, it was later expanded and published as a book in 1957. Benson recorded his still raw and vivid memories in 1945:

> Gona is a hard three hours walk west of Buna on beaches of soft yielding sand, and that before July 1942 it was one of the most beautiful stations in New Guinea, a land most prodigal in lovely settings.

If you could imagine a completely tropical Sydney Botanical Gardens alongside a lovely sweep of black sand and blue water, with a couple of small coral islands to the east and reefs running out to the west; and a creek spanned by a log bridge cutting the gardens in two, Kikiri on the west and Jamburadari on the east; there is the setting of Gona. In the garden of Jamburadari are most of the buildings and activities of the Mission—the great well-proportioned Church of All Souls surrounded by paths and shrubberies, the football and cricket field, teacher's [sic] houses, and Mission Boys' houses, and three schools, Senior, Intermediate and Kindergarten. All these buildings and the Mission workshop are of native material, and so sit rightly in the landscape. The Sisters' House, 'Jamburadari' itself, is of sawn timber framework carrying an iron roof, which is catchment for the water supply. The framework is filled in with walls of sago leaf lined with sago stalk like fluted panels of yellow oak, so that it too is really a native house of two story's [sic], built on a concrete foundation and the red-painted roof settled well into the picture, especially as round houses are the flower beds proper, as well as the flowering shrubs which are general to the whole station.

From the beach about 100 yards away, the broad path to the Mission travels through the coconut plantation of the village of Bepore, our fence being marked by an arch of Bougainvillea against which the little dispensary, where Sister Hayman attended the daily sores and other ailments of outpatients and school children. The broad path leaves Jamburadari House on its left and marches right into All Souls School, i.e., the Senior School. St Christopher's (Intermediate) is on your left incline; and St Nicholas' (Kindergarten) on your wide left, with the junior playing field between and half a dozen shade trees to dapple it. Away on your wide right, as I have said, is the great playing field and beyond, on the bank of the creek, stands the Church.

On the western, or Kikiri, side of the creek is the hospital and the doctor's house, with accommodation for white patients when need arises; while the native hospital has its kitchen and attendant's [sic] houses adjoining and there is a house for two old native teachers ... Here life went on its peaceful ordered way, and we were indeed a

happy community in 1941, when war entered the Pacific . . . we were
still three, Sister May Hayman (nurse), Miss Mavis Parkinson (teacher)
and myself.[10]

•

Both Mavis Parkinson and May Hayman would write letters to their
loved ones back home during their flight from the Japanese.[11] Mavis's
long letter to her mother, dated 5 August 1942, was published in the
Queensland Times on 5 May 1943; she addresses it 'Dearest Mummy'.
May's detailed letter was to her sister Viola who lived in Canberra. Her
letter of fifteen pages was written in pencil in small neat handwriting on
quarter folio notepaper; with letterhead in red ink 'Australian Comfort
Fund (Victorian Division) *With which is affiliated the R.S.L War Service
Fund*'.[12]

The opening paragraph to May's letter to Viola, dated 4 August,
tells of their current situation, two weeks after the Japanese invasion,
with the next paragraph detailing the day before the Japanese arrival,
describing their idyllic paradise.

> In our bush hideout: ND
> 4th August 1942.

Dear Vi,
With plenty of time and tons to tell you, our troubles now is that we
are entirely cut off from any communication with the civilised world,
however, I'll start a letter and hope that by and by there will be a way
of getting it through to you. We have no idea what is happening even
in this Northern Division; therefore we have no knowledge of what
lies before us. When next I see Nathaniel (evangelist in charge of Siai
near where our camp is) I'll give him what I have written out for you
about our recent adventure and he can keep it by him and forward
to you later when the war is over if anything should happen to us;
for it would be a shame if our recent adventures were never told. Of
course, there must be many others even more thrilling and certainly
more gory, for we have not so much as seen a dead bird, nor have we

suffered anything more than a few scratches and many insect bites, but it has been very terrifying and nerve racking never the less. I shall try to describe it for you starting just one day before our flight [escape] so as to provide the perfect contrast.

Two lads, one in charge of some P.I.B.s and one a spotter [Sergeant Lyle Hewitt and Corporal Harry Palmer] were staying with us on their way through (I have made mention of many other similar visitors, some we saw more often than others, or detained them longer if sick so that our home became a half-way house which we liked to think was a home away from home for one and all). This particular evening 20/7/42, both Sister and I had on our pretty long dresses; dinner was a gay meal and our lovely polished table with its pretty mats and beautiful flowers did not fail to call forth the usual compliments. When the house boys had finished the dishes, they brought us the hanging tilly from the kitchen and with deck chairs and cushions, gramophone and chocolate we went down to the front lawn. This scene was even prettier for the bright light showed forth the many soft ferns on the trunk of the oil palm under which we reclined. 'I don't suppose many places in the world today could afford to show as much light as this' someone was heard to remark. How safe we all felt—alas! What a change came upon us before the next 24 hours had passed.[13]

9

'Under heavy bombardment. Smashed radio. Evacuating'

Reverend Benson recalled seeing the Japanese invasion fleet just east of Gona, shortly after the Japanese aerial attack against the ANGAU radio station at Buna: 'It had been an ordinary sort of day . . . in the afternoon I was in the workshop repairing a small deck chair which I used when travelling on the six-foot by four-foot decks of our local canoes. Suddenly I heard cries of fear from the beach, and a second later a boy rushed to the door, shouting: "Father! Great ships are here".'[1] He hurried to the beach and looking out across the bay, where normally the only vessel to be seen was the mission ketch, he saw a Japanese cruiser, three destroyers and two large troop transports. The Japanese convoy had arrived just east of Gona at Basabua.[2] Benson recalled:

> My mind must have been numbed, or in some way out of order, for in the next ten minutes I did several stupid things. I remember I went back to the workshop, picked up the repaired chair and walked across with it to Kikiri, saying: 'I might as well put this away.' While at Kikiri I took my old white cassock off the nail where it hung alongside a good new one, rolled it up and pushed it into the small canvas satchel which I, or my boy, Alban, always carried over our shoulders when on a journey. It contained my Office Book, a cheap watch in a tin box (for protection from the damp), a pocket compass which Lieut.,

Dickenson[i] had given me as a parting gift (this later saved our lives), a few sticks of trade tobacco, pencil and notebooks, a couple of spare handkerchiefs and other odds and ends. I shut the door as though I were off on a usual journey, and, in a sort of daze, walked down the path towards the bridge. With ideas of our fellows soon taking Salamaua and Lae again, I thought the ships might be ours, carrying troops for the job, but that meeting with [Japanese] aerial opposition they had returned down the coast. People were streaming away along the bush tracks through the swamps which lie all along behind the beach strip. They were carrying what they could of their poor simple possessions, sleeping mats, clay cooking pots, little pigs and babies.[3]

Benson went in search of Mavis and May and found them in the dining room of the mission house sewing torn khaki shirts and shorts belonging to Sergeant Lyle Hewitt, a 21-year-old painter from Ascot Vale, and Corporal Harry Palmer, a 22-year-old grocer from Nullawarre, both from Victoria. Each had signed up with the 39th Battalion but on arriving in New Guinea had volunteered to join the NGAWWC. They were based at Ambasi but had come down to salvage the radio from a downed American aircraft located near Gona—possibly the aircraft flown by Lieutenant Dickinson.[4]

•

Earlier, Private Paul Lafe of the 1st PIB had been ordered by Sergeant Samai to take up a position on the Sanananda track between Gona and Buna, the Papuan private recalled in pidgin English which was later put to paper:

On the way I met Lieutenant Wort and passed on a message to him from my platoon sergeant. It was lunch time, and Lt Wort gave me some bread. After lunch, at one o'clock, he gave me a message to take back to

---

i   Dickenson was an American pilot who had been shot down on 23 May while returning from a bombing mission against Lae. His co-pilot and one of his gunners were killed outright, and only after the three surviving crew members bailed out did the wounded Dickenson bail out near Gona; he was nursed back to health by Sister May Hayman and soon after placed on a ship bound for Port Moresby.

my base, and a loaf of bread which had been cooked by the company cook . . . On the way back to Gona along the Sanananda track I came onto the beach and saw a warship in the bay. I asked two local people. 'Who does that ship belong to? Does it belong to the Japanese?' They said, 'We don't know, we think it might belong to America.' . . . I went along the beach and as I was walking along a Japanese plane flew over my head. After it had gone, I looked out to sea again and there were ships coming into the harbour, with two destroyers plus gunships on either flank. They lined up in the bay. One of the local women standing on the beach gave me a coconut and a yam for food, and I then started back to inform my platoon commander of the coming of the Japanese. I had just crossed over a small creek when the Japanese started to shell the area.[5]

•

At Gona, Sergeant Hewitt and Corporal Palmer had joined Benson and Mavis, who had by now rushed to the beach to watch the ships. All were unclear if the ships belonged to the Japanese or Allies 'when the two outside destroyers steamed off at full speed with their guns blazing, Miss Parkinson cried, "Scrummy! (her favourite word) a real naval battle, and here we are actually watching it. I do wish I knew if they are our ships!" One of the destroyers veered off straight out to sea while the other disappeared round Basabuga [sic Basabua] point. We still thought the two were off to meet Jap opposition either from sea or air.'[6]

It was around 3.30 p.m. when the Japanese warships fired several shells into the foreshores east of Gona in preparation for the landing of troops—there was no disputing now that the ships were Japanese. May, who was at the time still in the kitchen, wrote what happened next:

I had started on the pudding, so I did not tear off with the others, but when 15 minutes later I heard bombing and shelling, I too ran down to the beach and joined Sister, Father and two soldiers, Godfrey, our head teacher, and three brave but frightened mission boys (everyone else had either fled or were on the way by this time). A naval battle, what a thrill! (a shell could easily have been plomped right in the middle of us, but we were still not aware as to what was really happening). Were those two big transports just outside the reef American or Japanese and why the shelling and gunfire between the four or five destroyers which were darting about . . .

As we watched, old Harry (native teacher) came up from the nearby village (old Harry <u>never</u> hurries, even now he strolled up and stood with us awhile). We asked him about the village people, and he replied, 'Oh they all go along bush quick time, no shut em door.' Now a native never leaves his house without first barring his small door, so we knew that the general panic must have spread like wild fire. Harry strolled on his way to his house on the Kikiri side of the station and Godfrey and the boys came with us as we moved back to a new deserted station where we packed things, because it looked as if a landing might be made not so far away for two small boats had been lowered.[7]

Mavis also recalled with fear upon realising that the ships were Japanese and they were about to land in force, writing to her mother a few weeks later: 'The Japanese put down dinghies and men got into them, so we decided we'd better move to a healthier spot.'[8] Father Benson also recalled the Japanese 'turned their attention to us, and a barrage of fire swept the beach-strip ahead of the landing troops. Shells came screaming on to the Mission buildings.'[9] Hewitt and Palmer rushed down to the water's edge to confront the landing, but Benson pleaded with them not to open fire as innocent people at the mission would likely be killed in retaliation. They agreed and headed to Buna to join the small ANGAU radio party. Benson recalled in 1945: 'I still think my advice was the best in the circumstances . . . I admired [their] coolness on that day, standing alone in face of a whole hostile army.'[10] They would not make it to Buna and would, like the missionaries, find themselves trapped behind enemy lines; weeks later they would rejoin the Gona mission party in their final bid for freedom.[11]

Benson, Mavis and May urgently gathered together essentials. Mavis wrote to her mother:

We rushed up to the house, grabbed a box and flung as much as we could into it, our nicest dresses, some undies, comb, toothbrushes, soap, shoes, etc. The boys helped us fill some kerosene tins with tinned meat and vegetables; we got a few mosquito nets and ground sheets. May had just finished making the pudding for dinner, chocolate blanc-mange, so we ate that up in a hurry, and some sandwiches from the afternoon tea tray which was still there. Our house was probably as untidy as it has ever been, freshly ironed clothes everywhere with our parachute sewing all over the place, and the tables strewn with soldiers' khaki shirts and shorts we had been mending and fixing the sleeves of. Then after we'd been through collecting the things we needed, it looked as though a cyclone had hit it . . . Our mission-boys were so frightened, but so brave, and carried our things for us along the only road we could take—the mission road to Kokoda.[12]

•

Lieutenant Champion was still on the beach at Buna looking towards Gona through his binoculars as the Japanese began to shell the area around Gona. By now he was joined by Lieutenant William Wort and Sergeant Harry Bishop both with the 1st PIB, who with their men had been conducting a routine patrol. Champion recalled: 'I collected all codes, ciphers, and defence papers, together with a bag of each from the office safe, and then one of my beach patrols from Sanananda area came in to report that troops were landing in that area, I immediately burnt all secret documents.' Just then he heard what were clearly several Japanese aircraft coming in from the sea, so he decided to evacuate the station. 'On returning to the radio station I found the radio equipment destroyed, and the spotter personnel having already evacuated. I immediately sent a runner after Pte. [sic Sergeant] Harper to ascertain if he had transmitted my message to VIJ; Harper sent word back that he had sent the message eight times without getting any acknowledgement from Moresby.'[13]

Signaller George Clasby recalled: 'We were strafed by a Jap plane again and . . . then quite a few planes came over, so we thought it was "on", so we sent a message, and up and off!!!'[14] The ANGAU war diary records on 21 July: 'Signal to Awala from ADO Buna

(Lt. F.A. Champion) at 1700 hrs. "Under heavy bombardment. Smashed Radio. Evacuating".'[15]

•

It was also now that the Anglican missionary ketch, the *Maclaren-King*, was approaching just east of Buna. It was carrying stores for the mission stations and May Hayman's fiancé, Reverend Vivian Redlich, who had been recuperating at Dogura. Having recovered from his illness Redlich was returning to the mission station at Sangara; now with the others onboard he saw and heard the Japanese invasion and they quickly anchored close to shore in Oro Bay.

Reverend Redlich was described as a 'very thin man, not very strong, and inclined to discipline himself into doing things that seemed to be beyond his strength. His eyesight was weak, and he wore very thick glasses. He had an impulsive manner of speaking which sometimes brought words tumbling out in an embarrassing splutter.'[16] After he had proposed to May Hayman earlier in the year he had stopped halfway between Gona and Dogura at a mission station at Wanigela, and 'he came along the beach with eyes shining and face beaming, almost shouting the good news, "May and I are engaged".'[17]

Now, with an enemy invasion taking place just kilometres away, he and his men unloaded the 15 tons of stores during the night, hiding them in the nearby jungle. With this completed, early the next morning Redlich ordered the boat to sail back to Dogura; he would stay behind to help his parishioners and find May. He stood alone on the beach just as dawn was breaking and watched the schooner rig its sails and head out of the bay on its way to the relative safety of Dogura. Within minutes, he turned his back on the beach and headed inland for Sangara mission station.[18]

10

'The damp soil was your bed and the rotten logs your pillow'

At 4.p.m., the shelling ceased—just east of Gona large numbers of Japanese soldiers scrambled down rope-net ladders from the large transport ships, the *Ryoyo Maru* and *Ayatosan Maru*, with rifles strung across their backs. Obviously well practised and rehearsed, they quickly boarded several waiting barges and headed for the beach.[1]

One of these soldiers was 27-year-old Sergeant Imanishi Sadashige, a veteran of the war against China; he had returned home to become a school teacher but was soon back in uniform with the 144th Regiment with Japan's entry into the Second World War.[2] Hours before the invasion, he had been crouching in the dimly lit hull of the transport *Ayatosan Maru*, and like most of his comrades knew nothing of their enemy other than recalling that 'Australia is the destination of British criminals, so they must be very cruel, and we have to be very careful . . . I also had this premonition that the battle we were going to might be something very tough, like we would eat soil in the ground. It was exactly as I expected.'[3] Indeed, as Sergeant Imanishi and his men climbed down the rope netting they did so uncharacteristically in silence: 'No one spoke except when an instruction was given, the dominant sound the whirring of motors driving the barges towards shore. Normally Japanese soldiers were chatterboxes; now there was silence, with everyone alert. Barges hit the shore in succession, each with a grating thud. Men leapt out with their knapsacks, splashing through the last metre or two of the ocean journey and up the black sand of Gona beach, well-drilled in the landing procedure that had dominated their recent training.'[4]

Not only were troops disembarking but many bicycles were also being unloaded from the barges—the initial advance off the beaches and into the hinterland would rely heavily on them. Japanese Lieutenant Nose Munekichi, commanding No. 3 Company, I Battalion, 144th Regiment (I/144th Regiment) recalled that every man in his company had a bicycle in order to push forward at the greatest possible speed. As Nose and his men were landing, close by was Sergeant Major Tanaka with the Sakigawa Transport Unit who was tasked with selecting a suitable landing and assembly area for the trucks still aboard the *Ayatosan Maru*. The rest of his men were still aboard the ship and getting the first of the trucks ready for lifting out of her holds and onto barges—speed was of the essence. While a few were soon unloaded and ready for service at the newly established assembly point, it was not long before large waves began to come in and the loading of the remaining vehicles was disrupted—the unloading would continue at first light the next morning.[5] The unit's log reports: 'In accordance with SAKI Op Order No. 21, SM [Sergeant Major] Tanaka and 2 men landed with the 2nd wave at 1750, to select the location of vehicle landing point and vehicle assembly place. The personnel remaining on the ship are preparing to unload the vehicles. Speed is a matter of great importance in this. At 1630, each man received food for tonight's meal and tomorrow's breakfast. This is to be carried on the person. 2000 hrs. As the waves were very high, it was extremely difficult landing the vehicles of No. 3 Sec. Therefore, landing vehicles was suspended . . . Personnel slept.'[6]

●

Benson's party had left Gona just as the first of the Japanese troops landed about 2 kilometres east of the mission station. He recalled, 'our nice hot dinner, Miss Hayman's daily delight was still in the oven, and the soldier's [*sic*] shirts and trousers awaiting repairs laid out neatly on a side table. I wondered what the Japs would make of it.'[7] Their immediate destination was the township of Popondetta located 20 kilometres inland; from there they would continue onto the mission stations at Sangara and Isivita. Within hours, however, the advancing Japanese would almost catch up with them after darkness set in.[8]

•

Meanwhile at Buna, lieutenants Champion and Wort watched as the Japanese marines (5th Special Naval Landing Party [No. 5 SNLP]) landed at Sanananda Point—about 3 kilometres west of Buna—sometime after 5 p.m. This small headland was the shipping terminal for the Sangara rubber plantation, representing the closest point on the coast to Kokoda Station. It was not long before these crack troops were fanning out from their beachhead. Champion and the others evacuated Buna and made their way towards Awala. They had barely cleared the village when Japanese aircraft bombed the station. Champion wrote in his report to ANGAU:

> Lieut. Wort, Sgt. Bishop and myself then retired to Giruwa village at the rear of Buna, we waited there until 1745 hrs. and heard heavy explosions coming from the direction of Buna Station. Not having received any acknowledgement to my messages and fearing the possibility of being cut off by the enemy we decided to make for Awala, the nearest radio station, a distance of approximately 36 miles [58 kilometres] along the main Kokoda road. A Police runner was also dispatched to Awala with a letter to the District Officer [Grahamslaw]. On arrival at Soputa a PIB Cpl. caught up with us and reported that the japs were coming ashore in barges, we had a short spell, and then proceeded to Popondetta, where we found the spotters with Capt. Austen (Govt. Native Coffee Plantation). Capt. Austen gave us a meal, and asked me if he could return to Sangara, collect some stores and retire into the mountains. I told him it would be far better if he came with us to Kokoda, but he complained about his bad leg and said he could never make the trip. I suggested we had him carried, but he said he would rather go into the hills, unfortunately I granted his request.[9]

Major Bill Watson, commander of the 1st Papuan Infantry Battalion, was an unsung hero of the Kokoda Campaign.

Captain Harold Jesser, 1st Papuan Infantry Battalion, would be among the first to confront the Japanese.

Captain Bartor Faithorn (left), Corporal Jack Wilkinson (centre) and Captain Thomas Grahamslaw—Wilkinson and Grahamslaw were in the thick of the early fighting.

Captain Samuel Templeton, commander of 'B' Company, 39th Battalion, was much loved and respected by his men and known to all as 'Uncle Sam'—he was killed following action at Oivi on 26 July 1942.

Corporal Francis Tutuveta (here as a sergeant), centre, who witnessed the Japanese landings and rushed to find his commanding officer to tell him of the news.

Corporal John 'JD' McKay, who commanded No. 1 Section, 7 Platoon, 'A' Company, was in the thick of the fighting during the second battle for Kokoda.

Corporal Reg Markham with 10 Platoon, 'B' Company, who with his men had a narrow escape from the Japanese during the first battle for Kokoda.

The legendary Sergeant Katue (left), who remained behind enemy lines waging his own war against the Japanese and village collaborators—here he is pictured with Captain Grahamslaw in October 1942.

Lieutenant Arthur 'Judy' Garland, commanding 10 Platoon, 39th Battalion—he and his men were the first to confront the Japanese during the first battle for Kokoda.

Lieutenant Colonel Bill Owen was killed within days of flying into Kokoda, defending the plateau and its airstrip from several Japanese assaults.

Lieutenant Douglas McClean, 16 Platoon, 'D' Company, 39th Battalion (here as a major), was among the few to fly into Kokoda just before the Japanese launched their attacks against Oivi and Kokoda.

Lieutenant Bert Kienzle, here as a captain on leave in Australia after the Papuan Campaign—a true legend and hero of the Kokoda Track.

Lieutenant Arthur Seekamp, commanding 11 Platoon, 'B' Company, 39th Battalion, was near the battalion's commanding officer Lieutenant Colonel Bill Owen when he was mortally wounded during the first battle for Kokoda.

Lance Corporal Alexander Lochhead (here as an officer) with 9 Platoon, 'A' Company, 39th Battalion—during the second battle for Kokoda, he and his men faced the brunt of the Japanese attacks.

Staff Sergeant Jim Cowey, 'A' Company, 39th Battalion, who volunteered to stay behind on Kokoda Plateau to make sure the men of 9 Platoon got out—he was worshipped by the men.

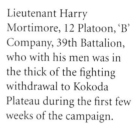

Major Allan Cameron, temporary commanding officer of the 39th Battalion after the death of Bill Owen—he ordered a controversial attack to retake Kokoda Plateau on 8 August 1942.

Lieutenant Harry Mortimore, 12 Platoon, 'B' Company, 39th Battalion, who with his men was in the thick of the fighting withdrawal to Kokoda Plateau during the first few weeks of the campaign.

Private Bernie Hanlon, 'D' Company, 39th Battalion, was mortally wounded during the second battle for Kokoda—his only concern was not being a burden to those around him.

Private William 'Snowy' Parr at Eora Creek with Private Harold Bradbury— during the first battle for Kokoda, Parr and his mate Horace Hollow remained behind to hold back the Japanese, enabling many to escape death.

Sergeant Major Joe Dawson, 'B' Company, 39th Battalion, seemed to be everywhere during the fighting and kept a diary, later writing a book detailing his experiences during the war.

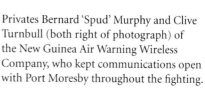

Privates Bernard 'Spud' Murphy and Clive Turnbull (both right of photograph) of the New Guinea Air Warning Wireless Company, who kept communications open with Port Moresby throughout the fighting.

Medical officer 'Doc' Geoffrey Vernon, another legendary hero of Kokoda, who at great personal risk treated the sick and wounded during the fighting for Kokoda and the track.

Major General Basil Morris, who commanded New Guinea Force during the early stages of the Japanese invasion of New Guinea.

Private Henry Evans and Sergeant Les Martorana, 'B' Company, 39th Battalion, were continually in the thick of the fighting.

The only known photograph of Lance Corporal Sanopa of the Royal Papuan Constabulary (taken in August 1972), who fought with the Australians and was instrumental in getting the men from 'B' Company out of Oivi when they were surrounded by the Japanese—standing next to him is Sergeant Les Simmons, who fought with Sanopa during the second battle for Kokoda.

A rare photograph of 'B' Company, 39th Battalion, on 7 July 1942, setting off to cross the Kokoda Track—they were the first Australian troops to do so.

Wounded of the 39th Battalion on the Kokoda Track in mid-August 1942 making their way back to Port Moresby.

Father Vivian Redlich of the Sangara Mission Station arrived back near Buna in a small boat just as the Japanese invaded— he then attempted to rescue his colleagues and his fiancée, Sister May Hayman.

Lay preacher John Duffill was attached to the Sangara Mission at the time of the Japanese invasion.

Father James Benson, head of the Mission Station at Gona—the station was immediately targeted by the Japanese invasion.

Sister May Hayman from the Gona Mission, who would write a long letter to her sister in Canberra during her attempt to escape from the Japanese over a three-week period.

Sister Mavis Parkinson of the Gona Mission Station would, like Sister May Hayman, write a letter during her attempted escape from the Japanese—her letter was addressed to 'Dearest Mummy'.

The much-loved Father Norbert 'Nobby' Earl of the 39th Battalion, who comforted the wounded and dying during the thick of the fighting throughout the Kokoda Campaign.

Reverend Henry Holland of the Isivita Mission Station who, with the party from Sangara, would attempt to break through the Japanese lines to reach the Australian forces at Kokoda.

Sister Lilla Lashmar of the Sangara Mission Station would, like others, attempt to break through Japanese lines to reach the Australian forces then thought to be at Kokoda.

Sister Margery Brenchley of the Sangara Mission Station—within 24 hours of the invasion she and others from the station would be trapped behind enemy lines.

Colonel Kusunose Masao, commander of the Japanese 144th Regiment, the main combat force that invaded Gona and Buna on 21 July 1942.

The coffee mill at Popondetta, where Sisters Mavis Parkinson and May Hayman spent their last night before being brutally murdered by the Japanese the next day and left in a shallow grave.

Sub-Lieutenant Komai Uichi beheads Australian commando Sergeant Leonard Siffleet. Uichi was responsible for several beheadings associated with the Gona and Sangara parties.

Sergeant Sadashige Imanishi was one of the few Japanese soldiers to survive the Papuan Campaign—he later provided a fascinating account of his experiences.

A rare photograph of Japanese troops of the 144th Regiment in New Britain, before leaving to invade Papua.

Captain Louis Austen with ANGAU had been a master of a coastal
vessel and now managed the coffee and rubber plantation at Higaturu;
he had earlier sent his wife to Australia for safety.[10] He had developed a
tropical ulcer in his leg making it difficult to walk and he did not want
to slow down Champion and his men. He would quickly discover his
safe refuge near Higaturu was no such thing and would soon join up
with the refugees from Sangara mission station in a desperate attempt
to escape the Japanese.

•

Andrew Duna and the other villagers at Buna were also escaping from
the invading Japanese:

> As the [first] plane came very low, it started to fire its machine guns and
> went ta, ta, ta, ta, ta, ta, ta, ta, like coconuts falling from the trees, and
> everything was totally smashed. Wilfred and I were near a house with
> an iron roof and we felt that the machine gun was going to destroy the
> roof of the house and bring the house down to the ground. So, Wilfred
> and I hid under some planks of timber that were laid on top of one
> another nearby. We were hiding there when the plane came and fired
> its guns and then passed by. Then it returned and fired at the station
> again. I came out from under the planks first and pulled at Wilfred's
> leg saying, 'look, if we stay here the bombs will come and kill all of us,
> so let's run away'. So, I pulled him out and ran to the sea. Wilfred and I
> left all our loincloths and our waistbands, armbands, everything under
> the planks. We just ran naked into the sea and dived under the water.
> All other parts of our bodies were under the water with mouths shut,
> though the noses to breathe and eyes to watch the planes were in air. It
> was like lying in a grave, except we still breathed. Each time the planes
> came over, we dived under the water . . .
>
> The firing of the guns and the explosions of bombs brought all
> the clouds of the skies down and touched the earth and all living
> things seemed to be crushed to dust. All the clansmen who were brave,
> courageous, and strong in the previous day appeared to become like
> babies in their first day out of their mother's womb at the arrival of

the Japanese. It was as if the landing, gun noises, and the actual terrifying sight of the ships that covered the wide horizon of the bay had removed the bones of the people. They could not run even if they tried to, for it was a unique disaster beyond anyone's memory.

[It was] as if you had a dreamlike spirit chasing you and you want to run, [but] you cannot run, and the spirit catches you. It went just like that. There was a great panic . . . There was not time to go to your village to gather your family or collect your valuable belongings. Wife ran naked without her husband and children. Husband ran naked without his wife and children. A child ran without his parents. And even if he or she who was with his small ones, he or she deserted them. All ran in different directions into the bush. Some ran for cover like rats and bandicoots in the Kunai grass. The night fell, and each individual slept either in the grass or under the trees. The damp soil was your bed and the rotten logs your pillow. You went to sleep wherever you happened to run that night.[11]

●

Back at Gona, it was not long before a Japanese scouting party led by Lieutenant Ida entered the mission station. He approached the main residential building and gently nudged open the door with his boot, entering cautiously. The first thing he noticed was the faint smell of perfume but as he scanned around the room, he saw it was empty. It looked like whoever was last there was sewing khaki uniforms which were laid on a table—needle and thread still embedded in the cloth. He also noticed some women's clothing lying nearby. On entering the kitchen, he saw two teacups and picking one up, noticed the remaining tea was still warm.

Ida ordered his men into action: 'They can't be far. Look for them.' Now the telephone rang, and on picking up the receiver he heard a flustered voice say in English before hanging up, 'Head for Kokoda immediately!'[12] Ida and his men searched the house while ordering others to search the nearby huts and gardens. His men entered the mission school and gathered up the children's exercise books and turned them over to officers of the dreaded Kempai (Military Police), who quickly searched them for any military information—it seemed that the residents had made good their escape.[13]

•

Captain Sam Templeton had reached Awala in the afternoon having made sure all the stores from the *Gili Gili* had been transported to Kokoda Station. There he came across Captain Grahamslaw and it was not long before they 'heard but disregarded a distant rumbling noise which seemed to emanate from the massive banks of cloud, the seat of tropical thunder, in the direction of the coast. The same rumbling noise went unheeded by the troops Templeton had left at Kokoda.'[14] Grahamslaw and Templeton were discussing plans to conduct a patrol the next day towards Morobe when they were interrupted by Jack Mason, a local coffee planter and now radio operator with ANGAU, as recalled by Grahamslaw.

> On 21 July I walked from Kokoda to Awala . . . Captain Templeton said he wanted to visit Morobe and [I] agreed to go with him. I explained that as we had no ships it would be necessary to walk and that the return journey would take about three weeks. We were discussing ways and means when Jack Mason, who was crouched over his beloved radio, called out that Corporal Hanna of Ambasi was on the air with an urgent message. I took over from Jack. Hanna informed me that enemy ships were shelling Buna. I instructed him to have a good look at the ships and what they were doing and report the results to me. He came on the air about ten minutes later with as much information as he could glean, which I immediately transmitted to Station VIG, Port Moresby. I instructed Hanna to stay at his post as long as he considered it safe to do so and to call us at hourly intervals, or any other time he had anything to report. I assured him we would maintain in constant watch. In the meantime, Templeton signaled his troops at Kokoda to set out for Buna forthwith and he himself left Awala to join them . . . McKenna, Brown, Mason and myself took it in turns to listen throughout the night, but nothing further was heard from Ambasi. We also made efforts to call Buna, but without success.[15]

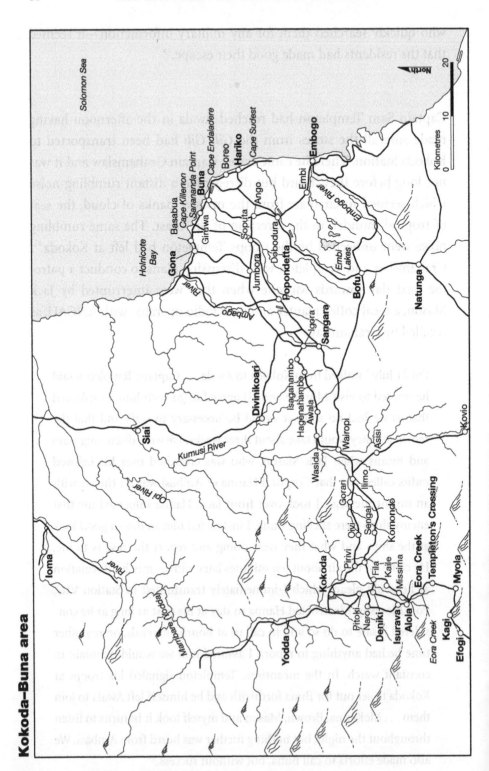

Kokoda–Buna area

Manning the station at Ambasi, about 50 kilometres west of Gona, was twenty-year-old Sergeant Robert Hanna from Walwa and 21-year-old Private John Holyoak from Kerang, both in Victoria. They were members of ANGAU and with their mate Barry Harper had joined NGAWWC to watch out for any Japanese activity along the northern coastline.[16] A week later, the two coast watchers Hanna and Holyoak were involved in a firefight with a Japanese patrol that had been sent out to hunt them down and destroy their radio; their position had been betrayed by two men from Senani village near Ambasi. The two Australians managed to escape and made their way south-east towards Kokoda. Within days they came across Lieutenant Arthur Smith with his twenty or so men of 'B' Company 1st PIB who were also falling back from Ambasi towards Kokoda. In a few weeks time, they, along with several American airmen who had bailed out from their stricken aircraft and had joined up with Smith's party, would join the Gona mission party, all trapped behind enemy lines.[17]

•

Meanwhile at Kokoda, Lieutenant Arthur Garland recalled getting word of the invasion from his OC: 'Captain Templeton contacted battalion through brigade, and they confirmed that the Japanese were landing at Buna. When Sam got confirmation of the Japanese landing, he sent 11 and 12 Platoons with 2i/c of the company, Captain Cathcart Stevenson, forward to seek out the Japanese. His instructions were for these two platoons to intercept, harass and fight a rearguard action ... Their role was to delay the Japanese until reinforcements arrived.'[18] Lieutenant Seekamp and 11 Platoon advanced towards Awala; while Lieutenant Harry Mortimore, a 28-year-old bread carter from Red Cliffs in Victoria and a veteran of the Middle East Campaign with the 2/14th Battalion, now leading 12 Platoon, was to take up a position at Gorari located between Awala and Kokoda. Templeton ordered Lieutenant Garland and 10 Platoon to remain at Kokoda to defend the airstrip—they would also act as the company reserve.[19]

•

May and the others from the Gona mission were now approaching a small garden house 6 kilometres from the station and about 15 metres off the mission track to Kokoda: 'We put up our nets and after saying evensong with the boys we settled down for the night, the boys going on to another house which they said was close by. Just then another pupil teacher (Robinson) arrived, he had remained hidden behind the hospital to see what happened, and he told us of men whose talk he did not know who were occupying our houses ... The boys wanted to take us with them to the next house, but we decided to stay and arrange for them to come to us at daylight.'[20]

Father Benson must have thought back to a few months earlier, when he had tried to get May and Mavis to leave for Australia, disregarding Bishop Strong's directive. Indeed, a number of official broadcasts were made encouraging those still in northern Papua to leave; on one such occasion the announcer pulled no punches imploring them: 'For you people on the north-east coasts, I have no definite instructions for you. But if you don't want to leave your bones on the beaches, I think you had better clear out too.'[21]

Benson had been against the bishop's directive and at every opportunity tried to get May and Mavis to leave for Australia; he recalled in 1945:

> Our first touch of war at Gona came soon after the fall of Rabaul in late January 1942, but for several months there was little more than an increase in the number of planes to be seen up and down the coast. The bombing of Salamaua [North-east New Guinea] brought much excitement in the form of about a dozen great canoes from the Waria River coming into our bay one evening ... sails against the sunset, bringing some thirty or so bearded and sunburnt refugees who stayed with us that night; sleeping all over the place, and, next morning, began the five days walk to Kokoda, whence planes took them to Port Moresby and so to Australia. From that time, I began to get really anxious and I rather pestered the Bishop to order all the women missionaries away to the safety of Australia, or at least to send my two sisters away from what had clearly become a danger zone. If the Japanese advanced from

Salamaua, the first Government station in Papua, Buna would be their objective, and we at Gona could not hope to get off scott [sic] free . . .

There were military wireless signal line stations at Buna and near Ambasi, our outstation 30 miles to the west, and the soldiers in their comings and goings between the two places always made the Mission their half-way house, and we often had them for the night. From them, and also I think from regular broadcasts, we heard that it was the intention of our military . . . to drive the Japs out of Salamaua and Lae before September; so, from time to time I took heart of hope that the evil would be stayed.[22]

Even so he still worried and, at one point, Benson thought he had finally convinced May and Mavis to evacuate to Australia. He organised several carriers to take them to Kokoda, from there they were to fly to Port Moresby and then Australia. Benson recalled: 'I was happy and content about the Sisters and their ultimate arrival safely among their dear ones at Canberra and Brisbane . . . But it was not to be . . .'[23] Even before reaching Kokoda, they had returned to the mission station, determined to stay come what may. Benson wrote of their return being like a bombshell exploding. The bishop told Mavis, given her age, she would need permission from her parents to stay, so she sent them a cable pleading with them, 'Please let me stay!'—they reluctantly relented.[24] Benson recalled how jubilant the locals were with their return, especially the children: 'I went back again to my rooms at Kikiri, the children returned to school again in full force next day, for it would take more than mere rumours of wars to keep them away if Sister were at home, and station life was quite back to normal at the end of the week . . . So we were quite "As you were" again.'[25]

Captain Thomas Grahamslaw had also unsuccessfully tried to convince the mission women from Gona and Sangara to leave Papua when most of the other Europeans had been evacuated. He recalled fondly years later of his visits to Gona: 'Mavis Parkinson was an attractive young woman in her early twenties and was engaged to a lieutenant in the Australian Army stationed at Port Moresby. May Hayman, who was several years older, was engaged to an Anglican missionary named

Vivian Redlich. They were high-spirited, intelligent, young women and it was always a pleasure to call on them during my occasional visits to Gona for discussions with the missionary in charge, Reverend James Benson.'[26]

Like the missionaries at Gona, those at the Anglican mission stations at Sangara were located close to the main Kokoda Track between the coast and Kokoda, and at Isivita to the south-west, were now in danger from the Japanese landing. The gentle and good-natured 62-year-old Reverend Henry Holland from Grenfell in New South Wales was at Isivita with John Duffill, a layman of the church. While at Sangara was Sister Margery Brenchley, the mission's nurse, aged in her twenties from Brisbane; 47-year-old Sister Lilla Lashmar, the station's teacher, from Kangaroo Island in South Australia; along with Lucian Tapiedi, a 21-year-old Papuan teacher–evangelist—all remained blissfully ignorant of the imminent threat to them. Within hours, the Sangara missionaries would be heading for Isivita in full flight from the quickly advancing Japanese.[27]

11

'It gave us rather a horrible feeling having them so near'

The messages from Lieutenant Champion and Sergeant Harper from Buna had been relayed to Port Moresby by Sergeant Robert Hanna at Ambasi and Private Jack Mason at Awala. However, authorities there were already aware of a likely imminent Japanese invasion of Buna as early as 17 July. That day reports came in of 24 Japanese ships in Rabaul harbour, with several assessed to be transports, while close by Japanese troops were observed rehearsing landing operations—their likely destination: Buna.[1]

There was some concern about speeding up Operation Providence to construct an airbase near Dobodura, but as the arguing continued about the destination of these ships, confirmation came in on 20 July by a lone American four-engine B-17 Flying Fortress bomber, piloted by Lieutenant Don Tower of 435th Bombardment Squadron (affectionately known as the Kangaroo Squadron). He and his crew had set out on patrol near Rabaul and when his message about the convoy was received by Allied Air Forces (AAF) Headquarters, and its heading plotted, they assessed it was heading for the northern coastline of Papua—Buna. All available B-17, B-25 and B-26 bombers in northern Australia were now ordered by Lieutenant General George Brett, commanding the AAF in the South West Pacific Area (SWPA), to be made ready to fly to Port Moresby.[2]

On the morning of the invasion another B-17 spotted the convoy but it soon lost sight of it due to heavy cloud cover. Another bomber was later sent out to find and shadow the flotilla, but it would be some hours before it could hope to contact the convoy. Later, with the news relayed by radio by Hanna and Mason that enemy ships were now off Gona, AAF immediately dispatched six B-26 Marauder twin-engine bombers based at Port Moresby to strike. By 6 p.m., five of these bombers engaged the convoy at a height of 2000 metres, just as darkness set in, with one crew reporting a direct hit 'with a 500-pounder' against the stern of one of the transports. Private Toshiaki Sugimoto, with 2 Platoon, Takasago Volunteer Unit, recalled having just left the larger of the two transports, the 9780-ton *Ayatosan Maru*, when enemy aircraft swooped down with one scoring a direct hit on the ship. Close behind, another sortie, this time of five B-25 twin-engine Mitchell bombers also flew in to attack the convoy, but by the time they arrived over the target area it was too dark to see the ships; they jettisoned their bombs and headed back to Port Moresby. The convoy was now free to continue landing troops, artillery and stores unmolested, although the trucks could not be unloaded until first light.[3]

•

Meanwhile, Corporal Francis Tutuveta, leading a section of Lieutenant Wort's men of the 1st PIB, had been out on patrol and in the late afternoon was approaching Buna when the B-26 bombers targeted the Japanese convoy. He later reported: 'My section was sent up to Bakembari, but I met Sergeant Haria who gave me a message that I was wanted urgently back at Buna, so we proceeded down the beach back towards Buna. I didn't see any Japanese boats, and I was walking along the beach and rounded a point and all of a sudden there were ships there, and Allied bombers were overhead dropping bombs, and this was the first indication that I had that the war had started in that area.' It was now that the Papuans' concept of fighting and their view of the white man's war came to the fore; Corporal Tutuveta continues: 'One of my men wanted to go back to his village. I told him he was lucky because his village was close but mine was a long way away, so I and the rest of the men would have to stop and fight . . . At this early time in the war, I didn't regard this as desertion but rather as the normal thing. The man didn't want to fight—well, that was his business.'[4] Tutuveta and his men retired further inland.

Nearby Private Paul Lafe was making his way off the beach still munching on a yam given to him by one of the local women; he was intent on finding his CO (commanding officer).

By the time I got back to the headquarters position Lt Wort and the platoon had gone, so I raided the store and took some biscuits and 200 rounds of ammunition. I went back along the track to try and locate Lt Wort. At this stage an Allied plane flew over. This plane made a bombing attack on the Japanese ships . . . Immediately after this a flight of eight Allied planes came in . . . but the [Japanese] were putting up a lot of anti-aircraft fire. One of the planes pretended to crash and fell towards one of the Japanese ships. When it was close to the ship it leveled out and dropped its bomb right in the middle of the ship . . . By this time, it was about 5.15 pm and as the Japanese landing boats were in the water, I thought it was time I left, so I started to walk back to report to Lt Wort. I was frightened to use the track, because the Japanese were shelling the area, so I took off into the bush. I didn't know the country, but I knew I was headed towards Kokoda.[5]

•

The Japanese invasion force of 4000 men was commanded by Colonel Yokoyama Yosuke, who was the CO of the 15th Independent Engineer Regiment. His force was given the name 'Yokoyama Advance Butai'.[6] Yokoyama, while sailing to Rabaul a week earlier, had issued a nonsensical order to his men: 'From today, we are entering an area subject to air attack. Hereafter, there will be no more exercises; any attack will be the real thing. Get out on deck before the enemy's arrival. Those who are slow will be regarded as cowards. When sinking, remain calm until the water touches the feet, and when in the water, take the necessary precautions. Those who hurriedly jump into the sea will drown. When in the water, sections or platoons should gather together and sing military songs. All must be calm, even when awaiting rescue for perhaps two days and nights.'[7] One can only imagine the reaction of the Japanese naval officers and their sailors on hearing this absurd order from the officer of engineers.

The combat arm of Yokoyama's force that was to initially invade Papua numbered around 1000 men; consisting of the I/144th Regiment (586 men); No. 5 Company, II/144th Regiment (165 men); No. 7 Company, II/41st Regiment (165) and other elements in support—all under the temporary command of Lieutenant Colonel Tsukamoto Hatsuo. Supporting this force were also two companies from the crack marines from No. 5 SNLP (numbering 236 men) led by Commander Tsukioka Toroshige, but most of these men were tasked with establishing and defending a landing base and assisting the engineers in building the airfield near Buna which was to be operational by 12 August. However, a few platoons appear to have been made available to support the advance as several Australians recorded at the time that some of the Japanese attacking them were clearly marines.[8]

The composition of the 144th Regiment at the beginning of the war reflected the general profile of Japanese infantry regiments at the time. Regular officers accounted for around 15 per cent of all officers with reserve officers making up the rest. Long-serving enlisted men, like the veteran of the China Campaigns and recent school teacher Sergeant Imanishi, accounted for around 20 per cent of NCOs, with other ranks a mixture of regulars and conscripts. These men and reserve officers originally relied on the combat experience of the veteran NCOs who had seen action in China. However, by the time these troops landed in Papua, most were veterans themselves having fought on Guam, Malaya, New Britain and North-east New Guinea.[9]

Tsukamoto's initial objective was to take Gona, Buna and Kokoda Station and its airfield. He would then advance into the Owen Stanley Range just south of what would become known to the Australians as Templeton's Crossing, south of Isurava. He was to report on the feasibility of advancing in force to Port Moresby using the track. Tsukamoto was an old-school army officer, hot-tempered, finding fault with his officers and men when no fault existed and was known to hit the sake bottle too often. By all accounts, most of his officers and men loathed him. Indeed, later in the campaign while his men were starving, he failed to provide them with food, but he did manage to supply them with sake.[10]

Also committed were men of Yokoyama's 15th Independent Engineer Regiment, who were to clear roads and tracks, to construct depots and to begin construction of the airbase at Buna—they could also be used as combat troops. To further assist the engineers a company of Formosans of the 15th Naval Pioneer Unit were made available. Also attached was No. 1 Battery, 55th Mountain Artillery Battalion, which consisted of sixteen guns, mostly 70-millimetre and 75-millimetre calibre, well supplied with ammunition, along with No. 2 Battery, 47th Field Anti-Aircraft Battalion. The combat force was supported by a further 2000 troops, extensively equipped with heavy machine guns and mortar teams. In addition, about 1200 natives from Rabaul had been press-ganged as carriers along with around 450 packhorses.[11]

Once the initial objectives had been taken, and if it was decided that an advance across the mountains to Port Moresby was viable, additional troops would be sent with command passing to Major General Horii Tomitarô, who commanded the South Seas Force. This force was built around the 144th Regiment, commanded by Colonel Kusunose Masao. Major General Horii was described as a 'small, plump and bespectacled figure, he campaigned with his troops, and directed operations from headquarters never far behind the most forward outposts. His troops saw him occasionally astride a carefully groomed white thoroughbred, a remote, powerful and dignified being.'[12] Within months, Horii and his horse would perish in the jungles of Papua.

When the remaining battalions of the regiment were landed at Gona, the total Japanese troops available to Horii for his attack against Port Moresby would number around 13,500 troops, but of these just 7300 would be available for combat duty. The non-combat elements would be used for logistical support, including road and airfield construction and the building and manning of defensive positions along the coastal lowlands to defend their beachhead and lines of supply. Even so, only about 2500 of the combat troops would be made available to conduct operations along the track in their attempt to capture Port Moresby from August to October.[13]

While the Japanese of the III/144th Regiment were mostly responsible for the massacre of Australian prisoners in the Tol and Waitavalo
plantations, some of Horii's troops of the I/144th Regiment now
storming ashore at Gona, along with the supporting troops, were also
likely responsible for the execution of Australian prisoners elsewhere
in New Britain. Troops of this regiment would soon become involved
in the murder of more Allied prisoners and civilians, including the
shooting, bayoneting and beheading of women and children. Within
weeks, the Japanese troops of the II and III battalions, 144th Regiment,
would be pushed into the battle along the Kokoda Track to annihilate
the Australians who by mid-August would be stubbornly holding the
line at Isurava.[14]

•

Within hours of the landing the Japanese were heading inland to
conduct rapid company-sized advances along the vehicular road
to Soputa—about 10 kilometres inland south of Buna. From there,
advanced elements of Yokoyama Advance Butai would disembark and
head for Kokoda Station, either on foot or bicycles, using all available
tracks. This not only enabled a rapid advance, but crucially a concentration of his force for a 'knock-out blow' against an enemy force he
had correctly estimated was small with little or no combat experience.[15]

At this point Sergeant Imanishi with the No. 2 Company, I/144th
Regiment, commanded by Lieutenant Takiishi Taneshige, recalled:
'There was little resistance. Soon after we landed, Australian aircraft
attacked, but we escaped into the jungle. We headed straight for
Kokoda.'[16] Indeed, by 5 p.m. Captain Ogawa Tetsuo and his No. 1
Company, I/144th Regiment (numbering 135 men) had been loaded
onto several trucks along with their bicycles and were heading for
Soputa. Beyond this village the road devolved into several narrow
tracks and the men would continue their advance on bicycles or on
foot. His company was also supported with a 70-millimetre field gun; a
platoon of the battalion's machine-gun company; a platoon from No. 1
Company, 15th Independent Engineer Regiment; and elements of No. 5
SNLP. Helping to guide him were some local villagers who had warned

Ogawa that 60 Australians had taken up a position at the major river crossing at the village of Wairopi, just west of the south to north flowing Kumusi River. The village was named after the bridge suspended by wire cables across the river and was pidgin for 'wire ropes'. Wairopi was located 15 kilometres further south-west of Awala. In all, Ogawa's force numbered around 250 crack veterans who would, over the next week, confront the 100 or so inexperienced young Australian militiamen of 'B' Company, 39th Battalion, and a handful of men from the 1st PIB and RPC, all dispersed over a considerable area.[17]

•

Major Watson's three companies of the 1st PIB were distributed from Ambasi to Buna and were led by three Australian officers and three Australian NCOs. At this point, Lieutenant Arthur Smith and 28 Papuan troops from 'B' Company were in the vicinity of Ambasi, located on the coastal strip about 50 kilometres west of Gona. Lieutenant Wort's 'C' Company was still making its way to Awala, having left Buna with Champion; while 'A' Company led by Captain Jesser, accompanied by Major Watson, on hearing of the invasion moved down from Wasida just a few kilometres west to Awala—to confront the Japanese.[18]

Watson and Jesser arrived at Awala after Grahamslaw and his small party had left the village to conduct a patrol towards Buna after dark. Grahamslaw later recorded in his report the arrival of Warrant Officer Harold Yeoman, a 38-year-old accountant of Salamaua, just before they left.

At 1730 YEOMAN arrived and reported that one BUNA native policeman had brought information to the effect that the Japs had actually landed at BUNA and GONA in force and that the A.D.O. BUNA (Lieut. CHAMPION) and staff had evacuated the Station and were proceeding to AWALA. Lieut. McKENNA immediately volunteered to go towards Buna with a view to ascertaining the disposition of movements, if any, of the enemy. I then decided to take a party consisting of McKENNA, YEOMAN and myself together with 9 police. Before departing I instructed W.O. [Gerald] BROWN to remove all stores and important papers from AWALA in the direction of KOKODA, and to establish a food dump in the vicinity of WAIROPE [sic] from which point there is a back road to KOKODA. Lieut. [Clendyn] SEARLE and Private MASON were to remove the teleradio set to a place to be decided by Major WATSON and Capt. TEMPLETON. I instructed my men to be guided by any decision arrived at by these officers, both of whom are experienced soldiers. Left AWALA about 1900 and met CHAMPION and BUNA personnel about half an hour out. Also passed BUNA detachment of P.I.B. on their way back to AWALA.[19]

Grahamslaw instructed Champion and his men to report to Major Watson, who was making his way to Alawa from Wasida. Then he, Lieutenant Richard 'Jack' McKenna (a 30-year-old assistant resident magistrate of Port Moresby), Warrant Officer Yeoman and the nine constables of the RPC pushed on and soon reached the native hospital at Isagahambo, about 5 kilometres east of Hagenahambo.[20] Grahamslaw recalled in his report: 'Reached ISAGAHAMBO about 2100. At this place W.O. BITMEAD had established a native hospital (300 patients) which he was running with the help of W.O. BARNES.'[21]

•

Private Paul Lafe of the 1st PIB had pushed further inland and soon found himself wading through numerous swamps. His stomach must have been rumbling as he had had nothing to eat since finishing a yam hours earlier.

As I came out of the swamp into the bush country, I met a small schoolboy, that led me towards Kokoda, and I set off along the path. I continued along the track until I reached a patch of heavy jungle. There I met Corporal Buga, one of the Mambare men. He knew I had been left behind and had come to look for me. He was also looking for another man, Private Wagu, who had been sent back by Lt Wort to climb a tree and observe any movement along the track. We tried to find Pte Wagu, but we couldn't find him anywhere, so we started back.

By this time, it was night, but there was a good moon and we could walk easily. We came to a big coconut tree at the side of the track and saw someone standing there. We stopped and watched, and we could see by the shape of the hat that it was an Australian, and I knew we had found Lt Wort. I called out and told Lt Wort that I had come back. He asked me if I had seen Private Wagu, and I told him no, we couldn't find him. 'Where are the Japanese?' Lt Wort asked. I told him that all the Japanese had landed and were along the beach between Buna and Sanananda. We then moved back, myself, the platoon sergeant and Private Moha . . . We rested at about four o'clock in the morning and at about five we got up and continued along the track. By the time it was light we came to a small village and the local people gave us food. Then we left the track and cut through the bush.[22]

•

Earlier, the small party from the Gona mission station had settled into their overnight refuge, finding sleep difficult. Father Benson recalled taking up a position believing that they were safe as the 'japs would be too busy establishing themselves on the beach to bother coming so far into the bush until daylight'. They laid out their bedding in a 'little shelter—four posts holding a sago leaf roof and with a floor of split palm stalks—we spread out our sheet of canvas and rigged a mosquito net. In those swamps behind Gona I am convinced was the original home of the Anopheles mosquito, and they are still the only creature that really flourishes there.'[23] Their carriers had already gone ahead to the nearby garden house. He was soon to be proven wrong about the Japanese being preoccupied with establishing their base on the beach— Captain Ogawa and his men had other priorities. May wrote of what happened a few hours later to her sister Viola:

We could not sleep . . . and when the moon came up, we thought perhaps we had better push on to Isivita after all, so we went looking for the boys and called to them but could not get any reply, so we decided to turn in again and wait. Off came our shoes and under the nets we scrambled. But our brains worked overtime, and thoughts ran thus: If the Japs are making our station their headquarters there is bound to be action of sorts tomorrow . . . shall we set out without our boys: No, that would not do for then we would be deserting them: we must wait until they come in the morning. So again, we tried to sleep, this time voices along the track to Kokoda disturbed us . . . Having put on our shoes for the umpteenth time we stood about wondering what to do— More voices, this time we called . . . first in English than [sic] in Notu [sic Motu], but only silence reigned . . . Were they Papuan voices? It was hard to tell, maybe they were Japanese, we stood listening, the suspense was dreadful, very bad for our morale . . . We thought we heard the clunk of a bayonet and once Sister [Mavis] saw a torch flash.[24]

Benson also recalled, 'soon we could see lights flashing, apparently two electronic flash lamps, and we knew our boys had no torches, it must be Japanese. By this time, we were out from the net and standing alongside the little house talking in the softest whispers; my blood seemed frozen in my veins with fear, as I prayed, they might not see the little turn off the track to our garden house. Presently the lights passed, and we heard the voices along the road now between us and our destination at Sangara.'[25] Mavis also wrote of her fear in her letter to her mother: 'It gave us rather a horrible feeling having them so near and we stood there expecting to see them come up our path every minute and to get a bayonet or bullet in our ribs. May and I thought we'd like a run for our money, so suggested that we should wait our chance of getting over the Kokoda road and into the bush on the other side.'[26] Benson himself recalled, 'I said to the girls: "The best thing now is for me to go out on the road and explain that we are the Mission staff".'[27] Mavis and May would not hear of it, with May telling him: 'You do no such thing . . . If you appear on the road you will have a bayonet in you and then what about us?'[28]

May later wrote to Viola that she and Mavis were intent on escaping the Japanese, suggesting to Benson: 'Let us nick across the Kokoda track and hide out in the bush behind those villages away from the belt of territory.' Benson replied: 'That would be madness, we would get lost there.' 'Yes, maybe we would,' said May, 'but let's try, maybe we would find some native gardens, there must be gardens there and there certainly are rivers. Anyway, it's going to be a hot spot here.' With this they got moving—May continued her letter: 'We hurriedly tied up our nets and blankets in a ground sheet and took a tin of biscuits and chocolate and Father's little billy and his walk about bag. What a treasure store it proved to be . . . Grasping our bundles in true refugee style and leaving our cases of clothes and tins of stores and lamps, we stole along the path and nicked oh so quickly across the Kokoda track and so into the pathless high grass which we hoped would hide us.'[29]

Benson led the way, carrying the largest of the bundles. As they crossed the road, they saw the torches of the Japanese patrol flashing along the road leading to Sangara. They disappeared into the tall thick grass and swamp country on the other side of the road.

The strip of country between the coast and the northern foothills of the Owen Stanley Range was—then as now—rough and stifling hot. The only 'easy' way they could get around was to use the many paths that had been established over the years. The terrain is relatively flat and 'perpetually swampy. It is subject to widespread inundation with each daily deluge. From its spongy ground rises a dense jungle, dank and fetid, broken occasionally by patches of kunai, and intersected by native pads connecting the villages.'[30] It was through this quagmire that the small party was now forced to negotiate—where possible avoiding any tracks. Obviously, Isivita and Sangara missions were no longer an option, so Benson, using the compass, led them south-west towards the Lower Kumusi River where there was a mission outstation at Siai, which they used when out conducting missionary work. Benson distinctly remembered repeating the Lord's Prayer and stating to May and Mavis, 'let us give ourselves into God's keeping, and surely we shall be well.'[31]

They stopped for the night at a fallen tree but awoke early. May wrote: 'Oh it was hard work pushing through that tall coarse grass which in places came above our heads. At last about a mile in, we came to the edge of the bush, tall timbers hung with vines . . . never before had we been off the beaten track. We sat on a fallen log and waited for light, then we pushed down a biscuit, ate some chocolate, drank water from Father's billy, tied up our bundles better, then on we pushed.'[32]

•

Meanwhile, the missionaries at the Anglican mission stations at Sangara and Isivita remained ignorant of the approaching danger. Also, unknown to them, their shepherd, Reverend Vivian Redlich was also heading for Sangara mission.[33]

12

'Scrummy, scrummy . . . I wouldn't have missed it for anything'

•

During the early morning hours of 22 July reports of the Japanese invasion of Gona and Buna were flooding into Allied headquarters in Australia. Major General Morris at Port Moresby was informed that arrangements were being made to fly 50 tons of supplies and ammunition across the mountains; nothing would come of this. He immediately ordered the remaining three companies of Lieutenant Colonel Owen's 39th Battalion to prepare to leave for Kokoda, with one company to move out the next day—23 July. They would have to make their own way across the jungle-covered mountain range on foot, following the meandering Kokoda Track.

Owen was told that if he could not prevent a Japanese advance to Kokoda he was to retire to fallback positions and prevent any further penetration towards Port Moresby. That said, he was informed that it was unlikely that the Japanese would attempt to move against Port Moresby from Buna or Gona, and that they were likely tasked with establishing an airfield in the area—as well as possibly capturing the small airfield at Kokoda as a forward base for operations.[1]

•

Overnight, the command of the AAF planned 81 sorties to be flown the next day against the Japanese ships now anchored between Gona and

Buna. The main thrust would be several coordinated strikes consisting of eight Bell P-39 Airacobra fighters, six B-25 and six B-26 bombers. In all, around 48 tons of bombs and 15,000 rounds of ammunition would be expended during these operations.[2]

The first Allied attack that day occurred at 6.30 a.m., when a lone twin-engine Lockheed Hudson light bomber, piloted by 25-year-old Australian Flight Lieutenant Lucius Manning from Bullsbrook in Western Australia, with 32 Squadron, Royal Australian Air Force (RAAF), attacked the convoy. Manning's solo attack enabled the Japanese to focus all their anti-aircraft fire against him, greatly reducing his ability to focus on his target as he was forced to fly erratically to avoid being hit. Even so, he descended upon the convoy in a low-level bombing run at a suicidal height of just 400 metres above one of the transports, but on releasing his four 250-pound bombs, to his disappointment, he saw the closest exploded 70 metres beyond the target.[3]

Next was American pilot Lieutenant Robert Debord with the 435th Bombardment Squadron flying a B-17 Flying Fortress who came upon the convoy at 7.15 a.m. He was to bomb the convoy and then orbit above, keeping it in contact. He initially made a bombing run at 3000 metres against a fast-moving destroyer, he flew into a 'cloud' of intense anti-aircraft flak—all aimed at him. He dropped five of his 300-pound bombs but missed and now targeted his final bombs against one of the anchored transports. His bombardier, Sergeant Richard Olson, positioned the aircraft for an oblique run across the largest of the two, and dropped their remaining nine bombs and watched as the 'bombs straddled the ship in a line of bomb splashes, the exultant bomber crew saw one bomb detonate amidships, followed by a spurt of flame and smoke. Debord continued to orbit the area in fulfillment of his . . . mission, observing that the vessel he had bombed was burning, listing and settling in the water.'[4] He had hit the *Ayatosan Maru*, which was disabled by uncontrolled fires and then abandoned in shallow water. From that moment on she became a local landmark to troops and airmen alike known as the 'Gona Wreck'. This had been a significant hit against the Japanese as most of her cargo was still onboard, including several trucks which were now submerged in the flooded holds.[5]

The Sakigawa Transport Unit log records this attack: '0720 hrs . . . [a] Boeing B-17 came in . . . impudently evaded the [anti-aircraft] fire, and calmly soared over the *Ayatosan Maru*, dropping countless bombs. The heavy bombs screeched as they fell, dropping all around the ship, and almost lifting the ship from the sea. One bomb struck No. 4 hold, which was loaded with crude oil. The Fire Extinguishing TAI [party] worked valiantly. Amn [ammunition] of A/A guns on the bridge was dumped into the sea because of the danger. The situation was desperate.'[6] With the bulk of their vehicles having gone down with the ship, the Sakigawa Transport Unit had just seven vehicles ashore, including a motorbike with sidecar and a light armoured car. They would now have great difficulty in fulfilling their role supporting the advancing infantry, engineers and artillery, even if roads could be constructed in the hinterland of the surrounding lowlands.[7]

It was now around 9 a.m., and a combined strike force, consisting of five B-25 bombers of the 3rd Attack Group in the first wave, and five B-26 bombers of the 22nd Bomb Group five minutes behind them, launched their attacks. Seeing the *Ayatosan Maru* already aflame and settling in the water, they focused on the remaining transport—the *Ryoyo Maru*. As the B-25s came into view they were targeted with clouds of flak and, flying at 2000 metres, all missed the target. The next wave, accompanied by American Brigadier Kenneth Walker, consisting of the B-26 bombers, flew in at about the same height and bombed the already burning *Ayatosan Maru* as well as hitting the destroyer *Uzuki*, which was then tied up beside the burning transport, evacuating casualties and saving supplies—the destroyer was soon on its way back to Rabaul for repairs.[8]

Shortly after, six P-39 fighters from the 80th Fighter Squadron, led by American Captain Philip Greasley, which had been escorting the bombers, dived upon the barges transporting men and supplies to the beach. With their .5-inch and .3-inch machine guns blazing they strafed the small vessels. While these aircraft also had twin 20-millimetre cannons—perfect for sinking barges—they had unfortunately not been loaded with ammunition. Even so, this attack must have resulted in several casualties among the crews and soldiers onboard, but only one barge was reported sunk.[9] Sergeant Major Tanaka of the Sakigawa Transport Unit had just returned to the *Ayatosan Maru* to help salvage what he could when the P-39s struck as reported in the unit's log:

> At this time, the greater part of the HQ HAN commanded by SM Tanaka, who returned to the ship . . . after selecting the vehicle landing point, was waiting within the ship. Valuable ship's papers in the hold, office baggage and essential equipment were taken out and quickly loaded in a small boat. Two guards were posted to guard these after landing. As the fire was spreading, it was decided that all personnel would abandon ship and land. Our wounded comrades were carried past us onto the deck. Like a typhoon came the low-flying spitfires [Airacobras]! They strafed from about 50 metres the personnel making for land in motor boats. The ship A/A fired bravely, and those who crossed the line of death are truly flowers of the soldier's spirit. We shot down 2 enemy planes.[10]

As these American pilots came in low, they were targeted with heavy anti-aircraft enfilade from guns positioned on the ships and those ashore. Lieutenant David Hunter's P-39 was hit. Wounded and suffering from burns, he came out of his dive and jettisoned his cockpit canopy, which almost hit the plane of his wingman, 2nd Lieutenant Danny Roberts. Hunter was forced to ditch his aircraft a few hundred metres from shore and, abandoning the sinking aircraft, he swam for the beach—and the waiting Japanese. He made it ashore close to the barges he had just moments before been strafing. Lieutenant David Hunter was captured and sent on to Rabaul and once there interrogated and soon after beheaded.[11]

Lieutenant Robert Debord and the crew of his B-17 were still circling high above the convoy and reported that all ships, except for the still burning *Ayatosan Maru*, were now heading out to sea towards Rabaul. When the next squadron of B-17s from the 19th Bomb Group arrived over Gona at around 10.30 a.m., at a height of 8000 metres, they looked below and only saw the stricken *Ayatosan Maru*. They had been tasked with the 'total destruction of the convoy' so they headed out to sea and when they reached the convoy, they dropped their bombs upon the fast-moving ships, including the *Ryoyo Maru*, which still had onboard its packhorses—all bombers returned empty-handed. Several raids were made throughout the day against the Japanese beachheads around Gona and Buna and these aircraft now had to fight off Japanese Zero fighters from Lae.[12]

•

Australian 31-year-old pilot officer Warren Cowan from Adelaide with No. 32 Squadron, RAAF, had taken off from Port Moresby in his small twin-engine Hudson bomber A16-201 on a mission to locate the departing convoy. He soon radioed in that he had spotted two Japanese cruisers heading for Rabaul and was going in to bomb them at low altitude, but before he could do so he was jumped by nine Japanese Zeros who were escorting the cruisers. The Zeros dived on the lone slow-moving bomber, among them was Japanese ace, Sub-Lieutenant Sakai Saburō. He recalled the single-sided dog-fight as the Hudson pilot banked his aircraft so his gunners had maximum coverage of the attacking fighters, at one point flying into the Zeros head-on.[13]

For over ten minutes the Zeros flew around and poured bullets into the bomber—each anxious to claim a certain kill. Cowan's gunners, 24-year-old Sergeant Russell Polack from Sydney and twenty-year-old Sergeant Lauri Sheard from Adelaide, returned fire, but it was only a matter of time—Sakai moved in for the kill and took out the Australian rear gunner, and soon after Cowan's petrol tank was ignited and ablaze. By now they were flying overland, and the Zeros followed the stricken bomber as it descended, tearing into the jungle, its wings ripping off before it exploded. Sakai, who would survive the war with 28 confirmed kills—but he is believed to have downed at least double that number— wrote in his biography how he and his comrades admired the Australian flyers, writing that Cowan was the best opponent he met while fighting over the skies of New Guinea. The gunners, who also acted as radio operators, were kept so busy during the fight that they had no time to send a message and their fate remained unknown for many years. The wreckage of Cowan's Hudson was found after the war near Popoga village, close to Buna, and the remains of the crew were recovered. The RAAF only became aware of the details of the dog-fight and crash after Sakai's biography was published in 1986.[14]

•

The Gona mission refugees heard the ongoing Allied bombing raids throughout the day, while they fled deeper into the bush. May recalled in her letter to Viola:

> As we expected, not long after dawn over came the planes. Such bombing and shooting—19 raids we counted that day, nothing could possibly be left of our lovely station. On we pushed, not seeing anything, but hearing more than enough to tell us of the havoc which was being caused by our Australian bombers, Japanese anti-aircraft their fighters etc. Many a time we crouched between the sheltering flanges of the huge trees whilst dog fights took place practically over our heads. The earth trembled when the biggest bombs fell, or planes crashed. On we sped using (now this is our biggest piece of good fortune to date) a compass which had been given [to] Father not so many weeks before by an American airman who stayed with us after his crash not so far from our station.
>
> About noon we came to a river and judged it to be the one which turns and twists and comes out near our station [likely the Amboga River]. We could not have been more than about 3 or 4 miles [5 or 6 kilometres] from Gona: however, we felt safer, the sound of the fighting seemed not quite over our heads, so we put up our nets and rested, but not for long, because it was impossible to rest in mind at any rate, so on again until about 3 or 4 o'clock when we began to feel terribly lost and as if we might be going round in circles. So when we arrived at a huge scrub-turkey's nest near a big tree, we leveled it out a bit, removing some of the largest sticks, put down our ground sheet, erected our nets, ate another biscuit (coffee) and a ration of chocolate . . . drank some water and tried to sleep, but added to the noises of the battle (raids were not so frequent) were those of the bush creatures, birds of all sizes; this we could only guess for they kept well above our heads in the leafy tops of the trees.[15]

Benson also recalled with candour his growing fears, which the two missionary Sisters tried to alleviate:

> After Evensong, we lay under our nets and began to run over the events of the day and consider our position. I was by far the most nervous and fearful member of the party and Sister Hayman rebuked my fears in a lovely way. She said, 'Father, why are you afraid for us? Last night when we made our decision to trust ourselves to the jungle rather than give ourselves up to the Japs, you yourself commended us all to God's keeping, and you blessed us. Well just leave it in God's hands. What is the good of giving ourselves to God if we are going to worry about it afterwards? All we can do is to do our very best, and we are doing that.'
>
> There was also a characteristic speech by Miss Parkinson: 'Golly, think of it. In the past twenty-four hours I've seen a naval battle, been driven out of hearth and home, crossed the enemy lines, been lost in an impenetrable forest, on the edge of a first-rate aerial bombardment, and now I'm one of the babes in the wood. Me! Who feared I was going to die without adventure; Scrummy! Scrummy! If I do die tonight, I've had a day's adventure anyhow. I wouldn't have missed it for anything.'
>
> 'Yes, my dear', said May rather sleepily, 'that aspect of it sounds all right, but you must admit it was pretty terrible being so close this morning when we were near the beach and that big drom bopped.' We were all immediately awake with laughter, and never again could any of us speak of a 'bomb dropping', it was always a 'drom that bopped'.[16]

13

'. . . two shots, followed by a terrific burst of firing'

With the early hours of 22 July ticking over, Major Watson and Captain Jesser and their men of the 1st PIB had made their way to Awala and were tasked with trying to slow down the Japanese advance halfway between Buna and Kokoda.[1]

At this point, Grahamslaw and his men were preparing to leave Isagahambo where Warrant Officer Harry Bitmead, a 32-year-old medical assistant, was treating his native patients. This native hospital was located on the Awala–Buna track. With Bitmead was Warrant Officer Donald Barnes, a twenty-year-old pharmaceutical chemist from Kensington Park in South Australia and 48-year-old Private Harold Chester with ANGAU, who was usually based at Ioma to the west. Chester had arrived with several native carriers loaded down with bags of rice heading for Awala. Bitmead told Grahamslaw that he had sent Papuan troops out to scout along the narrow Sangara–Buna track, which ran parallel but south of the main Awala–Buna track (further west both converged and joined to form the single track leading to Wairopi). Grahamslaw instructed Chester to continue to Awala with his carriers, and then proceed back to Ioma—he was to use his discretion whether to evacuate his position if the Japanese approached.[2]

Grahamslaw now instructed Bitmead to pack his medical supplies and fall back to Wasida, which lay just behind Awala, as the Japanese must be close; Bitmead agreed to send Barnes back, but requested he be allowed to stay to help evacuate his patients. Grahamslaw recalled:

110

'I instructed . . . Bitmead, former Administrations Medical Assistant who was in charge of the native hospital, to send his patients back to their villages and fall back to Wasida. I stressed that soon his services would be needed to tend the wounded. However, Bitmead—a dedicated man—prevailed on me to let his assistant go to Wasida with medical supplies while he personally saw to it that his patients got to safety. I stationed a police constable on the track below the hospital with instructions for him to tell Bitmead if he saw signs of the enemy. Unfortunately, the constable later fled to his own village'.[3]

Grahamslaw and his party pushed on towards Buna along the main track with McKenna and three constables up front, Grahamslaw and three other policemen ten minutes behind them, and bringing up the rear, Yeoman and the three remaining constables.[4] They soon crossed Arehe Creek where they stopped for a smoko. Grahamslaw recalled:

By this time, it was early afternoon and we were feeling in need of a meal. Our journey had been interrupted a number of times by Zeros which were flying up and down the track, at a height of a few hundred feet. Whenever we saw one approaching, we would leave the track, sit down in the undergrowth, and resume our journey when it departed. In order not to attract attention from either enemy aircraft or troops, we moved about 200 yards [about 200 metres] up stream around a bend, where we lit a fire under a canopy of trees. At Arehe the road branched off in two directions—one to Buna and the other to Popondetta. Two constables . . . were posted on the Buna Road and two on the Popondetta Road, about a quarter of a mile distant, with instructions to squat in the undergrowth and watch for enemy movements. If they saw any sign of the enemy, they were to report back to us. If circumstances did not permit this to be done, each was to fire a warning shot and then decamp. Tea was made, and we were relaxing in the shade—McKenna seated on one log . . . with the open tucker box between us. Before we could commence, without warning, we heard two shots which were followed by a terrific burst of firing.[5]

Grahamslaw and McKenna immediately bolted into the jungle scrub; at the time Yeoman and his three constables were still bringing up the rear and were a few minutes from the bivouac. Grahamslaw and McKenna tried to rejoin the track further south but had become lost. Indeed, Grahamslaw lost sight of McKenna who was leading the way. Grahamslaw recalled in his report to ANGAU a few months later that he was following as fast as he could when his rifle 'caught in some undergrowth and caused me to fall heavily'.[6] By the time he got himself together, McKenna had disappeared. Meanwhile, Yeoman and his men fell back along the track, avoiding the Japanese. Grahamslaw continues his narrative:

Months later I learned that the leading elements of the Japanese were on bicycles, and they were almost on top of the police before being seen. All the police could do was to fire a warning shot and then flee into the jungle. The Japs must have thought they had run into an ambush and hundreds of them opened fire. Unfortunately, the fusillade caused someone in our party to panic, and before I could do anything about it, McKenna and I were left to our own devices . . . Shortly after nightfall I made a cautious inspection of the main road some miles on the Kokoda side of Arehe Creek crossing. By this time the main body of enemy troops had passed. They were being followed by native carriers brought from Rabaul by the Japs. The carriers were in groups of what appeared to be between 20 and 30, with Jap guards at the front and rear of each group. The natives were silent, but I could distinctly hear the guards calling out to each other. Perhaps they were doing this to keep about the same distance between each group. It was quite an experience listening to voices gradually becoming louder and then just as gradually dying away. Deciding this was no place for me I crawled back into the jungle and then proceeded to walk in what I hoped was the direction of Sangara Mission. I had no compass to guide me and the dense rain forest country prevented me from seeing the stars.[7]

•

Corporal Francis Tutuveta and his men were making their way from the beach back to Lieutenant Wort: 'In the morning [22 July] we heard the Japanese moving down the main track towards Kokoda, so we broke bush and moved parallel to the track and got into Sangara. We reported to the Kiap [patrol officer] and police at Sangara that the Japanese were coming, but the Kiap wouldn't believe us, so I and my section said, "You can stop here if you want to, but we're moving back." So, we moved back and eventually joined up with Captain Jesser and Lieutenant Chalk.'[8] On arriving at Awala, Captain Jesser asked Corporal Tutuveta had he seen the Japanese? He replied, 'No, I haven't seen any Japanese soldiers. I saw their ships on the beach, and we moved back and slept in the bush and then we heard them coming down the road.'[9]

Watson wasted no time and sent forward several patrols from Awala, the strongest of these was led by Jesser and Chalk with 35 Papuan troops, including Tutuveta and his men. They left Awala just after 11 a.m., and early in the afternoon contacted Bitmead who was still at his native hospital at Isagahambo. Bitmead told them that Grahamslaw and his men had passed through earlier. Chalk later wrote in his report:

> Received orders from Major Watson regarding role in Buna area. Left Awala 1115 hours arrived at Isagahambo 1400 hrs. Contacted W.O. Bitmead, Medical Orderly A.N.G.A.U. who told us he had posted 100 carriers . . . along Buna track from Sangara, to fall trees across the track with the intention of impeding the enemy's advance, also to gain information regarding their movements in the Sangara area. 1430 Capt. Jesser left to make recce of Higaturu area and to select observation points on a high feature overlooking Buna. Remainder of force proceeded to Sangara to await the arrival of Capt. Jesser. Arrived Sangara 1500 hours. Three scouts were posted half [a] mile along Buna track. 1700 hrs., Capt. Jesser arrived Sangara. He advised Lt. Chalk that the enemy had advanced along the track on bicycles and had taken our scouts by surprise. Force moved to a position on the loop road to Isagahambo, where it was possible to cover both tracks to Awala.[10]

Corporal Tutuveta recalled that as they began to leave Sangara they heard a 'motor bike coming down the track, so we all dived into the bush and the Japanese arrived. Jesser sent me out to scout during the night, and I remember that it rained very heavily and in the morning [23 July] the road, and all the bush around us, were full of Japanese.'[11] Meanwhile, Lieutenant Chalk and ten of his men had returned to Isagahambo to warn Bitmead of the Japanese approach. At this point Warrant Officer Harold Yeoman, who had been with Grahamslaw's party when they were attacked by the Japanese, had made his way back to Chalk's position.[12] The young lieutenant later reported: '1815hrs W.O. Yeoman contacted force on track to Isagahambo, the enemy at Arahe [sic Arehe] at mid-day . . . 1830 hours arrived at Isagahambo. Bitmead was not there his personal boy advised that Bitmead had gone to buy food East of Sangara. 1915 hrs. Capt. Jesser arrived [at] Isagahambo, with food he had been given by Mission personnel of Sangara, whom he had contacted earlier in the afternoon. Capt. Jesser had posted three scouts on the Sangara track to observe any enemy move-ments.'[13] Bitmead had arrived at Sangara and warned the missionaries there of the approaching Japanese and told them to clear out. Within the hour, Sisters Margery Brenchley and Lilla Lashmar, along with Lucian Tapiedi, were heading for Isivita Station, having already sent a runner to Father Holland based there to warn him of the imminent danger.[14]

On the other side of the Owen Stanley Range, Lieutenant Colonel Bill Owen, along with his remaining companies of the 39th Battalion, were close to Ower's Corner. Owen's men were to push through the moun-tain range to reinforce Sam Templeton and his men of 'B' Company. Owen himself was about to fly into Kokoda to take command of Maroubra Force. Hearing this, Templeton was now forced to wait for him at Kokoda, so he could brief his CO of the situation and troop dispositions as known, not just those under his command, but also those of the Japanese.[15] While Captain Sam Templeton was anxiously awaiting the arrival of his CO, unknown to either, Owen's flight would be delayed, and he would not arrive until the next day.[16]

That night, Lieutenant John Chalk, with Corporal George Meta and three other members of the 1st PIB, moved back along the track to determine whether the Japanese had occupied Sangara in strength. Chalk and his men took up a position among some thick scrub and observed several Japanese in and around the village. The Australian lieutenant later reported: 'The enemy were in occupation of Mason's house and out-buildings, and could be heard talking etc. No estimate of enemy strength could be obtained. Force then withdrew, demolishing bridges en route, and erecting barricades across track.'[17]

•

Warrant Officer Harry Bitmead, who had been out east of Sangara looking for food for his patients, had been captured by the Japanese. Over the next few days he endured psychological torture, as more than once he was led out before a firing squad and as he braced himself the Japanese would break into laughter, and then drag him back to a small filthy hut. He later told Doc Vernon of his experience with the Japanese execution squad: 'While in the hands of the Japs he suffered great indignities and was in constant danger of being shot. Time after time, he told me later, a squad of five Mongols leveled their rifles at him and clicked the triggers, but the barrels were unloaded, and his imminent death postponed. Their object in this . . . was probably to get him in the right state for questioning and, all probability, they were awaiting the arrival of some English-speaking Jap Officer to obtain information about our troop movements. His ordeal ended in utter loss of consciousness.'[18]

•

Back in Australia, news arrived from George Johnston, an Australian correspondent then with the *Sydney Morning Herald*, the Melbourne *Age*, and the *Daily Telegraph* in London. He was based at Port Moresby at the time of the Japanese invasion and reported on 22 July:

> The significance of the Gona landing will no doubt become clearer
> in a few days. Buna is almost due north of Port Moresby—120 miles
> by air [190 kilometres]—and is a small but fairly important native

administration and mission centre. A good foot track leads through undulating jungle country to Kokoda, 60 miles to the southward; and then a much tougher foot track leads over the Owen Stanley Range, through a wide, 6000-foot [1800-metre] pass known to New Guinea air pilots as 'the Gap', and on through terrible mountain jungles to Moresby. With the exception of a small stretch between Buna and the Kumusi River (less than half-way to Kokoda) the track is impossible for mechanized transport, and so it seems unlikely that the Japs can hope to attempt any overland invasion of Moresby by pushing south-ward through the mountains, with Buna as a supply base. It is true that Buna has what Lae and Salamaua have always lacked—a *direct* link with the main Australian base [Moresby], but it seems more logical that the landing has been made to gain control of the comparatively flat North Papuan coast, with its limitless possibilities for the estab-lishment of many good, large airfields and landing strips over a wide area of dispersal and within 30 minutes' flying time of Moresby. This new move by the enemy may be the curtain-raiser for almost anything. Perhaps, even the long-expected Battle for New Guinea.[19]

One can only imagine the reaction of May Hayman's and Mavis Parkinson's loved ones on reading the news that the Japanese had launched their invasion just off the coast from the Gona mission station.

14

'We only had rifles'

By 3 a.m. the next day—23 July—Lieutenant Chalk and his small party had arrived back at Isagahambo where Jesser and his men were waiting for him. Chalk later wrote in his report: 'As the only means of communication with C.O., at Awala was by runner, and as this means was not satisfactory, Capt. Jesser returned to Awala to report on the situation. 0530 hrs. Bitmead's house containing medical stores etc., was demolished, and force withdrew to Hagenahambo where defensive positions were taken up. Road barricaded en route.'[1]

Meanwhile, Private Lafe and his small party of the 1st PIB made an appearance at Awala, having earlier reported to Lieutenant Wort of the Japanese positions. 'We met the forward sentry of the company position, and he took us to where Captain Jesser was waiting. I reported my information and after we had some food, we continued back to the company headquarters area where we reported to Major Watson. The headquarters was at Awala, at the Government station, where there were gardens with plenty of food.'[2] Captain Jesser now led a patrol out towards Tonana, along Ioma Road, to help cover their north-western flank.

A few hours later Chalk and his small party at Hagenahambo were reinforced with a party led by Lieutenant Wort, Sergeant Harry Bishop and Warrant Officer Jack McWatters. In all there were now about 35 men at Hagenahambo. Also present was Corporal Tutuveta, who went out to scout the Japanese positions up front as had Sergeant Katue of the 1st PIB. Removing his uniform, Katue disguised himself as a local and moved around and through the Japanese positions, collecting valuable intelligence on enemy strength and dispositions. This enabled the Australian and Papuan troops to redeploy to further slow down the enemy advance. A member of his battalion later recalled: 'We got a hero, we got a spy.'[3]

•

Sergeant Katue would spend almost three months behind enemy lines collecting intelligence, killing Japanese troops, organising resistance and burning food stocks that might be of use to the enemy. He also dispensed with summary justice shooting two tribal leaders who were urging their people to support the Japanese. He even managed to capture a Japanese radio, which was shortly after passed on to the Australians. On his return to the Australian lines, with one Japanese prisoner, he presented the rank insignia from 26 Japanese officers and NCOs who he had killed—he stated he found nothing on the private's uniform worth taking. Australian newspaperman, Geoffrey Reading, with Sydney's *Daily Mirror*, interviewed Katue in Port Moresby shortly after his return to Australian lines, recording for his readers back home:

He moved through the green jungle silent as a shadow, and, as perhaps the Japanese one day will tell you, he was a kind of shadow—the shadow of death. Sometimes he struck without warning, and then death was swift, clean, and painless. But sometimes he made his presence known, and on these occasions the Japanese soldiers went quickly to the abode of their ancestors and their gods with one terrible image burning through their minds—a slow mirthless smile, and a cold dark eye squinting along the barrel of a rifle.

For ten years Katue had served in the native constabulary, and then, in June 1940, he enlisted in the Papuan forces. At the time I spoke to him he had shot dead twenty-six Japs. No man in New Guinea, white or black, had accounted for more of the enemy than that. Sergeant Katue was about five feet seven tall, with close-cropped fuzzy hair. He was as black as the ace of spades. In each ear were three holes, but he no longer wore the savage decorations for which, in his boyhood, the holes were pierced. On the right sleeve of his tunic he wore a sergeant's stripes, his own, a badge of rank taken from a Jap marine he had slain, and two Jap lieutenant's [*sic*] strips [*sic*]. On his left arm he wore another marine's badge and thirteen Jap stripes . . .

On patrol in Japanese-held territory, shortly after the enemy had landed at Gona and advanced on Kokoda, Katue saw three Japs on bicycles approaching a village. He ordered the two police boys who were under his command to hold their fire—for he rather prided himself as a trigger-man—and thrust the muzzle of his rifle through the undergrowth. Three shots rang out, and three Japs fell.

Moving swiftly from village to village Katue recruited his own native army. By the time he arrived at a mission station occupied by Japs, his force numbered fifteen. Katue here drew a bead on a Jap who was up an orange-tree looking for fruit . . . At the sound of the shot and the thud of the Japanese body, sixteen Nips came racing out of the mission house. Four were picked off as they ran, and the remainder fled in disorder into the jungle. Katue got to work with needle and thread again.

Then came village after village, but no Japs. The monotony was getting on Katue's nerves. At one village, which the sudden enemy advance had forced Australians to abandon, Katue set fire to a large food dump. Six Japs came up the track to investigate, and Katue shot the lot. They were buried by villagers. He returned to an Allied jungle post for fresh supplies, ammunition, and tobacco. Then the dusky army went back to the jungle.

One of Katue's men had the misfortune to be captured. Katue drew up plans and laid an ambush. As the prisoner was being led away Katue shot the guard and released the unhappy soldier. Later this man proved such a good shot that Katue held a solemn ceremony in the heart of the jungle and promoted him acting-lance-corporal-without-extra-pay.

Sergeant Katue brought back to Port Moresby a large quantity of captured Jap equipment, including Tommy-guns and rifles. Then he started making love to other Fuzzy-wuzzies' wives—the old, old story. What woman can resist a uniform, especially when it encases a warrior of the calibre of Katue? Katue went back to the jungle with a pack of irate husbands on his heels. Anything for a quiet life![4]

Sergeant Katue was awarded the Military Medal for his actions—the first of many to be awarded to the men of the PIB by war's end.[5]

•

Five Douglas A-24 Banshee single-engine dive bombers from the 8th Bomb Squadron appeared in the late morning over Gona and bombed the Japanese barges on the beach. Providing air support to these vulnerable twin-crewed bombers, which had a top speed of just 400 kilometres per hour, were four P-39 fighters from the 35th Fighter Group with a top speed of around 600 kilometres per hour. All feared that the highly agile Japanese A6M2 Zero fighters, with a top speed of 570 kilometres per hour and with a tight turning circle, might be in the vicinity, however, the Zeros did not make an appearance and, after conducting their bombing run, all Allied aircraft returned safely to their base at Kila, also known as 3-Mile Drome, the original civil airport at Port Moresby which was now being used by several fighter squadrons.[6]

•

By 4 p.m., Chalk and his small party were waiting at their ambush position near Hagenahambo about 1 kilometre east of Awala, on the eastern side of a creek. Soon a runner arrived with a message from Watson, 'You will engage the enemy.'[7] Wort ordered Corporal Meta to go down the track towards Sangara to watch out for the Japanese. The corporal took up a position in some thick scrub with a view of the track. It was not long before a lone Japanese scout was seen advancing cautiously up the path, the man stopped, seeming to sense danger and quickly retreated. To Meta's relief he was soon joined by Corporal Tutuveta and four of his men. Informed of the Japanese approach, Tutuveta and the others withdrew to warn of the Japanese advance.

Soon, elements of Tsukamoto's force were seen coming up the track, heading straight for the ambush position. Chalk waited before giving the order to fire—surely all were anxious with fingers squeezing triggers. 'Fire!' yelled the Australian officer and with this the men poured lead into the advancing Japanese. The burst of fire from around 35 rifles took the Japanese completely by surprise and their lead elements stumbled and fell. However, the Japanese quickly recovered and replied with rifle, machine-gun and mortar fire.

Lieutenant Chalk recalled: 'The Japanese eventually arrived, preceded by native carriers, so I had to hold my fire until the Japanese soldiers came into view. I gave the order to fire and the Japanese immediately swung into action with mortars and woodpecker machine guns.'[8] Corporal Tutuveta also recalled: 'We only had rifles, and we opened fire on the Japs [and they] scattered everywhere and when they returned our fire, we retreated across the wire bridge . . . and then cut it down.'[9] The men of the 1st PIB inflicted several casualties against the Japanese, as described by historian Phillip Bradley. 'The Papuans unleashed a hail of small-arms fire . . . at close range. Several Japanese troops fell dead, but the [Japanese], in their first action of the campaign, responded quickly and began firing mortars onto the ambush position. It was time to leave. The PIB men dashed for the footbridge over the creek and chopped it down when the last man was across.'[10] They made their way back to Watson's position at Awala.

Earlier, at around 11 a.m., Lieutenant Seekamp and his men of 11 Platoon had arrived at Awala after their forced march from Kokoda. As the strong Japanese force pushed Chalk and his men back, Watson ordered Seekamp to hold his position while elements of the 1st PIB fell back on Ongahambo, about 12 kilometres west of Awala along the same track. Seekamp and his men were eventually forced to withdraw to Wairopi along with Watson and his men, taking up a position along the western bank of the Kumusi River.[11] Thirty-two-year-old Sergeant Les Martorana from Bentleigh in Victoria, recalled: 'While we were guarding the river crossing they [Watson's men] set fire to the stores at Awala, petrol, ammunition you name it . . . and this is going boom, boom, boom . . . we didn't want to move the fellas all out in one mass, in case there were Nips with machine guns, which there were. Moved two at a time to cover people. It would start getting dark at 5 minutes to 6:00 and then at 6:00 it would go black . . . We passed through at about 6.15; as we passed through Awala it was just red embers.'[12]

•

The Japanese at Gona and Buna were busy establishing their head-quarters and supply depots and consolidating their beachhead. Japanese engineers, troops and native labour parties were constructing fortified positions and strong bunkers and anti-aircraft gun positions along the coast, with work begun on expanding the small airfield at Buna for major operations. A wharf was also being constructed at Buna to help with the landing of supplies. Another base was under construction at Sanananda, which would become the main Japanese field hospital. Just beyond, Sergeant Major Tanaka and his men of the Sakigawa Transport Unit were busy expanding and pushing roads inland; within days they had constructed a main road connecting Gona, Sanananda and Buna. The unit's log records that elements of the unit had also pushed about 10 kilometres inland from the landing place, heading towards Soputa:

> Our duty to reach the front line would not let us rest for one moment . . . The surface of the road became worse, and except for one or two leading vehicles, the cars could not advance by their own power. All personnel covered with mud and sweat and needing sleep, bravely carried on . . . We spread logs for a distance of 30 metres and smoothed out the unevenness of the surface, but the vehicles still slid, and advance was not facilitated. Finally, tractors were used, and we reached an open space. This took five hours and a half . . . Since the night before landing, we have not slept. The difficulties of the roads and their repair are beyond description. All officers and men realised their duty and proudly carried on.[13]

The difficult swampy terrain beyond the coastal fringes would require a rethink about Kokoda Station being a main supply depot. Even so, the ground beyond the coastal swamps was relatively good going, and the Japanese would eventually build a road that trucks could use, most of the way to Kokoda. However, the Japanese were desperately short of transport aircraft and the airstrip at Kokoda would play no significant logistical part in the Japanese attempts to cross the Owen Stanleys.[14]

15

'Our swags were much easier to manage now . . .'

Captain Thomas Grahamslaw was still trying to make his way to Kokoda, having avoided death or capture from the Japanese, he was now hopelessly lost in the scrub.

The following morning [23 July] I found myself near the main Buna–Kokoda Road again, which indicated that I must have walked in circles during the night. I could hear Japanese voices and the sound of marching footsteps. As I squatted in the undergrowth pondering what to do, I heard a rustle and saw an Orokaiva native crawl past in the direction of the road. I subsequently found that it was common practice for natives to do this, and they usually succeeded in observing what was going on, without themselves being heard or seen. I was tempted to make myself known to the native but decided he might panic and attract attention to me. By this time, I was in no condition to make a speedy exit. I waited for a lull on the road and then had a quick look at it before crawling back into the undergrowth.

In the late afternoon, finding myself at Arehe Creek several miles above the crossing, I suddenly remembered the tucker box, which our party left behind when we fled. By this time, I was very hungry. I made a cautious approach along the creek and was delighted to find the tucker box intact. Hearing noises at the crossing around the bend, I investigated and saw a number of Japanese manhandling a motor truck, which had bogged down when partly across the stream. I crept back to the box and was crouched over it helping myself to a packet of Army biscuits when two shots whistled past me. Apparently, I must have been seen while investigating the crossing. I gave a convulsive leap and dashed back into the jungle, with the sound of shots spurring me on. I kept going until sheer exhaustion caused me to drop to the ground and fall asleep.[1]

•

Meanwhile, the refugees from the Gona mission station were continuing their escape, unaware that the Japanese were already well forward of their position. In her letter to Viola at this point, May seemed to be cramming as much information as possible onto the page, perhaps worried she might run out of paper before concluding her story: 'We did not waste much time in getting away next morning [23 July] and strode out as fast as the undergrowth and prickly vines would let us. These long (1 or 2 yards) saw-like arms seemed to pull us back even more than yesterday and seemed to divert our course to a much greater extent, but we had the whole day before us so were not too cast down until we came to swampy jungle and try as we might at every direction, we seemed to meet swamp.' She wrote that they were clearly lost in the lowland putrid swamps, a truly frightening prospect: lost, never to be seen again, their bodies never to receive a Christian burial; she continues her letter: 'Surely, we must be able to skirt these swamps, let us even turn almost to retrace our recent steps. This we did, and we kept out of the swamp and gradually by aid of the compass (which we continually held open now) we began to bear again in the direction which should eventually bring us out onto some of the tracks which led to Siai. How often we thought we had found a path, only to find it petered out before 4 or 5 yards were traversed.'[2]

Mavis also recalled with despair to her mother: 'To our dismay, we were getting into a sago swamp, and only if you've been in this country could you know what that means—prickly, almost impenetrable undergrowth, and slushy mud underfoot into which it is possible to sink up to one's waist and even neck, and always the fear of crocodiles. Everywhere, North, West and South, was the swamp and for the first time I felt maybe we'd never get out of the jungle—it seemed so hopeless.'[3]

May continued her letter to her sister writing what happened after they had managed to get clear of the swamps.

When following one of the more likely paths, we found a native foot mark—what a relief—now we must not lose this path for it surely must lead us somewhere—there is a dog's paw mark also. Now none at all, but not far away there was another and almost before we knew it, we were on quite a good path. Our hearts were much lighter now for really Father's fear of being lost in the trackless jungle is a very real one.

Presently we came to quite a big stream of water, here we stayed awhile, sent Father further along, took off our clothes and had a bonza swim, for in Father's little bag he had some soap and we had our toothbrushes. We washed our clothes (except dresses) joined Father, ate some more biscuits and chocolate then said mattins. Yesterday's had been said while crouching behind a big tree after a dog fight. With what thankfulness we praised God this morning—surely God was guiding and caring for us.

Our swags were much easier to manage now that we were on a real path. Presently we heard voices and came upon a group of bush people, some we knew for they had been patients of Gona. They cooked us some sweet potatoes and we really enjoyed them. On again but this time we had natives to guide us and carry for us. These people had erected a rough bush shelter for they were afraid to stay in their village as there was a main Government track through there and someone had encountered two Japanese . . .

Needless to say, we did not sleep in Vivisoini nor Senani rest houses, but went on to Biri, even there the people did not welcome us, and we began to realise that being white people the natives felt we might endanger their existence should the Japanese come and discover them befriending us. However, there was a man from a little village quite off the main track and he was very taken that we should go on and sleep there. This village we found to comprise two native houses and their usual little roofed platform where the big men sat at the time of a feast.

We asked if we might put up our nets there rather than the dirty old windowless house of a native. They cut long grass to form a mattress for us, but alas it was not much softer than the scrub-turkey's nest, but we felt quite safe and that was the best feeling we had had for a long time.[4]

•

It was not only May who was coming to the realisation that the reign of the 'white man' was coming to an end. Twenty-four-year-old Lieutenant Alan Hooper from Wynnum in Queensland now with the 1st PIB, was based in the Ioma district just north-west and wrote at the time: 'The Gona landings sped many indentured or casual labourers back to their tribal area. Wild-eyed, they spread horrific tales of enemy brutality throughout the Northern Division. The arrival of shiploads of [Japanese] soldiers, packhorses, anti-aircraft guns, equipment in vast quantities boggled their minds.' The tribal old ways had obviously laid just below the surface and quickly re-emerged to gain dominance, especially among those seeking power and leadership roles. 'Orokaiva renegades and power-seeking sorcerers intimidated loyal villagers and were quick to kill for payback or for prestige. Those reluctant to obey the Japanese or exchange crops for worthless invasion money courted death. Natives willing to act for the enemy as captains were given descriptive armbands. Seemingly, the rule of the white masters had ended forever. I was outranked, out-maneuvered and, like other Australians in the district, regarded as a potential or an immediate liability.'[5] Indeed, the Orokaiva people were known to be fierce and were feared throughout the region—they were only 50 years removed from cannibalism and, if that was not bad enough, they had practised 'living meat', in which they had tied their prisoners to a tree and, as meat was needed, cut slices from buttocks or legs, plastering pandanus leaves over the wounds; some of the poor wretches, Father Benson had learned, 'would live in agony for two weeks'.[6]

That said, Peter Ryan, an eighteen-year-old warrant officer with ANGAU, who worked closely with the 1st PIB, recalled that while the 'pre-war relationships of white master and black servants were shaken' he also observed 'a different sort of white man was seen for the first time in the Australian soldiers whose humanity, informality, and willingness to labour in the sun and in the mud were in contrast to the rigid allowances of many of the pre-war residents'.[7] However, not all Australian soldiers would display regard for the locals and the carriers who were assisting them in the fight against the Japanese, especially in the early days of the Kokoda Campaign.[8]

•

Back in Australia, the public was receiving additional reports on the Japanese invasion. Chester Wilmot with the ABC had returned from covering the Australians fighting in Greece and North Africa and broadcast the following from 4QG radio station in Brisbane on 23 July 1942.

The Latest Japanese Attack in New Guinea

As you all heard in the news tonight, the lull in New Guinea has ended. The Japanese have made a fresh move. For the first time they've landed in Papua as distinct from the Mandated Territory of New Guinea. They've established themselves at the eastern end of the one track which leads across the island to Port Moresby only 120 miles [190 kilometres] away. They haven't yet landed a force large enough to enable them to launch a serious attack on Port Moresby ...

This invasion force was made up of warships escorting enough transports to carry the equivalent of an Australian Brigade group. It is reported that not more than 2500 troops and their equipment have landed, and this suggests that the landing force was a mixed Japanese regiment of infantry with supporting artillery.

Late on Tuesday our reconnaissance picked up this invasion force some distance out from Buna. By then it was too late for the Allied Command to swing a formidable bomber force into action against it before dark. Our bombers did what they could, and one large transport is officially reported to have sunk.

Under cover of darkness the Japanese reached Buna and by dawn their landing was already in progress on the beaches near the Gona Mission. But it is known that there were no Allied land forces to oppose the landing. From early morning our aircraft bombed and strafed the Japanese forces as they continued to ferry troops and equipment ashore in landing barges. Apparently, the Japanese were protected by Zeros operating from Lae and our aircraft were not able to stop the landing. It is significant that the communique claims that only one barge was sunk. Either the Japanese gained temporary local air superiority or else most of their troops were landed before daylight. Certainly, this is the cheapest success the Japanese have had since they took Rabaul. In getting Lae and Salamaua they lost a large number of ships as a result of the RAAF's bombing and when they attempted to gather an invasion force to push south towards Buna in mid-March, American bombers sank or badly damaged at least 23 ships . . .

So long as the Japs were only in Lae and Salamaua, they couldn't make any direct attack on Port Moresby, as there is no suitable track across the 13,000 feet [4000 metre] high Owen Stanley Range. But from Buna a rough track does lead over mountains only a few thousand feet high and it would be possible to get a small force across it. I'm told by people who've been there that this is only a rough mountain track and that it's suitable for vehicles for only part of the way. But we must remember that the Japanese travel light and have an extraordinary capacity for getting through apparently impassable country.

It is too early to say whether this is the first step in an attack on Moresby. The approach is very difficult and the force at present isn't anything like adequate. A force this size would have had no chance of attacking Moresby successfully four months ago. Since then the garrison has been considerably strengthened by Australian troops and American forces. But if they continue to bring troops into Buna and attempt to move a force round into the Coral Sea then it will be a different matter. But at present it appears that this move is merely an attempt to protect their air bases at Lae and Salamaua and to forestall any attempt by the Allies to get a secure footing on the eastern coast of New Guinea. Buna is the last place where we could have established a forward base for a counterattack against Lae. Three weeks ago, we made a night raid on Salamaua with land forces [Australian Independent Company raid]. Since then Japanese reconnaissance planes have been actively watching any moves by our land forces in south-eastern New Guinea. This is their reply—it is to be hoped that they are not going to have the last word. We cannot afford to leave them in undisputed possession of Buna.[9]

Mavis's parents and family, who were based in Brisbane, must have been distressed to hear this broadcast and the ongoing references to Gona mission. Only months before they had reluctantly agreed that Mavis could stay at Gona, after she had pleaded for their blessing to remain there with May and Father Benson.

16

'What's the state of your underpants, Sarg?'

By early morning of 24 July, Lieutenant Seekamp and his men of 11 Platoon, along with Watson's small party from the 1st PIB, were on the western side of the 20-metre wide Kumusi River at Wairopi, having destroyed the bridge behind them. At 9 a.m., they received a message from Captain Sam Templeton at Kokoda, stating that he had heard a radio report that between 1500 and 2000 Japanese had landed at 'Gona Mission Station. I think that this is near to correct and in view of the numbers I recommend that your action be contact and rearguard only—no do-or-die stunts. Close back on Kokoda.'[1]

•

At 10.30 a.m., Captain Stevenson, Templeton's 2i/c, arrived at Wairopi with Company Sergeant Major Joseph Dawson. The young senior NCO recalled the miserable conditions as they moved forward to confront the Japanese: 'It never stopped; rain, rain, rain. You got wet . . . Everything got wet. We had the haversack, and I think the things in that kept reasonably dry. They had a dampness about them when you opened it up. It rained all the time. Everything was wet. You were in wet clothes, and when you got around you were covered in mud; terrible. Then you had the mozzies. The jungle was very hard to move through, and there were leeches, spiders, you name it. No one liked moving through there, but we got into the habit later on. We used to move through the scrub, with difficulty—very thick.'[2]

Lieutenant Mortimore and his men of 12 Platoon were near Gorari, about 7 kilometres west along the same track. It was at Gorari that Watson had set up his headquarters. Stevenson now ordered Seekamp to prepare to fight another rearguard action, and when attacked in strength to withdraw along the track. Sergeant Major Dawson recalled: 'Our small force took up a defensive position under cover along the bank of the river and were told to hold fire. I swapped my rifle for a Thompson with a 50-round drum magazine and [had] taken a spot among the greenery just to the right of the bridge. Al Collyer was nearby.'[3]

About midday, Captain Jesser with the 1st PIB and his small party who had been out scouting round the Japanese to the north-west, were now forced to swim the river at Wairopi as the bridge had been demolished. Jesser reported the Japanese had spent the night at Awala and, as of 7 a.m., had made no advance from there. Jesser had also encountered the mission people from Sangara, who, like those from Gona, were now refugees; they were trying to reach Kokoda Station. He provided them with the details he had of the location of the Japanese before heading back to Wairopi.[i] However, the Japanese were not far behind him and, by 2.30 p.m., they emerged on the east bank of Kumusi River.

Corporal Tutuveta recalled the arrival of the Japanese on the far bank of the Kumusi River, who opened fire on the Rest House. He and his men moved into the garden area as the enemy occupied the rubber plantation on the other side of the river. The Papuan troops stood in the garden area watching the Japanese, who did not see them as they were not fired upon: 'We were not camouflaged—all we had were our lap laps and rifles. At this stage Australian troops moved in, and they asked us, "Where are the Japanese?" and our reply was, "Well, you be quiet for a moment and you'll hear them." So they shut up. Sure enough, you could hear the Japanese chattering away amongst themselves . . . My line was relieved and ordered to move back, and we retired to Kokoda Station.'[4]

Sergeant Major Dawson recalled: 'The Japanese appeared on the eastern side of the Kumusi at about 2.20 p.m. We could see them at the bridge entrance. First one scout, then another . . . then a third joined

---

i   For his ongoing scouting and patrolling during the first week of the invasion, Captain Harold Jesser was awarded the Military Cross.

them. They seemed to be having a conference.' Unfortunately, one of
his men with a Lewis gun had an itchy trigger finger and opened fire
against the Japanese before the order was given: 'I saw one scout go
down but I'm not sure what happened to the other two. We had no
mortars, but they did, and they brought them into action very quickly.
With reasonable accuracy numerous bombs landed close to and behind
our position. It's true to say I really didn't like being in the thick of the
action. We continued to fire at any head that appeared on the opposite
bank and also in the direction of their mortar smoke, but their mortar
barrage only got heavier.'[5]

The Japanese attempted to cross the river using several rubber boats,
supplied by the accompanying combat engineers, but the Australian fire
repulsed the attack and the Japanese fell back. Dawson recalled: 'We'd
fire and keep firing at them. And then we'd get machine gun fire back
at us. But this went on for quite a while, but eventually . . . you could
see along the river the trees moving, because obviously the Japs were
looking for another place to cross the river.'[6] The Japanese troops quickly
moved upstream and made an unopposed crossing, forcing Seekamp
and his men to retire before they were cut off. Dawson was still holding
his position when a 'runner slithered up through the undergrowth and
by way of greeting said, "What's the state of your underpants, Sarg?"
Before I had a chance to reply, he went on to say that Captain Stevenson
wanted the company headquarters to move back and join 12 Platoon at
Gorari.'[7] These men quickly moved back to take up a defensive position
near the village, however, several men became separated and were never
seen again.[8]

Among the Japanese crossing the Kumusi upstream a few hours
later was Sergeant Imanishi with elements of No. 2 Company who were
coming up behind Ogawa's No. 1 Company of the I/144th Regiment.
During the afternoon of the invasion, Imanishi had been crouching
in the *Ayatosan Maru*, thinking of the terrible fate that awaited him at
the hands of the Australian convicts. He now recalled as he crossed the
river: 'There was some resistance and a few casualties. But I was a bit
behind. I had to carry my bicycle on my shoulders across the Kumusi.'[9]
He recalled that at this point: 'I was hoping to get on[to] . . . a flat area

and put some bags on it. I carried the bicycle and climbed up a steep hill. I was so thirsty. Then someone said, "Look at that! He carried his bicycle to here".[10] He jettisoned the bike.

•

Back at Kokoda, Lieutenant Brewer had been establishing a supply depot at Deniki, located south in the highlands, 400 metres above the plateau and about 8 kilometres south of Kokoda. He wrote in his report to ANGAU: 'I instructed Lieut. [William] Graham to move all stores to DENIKI in case of withdrawal. Signalers and myself moved the radio to a position of safety in the hills at rear of the Station and then established communications . . . At 1630 hours Lieut. Searle, W.O. Brown, W.O. Yeoman and four signalers arrived from Awala with stores and radio . . . Lieut. Searle, reported that Capt. Grahamslaw, Lieut. J.B. McKenna and W.O. Bitmead had been cut off by the Japs. I assumed command in Capt. Grahamslaws [sic] absence.'[11]

During the late afternoon of 24 July, Lieutenant Colonel Bill Owen climbed into a RAAF Lockheed Hudson twin-engine bomber and made the twenty-minute flight from Port Moresby to Kokoda in advance of his men. Waiting for him was Captain Templeton who quickly briefed him of the situation. Likely accompanying Owen on his flight were two spotters with the NGAWWC, 21-year-old Private Clive Turnbull from Junee and 21-year-old Private Bernard 'Spud' Murphy from Wentworth Falls, both in New South Wales; along with their heavy radio gear including transmitter and generator. They were to relieve the two signallers from the 39th Battalion, 22-year-old Sergeant James Craddock from Berrigan in New South Wales and 27-year-old Corporal Robert Skinner from Princes Hill in Victoria.[12] Murphy recalled their arrival at Kokoda:

There were no native carriers for our wireless gear. The carriers initially allotted to us only minutes before [had] been released from the Kokoda prison—and given the cover of darkness 'they took off like the Watsons'. Both of us had just been discharged from dysentery camp and were not fit to haul all the gear which included the transmitter, receiver, batteries and battery charger as well as our own clobber. Then an officer arranged for 8 police boys to do our carrying. They were great. We set up on the edge of the Kokoda plantation and made contact with Moresby. Eureka! All was well. Well, for a matter of hours anyway, then the Japs were everywhere. Over the next two days we shifted half a dozen times ending up at Deniki.[13]

Radio communications remained unreliable. The army's 101 small radio set—unlike the larger civilian AWA (Australian Wireless Association) set used by Murphy and Turnbull—was largely ineffective given the terrain between the north and south coast; communications were only possible during the most favourable conditions. To help rectify this situation a single telephone line would trace its way back to Port Moresby alongside the track; it would be the only 'sure' line of communications with the outside world.[14]

Also at Kokoda was Jack Wilkinson, who was looking after the wounded and sick. He was able to evacuate most of these men onboard the bomber that had flown Owen and the spotters into Kokoda, while others were led back to Port Moresby over the Kokoda Track by William Graham, a plantation manager of ANGAU.

I sent five people back by the first plane to land at Kokoda, just before the strip closed permanently. One could not walk, several had some type of fever (we only had quinine for malaria, and I advised every man to take some before any action). As I only had a few minutes to get them on the plane I sent no records with them. I sent another lot back with Mr. Graham, walking to Moresby. Mr. Graham was a plantation manager and had a lot of experience in the country. He was over 55 at the time and I asked Colonel Owen if he thought it would be advisable for him to go back and take the chaps I had in hospital with him and look after them en route. He agreed, as we both knew that a battle was close, and we had little hope of holding if the figures given for the enemy were correct . . . Feel scared of having battle casualties to look after alone. I got word of Harry Bitmead, missing. Also Tom Grahamslaw and Jack McKenna . . . Captain Templeton had been

very busy walking between the advanced platoons and Kokoda, and I
had to dress his feet several times. They were in a very bad condition.
The last time I gave him some plaster and a block of chocolate I had
saved up. He never returned.[15]

Within an hour of arriving, Lieutenant Colonel Bill Owen,
accompanied by Captain Sam Templeton, were both moving out of
Kokoda to Gorari, reaching the small village at around 2 a.m. the
next morning.

•

During the day several sorties were flown against the Japanese beachhead at Gona and, to the relief of the Allied bomber crews, the Japanese
Zeros failed to make an appearance. The absence of Japanese fighters
over the previous few days led to some complacency. When fighter
escorts for another bombing raid by A-24 Banshee dive bombers failed
to appear, the commander of the sortie decided to complete his mission
regardless with just one P-39 providing fighter support. If the Zeros
had made an appearance the fast and manoeuvrable Japanese fighters
would have 'chewed up' the relatively slow-flying dive bombers. The
sortie successfully bombed the mission station at Gona, amid heavy
Japanese anti-aircraft fire, and all returned safely. It would be a totally
different story the next day when the Japanese Zeros from Lae made an
appearance.[16]

•

Captain Grahamslaw, having managed to avoid death or capture from
the Japanese while trying to retrieve rations from the tucker box, had
reached the Amboga River, enabling him to get his bearings relative to
Sangara mission.

I followed the course of the river until I came across a native track.
This led me to a garden where I saw a native woman with a baby at her
breast. When I spoke to her, she started to shout, and almost immediately a man materialised with a tomahawk in his hand. I spoke to him

in the Motu language, but he shook his head and advanced on me with the tomahawk. I then drew my revolver and he backed away. As I couldn't get any sense out of him, I stood aside and allowed him and the woman to depart.

I was now reaching the stage where hunger, instead of self-preservation, was dominant. I helped myself to a cob of corn, adjourned to the track leading into the garden and seated myself in the under-growth, a few feet from the entrance, feeling reasonably certain the owners of the garden would investigate me when they learned of my visit. Soon afterwards, I saw two men approaching, with pig spears in their hands. I waited until they were within a few feet of me before showing myself. They turned and ran while I kept calling after them in Motu. Fortunately, my words penetrated, and they stopped. Then there was a welcoming shout from one of them. He turned out to be a Mongi village man named Peter (I forget his native name) whom I had known in Samurai when he worked for a European carpenter named Young.

Peter told me that the Japs had already been to his village seeking carriers and food. His people had fled and were living in their garden places. When I told [him] about the incident in the garden, Peter excused himself and went to look for the man concerned. He returned with a large group of his village people, including the man, woman and babe. It turned out that the man could not speak Motu. He had never seen me before, and my unshaven and disheveled appearance caused him to conclude that I was Japanese. After Peter heard my story, he readily agreed to guide me to Sangara, and further inland if necessary.

We reached Sangara Mission in the mid-afternoon to find it deserted. However, we were able to contact several native children who told us that the European missionaries had departed for Isivita the day before. The children also told us that the Japs had visited the Mission . . . and fired a number of shots into the buildings. Sure enough, the evidence was there in the form of bullet holes in the corrugated iron tanks, and the roofs of the Mission buildings.[17]

The children also told them that McKenna had passed through the day before and had joined Captain Austen at Higaturu, and from there both had pushed further inland. Grahamslaw and Peter headed towards Higaturu to catch up with them—they spent the night at the small village of Isivita.[18]

Early that morning the missionaries from Gona had renewed their trek hoping to reach the relative safety of their outstation at Siai, located on the banks of the mid-Kumusi River, before deciding what to do next. They were making good progress moving away from the coastal region further inland. May recalled: 'We travelled along a good track, but we tired as the miles slipped slowly passed [sic] and were so relieved when at about 11 am, we met 4 boys from our own district, boys who had been carrying for Father John Livingston Yariri when he went to Siai the previous week. Two very readily offered to return to Siai with us. We had yet another night to sleep before reaching Siai.'[19]

Mavis also wrote in the letter to her mother that the locals warned them that the Japanese were in the area: 'They told us of the Japs on the tracks—more patrols, of course, and also told us, we were on the track to Siai; our outstation! Wasn't that lucky. Three of the men came with us to carry our swags and show us the way. We held our breath as we went along the tracks the Japs were patrolling, but all went well, and soon we passed through some villages . . . Even [so] we were fairly close to Gona, and all the time could clearly hear bombing.'[20]

•

Further south, on the track in the Owen Stanleys, Lieutenant Bert Kienzle had formed more carrier parties forward to Nauro, but only had supplies for 120 men for four days; additional parties were carrying similar supplies to Efogi. He had made his way back to Port Moresby and, on hearing of the invasion, stressed to Morris the need for more carriers and aircraft drops using Efogi and Kagi as drop zones. He wrote in his report for 24 July:

Met Maj-General Morris and Col. Pitt, have a first-hand account of the track to KOKODA, depots built, nature of country, tracks, numbers of carriers available etc. I urged for more carriers and orders were issued by H.Q. immediately for all natives to report at ILOLO on 25th July ex rubber plantations from SOGERI PLATEAU, together with available overseers. One of my last requests to the HQ was for the laying down of a telephone line from H.Q. to KOKODA or 'the front' where the enemy were being contacted. I also pointed out the necessity for obtaining the cooperation of the Air Force for dropping of supplies to selected grounds. EFOGI and KAGI were mentioned as possible areas. Arrived back at ILOLO about 2300 hrs. after a further session with Capt. Jensen, O.C. Native medical services requesting additional native medical assistants for the extended line from KAGI to 'the front'.[21]

17

'May and I took off our filthy dresses and washed them'

The next day—25 July—Owen and Templeton decided to make a stand about 800 metres east of Gorari, with Owen dispersing the available Australians beside the track in an ambush position, with some of the Papuans in the thick bush on their flanks. With Templeton in command, Owen returned to Kokoda to report the situation to his commanding officer Brigadier Bill Porter in Port Moresby and urgently request reinforcements be flown in to Kokoda. Meanwhile, Major Watson sent out two small patrols to report on the location of the Japanese. One was led by Corporal John Ehave, and the other by Corporal Meta. Private Lafe also climbed a tree forward of Gorari and reported seeing a large Japanese force, with a mobile field hospital already set up. Soon the patrols returned having located the Japanese—they were approaching the ambush position.[1]

It was not long before the Japanese walked out of the silence of the bush track into the ambush. The Australian and Papuan troops opened fire resulting in fifteen Japanese casualties—two killed. But soon the Australian and Papuan position was no longer tenable as they faced odds of around ten to one, and they were forced to fall back to Gorari— the Japanese quickly followed up.[2] Before 5 p.m., they engaged the Australians of 11 and 12 platoons along with the surviving members of the 1st PIB who had all set up another ambush position. Lieutenant Mortimore of 12 Platoon recalled:

We set up the ambush with the only Bren gun in the company on the left of the track and slightly in rear of the Lewis gun which was on the opposite side. The men on the LMG's [sic] [light machine guns] were changed every hour to keep them from losing any alertness but unfortunately the Jap scouts who were wheeling bicycles came around the first bend in the track just as the men on the Lewis changed over. The Japs didn't see my men, but they saw the movement of vegetation and that was enough for them—they dropped their bikes and dived into the scrub on the side of the track. I had told my men not to fire until they got the order from me and I was positioned at the Bren gun.

After a few minutes the Jap scouts came back onto the track and started to move forward again. Then, when nothing happened, the others started to follow them. I whispered to the Bren gunner to hold his fire as I wanted to get as many of them as possible onto the track before we opened fire. The leading scout was almost level and I gave the order to fire (Arthur Swords was No. 1 on the Lewis and he later thanked me for saving his life. He said he was looking down the barrel of the leading scout's rifle when I gave the order!) I was proud of my men's fire discipline because one of the hardest things to do in an ambush is to wait for the order to fire when the enemy is very close.[3]

Sergeant Major Dawson also recalled that the ambush at Gorari 'proved successful in as much as we killed quite a few of their soldiers and slowed down their forward movement'. However, it was not long before the Australians and Papuans were forced to retire again, retreating towards the next village along the track—Oivi which was located on a small plateau—just 16 kilometres forward of Kokoda Station. The battalion war diary recorded that, on arriving at Oivi, these men were 'very tired, and approx., six men missing'.[i][4] Sam Templeton now ordered Dawson to take two men and accompany Captain Stevenson back to Kokoda to tell Owen that they had taken up a position at Oivi.

---

i   Between 25 July and 15 August, eighteen men of the 39th Battalion were recorded as missing, presumed dead. Japanese records indicate that eleven of these men were captured and executed. No Australian troops captured by the Japanese during the entire Papuan Campaign would survive captivity—all were executed soon after capture.

Dawson recalled that communications were dependent on runners and word of mouth: 'There was a master radio set in Kokoda that was in contact with... Port Moresby... The only communication was between runners. Hand written notes sometime[s]. And that was hard in wet weather, and we didn't have any paper, anyway. So that's how communication was done and the same within our own platoon.'[5] Stevenson, Dawson and two others now set off for Kokoda.

> I grabbed my Thompson and off we went, taking turns as forward scout along the way. By the time Stevenson had delivered his informa-tion and we had had a quick cup of tea, it was dark and raining heavily. We had to trudge back to Oivi along a track with a few streams to cross under nightfall. A couple of these had native footbridges, which were simply a tall tree dropped across the river. One of these was fairly long and bounced quite a bit as you walked over it, so we decided to go across one at a time. Stevenson carried the Thompson, so he went first followed by another soldier. When they were across, I followed, telling the fourth member of our team to wait till I was on the other side. However, when I was about halfway over the log bridge started to sway; to save losing my balance and dropping several feet into the water, I slid down on my backside... and so did the bloke right behind me. He had decided to follow my tracks as he didn't like waiting alone. After a few whispered words of coarse language in his shell pink ear, we managed to get across together and continue on our way back to Oivi.[6]

The battalion war diary records: 'Capt., STEVENSON was sent to KOKODA to report situation to Lt. Col. OWEN arriving back at OIVI at 2200 hours. Lt. Col. OWEN ordered OIVI to be held at all costs—unless the Force was surrounded.'[7]

Some of the missing men from Wairopi and Gorari, or perhaps Grahamslaw and his men, were spotted by locals and reported to the Japanese as recorded on 25 July in the Sakigawa Transport Unit log: 'It was learned from native reports that there are three armed enemy soldiers in a native village 1.5 km away. All personnel went to seize these, except for Sgt MAEDA and twelve men who remained as guards. Guided by natives we searched for an hour but did not find them. Returned at 1730 hrs. The BUTAI, especially those on night duty, are to be on the alert.'[8]

●

At Kokoda Station, Lieutenant Colonel Owen was extremely troubled as his small force alone stood between Kokoda and the Japanese. His men of 'C' Company led by Captain Arthur Dean (a 27-year-old professional soldier from Adelaide) had three days before begun their crossing of the Owen Stanleys to Kokoda, the rest of the battalion was about to follow.[9] When Owen requested the urgent need to reinforce his small exhausted force, one response he received from Morris in Port Moresby was: 'Reinforcements not available. Remember tired Australians fight best.'[10] Owen's likely response to those around him on receiving this reply went unrecorded.

Accompanying 'C' Company was the battalion chaplain, Nobby Earl, and the men of the battalion headquarters, among who was twenty-year-old signaller, Kenneth Phelan, from East Malvern in Victoria with 1 Platoon. Phelan recalled their trek through the mountains: 'Here was the first example of mateship in adversity, soldiers constantly helping, supporting and encouraging their mates "to not give up" eventually all the sigs (signals) gathered on top [of a ridge] to collapse and rest . . . At Efogi we got the message of . . . how necessary it was to "hurry up and help the beleaguered B Company". The track now went straight up the main range . . . If the early part required fitness, courage and dedication (not to let your mates down), this was the ultimate test.'[11]

Coming up behind 'C' Company were the men of 'A' Company, who had on 25 July begun their trek across the mountains, led by Lieutenant Bert Kienzle. Sergeant Major George Mowat, a 47-year-old Great War veteran from Geelong in Victoria, who had received the Military Medal while serving with the 58th Battalion on the Western Front, was now with 'A' Company and scribbled in his diary a few days into the hard slog across the mountains: 'Trail rough, steep and slippery; arrived 18.00 Native Village. Good Meal.' A few days later he recorded: 'Today we rose to great heights. Crossed the OS Range at 7,500 feet [2300 metres]. Phew, what a climb. Had a lot of rain. Each day has been a bit stiffer.'[12]

By now Lieutenant Champion and Sergeant Bishop had made their way to Kokoda as ordered by Major Watson on their arrival at Awala days before. Champion wrote in his report to ANGAU: 'I spent [time] supervising the extension of the drome and at 1630 hrs. I left Kokoda with a line of rations for the forward troops at Oivi, having handed over the rations to Major Watson, I returned to Kokoda arriving at 2400 hrs.'[13]

Bill Owen at Kokoda had sent another urgent signal to Port Moresby requesting reinforcements be flown into Kokoda using all available aircraft: 'Clashed at Gorari and inflicted approximately 15 casualties at noon. At 5 p.m., our position was heavily engaged. And two tired platoons are now at Oivi. Third platoon ... at Kokoda ... Must have more troops, otherwise there is nobody between Oivi and Dean, who is three days out from Ilolo. Will have drome open for landing. Must have two fresh companies to avoid being outflanked at Oivi. Advise me before 3 a.m., if air-borne troops not available.'[14] He got no reply.

During the day, a formation of eight B-25 Mitchell bombers from the 3rd Attack Group, supported by a dozen P-39 fighters from the 35th Fighter Group, were tasked with slowing the Japanese infantry advance by bombing the tracks leading to Kokoda Station. This was the first sortie in direct support of the Australian and Papuan infantry trying to hold back the Japanese advance. However, the weather closed in and they could not accomplish this mission, so they continued on to their secondary target—Gona. They flew over the target at around 3000 metres when they were jumped by eight Japanese Zeros—attacking the bombers head-on. As planned, this tactic broke up the bomber formation with only two bombers completing their mission while the other six jettisoned their bombs and headed for home over the Owen Stanleys. The agile Zeros were in quick pursuit, hitting six of the slow-moving bombers (with a top speed of just 450 kilometres per hour), heavily damaging two, while one Zero was shot down, reportedly going down in flames and crashing near Dobodura.[15]

The Allied fighters were hampered in their mission of protecting the bombers, as six of the twelve fighters were fitted with bombs to perform the role of fighter-bombers, while the remaining six fighters were focusing on protecting the fighter-bomber sortie. Two American fighters were hit as they conducted their 'bombing' mission; Lieutenant Frank Beeson was piloting one of these planes but he never made it back to base and was posted as missing; while Lieutenant Hoger, wounded in the leg, managed to get his fighter back to base.[16]

●

The Gona mission party were finally approaching Siai village and made their way to the government rest house, located, as May wrote to her sister, 'well away from any track the Japs were likely to be exploring, we felt fairly safe'.[17] She was not to know that at this point her fiancé, Father Vivian Redlich, who she believed to be safely at Dogura, had already made his way to Sangara mission, intent on finding her and the other missionaries.

On arriving at Sangara, the local parishioners built Father Redlich a lean-to on a hillside near the village of Hondituru, close to Sangara, and posted people all around to watch out for the appearance of any Japanese. These same people also provided him with food and other essentials. No doubt, he spent his time worried and fearful not only for the missionaries at Sangara and Gona, but especially for May.[18]

May continued her letter to Viola:

> We sent a note on . . . asking Father John to come to meet us and also
> to send on a note to Government at Ioma (about 20 miles [32 kilo-
> metres] beyond Siai) and one on to Father Gill at Mamba, asking for
> some reading matter (we had 3 books with us) and some soap. Boys
> carried our things until we met Father John and some Siai boys. Such
> a greeting they gave us, general hugging and patting as I've never seen
> before between white and brown. We arrived at Siai mid Saturday, had

hot baths in enamel basins and Father John brought us a clean towel
and clothed us in his white cassock [sic] and alb [white linen cloak
traditionally worn by Christian clergy] while our dresses received a
much-needed drink. Oh, how lovely to be clean. Next, we sat down
to a well-cooked lunch of sweet potatoes and corn cooked in coconut
milk—most delicious. Papaws for dessert. When our dresses were
dry, we went across to the little church for Evensong. Then we were
treated to another meal of native vegetables. Again, our bed was a hard
one—1" slates [sic] with only a canvas covering, it was still too hard for
us. Next day the people went off to build our home in the bush. They
reported a very good hide out place when they returned that night. We
had 3 meals that day. Next day, they moved us into our 'hideout' about
½ miles [sic] [800 metres] from Siai—no tracks leading to it, so we
could not find our way out if we wanted to and no Jap could ever find
us. It's a lovely spot with tall timbers and the usual shrubs and creepers
and a stream close by.[19]

Mavis also wrote with joy to her mother of their arrival: 'As long
as I live, I shall never forget the welcome they gave us. They hugged
and patted us for ages, and actually cried over us—they thought
maybe we were dead. They took us on to Siai station and there we had
another demonstration, by the women this time. I was almost beginning to feel tearful myself.' Like May, a major concern for Mavis was
to bathe and to give their filthy clothes a good scrub, it made them
feel half-human; she continues: 'They brought us food and hot water
for a bath. May and I took off our filthy dresses and washed them
and while they dried May wore a Cossack of Fr. John's and I wore an
alb. I wish you could have seen us, particularly our heads—we had
no comb and after four days of walking through jungle—well, you
can imagine what it was like! The people decided the best thing to
do would be to build us a cottage in the bush, where we should be
hidden until things cleared up a little—we could still hear bombs
falling on Gona.'[20]

It was 4 and 5 August respectively when May and Mavis again put
pencil to paper to recall their adventures up until this point. They

remained at Siai for about two weeks, hoping to hear news that the Japanese had finally been forced to evacuate their beachhead.

•

Meanwhile, Grahamslaw and his Papuan guide Peter were also still trapped behind enemy lines. They were now making their way towards Higaturu to catch up with McKenna and Austen. They soon reached the friendly village of Seapareta and there they found Captain Austen along with native plantation manager Anthony Gors and his wife and seven-year-old son. Austen had brought a three-month supply of stores from Higaturu. McKenna had only 30 minutes before he left the village to make his way to Wairopi. A runner was sent out to find him and soon McKenna was back at Seapareta.[21] Grahamslaw recalled many years later: 'McKenna informed me that he had experienced no difficulty in getting to Higaturu within a few hours after we became parted. He had been stationed at Higaturu for several years and possessed an intimate knowledge of the area. On arrival at Higaturu he had teamed up with Austen. McKenna had no knowledge of Yeoman's fate but believed that the Buna police, who were with him at the time, would have got him out of trouble—this proved to be correct.'[22]

Grahamslaw and McKenna now sat down to discuss their options and decided to leave for Wairopi the next morning, taking with them a PIB soldier from Isivita village along with three locals to guide them. During the day some of the Seapareta natives built a hut just off the main track for Austen and his supplies.[23] Austen had already decided not to join them, as his age and injured leg would prevent him from completing the long journey, and he refused to be carried. He was sure that his supply of stores would last him and his small party until such time as they could be evacuated. Austen gave Grahamslaw a message to pass onto the naval officer in charge at Port Moresby, requesting that a launch be sent to Pongani in September to pick them up. Grahamslaw would eventually deliver this message, but he was informed, at this point, the request could not be granted.[24]

•

Earlier that day, Harry Bitmead, with the help of one of his Papuan orderlies, escaped from his Japanese captors. He had suffered four days of physical and psychological torture. Bitmead and his orderly made their way towards Sangara mission station and he was soon taken to the hideout of Reverend Redlich. Bitmead recalled many years later:

Saturday 25th July 1942 is a day I shall not easily forget. Early that day I had escaped from the Japanese mainly through the help of one of my Sangara Mission boys. Much to my surprise I learned from the natives that the Rev. Fr. Redlich, who a couple of months previously had returned very ill to the Mission Headquarters [at Dogura], was again in the district and in hiding quite close to the [Sangara] Mission House. Early on that Saturday afternoon fifteen Japanese soldiers and an officer told the natives that they would return on the following day to 'smash up the Mission', which was about fifteen minutes' walk away.

About six o'clock in the evening with a few natives, I left one of the villages to get in touch with Fr. Redlich. On my way to his hideout I passed the Mission House where one of the Church Councillors was on watch. The Councillor told me that the Japanese were going to wreck the Mission on the morrow, Sunday. Just on dusk I reached Fr. Redlich's shelter. The village people had built him a lean-to on the side of a hill and posted watchers along the track.

From Fr. Redlich I learned that in the Mission Boat he had arrived at Oro Bay as the Japs were shelling Buna. By working hard, he landed during that night fifteen tones [sic] of supplies and concealed them in the bush. He spoke of the tremendous struggle he had with himself on the beach. 'Would he return with the boat or not?' He admitted that his nature shrank from the sacrifice, and with sinking heart he stood on the beach and watched the boat that might have borne him to safety sail out of the bay. I feel that the high official who recently said that he considered Fr. Redlich's actions in allowing the boat to sail away without him ranks amongst the outstanding deeds of bravery in the New Guinea campaign has spoken the truth, and little other comment is needed.

After the departure of the boat, Fr. Vivian had made his way quickly to Sangara. He found Japs everywhere and about to destroy the Mission, so the frightened natives made a shelter for him on the side of a hill and set watchers along the track to give warning of any enemy approach. When I arrived at the shelter there was quite a crowd of natives round about. Fr. Vivian spoke to them thus: 'I am your missionary; I have come back to you because I knew you would need your Father. I am not going to run away from you. I am going to remain to help you as long as you will let me. Tomorrow is Sunday. I shall say Mass, and any of you who wish may Communicate'.

Shortly after dark he returned to the Mission House to collect some church equipment. He returned about midnight and told me that as yet nothing had been touched at the Mission, but that the Japs had told the people of their intention to destroy the place on Sunday.[25]

18

'Give me a thought sometimes . . .'

On 26 July 1942, Lieutenant Colonel Owen, still at Kokoda, was anxious about the condition of his pitifully small garrison, now numbering fewer than 80. Looking at his men, whose average age was around 21 (not the frequently quoted 18 or 19 years), he described them as 'pathetically young warriors'.[1] Indeed, JWB, who had been liberated of his two bottles of whisky by Captain Sam Templeton while in Port Moresby, recalled many years later: 'The 39th Militia Battalion was the mother of us all, and it gave 1500 half-trained, 18½-year-old, beardless youths pride in the battalion. Now on Kokoda Day, when the names are read out of those killed in action, I knew them all, and *still* see them as they were. They will never become old or embittered. Just laughing kids forever.'[2] These kids stood between the Japanese and Kokoda Station and the track that led south over the mountains to Port Moresby.

General Morris had only two transport aircraft available at 7-Mile Drome—two civilian Douglas DC-3s, with each being able to carry just fifteen men—half a platoon each. Captain Max Bidstrup, a 31-year-old manager from Wallaroo in South Australia commanding 'D' Company, was ordered to make one of his platoons ready for an immediate flight to Kokoda. However, in the end only one DC-3 was available. Lieutenant Doug McClean and his 16 Platoon were chosen to make the flight. The platoon would be flown in piecemeal. Unknown to all, McClean's platoon would be the first and only troops to fly into Kokoda as the pilots of the slow cumbersome transport planes became increasingly fearful—for good reason—of being jumped by Zero fighters. All other Australians would have to endure a hard slog across the Owen Stanleys using the Kokoda Track.[3]

Arriving at 7-Mile Drome with 16 Platoon was Sergeant Ted Morrison, a 23-year-old farmer from Foster in Victoria. He recalled: 'That morning (26th July) we were told to prepare to move out immediately and the whole company was taken to the drome in 3-trucks. There was a lot of movement on the drome itself with aircraft being serviced and American Negro engineers [96th Engineer Battalion] working on the landing strips. 16 Platoon was divided into two halves for the flight—one half (fourteen men) with Doug McClean, and me in charge of the other (fifteen men) with the platoon's two Bren guns which were still packed in their boxes.'[4]

Bidstrup recalled many years later how he had come across these most prized machine guns: 'There's a story about how I got those Brens. The night before we were due to leave . . . there's a truck landed up to my Company Headquarters and the bloke asked for the whereabouts of Brigade Headquarters. And I said, "Why do you want Brigade?" He said, "I've got some guns for him, six Brens." I said, "Right here." So, I scribbled a signature and took the guns.'[5]

Lieutenant McClean and his men climbed aboard the DC-3 with half of his platoon and were soon in the air. At around 10 a.m., the DC-3 and McClean's men landed at Kokoda—given the turbulence several men had been violently sick, vomiting into their helmets. The young lieutenant recalled orbiting Kokoda airstrip waiting for it to be cleared of obstacles: 'The flight only lasted 20 minutes but we had to circle Kokoda airfield about ten times because our men on the ground were uncertain who we were and would not remove the obstacles they had put on the runway. While we were circling seven Zeros (probably heading for Moresby) flew by, but thanks to the clouds over Kokoda they did not see us. Eventually the strip was cleared, and we landed and were met by Colonel Owen.'[6]

Owen approached the men, who were stricken with airsickness, as they deplaned and told Doug McClean: 'Sorry I can't give you a spell, Mac. B Company is in trouble at Oivi, and I'll have to send you off right

away. It's half a day's march.'[7] Owen told his young lieutenant he would
send on the rest of his platoon as soon as they landed—which would
be some time behind them as the lone DC-3 would have to fly back to
7-Mile Drome to pick them up.

•

Oivi village was located on a plateau that protruded from the Owen
Stanleys at a height of about 250 metres above sea level, separating the
Kumusi and Mambare rivers—the Mambare River being the largest in
the district. The plateau was predominately covered with dense rainforest and tangled undergrowth, trees and vines. It was at Oivi that
Captain Sam Templeton and his small force were going to attempt to
hold up the Japanese advance towards Kokoda.[8]

Templeton and his men of 11 and 12 platoons (numbering around
60 men) along with Watson and the remaining men of the 1st PIB and
RPC (together numbering around 30 men) were digging in close to the
village. All knew they had no chance of stopping the Japanese advance,
not only because they were heavily outnumbered, but they knew the
Japanese were well supported with heavy machine guns, mortars and
small-calibre mountain guns, which could quickly be broken apart
for ready transport by mules or men and reassembled within minutes
when required. The best the Australians and Papuans could do was
inflict as many casualties using 'fire and retire', meaning they'd fall back
to another defensive position further down the line at the last moment
and repeat the tactic. This would buy time for reinforcements to reach
them using the track and hopefully aircraft landing at Kokoda itself.[9]

Captain Jesser with nine of his men of the 1st PIB had deployed
along a parallel track to the south to guard against any Japanese flanking
movement from that direction. Sam Templeton's men were 'hollowed-
eyed and exhausted having had little sleep or food in four days'.[10]

When McClean and his men made their appearance at Oivi, it
must have been a welcome sight—even though his party consisted of
just fourteen men. Templeton now had around 100 men manning his
position; more importantly, for the men's morale, they were no longer
alone. McClean recalled their arrival at Oivi: 'As I arrived Templeton

said, "Would you like a cup of tea for your men?" I said, "Yes, give it to the men, but I'd be very pleased if you would show me where your gun positions and where the defences are." So we walked around for about 20 minutes.'[11] McClean told Templeton that the other half of his platoon was a few hours behind them. The young lieutenant must have been concerned about the position they were being ordered to hold. The troops manned a perimeter along the edge of the plateau which was covered in thick jungle. There was no way of seeing the enemy until they 'were right on top of you'. Thirty-one-year-old Corporal Richard Stent from Gisborne in Victoria and his section had the unenviable task of manning a forward post located in the jungle across the track below a clearing to warn of the Japanese advance. McClean and his men were assigned a position on the plateau just forward of the main body to help support Stent and his men.[12]

•

A few hours earlier, Sergeant Morrison and the second half of 16 Platoon were finally boarding the DC-3 at 7-Mile Drome with their freshly issued Bren guns. He and his men would land at Kokoda at around noon.[13]

After about an hour and a half the Douglas came back and it was our turn. Just as Alf Scarborough's section was starting to scramble aboard, the pilot asked me: 'Has the weight been checked?' adding that he had had a lot of trouble landing at Kokoda on the first trip because of the heavy load. So, I simply said, 'Yes, weight correct' (though it was obvious that with one extra man and the just-issued Brens still in their boxes we would certainly weigh more than the first plane-load). During the flight (a bumpy one) we took the Brens out of their boxes and cleaned the packing grease out of them.

Colonel Owen was waiting to meet the plane at Kokoda, and when he saw me clamber down, he said: 'What the devil are you doing here, Pinhead?' (Pinhead was what Bill Owen nicknamed me back in the days when he was my company commander in the 22nd Militia Battalion and he used to come and play cards in our tent.) Anyway, after we'd exchanged a few words of greeting he said, 'You'll have to get straight on to Oivi and join Lieutenant McClean there'. Not having a clue where Oivi was, I said, 'Oivi: where's that?' Colonel Owen simply said: 'Just keep going along that track and you'll get there!'[14]

Near Sangara mission station, Reverend Vivian Redlich, true to his word, was preparing for an early morning Mass, even though the Japanese were due to arrive at Sangara mission, not far from his hiding spot. During the morning hours, a local constable and 'sorcerer' named Embogi, who had considerable influence over the people, had gone to inform the Japanese of the whereabouts of Redlich and Bitmead.[15] The young Australian Warrant Officer Harry Bitmead, who admitted to not being an Anglican himself, clearly admired the devotion of Reverend Vivian Redlich and the other local missionaries to their parishioners:

Shortly after dawn he woke me up saying. 'There is a big number of people here. I am going to say Mass. He began to vest and was nearly finished when a native boy rushed up to us crying out 'Father, Doctor, go—do not wait! During the night Embogi came and had a look at where you are, and he has just gone to tell the Japs because he wants them to come and kill you and Mr. Bitmead.'

There was a dead silence. I looked at Fr. Vivian. He bowed his head in prayer in a few moments and then said to the people: 'Today is Sunday. It is God's Day, I shall say Mass. We shall worship God. Why has Embogi done this? Does he hate us? Have we ever harmed him?' From here and there among the crowd came the reply: 'Embogi is not a Christian.' Turning to me Fr. Vivian said: 'Will you remain for Mass?' 'Yes' I replied and remained. I do not think I have ever witnessed a more devout congregation. The fervor expressed on those faces would have equalled that of the early Christians assisting at Mass in some hidden catacomb. Like those early Christians, these New Guinea Christians were assisting at Mass at the risk of their lives. The dense silence of the jungle was broken only by the sound of the Priest's voice praying for his people. Then came the rustle of movement as those brown feet moved near the Altar at the time of communion. It was really edifying to witness each native present Communicate in such a devout and recent manner . . .

After the Mass the people quietly dispersed. Father Vivian and I moved on. The following day it became necessary for us to part. With sorrow not unmixed with feeling of deep admiration for his courage, I bade him farewell and good luck! He was going to remain with his people moving amongst them. My own duty bade me to escape.[16]

Before Bitmead left, Reverend Redlich gave him a letter, asking him to pass it on to Bishop Strong. It read: 'I am back in my own district and not far from fun and games. I have not yet contacted directly any of the staff but know for certain that Margery, Lilla and John are somewhere about and that yesterday they were safe . . . Big upset, of course. I've contacted some of my people, but they are too scared to have me near—however, I shall keep in touch with them as much as possible. I could not have Eucharist on St. James' Day owing to the scare but did on Sunday in the bush.' Undoubtedly a major worry was the whereabouts of his fiancée, May, who was now located about 30 kilometres west of his position at Siai. He went on to inform the bishop: 'The place near my home has been busted up and I think mine, too, by now—I have visited and got some stuff out in the bush and rescued chalices, etc. I shall try and carry on my job . . . Give me a thought sometimes but don't worry, I'm prepared for whatever might happen.'[17]

19

'Grab yourself some headlights, fellas'

Back at Oivi, Doug McClean and his men of 16 Platoon were settling into their forward position as instructed by Templeton who had received orders from Owen that he was to now hold his position 'at all costs unless surrounded'.[1] Just before the Japanese launched their attack, he recalled seeing: 'movement coming around the side of the hill. And sure enough enemy, about six feet tall, big strapping-looking blokes with foliage stuffed down their belts. And so when they paused, they rather looked like bushes. Wonderful field craft; they were very, very good, and very hard to hit.'[2]

It was around 4 p.m., when Japanese Captain Ogawa launched his attack against Templeton's position. Along with his own No. 1 Company, I/144th Regiment, he still had with him elements of No. 5 SNLP, a platoon of combat engineers, a mortar platoon and at least one mountain gun—his force had likely increased with additional reinforcements to around 280 men; odds approaching three to one in his favour. Corporal Stent and his section in the forward position were quickly targeted by Japanese marine scouts who were directing fire from a Juki heavy machine gun against them. Before being forced to retire to the line above, Stent and his men killed the scouts and, as they fell back, several Japanese marines charged their position, but they got out just in time. Now the plateau was targeted with Japanese mortar bombs—the Australians could not respond in kind as they had no such weapons. The mortars, along with heavy machine guns and at least one mountain gun, gave the Japanese a significant edge against the lightly armed Australian and Papuan troops.[3]

Using what would become their standard tactic when assaulting Australian positions, the Japanese, well camouflaged in jungle-green uniforms with steel helmets garnished with local vegetation, initially conducted a frontal assault, taking full advantage of the terrain and vegetation, attempting to draw the enemy's fire so their positions could be identified. Assisting them were nearby feints or deliberate attacks along the Australian front. Meanwhile, stronger combat elements attempted to cut their way through the flanks, skirting around the Australians, probing ceaselessly for weak spots, either to force the Australians to withdraw or to annihilate them in a surprise attack from the rear.[4]

Doug McClean recalled the fighting as it broke out: 'We had a most tremendous mass misinformation about the Jap being a little fellow, and the first Jap I hit under the ear with a grenade was six feet two inches and fifteen stone, with a silver anchor on his belt, meaning that they were marines [No. 5 SNLP]. Their movement in the bush had to be seen to be believed, because they'd just vanish! Their field craft and movement was magnificent.'[5] The Japanese assault was initially halted by Doug McClean's men in their forward position, but soon they were outflanked and forced to fall back to the main position on the plateau. The Australians and Papuans formed a tight 50-metre perimeter. Both sides maintained a desultory fire during the afternoon, with some Japanese troops pressing to within a few metres of the Australian line before being killed. Sam Templeton knew that if the Japanese overran his position at Oivi, Lieutenant Garland and his 30 men of 10 Platoon at Kokoda could not hope to defend the airfield. With this, the 'gateway' to the Kokoda Track as it entered the mountains would be open to the Japanese.[6] Sergeant Les Martorana recalled once the enemy 'knew we were there, they started to send troops around onto our right flank and there was a machine-gunner there'.[7]

About 5 p.m., there was a temporary lull in the fighting, and Captain Templeton went out alone to examine the rear defences and to bring in the second half of McClean's platoon, led by Sergeant Morrison, who by now must have been close to arriving. With the lull in firing, Templeton feared these men might become victims of a Japanese ambush. Lieutenant Harry Mortimore recalled Sam Templeton telling him at the time: 'In case they [Morrison] pull back along the track as it gets dark, I'm going back to meet them and bring them on.'[8] His runner, Private Edward Stuart, a twenty-year-old metal spinner from Collingwood in Victoria, also recalled Templeton giving his men instructions that if he did not return they were to withdraw when the situation was dire. 'I said to him,' recalled Stuart, 'Would you like me to go with you, sir?' Templeton, in his usual style, replied: '"No, laddie." So, I turned around and walked back and he went down the track.'[9] Templeton had no idea that their position was already surrounded by the Japanese. Soon after he left all heard a short burst of machine-gun fire to the rear.[10]

Sergeant Martorana instinctively knew his OC was in trouble. He turned to their guide, Lance Corporal Sanopa of the RPC, and two of McClean's men from 'C' Company—22-year-old Private Arthur 'Bill' Luxmoore from Hampton in Victoria and 21-year-old Private Henry Evans from Sandringham in Victoria—they all moved out in search of Templeton. However, when they were close to where they thought the firing originated, Sanopa halted, whispering: 'he could smell them'. Martorana recalled many years later: 'I got two men, Henry [sic] Evans and Bill Luxmoore and my guide, Sanopa to come and see if we could help Captain Templeton . . . Anyway, I put Henry [sic] and Bill on one side of the track and said don't fire until I tell you and then the Japs had just come around the corner. I didn't know how many there were. They were 200 or 300 yards [around 280 metres] from our position, so I said, "Right fellas, back!" By the time we'd come back, Nips had come down the spur overlooking our position. They were quick, and so many of them and so few of us that we didn't know what to do.'[11] Later a small patrol was sent out to find Sam Templeton, but these men became lost, with some later stumbling onto Sergeant Ted Morrison's party—just to the rear of Oivi. Captain Sam Templeton was never seen again by his men.[12]

The battalion war diary records: 'Capt. TEMPLETON walked around a corner of the track towards the rear with view to warning

the remainder of 16 Pl which was expected, to keep a sharp lookout. A
burst of fire was heard in the direction he had taken, and he was NOT
seen again. Neither was there any trace of his body.'[13]

•

With the disappearance of Captain Templeton, Major Watson of the
1st PIB was now in command of the shrinking defensive perimeter.
He believed the Japanese were weakest to their front. The bulk of the
Japanese seemed to be probing the flanks and had apparently crossed
the track to the rear, cutting off any means of escape in that direction.
This was confirmed with increased machine-gun fire from the flanks
and rear tearing across their position. Luckily, the Japanese were firing
high and wild as it was difficult to identify the Australian positions
along the plateau within the thick vegetation. Watson realised that his
perimeter was close to collapse as they were running low on ammunition and grenades. At this point, a burst of heavy machine-gun fire from
the rear cut through the vegetation next to Sergeant Allan Collyer and
Corporal Stent, confirming to them that the enemy had surrounded
their position, their line of retreat along the track back to Kokoda was
blocked by entrenched Japanese troops and machine-gun nests.[14]

The loss of 'Uncle Sam' Templeton, the father figure not only of
'B' Company but the whole battalion, was a huge blow to the morale of
the tiny force. His company sergeant major, Joseph Dawson, recalled: 'I
was deeply upset and saddened by the loss of Sam Templeton. I had a
great respect for him; he was a very courageous man. The pity was that he
did not get the opportunity to take his company as a whole into battle.'[15]

Captain Stevenson, Templeton's 2i/c, could not help but notice
that his men were physically and mentally spent; he nudged Watson,
pointing towards some nearby men who were obviously having troubles
trying to keep awake—the adrenaline of combat was wearing off—even
as the Japanese were pressing home their advantage in numbers. It was
not long before the Australians and the Papuans could hear the noise of
vegetation below their position being felled. The Japanese troops were
also banging their mess tins together, shouting out orders in English
to sow confusion into the ranks of their exhausted enemy, enticing

them to fire to give away their positions—the Japanese were masters of psychological warfare. Soon a newly installed Juki heavy machine gun, sited on the north-western flank, fired a short burst to make sure it was in working order—they were getting ready for an all-out assault.[16]

Sergeant Les Martorana recalled at this point, 'one of our men got up and yelled out for Mr. Watson. I said, "What are you doing?" He said, "I'm going to surrender." I said "What! Get down you silly bastard." Fortunately, he did because there was a machine-gun blast in front of us. I thought, "Gee, we're in a pickle now." This bloke said, "What are you going to do?" I replied, "I'm going to fight my way out!" He said, "You won't get out" and I said, "I'll get out all right." I turned around to Sanopa, our guide and asked, "Sanopa, will you go to Moresby with me?" "Yes Pavada," he replied.'[17]

Within minutes the Japanese launched their attack, as recalled by Watson: 'Enemy attacked in force on all fronts, under cover of dusk enemy had quietly encircled our position. Enemy in greatest strength in our rear. Enemy had about 20 L.M.G. in position and brought heavy fire to bear. Shooting mostly high and wide. Our L.M.Gs., held enemy below perimeter edge. At this state it was obvious that our force was greatly outnumbered ... Enemy brought trench mortars into action shots landing about 600 yards [550 metres] plus. Obviously enemy could [no longer] mortar plateau—own troops too close'.[18]

It was around 8 p.m. when Lieutenant McClean and Corporal Charles Pyke, a 22-year-old fruiterer from Noble Park in Victoria, crawled out towards the rear of their position and lobbed hand grenades into several Japanese machine-gun positions. Watson later reported that he and his men could hear the 'cries and groaning' of the wounded Japanese from this daring attack.[19] Sergeant Major Dawson also recalled, 'Doug McClean and another fellow moved out on our flank and around the Japanese positions and pelted a few grenades down on them. We knew they'd hit a target because there were quite a few yells and screams.'[20] Lieutenant McClean recalled the attack many years later:

We were surrounded by the Japanese early elements. By dusk they were building a platform to raise their gun to a position where they could fire upon the higher ground. And having heard the noise I decided to move out, creating a diversion on one side, and move out on the other. And arranged with the Police Boy, who said he could lead us in a round-about way to Deniki, avoiding Kokoda. And so I said, "When the explosions start, you move off." And I asked for a volunteer. A fellow named Pyke, Charlie Pyke, came with me carrying extra grenades and we attacked the place, killed the gun crew, and apparently startled the remainder of the force . . . the density of the jungle precluded them realising how few we were, so they weren't willing to push on . . . You don't get the shakes, but you sometimes think, "Was that me? Was I silly enough to do that?" But it was very effective, so I was highly delighted and pleased that it worked.[21]

Lieutenant Doug McClean was awarded the Military Cross for his actions and Corporal Charles Pyke received the Military Medal. They were among the first Australians to be awarded military decorations for gallantry during the Kokoda Campaign.

Shortly after, other Japanese troops were heard to call out 'Come forward, Corporal White!' and 'Taubada me want 'im you!'[22] Such calls had been going on since the battle started but were now increasing in frequency. Sergeant Major Dawson wrote, 'all that produced from us was a few grenades in their direction'. However, all knew that they were greatly outnumbered, and the mortar bombs continued to explode too close for comfort. Dawson continues: 'It was obvious the Japanese had indeed cut off our track to Kokoda; our position was now rather desperate—our ammunition was nearly gone, and our grenades were just about used up. It seemed to me at the time that we were on the verge of being wiped out. We were totally outnumbered and thought our only hope was to make a sudden charge along the track towards Kokoda and hope for the best.'[23]

It was around 10 p.m., and Watson knew that they were about to be overwhelmed by the Japanese. However, he knew trying to break out along the track to the rear would end in their slaughter. He called on Lance Corporal Sanopa who knew the area well; the Papuan NCO judged their best chance of breaking contact was by using the creek running below the plateau to their front where the Japanese appeared weakest. Watson agreed, and word was quietly passed along the perimeter: 'Major Watson, who was now in charge of the force,' recalled Dawson, 'had with him a Papuan policeman by the name of Sinopa [sic]. He told us he could lead us out through an area where the Japanese positions were the thinnest. The word was passed around to move out quietly in single file, holding the bayonet scabbard of the man in front as it was pitch black.'[24] Lance Corporal Sanopa led the men out of their perimeter to their front. Watson later reported: '2215 hrs: Force under C.O., P.I.B., withdrew to south [sic north], other exits too strongly held, and Kokoda track blocked. Intention to circle and regain Kokoda track and further engage enemy in daylight.'[25]

They pushed down into the creek, which at some places was waist deep and icy cold, through a ravine covered in thick scrub. It was now that heavy rain set in—a blessing as it helped them slip through the Japanese perimeter unseen and unheard. The men struggled on, with Sanopa leading them eventually up the right-hand bank into dense jungle, trudging up steep hillsides; in some cases the men had to stab their bayonets into the hillside just to help get a footing—the bush tore clothing and flesh alike. One soldier who inadvertently seized a handful of phosphorescent fungus was heard to tell his mates behind him: 'Grab yourself some headlights, fellas.'[26]

Major Watson also recalled: 'Intensely difficult and slow as force had to "break bush". Raining heavily—progress extremely slow. P.I.B, adj. [adjutant], suggested that force travel on compass bearing . . . as force could not regain Kokoda track, visibility nil. This plan was followed and possible only when personnel placed luminous leaves in hats and waist belts. Track crossed creeks and scaled steep slopes through very dense jungle. 0400 hrs: Halt called to await daylight, when it was found force only 2 miles [3.2 kilometres] from OIVI.'[27]

Lieutenant Mortimore also recalled their escape: 'Sanopa went off and he found a gap on the side; actually the village was a little way up from the creek; we came out of the village down into the creek and then we spent from, I think it was 10 o'clock at night until just about daylight next morning, going up that bloody creek.'[28]

Private Ronald Halsall, a 23-year-old welder from Euroa in Victoria with the Company Headquarters staff, also recalled: 'We had Sanopa, he got a MM. He was a very good scout. He'd lead you out ... say you got trapped. He'd know where to take you, up over a dry creek bed or something. He earned his MM, by gee.'[29]

Just on dawn, these men found that they had not made much progress, as recalled by Sergeant Major Dawson: 'When daylight arrived, we realised we had not travelled very far as we could still hear the sounds of battle at Oivi.'[30] The Japanese had obviously launched an attack at first light against the now vacated position. Many men probably joked (and hoped) that the bastards had killed each other in friendly fire! Watson's intention, recalled Joseph Dawson, 'was for us to move parallel to the Kokoda track, cut back onto it and join the troops left at Kokoda. It soon became apparent that was not possible; the jungle was impenetrable. We followed a different track instead and that brought us into Deniki. When we arrived there, someone gave me a 16-ounce [450-gram] tin of baked beans. My poor neglected stomach could not handle the food and I promptly threw up.'[31] Mortimore also recalled: 'We pulled in early next morning into a village which was possibly Fila. All we could do was knock a few coconuts down. That was the only meal we got and then we kept on going to Deniki. Sanopa saved two platoons and Doug's (McClean) troops from getting wiped out and was promoted and awarded the Military Medal for his actions.'[32]

•

Not all at Oivi had got the word to clear out. Six Australians were still holding their positions long after the rest of the men had gone. Among them was Corporal Charles Pyke, who had earlier gone out with Lieutenant Doug McClean to lob grenades into the Japanese positions to the rear. Close by was Private Arthur Swords, a 32-year-old farm labourer from Dandenong in Victoria of 'B' Company. Swords recalled that he and his mate 'Ocker' Taylor soon discovered they had been left behind.

> In the defensive position at Oivi, 'Ocker' and I with our Lewis gun had been detailed to cover a little track leading out of the village. At one

stage we got a warning order that we were to evacuate, but later that order was countermanded. So, we stayed put guarding our little sector without a clue as to what was going on behind us in the village.

At about eleven that night Bill Hoskins, one of the 16 Platoon lads, came over to us and asked where all the others had gone. We said we didn't know, and he said: 'Well there's nobody else around except you two and four of us, but I did see blokes moving out along a track over there.'

That news gave us a bit of a shock. We went and searched through the village . . . but no troops. Obviously, the others had moved out and forgotten about us. So, we decided that the only thing to do was for us to get out too, and we headed out along the track the rest of the blokes had apparently taken. We thought that the main track leading to Kokoda might already be held by the Japs and it seemed best to strike out to the side of it, but keeping parallel, and then cut back onto it ahead of the Japs. We set off in drizzling rain, but soon got lost because we didn't have a compass and clouds had hidden the moon.[33]

It was not long before they found the surrounding area blocked by Japanese medics attending to their wounded. Even though outnumbered, Pyke and the others decided to bluff their way out: 'We said we will go through, but we won't draw attention, we will just keep going, if we get challenged, just open with everything from the hip and keep going, that's our only hope . . . they were fixing up their wounded. They were yabbering. They didn't challenge us. I don't know why. I don't know if they were . . . confused, we weren't even challenged.'[34]

●

Sergeant Ted Morrison, commanding the second half of Doug McClean's platoon who had not been able to break through the Japanese attacking Oivi, took up a blocking position across the track leading back to Kokoda. He had been waiting for an opportunity to break through to 'B' Company, which he still believed to be at Oivi. Shortly after, a couple of men from the patrol that had been sent out earlier to find Sam Templeton stumbled upon Morrison and his men, telling him that by now Oivi was likely already overrun by the Japanese and that Templeton was likely dead. Morrison recalled: 'I decided that it was best to return to Kokoda and inform Colonel Owen of the situation. When we got back to Kokoda about 2 a.m. Colonel Owen approved my decision to return and sent me on a reconnaissance with a few others to try and find out what was happening at Oivi. But while we were still heading for Oivi a police boy caught up with us with a message from Colonel Owen. It was written on a sheet of toilet-paper and said: "Withdraw patrol through me to Kokoda at 1000 hrs. Be careful enemy do not catch up to you unexpectedly on bicycles." So, we returned to Kokoda again.'[35]

At Kokoda was medic Jack Wilkinson, who recalled at the time: 'Word of Oivi falling on 26th. Hope Uncle Sam got back all right. Was alone and a bit too game for safety, our troops surrounded at Oivi. We prepared to abandon Kokoda. All carriers had cleared out and a lot of police.'[36] Also, still at Kokoda was Lieutenant Champion who later recorded: 'On 26 July ... I received a message from HQ instructing me to report to Moresby immediately, Lt Col. Owen told me to catch the next plane to Moresby, but no further planes arrived, so I, together with some sick troops, left Kokoda at 2330 hrs. and I proceeded over the Owen Stanley Range to Moresby where, on arrival, I reported to Major-Gen. Morris.'[37]

The fighting at Oivi resulted in around 20 per cent of the Australian and Papuan force becoming casualties—killed, wounded or missing.

•

Thomas Grahamslaw and Jack McKenna had earlier that day parted company with Austen and his small party at Seapareta in their attempt to reach Wairopi and Kokoda. The men of the 1st PIB and their three guides had disappeared into the jungle before daylight and now they were relying on their trusted native tracker Peter. No one else from the village would accompany them from fear of the Japanese and they were informed by some villagers along the way that Wairopi and Kokoda were already in Japanese hands. Grahamslaw wrote in his report to ANGAU that their only option was to make their way to Port Moresby.

There were three routes in that direction. They rejected the route via the village of Tufi as it was also likely now in Japanese hands. The track through Rigo was also ruled out as it required a 2440 metre climb over Mount Obree. The only viable route was through Abau. With the decision made they left Seapareta at 0900 with 'one trade blanket a piece kindly donated by Capt. AUSTEN, 5 tins of meat, 6 pkts biscuits and 2 lbs trade tobacco, also from Capt. AUSTEN ... Reached BOFU at 1400 and camped for the day.'[38]

Peter guided them as far as Bofu but could go no further as he had a wife and child to think of and, with the Japanese all around, his place was understandably with them. Grahamslaw recalled many years later: 'Peter was a friend in my time of need, and his name lives in my memory.'[39]

•

After capturing Oivi, Captain Ogawa was now massing his troops for an all-out attack to take Kokoda Plateau and its nearby airstrip—the gateway to the Owen Stanley Range and the Kokoda Track running through it. Beyond lay Port Moresby.

•

It would be almost 70 years after Captain Sam Templeton's disappearance at Oivi that details of his fate emerged. In 2009 a Japanese veteran of the campaign alleged that the short burst of machine-gun fire that was heard from the rear of Oivi just after Captain Templeton moved out had wounded him. He was taken prisoner and his wounds tended to by medical officer Lieutenant Colonel Yanagisawa Hiroshi with the 15th Independent Engineer Regiment.

After his wounds had been treated, Captain Sam Templeton was taken to Lieutenant Colonel Tsukamoto, who was in temporary command of the combat arm of the invasion, and commanding the I/144th Regiment. During interrogation by this senior Japanese officer, Templeton provided no information other than to highly inflate the number of Australians at Kokoda to over 1000 men and did one better stating that the Australians at Port Moresby numbered around 80,000 when there were fewer than 8000. He mocked the Japanese senior officer stating: 'I wonder how many of you will see out the day. I'll be counting' and he started to laugh. Showing this defiance enraged Tsukamoto; he would not tolerate such insolence from his own officers, let alone a captured enemy captain. Tsukamoto's face 'went bright red, and he was very angry, to the point that he drew his sword, killing Captain Sam Templeton, thrusting his sword into his stomach'.[i] [40]

---

i   Reporting of the same period alleging that another Japanese soldier buried an Australian officer
      named Templeton near Oivi a week after the battle with a Japanese officer's sword still embedded
      in his stomach, is judged by the author not to be reliable.

PART THREE

THE FIRST BATTLE FOR KOKODA

20

'Passes over range must be secured'

During the morning hours of 27 July, Lieutenant Garland and his men of 10 Platoon were at Kokoda with Lieutenant Colonel Owen, they were soon joined by Morrison and his fifteen men of 16 Platoon along with some stragglers of 'B' Company. Also there was Lieutenant Peter Brewer of ANGAU and the two signallers from the NGAWWC, Bernard 'Spud' Murphy and Clive Turnbull. In all, Owen had just 50 men to defend Kokoda Station from a Japanese force now numbering around 250 crack troops, considering the likely casualties suffered at Oivi.

Owen remained unsure of the fate of Templeton and his men but knew that the enemy had apparently surrounded and attacked their position at Oivi, and that Sam Templeton had been reported missing in action, feared dead. He did not know at this point that, behind him in the foothills of the Owen Stanleys, the survivors of Templeton's 11 and 12 platoons, along with some of McClean's men and those of the 1st PIB and the RPC, numbering in total around 70 men, were making their way 8 kilometres south to Deniki—about 400 metres above Kokoda Station. Captain Jesser and his nine-man section of the 1st PIB would soon join them there.[1]

Owen decided that if he received no news from Templeton or Watson by 11 a.m. he would have to evacuate Kokoda and head south, climbing the Kokoda Track to Deniki. This village represented the first fallback position on the mountain track this side of the Owen Stanleys. It was here that Lieutenant Brewer had been building up his supply dump.

At dawn Owen ordered most of his small force to withdraw, while he and a few others remained, stacking as much of the supplies they could not carry into the village huts, preparing to set fire to the lot. Others went about trying as best they could to place obstacles on the airstrip. At 11 a.m., and with still no word from Templeton's force, those remaining at Kokoda set fire to the stores and left for Deniki. To their surprise, on reaching the village a few hours later, they found Watson, Stevenson and their men, who had arrived there an hour before. Owen was concerned to hear that Captain Sam Templeton was still missing.

•

Earlier that morning, Corporal Pyke and his small party had put the wounded Japanese and their medics behind them, but they were still lost and too close to Oivi for comfort. Private Swords recalled:

> In the morning the sound of rifle fire gave us our bearings in relation to Oivi—apparently the Japs were probing the village. It was just as well they fired some shots, because we could easily have blundered back there again. The day was mostly cloudy, so we couldn't keep our bearings by the sun, but we managed to get onto a high feature and recognize the terrain in the direction of Yodda and then head for Kokoda. Even so we kept getting bushed in the hollows and had to make for high ground time and again to get our bearings. Late in the afternoon we blundered onto a track which we reckoned must be the right one. Then we started to wonder if the Japs had already been along it (at that stage we weren't familiar with the mark left by their 'divided toe' jungle boots). Anyway, we set off . . . keeping proper patrol order and taking turns at forward scout. It turned out to be the right track and we reached Kokoda that evening.
>
> At Kokoda we found that some of the huts had been burnt down—their corner posts were still glowing hot coals. We decided it must have been our own scorch earth policy and not the work of the Japs. The tents we had camped in were still standing, just as they had been after our stay in the rubber Plantation after the hike over the Owen Stanleys. We picked over tins of bully beef looking for some that had not been

punctured with bayonets and managed to scrounge enough to eat. Then 'Ocker' and I took the 16 Platoon lads into our old tent. We felt that we were playing host to them. They had been flown into Kokoda only about 30 hours before and were then shot straight up to reinforce us at Oivi, so they knew nothing about Kokoda or the surrounding area whereas 'Ocker' and I were 'old hands'—we had been there for well over a week!²

•

At Buna, Japanese attempts to land reinforcements, along with additional equipment and supplies for Colonel Yokoyama's force, were met with mixed results. While one transport loaded with supplies got through on 25 July, four days later another two were less fortunate. One—carrying the balance of Yokoyama's 15th Independent Engineer Regiment—was sunk but most of the 263 men got ashore safely. Attacking aircraft forced the other transport to head back to Rabaul still carrying its full cargo of vehicles and supplies. A few days later another convoy was forced back to Rabaul before it reached Buna.³

•

Grahamslaw and McKenna left Bofu in the early morning hours of 27 July and by late afternoon had reached their next destination— the village of Natunga. Grahamslaw wrote of their reception by the villagers: 'Natives gave us a very noisy reception. We were the first Europeans to visit there since McKENNA patrolled the District from TUFI early in 1938. However, they provided us with food without cost when McKENNA explained the situation to them. Our scanty supply of tobacco was insufficient to pay our way, so we decided to live on the bounty of the natives as far as possible. We, of course, carefully explained to them that the Govt. would reward them for their assistance and for food provided when the next patrol visited them.'⁴ While they were at Natunga a village councillor from Bofu arrived with a note from Harry Bitmead, who had that morning left Reverend Redlich. Grahamslaw sent the runner back to Bitmead with a note that he and McKenna would wait for him at Natunga.

That morning Bitmead had left Redlich's hideout near Hondituru for Seapareta, where he had been told Captain Louis Austen was hiding out. On pushing further on to Bofu, he had been told that Grahamslaw and McKenna had passed through the village the day before; he was determined to catch up with them. Bitmead arrived at Seapareta in the afternoon and met Austen, Anthony Gors, his wife and their seven-year-old son; native guides brought in two American airmen whose B-25 bomber had been shot down by Japanese Zeros. Three crew members had failed to vacate the aircraft, including the co-pilot, 38-year-old RAAF Sergeant Edgar Hawter from Donnybrook in Western Australia, but three others managed to bail out. Two Americans, Captain Peter Bender and Sergeant Arnold Thompson, parachuted to safety, but 32-year-old RAAF Sergeant Ian Hamilton from Brisbane could not be found and was assumed to have been captured by the Japanese—the details of his fate remain unknown.

Bender and Thompson had landed near Isivita and were taken by friendly villagers to the nearby mission station where members of the Sangara mission, Father Henry Holland, Sisters Margery Brenchley and Lilla Lashmar, lay preacher John Duffill and Papuan teacher-evange-list Lucian Tapiedi, were located. Holland provided them with native guides to take them to Captain Austen at Seapareta. The next day, having received Grahamslaw's note, Bitmead and the American airmen left Seapareta to catch up with Grahamslaw and McKenna. Austen and the Gors were encouraged to join them but they were determined to stay put until the rest of the Sangara party, then at Isivita, arrived, they would then all make their way to Oro Bay where they expected to be evacuated by boat in mid-September.[5]

At this point a runner from Father Redlich also caught up with Bitmead just before he left Seapareta with a letter addressed to his father in England; he asked Bitmead to pass it on. The envelope had scribbled on it 'No Stamp'. It would eventually make its way to Australia and from there was sent on to his father, who was himself an Anglican priest in the parish of Little Bowden. It reads:

Somewhere in the Papuan Bush.

27 July 1942

My dear Dad,

The war has busted up here. I got back from Dogura and ran right into
it—and am now somewhere in my parish trying to carry on, though
my people are horribly scared.

No news of May and I'm cut off from contacting her—my staff OK
so far but in another spot.

I'm trying to stick whatever happens. If I don't come out of it just
rest content that I've tried to do my job faithfully.

Rush chance of getting word out, so forgive brevity.

God Bless you all,

Vivian.[6]

It is likely that within hours of writing this hurried letter to his father,
Reverend Vivian Redlich met his death at the hands of half-a-dozen
locals who killed him. In an investigation into his brother's death,
Patrick Redlich records in his book, *My Brother Vivian . . . and the
Christian Martyrs of Papua New Guinea*, that Vivian had just finished
writing a letter—likely the letter to his father—while sitting on
two large rocks next to a track. Reverend Redlich and a local guide
named Kipling Guveno walked up the track towards Ojahambi
village, arriving at Kogenata Creek where they stopped for a rest and
to drink the clean cool water. As they pushed on, they came across
a group of men with spears who immediately 'sprung at Vivian,
speared and knocked him down, and killed him. They did not bury
him on the spot but carried his body some distance and placed his
remains in a cave.'[7] Kipling Guveno managed to escape. The grave
was recently identified, and the body exhumed. The remains have
yet to be officially confirmed as those of Reverend Redlich, but it is
almost certainly him. It is hoped the remains will be conclusively
identified in the near future.[8]

Not far away, Japanese 1st Class Seaman Shin Shunji with No. 2 Company, Sasebo No. 5 SNLP, was relieved from duty and wandered over to look at a young American airman whose fighter had been brought down by Zeros. It is possible this may have been Australian Sergeant Ian Hamilton. Shin, like many of his comrades, had not seen the enemy close up before and was keen to have a good look at his enemy. He noted in his diary the major problems of supply due to the continued bombing by these young enemy airmen, forcing the Japanese troops to carry whatever supplies could be landed to the warehouse because of a lack of vehicles. The details surrounding the fate of this unidentified young airman remain unknown but after interrogation he was almost certainly executed. Indeed, the Japanese marines had an appalling reputation when it came to handling prisoners.[9]

•

Days earlier Lieutenant General Hyakutake, commanding the Japanese XVII Army, had arrived at Rabaul. He had since read several positive reports of the landings at Gona and on 28 July he decided to launch an all-out assault against Port Moresby across the mountains, using the Kokoda Track, even though no reconnaissance had been conducted regarding the way through the mountains. Indeed, at this point Colonel Yokoyama had not seen the track and his reports related only to the lowland terrain and their advance from the beachhead. He had not reported on the logistical problems that they would obviously encounter when trying to advance along the narrow mountain pass. However, Imperial General Headquarters now ordered the attack to go ahead regardless of what reconnaissance revealed of the passage through the mountains.[10]

Even before a cursory reconnaissance of the area had been made, the self-delusion of the Japanese military planners dictated an advance over the Owen Stanleys be undertaken to capture Port Moresby—victory disease had well and truly set in. Orders were issued from the Imperial General Headquarters in Tokyo that Port Moresby was to be captured within twelve days of Major General Horii's South Seas Force being committed to the battle: 'Port Moresby can be captured at a stretch if adequate provisions are provided for 12 days, that is, starting from Sambo [between Sangara and Awala], 4 days to Kokoda, plus 8 days to Port Moresby.'[11]

Major General Horii's South Seas Force was given the go-ahead to capture Port Moresby—soon he and around 10,000 men would be landing to reinforce Yokoyama's men of the Yokoyama Advance Butai. It was also planned that another invasion would occur along the most eastern part of New Guinea at Milne Bay on 25 August to capture the airfield then under construction; both attacks would act as a pincer movement to help 'strangle' Port Moresby from Australian control.[12]

However, the American landings at Guadalcanal on 7 August would throw these best laid plans into confusion. The landing of the US marines in the Solomons meant that the Japanese forces committed to the attack against Port Moresby would need to be reduced, with the bulk of Horii's South Seas Force to stay on the northern side of the Owen Stanley Range until the situation on Guadalcanal was resolved one way or another—his force might be needed to reinforce the fighting there. Historian Eric Bergerud wrote that with the invasion of Guadalcanal the Japanese high command quickly realised that the Papua and Solomon campaigns were essentially 'two parts of a whole—they were the two fronts of the same remarkable campaign that, in the truest sense of the word, turned the tide of the Pacific war. Just as its German ally saw dreams of empire turn to ash between July and December 1942, so did Japan's strategic position dissolve in the same fleeting months.'[13]

The main combat force to confront the Australians along the Kokoda Track would now total just 2500 men comprising the Yokoyama Advance Butai reinforced with the II and III battalions of the 144th Regiment and II/41st Regiment. While the Japanese landings at Milne Bay would proceed as planned, the destruction of Japanese forces there by the Australians in late August 1942 would come to represent the first defeat of Japanese land forces in the Pacific war.[14]

On the same day that the Japanese Imperial General Headquarters were giving the green light for extensive operations against Port Moresby from the north, MacArthur and Blamey refused to send reinforcements to New Guinea; they still failed to grasp the real situation playing out along the northern coast of Papua. Indeed, Blamey would not set foot in Papua until 12 September, while MacArthur would not put in an appearance until 2 October—three months after the fighting had broken out.[15] Blamey sent a message to Port Moresby on 28 July: 'Disturbed by enemy penetration in Kokoda area. Most vigorous action must be taken to establish block as far east as possible. Passes over range must be secured.'[16] Morris was being ordered to hold back the Japanese advance, but MacArthur and Blamey at this point refused to supply him with the troops, supplies, armaments and ammunition, along with air transports, that would enable him to continue the fight with any chance of success.

Historian David Horner summed up the situation: 'General MacArthur, in his *Reminiscences*, wrote that in anticipation of the Japanese attack in New Guinea, he "moved headquarters forward to Brisbane and then to Port Moresby. If I could secure Moresby, I would force the enemy to fight on ground of my selection—across the barrier of the Owen Stanley Range." Apart from his apparently faulty memory of the date of his move to Port Moresby, this statement is a distortion of what actually happened.'[17] In regard to MacArthur's overall abilities during this phase of the fighting, historian John Robertson succinctly assessed:

It is . . . important to assess MacArthur's generalship, which had serious limitations, for he did not lead his forces calmly and skilfully in the actual crisis of a battle against odds, as was seen in the Philippines campaign of 1941–42 and in the Papuan campaign from July to October 1942. His success after 1942 is not enough to earn him an accolade as one of history's great commanders, if the test of greatness is the ability to make skilful quick-thinking reactions to enemy moves, or the ability to defeat an opponent of similar or greater strength. For after 1942 MacArthur enjoyed great advantages. He had an intelligence system which informed him of his enemy's plans; in all his victories his forces were much stronger than his enemy's; he had ample time to prepare his plans, and he had the help of skilled staff officers in Washington who diverted him from some possible costly errors. On the other hand, after 1942 his abilities matched his responsibilities. He understood the American industrial machine, his great strength as a general lying in his ability to make most effective use of his country's overwhelming military superiority.[18]

MacArthur and Blamey were forced for the first few months of the Kokoda Campaign to react to the Japanese, failing to take the initiative. Indeed, at the height of the crisis, John Beasley, the Minister for Supply and Development, said after an Advisory War Council meeting in mid-September: 'Moresby is going to fall. Send Blamey up there and let him fall with it.'[19]

21

'Worn as no hat ever should have been worn'

Sixty-year-old Gallipoli veteran Captain Geoffrey 'Doc' Vernon arrived at Deniki on 27 July. Captain Noel Symington recalled Vernon as a 'very gallant medical officer. I first met him at Deniki. I ascertained that he'd been a medical officer in the First World War; he'd been awarded a Military Cross in that capacity . . . A very widely read bloke, quite opposite to Kienzle physically, but mentally, probably equally alert.'[1] Lieutenant Brewer knew Vernon well, writing of him in his official report to ANGAU: 'Capt. VERNON AAMC, heard that the Japs had landed at BUNA, came from KAGI . . . where he had been establishing a Dressing Station, to offer his services to Lt. Col. Owen. Note: Capt. Vernon has practiced medicine in Papua for a number of years . . . This sterling work among sick and wounded during operations is worthy of the highest praise.'[2] Sydney newspaperman Geoff Reading also wrote of Doc Vernon:

> Doc was a patriarch of Papua. A tall, lean man of about seventy years, he had spent a lifetime wandering among these jungles and mountains, and he declined to vacate them merely because a few wretched Japanese had invaded the land. When the civilian population was evacuated from Papua, Doc enlisted with the Angau unit, and assumed responsibility for the medical care of a large section of the native carriers in the Owen Stanleys. He spoke as familiarly of little-known trails in the hills as New Yorkers speak of Broadway, or Sydney-siders

speak of King's [sic] Cross. They were as real and as remarkable to him as the highways and byways we roamed when we were young. He knew most of Papua like the palm of his hand and asked what there was for him in the big cities of the south. He carried a roll of toilet paper with him, and rolled his cigarettes from this, preferring them to the tailor-mades that I offered him.[3]

That said, the Kokoda Track in July 1942 was as unknown to Doc Vernon as it was to the diggers now crossing it. A week before arriving in Deniki, Doc Vernon had reached Nauro as part of his inspection along the mountain track and had come across his good friend Bert Kienzle coming in the opposite direction. He scribbled in his diary:

> I went onto Nauro on 22nd July. It was accounted an easy walk, but I did not find it so. The ups and downs of the Owen Stanley Range were heartbreaking, and this particular day's journey seemed to have been designed to give a maximum of exertion. The track is really a native main road, probably centuries old, and it follows the native idea of road making. That is to say, it forges straight ahead taking the most inaccessible gullies and steepest slopes in its stride, distaining [sic] any idea of grading or following contours. I was told Nauro laid some 800 feet [250 metres] below Ioribaiwa which conveyed the idea of a downhill walk, but I had not taken in consideration the general cussedness of the Owen Stanley spurs or of native road planning. The path immediately fell down into a deep ravine, climbed out of that up a never-ending hill, and continued along a more or less level ridge which led us a dance over roots and boulders. Finally, it suddenly plunged down a breakneck descent to Nauro. Put in mathematical terms, the day's journey would result in a drop of 800 feet in altitude, but to achieve this it fell 900 [275 metres], rose 1000 [300 metres], and needed a final drop of 900 feet to achieve the level of Nauro Valley. So much for Papuan hill tracks! Multiply them by the number of days spent on the track and the unnecessary amount of climbing can be estimated.

On the way we pulled up for a rest, and while we were having some hot soup, Lieut. Kienzle, our OC passed on his way back from

Kokoda. It was a timely meeting and we swapped notes on the track as we drank our soup and he told me that the hospital at Efogi was crowded ... with sick carriers from the Kokoda end. Otherwise it was a lovely spring-like day. On the heights the air was fresh and invigorating, the trees quivered in a cool breeze, and the grass looked almost dewy. Here and there views of the surrounding ranges could be got, and the little outpost of Ioribaiwa, separated from our ridge by a deep gulf, was now far below us.[4]

After enjoying their soup and a brief discussion both men head off in the opposite direction, neither was aware of the Japanese invasion that had occurred the previous day. Vernon went on to record in his diary: 'Nauro was reached at 1500. The ANGAU OC Sgt. Osbourne, was quite alone here and spent much of his time doctoring up the carriers and the local sick. He wanted me to give him an NMO but none were available at the time and I told him he would have to evacuate his sick to Ioribaiwa where we had a central hospital for this section of the line.'[5]

On 23 July, Vernon passed through Menari before reaching the ANGAU post at Efogi—it was a difficult and exhausting slog. He wrote in his diary: 'I went uphill and over dale to Efogi passing through the old Seventh Day Adventist mission site which lies on the open slopes of the Brown River Valley. Efogi lies at the bottom of this and it is one of the most exasperating places to reach on the whole track. On arrival in the gorge, tired out after a day's climbing you find that the town planners of Efogi selected a small hill for their town, and a particularly nasty little hill at that.' Indeed, many consider this to be the worst part of the track, Doc Vernon continues: 'Its ascent seems to add the last straw to the day's exertions as you pull yourself up the rocks by roots and branches, just another of the insults that the range daily hands out to the hiker, doubly annoying when you find that you have to scramble down it again on starting the next day's trek. At its best (worst?), however, this little knoll is only an aperitif to a regular orgy of hill climbing as you continue on your way to Kokoda.'[6]

On finally reaching Efogi, Doc Vernon found, 'many sick carriers ... and an insufficient supply of blankets to keep them warm at night.

I sent the [Medical Orderly] ... in charge here who was ill back to base.'[7] Vernon stayed there the next day to help treat the carriers and on 25 July was conferring with Sergeant Hylton Jarrett (a 31-year-old engineer from Ramsey in Victoria) when a native runner arrived with a note informing Jarrett of the Japanese invasion to the north. Vernon recorded: 'Started at 0930 for Kagi in company with Sgt Jarrett, ANGAU station O.C. Just after leaving, we met a native policeman who handed Jarrett a letter. It announced the landing of Japanese troops at Buna ... This was the first intimation of invasion that had reached me.'[8] Turning to Jarrett, Doc said: 'I'll go on, there's no M.O. with those 39th youngsters.'[9] The near-deaf 60-year-old Gallipoli veteran immediately pushed on with Jarrett and a small party to Kagi. Vernon recorded at the time how they negotiated the steep descent from the village down to the Efogi River and then climbing the steep valley up to Kagi—at a similar height to Efogi—on the opposite side of the deep and narrow gorge.

> The track to Kage [*sic* Kagi] included ... very long ascents ... but after all you never really come to the top of a Papuan hill and you come to regard it as something unattainable. We toiled on through the forenoon heat and on arrival at the hilltop station got our first extensive view of the main Owen Stanley Range looming over the Brown River valley backed by Mount Victoria 13,300 feet [4050 metres] soaring over lesser peaks. At dusk, the great mountain grew shadowy and seemed to change into the figure of a giantess carved in stone, leaning back with her hands on her knees, a very prominent hump on each side projecting like an outsized in breasts, it lent a human touch to the grimness of the range. Jarrett had returned to Efogi, and except for my team, I was alone that night at Kage [*sic*]. It rained, I got wet through, and thick white mist closed in on the hut, but I built a big fire and read some home letters which had miraculously reached me by native carrier during the afternoon.[10]

Doc Vernon was now just two days from Kokoda and all going well he should arrive at Deniki the next day before descending into the Yodda Valley to Kokoda itself. At first light on 26 July Vernon headed off for Isurava.

I climbed up to the Gap and travelled down Mambare Waters. During the long descent through a bamboo forest, we met the first of our troops from the front toiling painfully up. A few had been wounded, others were sick or injured, and every man looked spent and seemingly disturbed by the rapid advance of the enemy, and the small numbers with which we could oppose them this side of [the] Range. They came from Wire Rope [Wairopi] and Oivi where clashes had already taken place . . . we [also] ran into a mob of carriers eating their lunch quite light-heartedly, either ignorant of or indifferent to the Japs ahead. We reached Iora [*sic* Eora] Creek by mid-afternoon, and here I obtained the first authentic news of the Japanese advance. There was an atmosphere of tension and unrest in the camp, the ANGAU OC was afraid that carriers would desert as the rumours of our retreat to Kokoda intensified, and that night a party of 30 to 40 did decamp. They were mostly Kokoda boys who were anxious about their friends in the valley and no doubt they just walked into the Japs and were cut off. Everybody was buzzing with information, true or false, from the front. Amongst those who had come in, and were adding to the confusion, was a PIB boy I knew well, who had apparently got separated from his detachment near Awala and [had] come back on his own, pretty scared by all he had seen and gone through. He told me our medical assistant Harry Bitmead, stationed at Isagahambo, had been caught and killed, his cook shot through the head, one of the medical boys having met with a similar fate . . .

The camp at Iora [*sic*] was badly sited; it ended a stage from Kage [*sic*] that was far too long and would have been better placed close to water and on more level ground . . . This would have exactly divided the distance between Kage [*sic*] and the more advanced post at Isurava. Iora [*sic*] camp was on a little side knoll high above the streaming white creek below, and the slopes were so steep and undercut that at night you had to be careful as one false step might have hurled you 200 feet [60 metres] into the chasm below . . . The approaches were very bad and one thought of the soldier's reply to a lady who asked how our troops went over the Range, 'Up on our hands and bellies, down on our backsides'.

We moved on ... [and] we met many sick soldiers, a party of tired officers and a stream of native refugees, the men carrying a few household goods and the women and children struggling after all the flotsam and jetsam of retreat. When at Isurava, about 1100 [hours], I found supplies were precarious and I was not even offered the travellers [sic] usual cup of tea. All these incidents proved the war was coming closer to me.

The track from Iora [sic] to Deniki leads up and down some very rough gorges, the northern face of the range being much rockier though it takes a more direct line to the Mambare Valley. From Isurava I had expected some fine views of Kokoda and Yodda, but thick mist hid everything from sight. In any case one sees little of the surrounding country from any part of the Owen Stanleys, the trees hem one in like a prison wall.

From Isurava to Deniki, the descent of the last slopes of the range begins and aided by a good many involuntary slides we made rapid progress. Three quarters of a mile short of Deniki, I found the first of the regulars camped on a grassy knoll, where Lieutenant Searle, an experienced wireless officer [with ANGAU] was in charge of signals. The news was not very reassuring, Kokoda had been evacuated the previous afternoon, and our most advanced troops were now at Deniki.[11]

Doc Vernon was shocked to hear that the front line was now at Deniki, just south of Kokoda Plateau and 400 metres above the station. During the late afternoon of 27 July Doc Vernon finally arrived at Deniki. The Official Australian Medical History of the New Guinea Campaign records it was not only the wounded that Doc Vernon had to attend to, but also the sick; he was busy 'attending to many men with painful and damaged feet, and others with malaria, no doubt relapsing attacks. Some were seriously ill from the combined effects of malaria and exposure to the cold and wet of the higher levels.'[12] Doc Vernon himself recorded in his diary:

On arrival at Deniki, I reported to the CO of the 39th Battalion, telling him that I was MO to the carriers and had come forward to see to their medical needs, but that if he wished to make use of my services for white troops, I would place myself at his disposal. He accepted and told me to stand by for orders. The 39th was without a Medical Officer, Sgt Wilkinson being attached as Regimental Medical NCO, and one of the ANGAU medical assistance [*sic*], WO Barnes, had joined up with them after receiving orders to withdraw before the advancing Japs from his post at Awala [Isagahambo]. I found the two men busy doctoring up men of the 39th; a large number of foot troubles and had evidently had a hard time during the last few days. Some were seriously ill from malaria and exposure to rain all night, yet every man was anxious to have a cut at Nippon. I spent a very cold blanketless night in the improvised hospital hut with the wind rushing through gaps in the floor and miniature shower bath that could not be turned off functioning through the roof.[13]

No doubt Owen and his men were relieved to see the arrival of the trained and experienced physician. Wilkinson and Barnes were especially relieved, with Wilkinson writing in his diary: 'Captain Vernon arrived out of the fog. Very pleased to see him. He had some instruments and dressings in two triangular bandages. He nearly got shot when first seen owing to his unregimental dress. Captain Vernon had shorts, which were really strides rolled up; a blue pullover with the arms tied around his neck and hanging down his back; a felt army hat, worn as no hat ever should have been worn, and a long newspaper cigarette in his mouth. A small dillybag and some army biscuits and tobacco in it. He saw me and spoke, "Jack, I heard there was some action up here and thought you may need some assistance. Where do I start?" What a man!'[14]

22

'. . . the Japanese have already penetrated 60 miles inland'

Corporal Charles Pyke and his men reached Deniki in the early hours of 28 July having spent the night at Kokoda as recalled by Private Swords, who was part of Pyke's party. They got up at first light and collected as much tucker as they could and set off for Deniki. Rain drizzled as they marched, and finally a few hours later they reached a clearing near Deniki. There they decided to stop for a rest, when suddenly they were surrounded—by mates from 'B' company. 'They had been alerted to our approach and were waiting in ambush on the track. They were relieved to see us as we were to see them instead of Japs. So, we went to Deniki village which was only a short distance further along the track and there we found the main body again. They were all surprised when we told them we had slept in Kokoda that night and that no Japs were there when we left. Colonel Owen plied us with questions and after we had told him all we knew he said, "We'll go back and re-occupy Kokoda".'[1]

Owen had earlier radioed Port Moresby that they had been forced to evacuate Kokoda Plateau and the airstrip, falling back to Deniki, but he now advised them that he was going back to Kokoda and requested that reinforcements be prepared to fly in and land at the station's airstrip. Leaving McClean and two of his sections at Deniki as a rearguard, Owen prepared to hurry back to Kokoda with 80 men of the 39th Battalion and around twenty men of the 1st PIB.[i] [2] Company Sergeant Major Joseph Dawson recalled that Owen 'decided we should move back and occupy Kokoda. After an issue of rations, ammunition and grenades, we headed back to Kokoda.'[3]

Doc Vernon and Jack Wilkinson both moved out with Owen and his men, heading straight for the plateau, even though Doc was supposed to stay at Deniki. Wilkinson wrote in his diary: 'We have 77 men all battle weary and suffering from exposure. Have had no sleep for three nights and feel rotten. Thank God Dr Vernon is here.'[4]

Indeed, Owen had seen Doc Vernon packing his supplies at Deniki for the trip to Kokoda. He turned to the old Gallipoli veteran: 'I think you should remain here at Deniki, doctor' said the CO. Vernon shook his head, 'Sorry, I'm rather deaf. I didn't hear you.' A case of selective deafness perhaps. Owen again said, 'I suggest that you should remain here at Deniki.' 'Nonsense,' said Doc Vernon, 'Where do you think the wounded will be—here, or down at Kokoda?'[5] Major Henry Steward, a 30-year-old physician from Melbourne and now medical officer with the 2/16th Battalion, would see Doc Vernon in action a week later and wrote of the Great War veteran: 'The Kokoda Trail saw many quiet heroes, none more impressive than this tough old warrior.'[6]

Doc Vernon soon arrived at Kokoda after the main force started to dig in as recalled by Wilkinson: 'We reached K [Kokoda] at 11 a.m.—no Japs. Dr Vernon supposed to stay at Deniki and take wounded evacuated from K. Left half of gear at D [Deniki]. Made old police house into RAP [Regimental Aid Post]. Peter Brewer dug up his three months' supply of grog and shared it out. Filled my water-bottle with whisky and water. Not game to drink it.'[7]

•

i   Historian Peter Williams assesses Owen likely had at least 130 men at Kokoda, possibly as many as 148; however, his estimate does not appear to take into account the ongoing casualties (including the missing) suffered by the 39th Battalion and the 1st PIB during the week-long fighting before the first battle for Kokoda or the two sections of 16 Platoon that remained at Deniki during the battle. Indeed, on arriving at Kokoda before the invasion, Templeton only had 101 men with him. Also, those at the battle consistently state around 80 men of the 39th Battalion and about 20 from the 1st PIB defended Kokoda, including extant diaries of the time. As such, this number seems more likely.

Fast approaching Kokoda from the north-east were the crack Japanese troops of No. 1 Company, I/144th Regiment, elements of No. 5 SNLP, the platoon of combat engineers and other supporting troops, including those bringing up mortars, heavy machine guns and at least one 70-millimetre calibre mountain gun, all tasked with capturing Kokoda Plateau and its airstrip. Also pushing up behind them were their comrades of the No. 2 Company, who had already crossed the Kumusi River and passed through Oivi.

Owen positioned his 100 men around his perimeter, waiting for the Japanese avalanche to hit.[8]

Back in Australia on 28 July, the ABC's Chester Wilmot broadcast another report from Brisbane on the Japanese invasion:

The Japanese Advance to Kokoda
Today's communique reports that the Japanese have already penetrated 60 miles [100 kilometres] inland in New Guinea from their new base near Buna. They are now almost half way to Port Moresby, but they have advanced over the easiest half of the route. Between them and Port Moresby towers the Owen Stanley Range and the lowest point in the Buna–Moresby track is almost as high as Mt Kosciusko [sic]. And what is more the next part across the Range is only a rough goat track along which men must advance in single file. It is ideal defensive country.

That's the description of it which I got at this operational base this afternoon. It came from an officer who was a government official in this area till the outbreak of the war. He was stationed at Kokoda, the next logical objective of the Japanese advancing from Buna. Six miles [10 kilometres] from Kokoda at the little native village of Oivi there was a clash between Australian and Japanese land forces within the last few days. However, the Japanese as yet have only met our patrols. They have still to get past the strong position which nature has given the Australians to hold in the Owen Stanley Range.

This officer told me a lot about this country over which the Japs have advanced so swiftly. He said that from Buna inland for about 25 miles

[40 kilometres] there is a good motor road, but it ends at Sangara. From then on, the only possible progress is by foot, bicycle or horse, but it is fairly easy going along the track or through the forest until you get to the thick timber and jungle between the Kumusi River and Oivi. Wherever there are clearings the natives have cultivated the rich soil very success-fully. There are some excellent coffee plantations run by the natives and near Kokoda there is a highly productive rubber plantation ...

According to this officer there is nothing at Kokoda beyond the aerodrome, the rubber plantation and the government station. Eight miles [13 kilometres] away there is the Yodda goldfield, where there is another small 'drome'. Aeroplane was the main means of communication with the outside world, but neither airfield is suitable for high speed aircraft. However, it seems that with Kokoda in their possession the Japanese could use it to ferry supplies in by air ...

This swift Japanese advance to the Kokoda district appears more dangerous than it really is. So far, they have not been opposed to anything but our light patrols. They have been advancing over the easiest part of the route. The mountain barrier and our main forces still stand between them and Port Moresby and they can only advance by one difficult mountain track. They have already received some reinforcements by sea to Gona. But the Jap force seems still small to fight its way across the mountains in the face of the opposition we have been preparing. Our bombers made only light raids yesterday, but they are helping to delay the Japanese consolidation. By their advance the Japanese have made it far harder for us to drive them out of Buna, but in spite of their progress a really dangerous threat to Port Moresby has not yet developed.[9]

Surprisingly, Wilmot was able to provide a rather up-to-date and relatively accurate summary of what was happening on the ground—albeit he describes the battle at Oivi along with other earlier fighting incorrectly as patrol clashes. He also assessed that as the main Japanese force had yet to land, any threat to Port Moresby looked like it could be contained. Indeed, it could be said that Wilmot was better informed than some senior Allied military commanders of the day.

23

'Rot boy! Bloody rot!'

Kokoda Station is located on a tongue-shaped plateau which stabs northward from the main mountain range. At its widest point the plateau is about 200 metres wide and it was here that the administrative area of the plantation and village was located. Owen placed the bulk of his force on the northern parts of the plateau facing the approaching Japanese. The sides of the plateau fall away sharply for about 30 metres to the valley floor and about 250 metres beyond its northern edge, the Mambare River runs in an east–west direction. Running parallel with the western side of the plateau in the valley is Madi Creek, a branch of the Mambare River, and just west of this creek is the Kokoda airstrip. Similarly running parallel with the eastern edge of the plateau runs Faiwani Creek, another subsidiary of the Mambare River. At the time a shallow drain also ran off the plateau to the east entering the river there. Located on the southern half of the plateau was the rubber plantation stretching back towards the mountains to the rear, overlooked by the village of Deniki 400 metres above, along the northern slopes of the Owen Stanleys. With enough troops it was a good defensive position— but Owen did not have a force large enough to defend it; he knew his position could easily be flanked to the east and west. The only way he could possibly deny the airstrip to the Japanese was to overlook it.[1]

On arriving at Kokoda, Doc Vernon recorded in his diary just before noon:

The night of the 28th and early morning of the 29th July will not easily fade from my memory. Kokoda is approached from the Range

First engagement at Kokoda, 28–29 July 1942

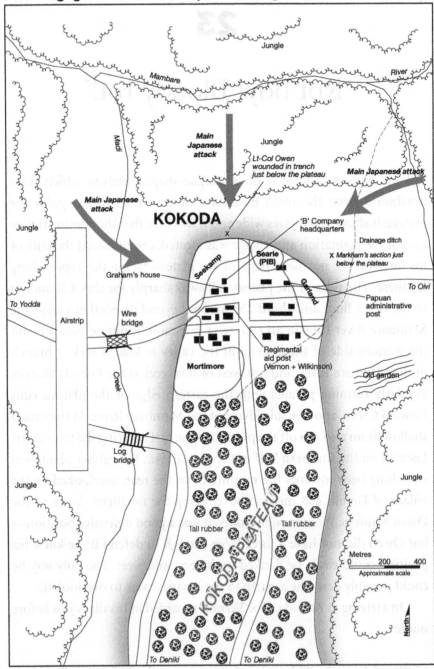

Jungle

Mambare

River

Madi

Main Japanese attack

Jungle

Lt-Col Owen wounded in trench just below the plateau

Main Japanese attack

Main Japanese attack

Jungle

KOKODA

X

'B' Company headquarters

Drainage ditch

Graham's house

Seekamp

Searle (PIB)

Garland

X Markham's section just below the plateau

To Oivi

To Yodda

Airstrip

Wire bridge

Papuan administrative post

Mortimore

Regimental aid post (Vernon + Wilkinson)

Old garden

Creek

Log bridge

Jungle

Jungle

Tall rubber

Tall rubber

Metres
0   200   400
Approximate scale

North

To Deniki   To Deniki

through a grove of rubber about three quarters of a mile [1.2 kilo-metres] in depth. The rubber trees, as deeply shadowed as a natural forest, suddenly give to the grass and gardens of the station where the buildings, all wood or native material and very inflammable, are dispersed, in orderly lines on the little plateau. Beyond them, on three sides, the ground falls away in an abrupt escarpment of some 200 feet [60 metres] that fronts two wide mountain streams junctioning at the northern end of the plateau, while the fourth side, our rear and main line of retreat to the hills, is closed in by the perfectly level rubber lands. It was expected, that the Japs would attack at several points on the escarpment, unless they chose to work round our position through the rubber.[2]

Cutting across the northern part of the plateau from the east was the Kokoda–Oivi track, which from the plateau continued west towards Yodda. Owen looked down the track to the east, Lieutenant Garland's 10 Platoon protected this approach, while defending the northern and western parts of the plateau was Lieutenant Seekamp and his men of 11 Platoon. Placed in between these platoons was 36-year-old Lieutenant Clendyn Searle of ANGAU, from Toorak Hill in Victoria, now commanding around twenty men of the 1st PIB. Covering parts of the western edge and rear was Lieutenant Mortimore and the men of 12 Platoon, digging in among the plantation trees and astride the track leading back to Deniki. The regimental aid post [RAP] was established just south of the administrative area.[3]

Lieutenant Garland recalled that after the men had regrouped, they reoccupied Kokoda and took up a defensive position around the perimeter of the plateau. 'At Kokoda plateau, Colonel Owen showed us what a fine soldier he was as he moved from section to section in each platoon encouraging the men to hold the plateau when the attack came.'[4] Corporal Reginald Markham, with Garland's platoon, recalled: 'The defense was in the form of a square with my section on the right-hand side, looking towards the point of the plateau and facing the way the enemy were expected to come.'[5] Indeed, he and his men were placed off the plateau, positioned slightly forward of the main defensive line, they were extremely vulnerable to any Japanese flanking manoeuvres.

Sergeant Major Joseph Dawson also recalled: 'We feverishly began setting up our defence positions, digging weapon pits with whatever tools were available—and there were not many.' Indeed, these men had to use empty bully beef cans, or those few with helmets used the head gear to scrape out holes in the ground. 'We were spread around the three sides of the Kokoda Plateau with a few troops covering our rear towards the track up to Deniki. Most of our automatic-strength Lewis guns and a couple of new Brens were located at the top of a ridge on the narrow end of the rubber plateau, where the track from Oivi came in.' It was there that the Japanese would most likely arrive. From his position Dawson could see the airstrip below the plateau to his left flank, which was 'strewn with drums and logs ... unfortunately, still had no mortars.'[6]

Meanwhile Doc Vernon was having a well-deserved rest—he would need it as within hours he would be treating the wounded coming in from the Japanese attack against the plateau; he recorded in his diary:

On arrival, I ... inspected and arranged the police house which had been turned into the RAP. In front of this was a large scorched area where a quantity of army and canteen stores had been burnt before the withdrawal of the 26th July. I was tired after the forced march from Efogi and want of sleep the night before at Deniki and I said I would have a rest at Graham's house near the RAP. Arranging to be called for the first casualty I selected a lounge and lay down in company with a fine ginger cat whose acquaintance I had already made when visiting the Graham's [sic] eight months previously. I fed the cat with pieces of scone; he seemed hungry and grateful for the snack and nestling up against me we both fell asleep. I hung my last few remaining treasures on a hook where I could grab them in an emergency, but eventually I had to leave them there for when the time came to retrieve them it was too late to enter the house as it was being riddled with bullets from a Jap machine-gun, posted just below it on the upper slope of the escarpment.[7]

It was just before noon when Owen radioed Port Moresby stating: 'Re-occupied Kokoda. Fly in reinforcements including 2 Platoon and four detachments of mortars. Drome opened.'[8] Two aircraft were already loaded and in the air heading for Kokoda and it was not long before the two C-47 transports—military versions of the DC-3—were circling the airstrip.[9] Onboard one of these aircraft was Captain Bidstrup, commanding 'D' Company, and his adjutant, 24-year-old Lieutenant Keith Lovett from Warracknabeal in Victoria. Distributed between the two aircraft were the men of 17 Platoon. Lovett recalled the flight across the mountains: 'During the short flight we were told to be on the lookout for Zeros which had been sighted in the area. The Bren gunners immediately took up window positions and one of them even smashed a window and poked his Bren through it ready to fire. The American . . . crew later said some nasty things about the damage to their "kite".'[10]

Bidstrup looked out a window of one of these aircraft as they circled Kokoda and saw Owen's men removing the obstructions from the airstrip. Bidstrup later recalled flying 'over the Owen Stanleys that morning [but] . . . the Yanks wouldn't put us down, because they reckoned there were Japs around. I could see our own troops on the ground at Kokoda. And I asked them to hang around; those people were clearing the barricades on the strip. No, they wouldn't, they went back.'[11] Among the men was Corporal Gordon Bailey, a 21-year-old sales assistant from Sale in Victoria, commanding a section of eleven men. He recalled many years later:

We got flown up and we were just about to come into land when they got a radio message to say that the Kokoda drome was in the hands of the Japanese and not to land. At the same time, he got a message to say that there were six Zeros in the area . . . I spoke to Ted Morrison afterwards and he said, 'I could have shot you bloody buggers out of the sky[,] we were all waiting for you to come in.' Whether they got the report tangled up, or something was wrong . . . There was no doubt that he [pilot] had received a message to say, 'Don't land', when in actual fact we could have landed. I don't know whether the Japs were up that end of the drome ... they might have been up the [other] end so you wouldn't have known anyway ... His [Morrison's] was the last aircraft to land on Kokoda.[12]

Both aircraft were soon back at 7-Mile Drome with Bidstrup and his men in a foul mood. Morris was waiting for them at the airstrip and the general's assessment of the employment of mortars must have been of concern to the young officer. His judgement would have a direct impact on the lack of firepower that the Australians would have in battle against the Japanese over the next few months. Bidstrup recalled on landing: 'And there's Basil Morris. "Believe you flew over?" "Yes Sir." "What's the track like?" I said that I was quite surprised. There were quite a few open spaces where I believe we could use mortars. And he said "Rot boy! Bloody rot! The mortar [bombs] would burst in the tree tops!"[13] As such, while the Japanese took into battle rifles, bayonets, grenades, light and heavy machine guns, mortars and mountain guns, the Australians went into battle with rifles, bayonets, grenades and light machine guns, even though Owen and his men, who had been on the ground fighting the Japanese for the past week, had specifically requested an urgent need for mortars.

•

During the rest of the day reports came in of Japanese movement to the north of Kokoda Plateau—but no attack was launched. Lieutenant Garland recalled their lieutenant colonel, like Sam Templeton before him, walked around their perimeter encouraging his men even though he must have been aware of Japanese snipers in the trees: 'At about four o'clock we saw the Japanese around the tree line about half a mile [800 metres] away. At that time, I did mention to Colonel Owen that he should take more cover. But he ignored my advice and continued to walk around the sections ... My platoon occupied a position with Corporal Markham and his section below the ridge and the other two sections along the top of the plateau. We expected to be attacked as night came on and, when that attack did not eventuate, we prepared for a dawn attack. But to our surprise the Japanese attacked around midnight.'[14]

Indeed, Corporal Markham recalled: 'At three P.M., when I had just about completed my inspection, a burst of fire (M.G.) came from the front. Needless to say, I moved quickly to my position of control and awaited events. From then until dark, there were odd shots and bursts from the Japs, but we with-held our fire so as not to disclose our position. A native, earlier in the day had informed me that the Japs "come close-up".'[15]

Earlier Sergeant Major Dawson had seen the Japanese moving up from the Kokoda–Oivi part of the track, recalling: 'They started moving around the end of our perimeter, firing odd bursts from different directions and throwing in a few rounds of mortar fire. At one stage, as I was moving round our position on the left flank at the rim of the plateau, I caught sight of a Japanese soldier looking round the airstrip. I took a shot. I don't know if I hit him, but he jumped and ducked for cover pretty smartly.'[16]

Just to his right, Lieutenant Seekamp and his men, who would face the initial assault along the northern edge of the plateau, continued to dig in; by nightfall they were anxiously awaiting the inevitable Japanese onslaught against their thinly held position. The 100 or so young Australians and Papuans were about to face a force outnumbering them around three to one; well supported with heavy machine guns, mortars and mountain artillery. Darkness came and shortly after midnight the Japanese announced their imminent intent by laying down a burst of heavy machine-gun and mortar fire against the plateau.[17] Bugle calls could be heard providing orders to the dispersed Japanese force.

•

Japanese Sergeant Imanishi with the regiment's No. 2 Company, who had earlier jettisoned his bicycle after crossing the Kumusi River, was one of the Japanese now advancing to support Ogawa's No. 1 Company, which would lead the attack against the Kokoda Plateau. 'We were ordered to occupy the airfield at Kokoda,' recalled Imanishi. 'No one knew there was a hill; we knew nothing of the terrain. But we were very good at executing night attacks. We had experience of this in China.'[18]

•

Grahamslaw and McKenna were still waiting at Natunga for Bitmead and the two American airmen, when at around noon a native guide arrived with one of the Americans, Sergeant Arnold Thompson. They brought with them a note from Bitmead saying that he was on his way but was making slow progress as Captain Peter Bender had a bullet in his ankle and had to be carried. Bitmead said that the few medical dressings he had been able to obtain from the medical orderlies were almost used up. Furthermore, he was having difficulty in obtaining stretcher-bearers for Bender.[19] Grahamslaw and McKenna decided that one of them should push on to Abau to get help for Bitmead's party, while the other would remain behind to take charge of their party. Since McKenna was familiar with the Managalasi country and was well known to the people, it was agreed he would stay with the small group while Grahamslaw set out for Abau; Grahamslaw wrote years later: 'I set out the following day, accompanied by a Dogura Mission native whose name I forget. He had been teaching at Sangara Mission and was separated from the European missionaries when the Mission was evacuated.'[20]

24

'Those rats are bad here'

Before launching their all-out attack against the Australian perimeter, groups of Japanese were targeting Corporal Markham's exposed position to the right, just below the plateau. He later recalled:

> The enemy did much loud talking and yelling, mainly trying to draw our fire, at times we did open up, when we thought . . . there was a possibility of getting a few. From time to time they did a bit of organised moaning—getting together in groups and yelling and howling—this I guessed, was supposed to break down our morale. It did, however, give me some idea of the Jap numbers. They obviously tried to make us think there were thousands of them, we judged them to be about three hundred strong . . . Then came the real thing—they got nasty and opened up with the whole works, mortar, M.G. rifles and .5's [sic] firing explosive bullets. Fortunately, their mortars were of poor quality for two or three burst uncomfortably close to us . . . one spattering light shrapnel on the back of my legs, but not causing any damage. Lead snipped off leaves, rather too close at times too.[1]

Markham's section was reinforced with 'four odds and sods of the unit . . . They consisted of one Canteen Sgt, a Postal Cpl, a Pay Sgt, and a Sig "spotter". Placing them in defensive positions close by . . . we awaited events.'[2] He later elaborated: 'my men . . . included extra men like the postal official, another fellow that had never handled a rifle in his life, a Salvation Army bloke . . . looking after the canteen and somebody else. There were three non-combatants. I said, "Well look men, you've got to learn to handle a rifle so if you've got to use it, you've got to use it, right?" They said, "Oh, we'll do our best".[3]

•

Just after midnight on 29 July, Owen and his men saw the main Japanese force in the moonlight moving cautiously up the steep slope along the northern perimeter held by Seekamp's men. They launched their assault, using fire and movement against the plateau as recalled by Sergeant Major Dawson:

> When they discovered where we were, they started charging up this slope . . . But the mortar fire was intense. Backwards and forwards, wondering where the next one was going to drop. There was a big gutter that ran across the middle of the plantation. I think that was to drain the water off, to keep it away from the trees. There were a couple of Sigs in there, and our fellows had tried to dig in around the perimeter, and we didn't have much in the way of tools, but they got a few holes dug . . . We had no mortars . . . The only thing we had was hand grenades and rifles, Lewis guns, and when Doug McClean got over, his team had a Bren gun. So that's what we did in the battle with the Japs at Kokoda. And the fight went on all night . . .[4]
>
> Being on the wrong end of a mortar barrage is quite frightening. You hear the cough-like sound as they are fired, then for a fraction of a second there is a swish of air, followed by the boom. Once you hear it your mind starts to think, "Will the next one blow me to bits?" or, "Will I lose my legs?" It's a long walk back to Moresby with no bloody legs.[5]

Captain Ogawa's No. 1 Company, I/144th Regiment, led the attack, supported by others who quickly followed up the initial assault, pressing the attack home. Sergeant Imanishi and his 130 or so comrades of No. 2 Company were closing in on Kokoda to support Ogawa's attack; he recalled many years later: 'We could hear soldiers' voices. Someone shouted "Charge!" then sounds of hand grenades and gunshots continued after that. It stopped sometimes, but again you hear sounds of twenty or thirty shots and then someone screams "Move and charge!"'[6]

Japanese Lieutenant Matsuoka, leading a platoon of No. 1 Company, complained that he needed to be at the front of the attack; his commanding officer overheard him and said, 'Well then, you go there.' He led the men up the escarpment yelling 'Charge!' He was among the first of the Japanese to be killed.[7]

Meanwhile, an unknown Japanese signaller with No. 2 Section, No. 1 Company, I/144th Regiment, was passing through Oivi and wrote in his diary: 'Looked over the old battle-ground ... The unit is reported to have made a night attack against Kokoda. Left ... at 2000, marching with difficulty over the muddy road ... the sound of battle was audible.'[8]

Lieutenant Seekamp and his men managed to repulse the first assault, while on Seekamp's right, Lieutenant Garland and his platoon where also in the thick of it; Garland recalled many years later, 'we threw grenades and fired at them, but it was very difficult to see being night you couldn't see much but you could hear the yelling every time a grenade went amongst them they yelled'.[9] Dawson also recalled the Japanese continued to charge, 'up the slope in the partial moonlight while a mist of rain fell. And they kept coming, yelling and screaming, charging up the slope, ready to die for their Emperor ... Apart from Japanese mortars, it was a small arms, grenade and hand-to-hand fight. The noise was deafening.'[10]

The Japanese were using a number of light 'knee' mortars to bomb the Australian positions, along with at least one 70-millimetre mountain gun which was used to great effect—Australian and Papuan casualties began to mount. Also, while the Australian and Papuan troops were outnumbered at around three to one, at the 'pointy end' they were likely outnumbered at far greater odds as the bulk of Japanese attacked at one point of the extended Australian perimeter, with other Japanese keeping the remaining Australian and Papuan troops pinned down. The odds against the Australians would significantly increase with the imminent arrival of No. 2 Company, I/144th Regiment.

Lieutenant Colonel Bill Owen was with Seekamp and his men, who were firing at the oncoming Japanese and lobbing hand grenades for all they were worth; it was then that he was struck by a bullet just above his right eye. Nearby was Papuan Private Lafe who saw Owen collapse to the ground.[11] On hearing that Owen had been hit, Major Watson immediately sent for Doc Vernon. Also near Owen was Sergeant Martorana who recalled his CO's mortal wounding.

> They put mortars, small field pieces, everything they could fire at us, and of course we lost a lot of fellas. We lost David Priestley and his gun crew; we lost two men I had put down near the drain that runs through Kokoda. Victor Holness[i] was one of those lost at the drain. We ran out of ammunition and there weren't many of us left. Lieutenant Colonel Owen asked me 'Can you give me a hand with this?' I said, 'Certainly.' It was a big box of ammunition and two dixies. He's got the ammunition in his left hand and using his right hand to carry the dixies. A historian said he was shot when he was throwing a grenade, but he wasn't. He was shot doing a good turn for the boys . . . They (the Japanese) were in the trees . . . I do believe that with all the shooting that was going on that (Priestley's) gun post had been wiped out . . . I remember Private [Jack] McBride and another (Jack Wilkinson) going out with a stretcher [to bring in Owen].[12]

One of Owen's Headquarters' staff, Private Halsall, also recalled: 'Colonel Bill Owen . . . got out of Rabaul. Overwhelmed they were there. Outnumbered to buggery. He got out of that and then within about a month after getting back to Australia, and after having a bit of leave and cleaned up and re-equipped, he was with us a fortnight and he was shot through the head . . . They were great at getting up trees those little Japs. They had special shoes. The big toe was separate in the rubbery shoe they had, separate from the other part of their foot . . . They get up there and they'd make a nest and they'd stay up there for a few days, living off their bit of rice in the pannikin on their waist . . . Poor old Bill.'[13]

---

i   Twenty-year-old Private David Priestley and 23-year-old Victor Holness, both from South Yarra in Victoria, are listed as KIA on 29 July 1942 having no known grave; the drain as described was almost certainly not the main drainage ditch that ran off the plateau to the east.

Doc Vernon was still asleep at Graham's house even though the whole area had erupted into an inferno of rifle and machine-gun fire with exploding grenades, mortar bombs and 70-millimetre shells. He recalled:

> By midnight, the firing on both sides had [apparently] become almost continuous. It was warm and comfortable on the lounge and I slept secure in the knowledge that I would be called when wanted. About 1 o'clock on the 29th, a hand touched my shoulder; it was Brewer with news that Colonel Owen had been wounded. The moon was now in full strength and shone brightly through a white mountain mist as I hurried with Brewer past the old magistrate's house, now head-quarters, where we picked up a stretcher and several bearers. We crept down a shallow communication trench leading forward to a firing pit at the very edge of the escarpment. The C.O., was propped up in a narrow place, struggling violently yet more than semi-conscious, quite unable to realize where he was or to help us get him out. Removal was difficult, but we got him onto the stretcher at last and carried him to the R.A.P . . . Lt. Col. Owen had received a single G.S.W. (gunshot wound) at the outer edge of the right frontal bone just above the eyebrow. There appeared to be no wound of exit and a little bleeding was controlled by gauze packing. Skull and brain of course had been penetrated. He was now quite unconscious, with occasional convulsive seizures, which lessened, as he grew weaker.[14]

Jack Wilkinson also recalled reaching their mortally wounded CO.

> I took a stretcher down to where he was lying but it was impossible to put him on it as it was too close to the enemy and on a steep slope. Major Watson and Dr. Vernon followed me down again and we managed to turn Colonel Owen and [with] Major Watson and myself pulling and Dr. Vernon pulling, we got him to the top of the plateau . . . there was a man there with a Bren, I think, and he kept a good look out . . . The enemy was moving round . . . I don't think I breathed until we got to the top, as we were very exposed . . . Colonel Owen weighed a lot and

my fingernails were driven back into my fingers with the strain. At the Aid Post, Colonel Owen was attended to by both Dr. Vernon and myself but we could not do much. He had a gunshot wound in the forehead above his . . . eye and the brain tissue kept bulging out; when it was pushed back the wound gushed blood. There was no wound of exit, so the bullet must have still been in the skull. We made him as comfortable as we could, and then other casualties came in.[15]

Major William Watson was again in command and, as the fighting continued into the early hours, the Japanese applied pressure along the whole perimeter, creating gaps in the defence which they began to infiltrate through, isolating Australian and Papuan positions. The perimeter of the small, confused and outnumbered garrison had begun to crumble; no one knew what was happening just metres away. Watson ordered Morrison's section that was in reserve near the assistant resident magistrate's house forward to reinforce Seekamp, but it was becoming hopeless as defenders and attackers were so intermingled that it was difficult to tell friend from foe in the darkness and mist that was now forming in the moonlight.[16]

Back at the aid post, Vernon and Wilkinson were treating the wounded and their position was being targeted by the Japanese heavy machine gunners. Wilkinson had to use a lantern to assist Doc Vernon and this light acted like a beacon drawing enemy fire. The young medic recalled many years later:

Somewhere along the line enemy with a machine gun had managed to get into a position where he could see the light at the Aid Post and was sending over quite a lot of fire. Eventually he cut one of the posts on the verandah and that end collapsed. My nerves were getting a bit frazzled. I remember one chap with a throat wound; the bullet seemed to miss everything of importance. He eventually walked back. I forget what the others had wrong with them, but they were all wounded . . . It was at this time that the celebrated story about Dr. Vernon and the rats happened.

I was doing some crawling around with my head down as the bullets swept over. Every time I held the lantern up to find an instrument Dr.

Vernon said, 'Now hurry up and don't be frightened. If you can't do it I will get someone else.' Just then a large lump of grass from the roof fell onto him and he said, 'Those rats are bad here.' Later on he saw splinters fly out of the wall near him and he stopped work for a moment and asked, 'Were those rats on the roof?' I said, 'No, bullets.' I had to yell as he was very deaf and could not hear the noise of the bullets . . . Years later Dr. Vernon and I spoke of that night and he thought his deafness was a godsend at times, as he could not hear the firing and did not get jumpy. He certainly moved fairly quickly when the splinters flew off the wall, and he said it was the first he knew that we were under fire at the Aid Post.[17]

Doc Vernon also recalled the situation at this point as Major Watson came in to check on the CO. Soon after, four or five walking wounded came in quick succession, who after treatment were told to make their own way back to Deniki. Wilkinson 'held the lantern for me and every time he raised it a salvo of machine-gun bullets was fired at the building. Owing to this particular enemy machine gun being as yet a little below the edge of the escarpment, probably just behind Graham's back premises, its range was bound to be too high and, while the roof was riddled, those working below could feel reasonably safe.' Doc Vernon, the Gallipoli and Great War veteran, added he was 'very glad to have Jack Wilkinson with me. He had been an old friend on Misima, and thanks to his professional capabilities, courageous demeanour, and his long military experience in Greece and Crete, I felt every confidence in him.'[18]

•

The two spotters and radio operators, Clive Turnbull and Bernard Murphy, were also in the thick of it. A major problem with their transmitter was that it made one 'hell of a racket' and they reckoned it could be heard kilometres away—they were probably right. Murphy recalled: 'The Japanese were never far away, but we kept the brigade traffic going back to Wonga and Rouna Falls. We were often under machine gun fire, or mortar attacks. Even the mountain gun had a go at us.'[19] Murphy and

Turnbull would continue to transmit messages while under fire, forced to relocate several times. This was no simple procedure as it required the packing and transportation of equipment—and trying to keep it dry. They finally lost their teleradio and transmitter to Japanese gunfire in early September just south of Isurava; each was awarded the Military Medal for their courage and resourcefulness during the early days of the campaign.[20]

25

'I told them with a smile, not to spread rumours'

About 3.30 a.m., Captain Stevenson and Lieutenant Brewer moved out from what had been the assistant resident magistrate's house—about 40 metres from the centre of the desperate hand-to-hand fighting that was breaking out. Stevenson reached a group of men in the darkness— yelling at them to move forward and throwing grenades over their heads to try to keep the enemy at bay. It was then that a devastating crossfire cut across both flanks of the group, while, from their right, someone began to throw grenades at Stevenson and Brewer. Stevenson suddenly realised the men he had been calling on for help were Japanese—such was the confusion of the fighting.[1]

The Japanese had broken through the northern perimeter. The Australian and Papuan troops were now forced to fall back. Wilkinson recalled that they 'could not carry Owen. Thought he was gone several times.'[2] Doc Vernon also recalled: 'At the point of our withdrawal he had become quite still and was on the point of death. He probably did not survive another fifteen minutes.'[3] Lieutenant Garland recalled Watson's decision to evacuate Kokoda: 'Major Watson . . . felt that the action had been going on long enough and it was around about four in the morning and he didn't want to be surrounded, the most important thing that Captain Templeton said to me was: "Whatever you do, you must defend the track, because the rest of the 39th Battalion is on the way over the ranges, so do not be captured, defend the track." Watson sensibly ordered a withdrawal.'[4]

Major Watson now ordered Lieutenant Garland and his men of 10 Platoon to fall back to form a line across the plateau to cover the withdrawal of 11 and 12 platoons. By now he had only two sections, as Corporal Markham and his section were still below the plateau. Before moving out, a runner was sent to contact Markham to tell him that they were falling back, but the man could not get through. Garland recalled his men shouted to him, but 'he failed to respond ... Our withdrawal from Kokoda plateau continued, platoon by platoon until we reached Deniki. That was my platoon's first action against the Japanese and one I will never forget.'[5]

Sergeant Major Joseph Dawson also recalled: 'They eventually over-ran us ... and so we were then ordered by Major Watson ... to move back to Deniki and it was absolutely chaotic because the Japs had got through our lines and we had lost a lot killed and wounded; the wounded had gone. They'd moved back along the Track. You didn't know whether [those around you] were Aussies or Japs. Anyway, we pulled out of there, and a few managed to get out through the scrub a few days later. And we got back to Deniki'.[6] Among the last to leave were Watson, Stevenson, Brewer and Morrison, just as Lieutenant Colonel Bill Owen was taking his last breaths.[i]

Meanwhile, Doc Vernon and Jack Wilkinson were preparing to get the last of the wounded back to Deniki as the first men began to retire off the plateau. At this point, Stevenson made an appearance, as recalled by Wilkinson: 'Captain Stevenson said to wait until I saw at least several lots go past and send some wounded with each lot. Bullets were coming through the roof of the Aid Post and also knocking splinters out of the wall. Double walls; fortunately, they were thick enough to stop most coming through ... We left Kokoda in the early hours of the morning in small batches. I waited until I saw Dr. Vernon get out and then I put a lot of dressings and things into a blanket and left also.'[7] Doc Vernon, however, was anxious to get his gear from Graham's house, as recalled by Wilkinson: 'Vernon tried to return to Graham's house for his gear

---

i   Lieutenant Colonel William Owen was the first Australian to be recognised by the United States for bravery in the SWPA; he was posthumously awarded the United States Distinguished Service Cross.

but managed to get him not to [go as a] sniper [was] there. Light mist is our saving.'[8] Doc Vernon also recalled:

I spoke of returning to Graham's house for my bag, but already it was a death trap and I was advised to let the Japs have my things. Before leaving, I spent some 5 to 10 minutes in the RAP during which we fixed up the Colonel, he was now dying, as comfortably as possible, moistening his mouth and cleaning him up. Then I stuffed our operating instruments and a few dressings into my pockets, seized the lantern, and went out towards the rubber. The rest of the medical equipment had to be abandoned, but it was not very extensive, and I think we saved all the instruments. Outside the mist had grown very dense but the moonlight allowed me to see where I was going. Thick white streams of vapour stole between the rubber trees and turned the whole scene into a weird combination of light and shadows. The mist was greatly to our advantage; our own line of retreat remained perfectly plain, but it must have slowed down the enemy's advance considerably, another chance factor that helped to save the Kokoda force. After a hasty look round the almost deserted plateau, I walked into the rubber. Firing was still heavy, coming I suppose from the Japs as many of our men had left.[9]

Helping to cover the withdrawal were Bren gunners Private William 'Snowy' Parr, a twenty-year-old textile worker from Wonthaggi in Victoria, with his mate, 31-year-old Private Horace 'Rusty' Hollow from Mildura in Victoria. They provided covering fire which helped the rest of the men fall back, but with each burst of fire the two men gave away their position and were forced to give ground. At this stage, around 25 Japanese suddenly appeared in a clearing close to Parr and his mate. The Bren gunners blasted the enemy troops at close range. Brewer said later: 'I saw Japs dropping.'[10] Parr thought he got about fifteen of them. 'You couldn't miss.'[11] Only after they had expended all of their ammunition did they finally withdraw, with Parr turning to Hollow, merely saying 'Come on Rusty' and with this they disappeared in the mist and darkness heading for Deniki.[12]

Doc Vernon had taken up a position rolling a newspaper with tobacco and within seconds was having a smoko, puffing behind a tree at the edge of the plantation.

I stayed a while on the edge of the rubber hoping to strike someone in authority, but as all the men were hurrying out to Deniki, I slowly followed them. I had not gone far before I felt uneasy at leaving the combat area while any troops who might have been wounded remained there. In the 1914–18 Sinai Campaign it was drummed into me that the place of the MO was at the tail of any retreating column in company with the Second in Command. I had many a scramble over the sandhills with 2 or 3 AMC men and no one else between the Turks, and us and usually found such hurried getaways somewhat exhilarating. Hence, at Kokoda, where my orders had been second hand, on reflection I thought I should remain for a while, at least till I had met some responsible officer, and I called to several withdrawing parties to ask if there were any officers amongst them. The men seemed neither to know nor greatly to care; their orders to leave had been definite enough and they were carrying them out.

By now I had gone nearly half a mile through the rubber, and I turned back and hid behind the trunk of a tree just at the edge of the Kokoda clearing, in sight of the RAP and station garden. Firing had almost died down, and the parties making for the hill were smaller and came less frequently. Finally, after a long period during which no one passed, and I was beginning to think I had better leave too, Major Watson MC, in company with Lt. Brewer and a couple of officers of the 39th, passed along the track.

I felt considerably relieved and leaving my hiding place called to Watson who said, 'Come on, we are the last out.' Actually, two men followed us a little later [Parr and Hollow]. I heard afterwards that the station was then full of Japs, but in the mist, I recognised no-one nor was I molested in any way. The major sent Brewer on ahead and [he] walked very leisurely through the plantation. At the time his dawdling rather mystified me but I put it down to his being very tired, but this was not the case for later he explained to me that he had dallied on purpose to see that all the men got out, and his subsequent good spirits as we got well away from the battle area showed me he had not turned a hair over the night's affair.

A mile and a half along the track, we passed 'Skinners' signal post; this had been hurriedly evacuated and several boxes of soldiers' treasures lay opened and abandoned. I was told to help myself, and thus, only an hour or two later, I more or less made up my involuntary gift to some Jap or other in Kokoda.[13]

William Watson, Cathcart Stevenson, Geoffrey 'Doc' Vernon, Peter Brewer, William 'Snowy' Parr and Horace 'Rusty' Hollow were the last to leave the plantation; all pushed on to Deniki. Vernon recalled the scene after the fighting as they moved on: 'It was an experience I would not have cared to miss, and among the impressions of that exciting night none stands out more clearly than the weirdness of the natural condition; the thick white mist dimming the moonlight; the mysterious veiling of trees, houses and men; the drip of moisture from the foliage and last the almost complete silence, as if the rubber groves of Kokoda were sleeping as usual in the depths of the night, and men had not brought disturbance and death to this quiet little Papuan outpost.'[14]

The survivors fell back, jaded and very dispirited. Sergeant Major Dawson recalled, 'upon reaching Deniki we regrouped and checked our numbers—the living, the dead, the wounded and the missing'.[15] Known casualties at this point were two killed—one being their CO, Lieutenant Colonel Bill Owen. Casualties for 'B' Company were soon shown to be thirteen men, with seven killed in action and one other dying from his wounds a few days later. In all it represented 17 per cent of the company. It is traditionally recognised that any force suffering over 10 per cent casualties had suffered a 'blood bath'. The casualties among the Papuan forces remain unknown, but of the twenty or so who had been at Kokoda, only ten had made their way to Deniki after the battle. Additionally, several men had been cut off and were missing. Most of these would be led to safety by Papuan corporal George Meta, arriving at Kairuku Station on Yule Island three weeks later and then crossing the Owen Stanleys to Port Moresby.[16]

The battalion war diary records that, after the battle, the total strength of all four Australian platoons (including the Company HQ) now at Deniki amounted to just five officers and 67 men, not including the ten men of the 1st PIB.[17] Using the original numbers of 'B' Company after crossing the Owen Stanleys, and including the arrival of 16 Platoon ('D' Company) as well as Bill Owen and his two signallers, the men of the 39th Battalion, who had been fighting the Japanese for just one week, had already suffered around 50 per cent casualties.

Wilkinson recalled finding 'several wounded on track and bandaged them. Reached Deniki after daylight.'[18] On arriving, he looked around at the scattered party of survivors: 'At Deniki there was a bit of reorganisation, and the wounded were sent back.'[19] Most of the Australians at Deniki were very young and, as recorded by the Australian official historian of the campaign, Dudley McCarthy, they 'felt very isolated; their enemies were the best soldiers in the world at that time in jungle warfare'.[20]

•

The pitifully young Australian troops may have felt out-gunned and outclassed, but the Japanese certainly did not think so as expressed in captured Japanese documents relating to the fighting at Kokoda on 29 July. Private Watanabe Toshi with No. 1 Company wrote at the time that he and his comrades were also feeling very much alone.[21] Another captured document relating to the fighting during this period stated: 'The [Australians] are skilled marksmen and expert grenade throwers' with another stating the Australians 'have greater fighting spirit ... [than] English, American and Filipino troops'.[22] Indeed, many believed that they had been doing battle with over 1000 enemy troops. Certainly, the Japanese did not get it all their way and, like the Australians who lost their commanding officer, Lieutenant Colonel William Owen, the Japanese of No. 1 Company lost their OC, Captain Ogawa Tetsuo, in the battle.[23] A captured Japanese diary belonging to 2nd Lieutenant Noda Hidetaka of III Battalion of the regiment was later translated; he wrote on 1 August 1942 while still on Rabaul:

Overcast, occasionally fine. Last night when the soldiers were chatting together, I heard them say that Lt [*sic*] OGAWA . . . Commander of No. 1 Company, had been killed in action. I told them with a smile, not to spread rumours but this morning, when I was walking on the North Side of the command group who were reading out the Imperial Rescript., 2nd Lt HAMAGUCHI confirmed that Lt [*sic*] OGAWA had been killed.

Being very surprised I hurried to the office and looking at the report found that in the KOKODA area our advance force, who have been engaged in battle with 1200 of the enemy had suffered unexpectedly heavy casualties.

I appreciate the fact that we shall meet up with various difficulties before reaching MORESBY. Many brave souls have been scattered to the winds and have not seen MORESBY except in their dreams. Alas they have gone, but uncompellingly, and now we reach on to MORESBY through the spirit of the departed. Surmounting all difficulties, we will carry out this great battle unfalteringly and with great spirit.[24]

Second Lieutenant Noda Hidetaka went on to record that he was concerned that he was too soft to take on the responsibility of command, providing a rare candid picture of a young Japanese officer in self-doubt.

The Medical inspection of those weakened by sickness was carried out to determine whether or not they are sufficiently fit for battle. The leaders of our company were present. Many commanders like to take into battle with them as many of their men as possible but, in contrast to this, I myself incline to leave behind many of those who are not really fit. Can it be that I am not sufficiently ruthless? It is a matter regarding which some self-examination is necessary. I am worried because I cannot unconcernedly overlook another's troubles and the feeling grows on me that as a commander I am lacking in sincerity. I feel that I am becoming detached from my comrades through insufficient mental discipline.

Diligent people talk of their hopes. Lazy people bemoan their misfortune. I will rectify my lack of mental discipline by diligence and industry.

At 1300 hrs had my inoculation with the 4th mixture. On the way back [I] . . . learnt that . . . Lieutenant TOKUHIRA has malaria. Since yesterday my head has been heavy and my nose stopped up and I feel as though I have a cold.

After the inoculation I thought I would read but couldn't concentrate so passed the time doing nothing. When a weak man starts thinking and examining his mind at quiet moments, he exhausts himself to the point of sickness without accomplishing anything. Why is my faith in myself so incomplete, it was not like that when I left school? That I should now be worried by matters temporal is due to the military environment.

As the great SAIGO said: 'Man is a mere nothing, Heaven is the great opponent.'[25]

Lieutenant Noda and the men of the II and III battalions of the 144th Regiment, reinforced with the II Battalion of the 41st Regiment, would soon be placed in several transports, leaving Rabaul to continue the fight against the Australians in the mountains of the Owen Stanleys.

26

'Every carrier is precious'

On Captain Stevenson's return to Deniki during the morning of 29 July he sent a signal to Port Moresby: 'Kokoda lost from this morning. Below the drome and road east of Oivi. Owen mortally wounded and captured. Templeton missing.' This message was then passed on to GHQ in Brisbane, which issued the following misinformation to the press: 'Gona—Allied ground patrols attacked and drove back the enemy from his advanced outpost positions.' The next day this was followed by: 'Kokoda—Allied and enemy forward elements engaged in skirmishes in this area.'[1]

Lieutenant Brewer, on arriving at Deniki, relocated the radio station, '25 minutes' walk to rear of Deniki. A second radio was installed at ISURAVA. I instructed W.O. Brown to proceed to ISURAVA to take charge of the carrier organisation.'[2]

Later that day Jack Wilkinson at Deniki recorded in his diary: 'Dr. Vernon, Don Barnes and self—worked all morning on wounded. Took up position on road and new section under Lt. McNamara arrived. Don Barnes left with wounded ... My nerves on edge ... Many others on edge. Troops dejected about Captain Templeton. He may still come back as some others have. He was Uncle Sam to all.'[3] Doc Vernon also recorded in his diary that, 'we reached Deniki at 0830. I checked the wounded and found several who had not passed through the R.A.P. at Kokoda. A bullet was extracted from the knee of one soldier ... We moved back 2 or 3 hundred yards to the rear of Deniki for cover, and here, many white troops came for treatment. We remained there that night.'[4]

Indeed, Wilkinson recorded that Doc treated Private Otto Menz, a 23-year-old labourer from Daylesford in Victoria: 'I think it was Otto Menz, [who] had a bullet in his knee and we operated in the village. A "45" bullet, one of ours, had hit the spoon and fork he had in the top of his legging and had ricocheted off upwards. It had entered his leg below the knee and then run around the knee and settled about 4 inches above it and about half an inch deep. Dr. Vernon cut it out while Don and I held the patient, who groaned a little but was really good. He later walked back to Moresby. All of the earlier wounds had both entrance and exit of the bullet. Otto was given the bullet as a souvenir.'[5]

•

Corporal Markham and his small party of men from Lieutenant Arthur 'Judy' Garland's 10 Platoon, who were last seen fighting below the northern slopes of the plateau, were making good their escape. Their mates now at Deniki believed their position had been overrun; they had called out to them just before withdrawing but received no reply; they were judged as killed in action. Markham would prove them wrong.

With the fighting appearing to die down on the plateau above, Markham and his men detected the sounds of the Japanese all around them. They realised that they were now alone; it was pointless to fight off a whole Japanese battalion with fewer than twelve men—the 'odds and sod' attached to his section had already made good their escape. He decided to bluff his way out of this predicament. They would climb onto the plateau and, in line, casually walk through the station into the rubber and to Deniki beyond. Remarkably, though they could hear the Japanese all around, in the darkness they were never challenged, and they moved through the administration area towards the plantation. They were soon in among the rubber and, having found the track, pushed forward, with Markham recalling they tried hard to avoid walking on the shells of the rubber seeds 'which lay thickly on the ground, and seemed to crack deafeningly, as we crept thru the now semi-moonlit plantation'.[6]

As they pushed deeper into the plantation, he recalled: 'Any moment during that twenty-minute walk, we expected to meet resistance; every clump of bushes was a machine-gun nest; every fallen log a Jap gunner; and as we walked, the slight rattle of the arms and clanking together of the drum mags., sounded like the clashing of symbols. Torture was in the minds of many, when one of our number started coughing. This happened at odd times throughout the whole hour's walk, and one <u>almost</u> inclined to believe, that had I given the order some would have strangled the culprit without compunction.'[7]

However, up ahead they saw Japanese soldiers who were setting up an ambush position—there was no way of knowing how many others were nearby. Markham and his men quietly retraced their steps down the track for a short distance and pushed into the scrub on their left. He later recorded in his diary:

That section of our journey will stay long in my memory. Scrambling over the sweet-potato-vine covered logs, disappearing at times from view, it's a wonder some of us didn't break our legs. It was more trying to the nerves than anything for we made such a 'hellava' din; what with dropping of rifles and pouches we imagined our number to be up at any moment; but the gods were with us, and our troubles had only just begun—before us literally a wall of vines and undergrowth. It was quite dark now too. There was nothing for it but to cut our way through; this we proceeded to do, using our bayonets for the job. Getting further into the scrub the moon's rays could be seen at intervals, thereby giving us a general idea of our direction. Hacking our way forward for about half an hour, we decided our position secure and rested . . .

Reforming [sic] once more into single file, we pushed, cut and dragged ourselves nearer to our destination—so we hoped anyway. It was still dark as we made our way with difficulty, blundering at times into stinging bushes and at others into small swamps. On striking the first swamp we decided that it was now safe to show the way with my torch and our progress was thereby made a lot easier. At least we no longer waded through the bogs not knowing whether we were at its widest or narrowest part. Coming to a very thick patch of barbed wire vine and not being able to see where it started or finished, we worked through it with difficulty. This finally accomplished, we decided as we were pretty near exhausted, not to go any further until daylight, which was not more than half an hour off.

With permission to smoke, the lads soon had a cig' rolled and lit, their looks of relief showing how they appreciated this luxury.

In the event of our becoming lost, which nevertheless seemed improbable, I checked our number of 'E' rations, and worked out a daily quota should it be required. Gradually the dawn approached and when we could see our way clearly, we set off once again, now taking our direction from the glow of the rising sun.

From then on, the way ahead was much clearer, and we were able to take the scrub in our stride. I knew there were about four creeks to cross so when the fourth was met we followed it upstream. Sometimes we were able to follow the bank but mostly we walked in the creek itself as climbing the banks all the time was too tiring. Our intention was to keep following the creek until we came to the track leading to Deniki.

On and on we splashed along the creek, wondering if we would ever come to the track. Once we received rather a shock when a wild pig that our splashing had disturbed, dashed from near us into the undergrowth with much crashing of sticks and brush. At long last, we saw the track in the distance. Stopping the men, I went ahead to see if all was clear and, finding it was, signaled them to close up.

One of the lads offered to go forward as scout so after he had gone ahead and signaled OK, we followed on.

Cautiously but speedily we went, for as yet we had nothing to indi-cate how far our enemy had advanced along the track. At about 1000 hours we heaved great sighs of relief when we saw halfway up, on a long steep section of the track, a member of one of our forward patrols waving us to come on. Needless to relate, we were not backward in doing so.[8]

•

The other companies of the 39th Battalion were making their way north-wards along the Kokoda Track through the mountains towards Deniki, including the battalion's Vickers Machine Gun unit ('E' Company) whose 100 or so men had exchanged their machine guns and equipment for rifles. The battalion war diary records for 29 July:

O.C., C Coy, R.M.O., and Sig. Off [Signal Officer] left EORA CROSSING at 1000 hrs with one sec [section] and moved to ISURAVA. Here—there were many conflicting reports as to the situation forward. The I.O. [Intelligence Officer] and the Section Commanded by Cpl. [Ronald] MCWHA was sent forward to ascertain the exact situation. The party arrived at DENIKI at 1800 hrs, and the section was immediately placed in posn [position] to strengthen the meagre defence. The I.O., advised Capt. DEAN by W/T [Wireless Transmission] of the intention to hold DENIKI and forwarded Major WATSON's request that C Coy come forward as soon as possible. The main body of C Coy, having been equipped from stores which had come forward by native carriers, and moved on to ISURAVA during the day under command of the 2i/c ([Kenneth] JACOB). A Coy moved up to KAGI, M.G. Coy ['E' Company] to NAURU [*sic* Nauro] and D Coy, less one Pl [McClean's 16 Platoon] to IORIBAIWA.[9]

With 'C' Company was Lance Corporal Kevin Whelan, a 22-year-old labourer from Healesville in Victoria, attached to 15 Platoon. Waiting for him at Eora Creek was a parcel from his uncle which had been carried up the line by carriers: 'My uncle, a cigar maker, sent me a box of cigars and it arrived with mail at Eora Creek which was getting pretty close to the "front line". It was pouring with rain and I knew that if I tried to carry cigars with me, they would get soaked, so I gave one to everybody in the platoon. There were just enough to go round, and we all lit up—you can imagine the smell of tobacco. And did Captain Dean blow his top! He said the Japs would be able to smell them for miles.'[10]

After the appropriate dressing down, they pushed on the next day to Isurava, and it was here that they came across some wounded and sick from Lieutenant McClean's 16 Platoon who had fought the Japanese at Oivi. Whelan recalled many years later: 'Next day at Isurava we struck some of 16 Platoon who had been flown over Kokoda with Doug McClean, and I will never forget the battle-weary look on their faces.

I was shocked. I had a yarn with Joe and Charlie Pyke—(Charlie won a MM at Oivi or Kokoda). I'd been mates with them since before the war and we used to go to parties and dances together. They started to fill me in about the Japs and I began to feel a little less brave.'[11]

•

By 29 July, Lieutenant Kienzle was back at Kagi: 'I sent Arms and Ammunition onto EORA CREEK as urgent requests for these supplies came in ... At 1615 hrs the first KOKODA/BUNA evacuees came in and gave us firsthand accounts of Jap landing at BUNA and [their] push to KOKODA. Telephone line has not reached us yet, connection as far as MANARI and expected to reach EFOGI tomorrow.'[12] With the fall of Kokoda, Bert and Meryl's home was now in Japanese hands; he wrote to Meryl:

> I am fit and well after the fourth journey on this track towards home ... Our home is in for some hot fighting and I am going to see what I can do. Don't worry about me dear—I'll look after others and myself to the best of my ability ... All I have with me is a change of clothes, 2 blankets and one boy. The rest of my gear is back at the end of the line. Every carrier is precious ... Wish this business could only end soon but fear it will last for years ... This fight is going to be tough. Old Doc Vernon is an old tiger. As soon as he heard of it he made straight for the Valley—he is attached to my unit ... Never thought I would have to not only help build and organise a big job in the army but also fight for my own home and properties. Wait until that day comes to a number of Australians in Australia. Hope it never comes to pass, but some people need shaking up. Trust my brother Wallace is safe.[13]

Back at Port Moresby there were now concerns about the morale of the carriers with the news that Kokoda had fallen to the Japanese, as recorded in the ANGAU war diary, '... it became known that the pressure of the Japanese at Buna and the subsequent capture of Kokoda had caused a serious rupture in native morale'.[14] Indeed, it was reported at the time by a central district officer close to Moresby that his patrol was a 'timely one. The natives were showing signs of restlessness and were under the impression that there was no Government. I soon disabused their minds on the idea. Every opportunity was taken to impress the natives with the fact that there was a Government. A strong Government. An Army Government. That they would be protected as heretofore but that they would have to work harder than before. That they would have to make roads and aerodromes if it was considered necessary.'[15]

•

Within hours of the Japanese occupying the plateau, the troops of No. 3 Company, I/144th Regiment, commanded by Lieutenant Nose Munekichi, were approaching Kokoda. Among these men was 2nd Lieutenant Onogawa, leading No. 2 Platoon, who recalled the heavy fog in the Kokoda basin; he was wondering if that was why the Australians failed to counter-attack the plateau. He was not to know that the Australian force at Kokoda before the attack had consisted of around 100 men and the survivors were in no condition to launch a counter-attack. Clearly it was becoming an established 'fact' to the Japanese that they were facing an Australian force numbering around 1000 men. Onogawa noticed with daybreak that all was quiet; all that could be heard was the odd burst of machine-gun fire. At 10 a.m., he was sent from Kokoda with 90 men—two-thirds of the company—to bring forward supplies along with bicycles. Three days later they returned to Kokoda with 70 bicycles and supplies for 135 men that would last just three days.[16]

The logistical bottleneck was already taking its toll even at this early stage of the Kokoda Campaign—every day the Australian militia held up the Japanese advance, was a further day that added to the Japanese problems of supply. The Japanese had limited resources and planned to be at Port Moresby within two weeks of committing themselves to its capture. At this point they had not even climbed the northern slopes of the mountain barrier—their schedule dictated that by now they should have been south of Isurava, where a detailed reconnaissance of the way forward would determine whether the attack against Port Moresby from the track was feasible—although the order had already gone out to capture Port Moresby using the Kokoda Track. However, they were still well below Deniki at Kokoda, apparently licking their wounds.[17]

Indeed, just as Onogawa and most of the men were being detailed to bring forward supplies, the Sakigawa Transport Unit around Buna and Sanananda were working on vehicle maintenance to push more supplies forward. During the afternoon these men divided their time between road construction and the unloading of supplies from the recently arrived *Ryoyo Maru*, *Kotoku Maru* and other vessels that had anchored just offshore. Priority was given to unloading food and ammunition, as all were concerned about the potential for Allied airstrikes; the eleven trucks onboard the *Kotoku Maru* were to be the last to be brought ashore. However, the worst fears of the Japanese were soon realised.[18]

27

'This was the first time a lone white man had appeared amongst them'

The US 8th Bomb Squadron conducted a sortie against the Japanese ships in the afternoon; they would pay a high price for their success. Seven A-24 Banshee dive bombers—the US Army Air Forces' version of the US Navy's slow but rugged Douglas SBD Dauntless dive bomber— were led by Major Floyd 'Buck' Rogers' squadron. They were to be supported by a flight of fighters, but both elements became separated in thick cloud cover over the Owen Stanleys. Knowing that he and his airmen no longer had fighter cover, and that the Banshee was no match against the Japanese Zero, Rogers continued his mission, knowing how critical it was to bomb the convoy now unloading.

As the clumsy and slow-moving bombers approached their targets, they were jumped by nine agile Zero fighters. Even so, all but one conducted a dive-bombing run against the convoy, focusing on drop-ping their bombs as opposed to dodging the Zeros all around them. Rogers was the only one to score a direct hit—his bomb exploding into an open hatch of the 6700-ton *Kotoku Maru*; the trucks and much of her cargo went down with her. Five of the six bombers never returned, including that of Major Floyd Rogers and his rear gunner whose aircraft was last seen on fire, crashing into the sea. Those flown by Captain Virgil Schwab and lieutenants 'Big Joe' Joseph Parker, Robert Cassels and Claude Dean also failed to return, along with their rear gunners, while another flown by Lieutenant John Hill was badly damaged but made its way back. His rear gunner, Sergeant Ralph Sam, died of his wounds shortly after landing.[1]

Lieutenant Parker belly-landed his aircraft on a beach near Ambasi—he and his rear gunner, Corporal Franklyn Hoppe, survived; while Lieutenant Dean also managed to make a successful forced landing nearby with his rear gunner, Sergeant Loree LeBoeuf. Lieutenant Cassels managed to bail out of his stricken aircraft behind enemy lines, but the fate of his rear gunner remains unknown. Within days, all five airmen had joined up with Lieutenant Arthur Smith and his men of the 1st PIB who were trapped behind enemy lines heading for Kokoda.[2]

•

Rogers and his brave airmen did not die in vain as they not only sank one transport they also forced the remainder to up anchor and head back to Rabaul with little of their precious cargo reaching the beach. This seriously disrupted the Japanese timetable, given their paucity of supplies. Indeed, Sergeant Ikeshima and his eighteen men of Sakigawa Transport Unit had been relying on the trucks and cargo onboard the *Kotoku Maru* to supply the forward troops. The next day they were forced instead to work on road maintenance, finding it difficult to get even a few picks and shovels.

The ongoing Allied airstrikes against shipping at sea and at Buna and Sanananda resulted in a critical shortage of food, ammunition, vehicles and reinforcements. To make matters worse, combat officers and men were now arriving at intermediate depots and helping themselves to their unit's requirements, disregarding the protests from the officers and men of the Sakigawa Transport Unit.[3]

Among the few Japanese who had managed to get ashore before Major Floyd Rogers' sortie was Private Teruoka Akira and his comrades of the Tanaka Unit, 55th Division Medical Unit, who were now pushing forward from Buna towards Kokoda. They had planned to march at night to avoid being targeted by Allied aircraft, but the dangers of becoming lost made this impossible and they had to march during daylight hours to ensure they remained on the main track. Over the next week most Japanese would notice increased Allied aerial attacks around Kokoda, Oivi and Buna, including its airfield.[4]

Japanese Imperial General Headquarters staff officer Lieutenant Colonel Tsuji Masanobu had left for Buna on 25 July but had been wounded onboard a destroyer that was attacked by Allied airmen. While recovering from his wounds back in Rabaul he reported his concerns to the commander of the 25th Air Flotilla and sent the following message to the Army Department of Imperial General Headquarters, clearly demonstrating the famous rivalry within and between the Japanese armed services: 'At the end of July, the enemy has air superiority over the Buna area. Although the navy's air strength amounts to only twenty fighters and thirty bombers, the realities of the situation are not passed on to army command.'[5]

•

It was not only the Allied airmen who were seriously disrupting the Japanese timetable and advance. The Australian militiamen of the 39th Battalion, and Australians and Papuans of the 1st PIB and RPC, had put up a good fight, sowing confusion among the Japanese commanders who now believed that they were facing at least a battalion, not just a company. This assessment was not solely based on the unforeseen fighting abilities of these few men, but also from the misinformation supplied by Captain Templeton just before his execution. As such, the Japanese commanders approached more cautiously than planned. Doc Vernon later wrote in his diary about the first battle for Kokoda, which brought the Japanese advance to a standstill for over a whole precious week.

> Looking back on the Japanese assault on Kokoda, I can now see that by withdrawing we took the wisest course. That we were considerably outmanned by the enemy was only too certain—we had but ninety combatants, not counting a detachment of the PIB, whereas the Japanese force was variably estimated at three to five hundred men. Besides this advantage in numbers they had others. Particularly in that our line of retreat was practically undefended and open to them had they worked around to our rear. In that case the entire force would

have been surrounded and capture or death the fate of every individual. By withdrawing in good time, we saved men who later held up the Japs till reinforcements arrived—a very good example of the military axiom that 'the only conclusive victory consists in the complete annihilation of enemy forces' . . . I was told that the Japs fell freely as they stormed the escarpment, but that there were too many of them to account for all. Their casualties must have been far heavier than ours—this was the case throughout the Owen Stanley Campaign— and I was given different estimates of 30 to 70 killed during the assault.[i] Taking it all round, though our early retreat prevented full resistance the results could hardly have been bettered. There was no point in further defending that desolate mass of mountains which lay behind us. Setting aside small clashes round Sangara and the more extensive delaying actions at Wire Rope [Wairopi] and Oivi the assault on Kokoda can be called the first pitched battle on Papuan soil.[6]

Doc Vernon also recalled that the most difficult job assigned to the carriers was only now becoming increasingly recognised as Australian casualties mounted.

The hardest work allotted to our boys was that of carrying out the wounded on stretchers. Right at the start of the homeward trail from Iora [sic Eora], there rose one of the roughest and steepest hills on the whole route, and even without a load it was a strain to clamber up the almost vertical slopes and flounder on over roots and boulders. A double set of bearers, eight in all, had to be sent as less could not have done the work. I tried always to keep the number of stretcher cases down to a minimum. As there was no general order for immediate evacuation, and Iora [sic] Creek was not then threatened in any way by the enemy, and rough as the nursing was there, nothing any better existed short of Moresby. There was a general wish to be moved back but I explained to several stretcher cases that if they waited a little longer at Iora [sic] they might become walking cases, and most

---

i   Williams assesses that the Japanese casualties amounted to 38, with 12 of these men KIA.

of them, realizing the strain put on the bearers, cheerfully agreed to wait. Only once did persuasion fail; a private soldier, who had been doing some wonderful juggling with his rifle, had managed to shoot himself through the foot. The wound was not serious, but it was very painful, and he insisted upon being carried back to Efogi. The nature of the wound stiffened my determination to save eight of my men such exhaustive work; he was told he could go back on foot if he did not wish to remain at Iora [sic]. He remained where he was.[7]

Captain Tom Grahamslaw had started his long hard slog across the Owen Stanleys to get help for McKenna, Bitmead and the two American airmen, Thompson and Bender. He later wrote of passing through a number of villages in his desperate bid to reach Abau: 'My story was invariably the same: that after the land hungry Japanese killers of men and seducers of women, had over-run Buna and Kokoda, I had decided to walk to Port Moresby by the quickest route to guide Australian soldiers who would kill the Japanese and restore the land to its native people.'[8] Overall, while the people appeared friendly towards him, he still had his doubts and wrote of his concerns almost 30 years later.

I would demand the production of the village constable's register. Then I would write something in it to impress the village constable. Incidentally, four years had elapsed since the previous patrol in this area by 'Mac' Rich from Tufi . . . The village people always provided sufficient food without demur. This was usually sweet potato, which was the stable [sic] food in the mountain regions. Sweet potato, without the benefit of salt, is most unappetizing. Your appetite goes after a few mouthfuls. However, it was necessary to eat about 5lb [2.3 kilograms] each day to keep going.

One of my main difficulties was persuading village people to supply enough firewood to keep a fire going at night. I did not possess a blanket, and at heights above 4000 ft [1200 metres] it gets almost unbearably cold at night. The mountain hamlets (there were no large villages) were built on treeless spurs (for safety reasons), and firewood had to be carried for a considerable distance—hence the understandable reluctance on the part of the people to meet my requests, particularly as I was unable to proffer payment.

Yet perhaps the most trying part of the journey was having to retell my story so many times in each village. Men returning from garden places late at night would insist on visiting my hut to see me and hear my story. On these occasions it was not good for my nerves to hear stealthy noises and then glimpse silhouetted figures peering at me from the ladder leading into the hut. I would sit up and, in a matter-of-fact voice, ask them what they wanted. Then my story would have to be told once again.[9]

On trekking across the mountains, he believed that if he were to tarry awhile in any one place his number would be up, as patrols had been few and far between. 'This was the first time a lone white man had appeared amongst them and there must have been the temptation to dispose of [me] at times. But I was aware that . . . natives rarely commit an act of this nature until they have discussed it among themselves at some length and formulated a plan, and I made a point of arriving late and departing at first light. In the high altitudes it was rare to see any sign of activity until the sun's warmth began to penetrate, and by that time I was well on my way.'[10]

PART FOUR

THE SECOND BATTLE FOR KOKODA

28

'A heap of boots that never dried out'

Major Allan Cameron, a 33-year-old lawyer from Elwood in Victoria, had commanded 'C' Company of the 2/22nd Battalion on New Britain as part of Lark Force, and like Bill Owen, he had managed to avoid capture. With a small group he had escaped from the northern coast after finding a small boat and, sailing undetected by the Japanese, made it to the coast of mainland New Guinea, landing near Buna. Not knowing the area, they trekked across country before coming across an ANGAU patrol and soon they were transported by sea to Port Moresby. Cameron was then promoted to Brigade Major of the 30th Brigade but with the death of Lieutenant Colonel Owen he was placed in temporary command of the 39th Battalion and Maroubra Force. He was now hurriedly making his way across the Kokoda Track towards Deniki.[1]

•

By midday 30 July, Captain Arthur Cyril Dean and his men of 'C' Company had arrived at Deniki with supplies and ammunition. Watson's men were sitting in water-logged weapons pits. One can only imagine the feeling of relief that washed over the surviving veterans of 'B' Company and the 1st PIB and RPC at seeing their reinforcements finally arrive. Even so, the battalion war diary records underwhelmingly: 'C Coy arrived at DENIKI at approx., 1200 hrs. Capt., DEAN then took command of all 39th Bn troops in area and became 2i/c to Major WATSON (comd., MAROUBRA FORCE).'[2]

Dean distributed his three platoons, with 13 Platoon placed forward astride the main Deniki–Kokoda track about a 10-minute walk beyond Deniki; 14 Platoon was placed along the track to the rear of the village; while 15 Platoon covered the right flank. Now settling into his position at Deniki was Lance Corporal Whelan and his mates of 15 Platoon, who had pushed forward from Isurava having smoked their cigars; he recalled being able to see the Japanese far below around Kokoda from his vantage point. 'When the clouds lifted, we could see the Japs moving about on the Kokoda air strip, but they didn't attack. Probably still licking their wounds and waiting for reinforcements.' At this point he was concerned as he had no weapon; he had been told to leave his Lewis gun behind before setting out, as Bren guns would be flown in to Kokoda. While he must have been pleased he did not have to carry his Lewis gun across the track, he was now at the front with nothing to defend himself with. 'Anyway,' recalled Whelan with obvious relief, 'the Brens must have come up with the carrier line because a couple of days later our platoon commander, Lieutenant [Stewart] Johnston, gave me a long wooden box with a Bren inside it. I'd never seen one before. "Johnno" told me to wipe all the grease from it and then he'd show me how to assemble it. I didn't know that in a few days' time I would have to use it for real, but I fell in love with it and nursed it like a baby.'[3]

The rest of the battalion was fast approaching, with 'A' Company arriving at Eora Crossing, 'E' Company making its way to Efogi and the remainder of 'D' Company reinforced with a platoon from No. 2 anti-aircraft unit, which had hurriedly been converted to a rifle platoon, arriving at Nauro.[4] Among these men was 21-year-old Private Stanley Barcham, from Box Hill in Victoria, who not only recalled the hardship of crossing the track, but also vividly the beauty of the rainforest:

Apart from the hideous business of climbing these mountainous mud heaps . . . when you got on the level . . . it was absolutely magnificent. They had these great big vines and they would come down and they were all covered in green and they would hang. God they were marvellous, different colours. And then you have got these butterflies. And . . . where the trees had died across the track . . . you could press them like a sponge . . . they were that rotten and they were that full of water, they just remained like that. If you didn't jump over them or hop over them your foot would go right through them. All covered in moss looking absolutely beautiful you know, it was a marvellous site [sic], nature is a wonderful thing. You used to feel that it was a shame that we were going to muck it all up . . . But that's man for you. Smashes everything up. The butterflies . . . were absolutely magnificent. These great blue ones . . . iridescent blue. I think the little devils used to know you were on to them because they used to go over onto a prickly bush or something and you couldn't go any further anyway. You could have got them if you had nets and all of this business . . . absolutely magnificent was the canopy of the green and everything, beautiful sight I thought, just to look at. To tread through was a different story . . . strangely enough not many animals were around, I didn't see any as a matter of fact. Seen plenty of birds, those beautiful birds they have got up there . . . They tell me there was a few sea snakes or water snakes in the rivers, never struck them either. The rivers were beautiful, stone cold you know.[5]

•

Meanwhile medical arrangements were finally being organised along the track. On 30 July, Captain John Shera, a 31-year-old medical practitioner from Brisbane with the militia 14th Field Ambulance, who had recently been appointed Regimental Medical Officer of the 39th Battalion, arrived at Deniki. Medical aid posts were entitled to fly a Red Cross flag at their positions, which theoretically meant they should be safe from enemy fire. The men chose not to fly the flag though as they were frequently among 'valid' military targets and they thought the enemy would mistakenly believe that a Red Cross flag was being used to disguise military targets. They also thought the pennant could be a perfect target for gunfire and bombing. Indeed, many chose not to wear the Red Cross armband as it merely made them better targets for the Japanese.[6]

Next day, Doc Vernon was heading back south along the track to help the walking wounded making their way to Port Moresby.

Wilkinson recalled: 'I was kept fairly busy until Dr Shera arrived, and Dr Vernon went back along the line. There were only enough carriers coming through for ammo, and light food. We eventually had a telephone and wireless set operating again. Instruments were only what the orderlies could carry. A couple of big banana leaves were shelter. From this time onwards, Dr Shera was in charge.'[7] Doc Vernon also recorded: 'About mid-day I was relieved by Captain Shearer [*sic*] A.A.M.C., the first medical reinforcement to arrive, and as he had been appointed to the 39th I handed over to him.'[8]

A day after leaving Deniki, Doc Vernon made his way to Isurava and there he took time to quickly scribble an update in his diary.

> I left rather thankfully for Isurava with something better in prospect than perpetually damp clothes and nightly roosts in the rain under a canopy of banana leaves . . . The kitchen [at Isurava] was the best spot in the hut; there was a roaring fire there day and night and one of the most cheerful cooks I have ever come across, a sergeant with a badly inflamed leg who volunteered to cook for the boys in spite of being a cripple. He was not provided with great variety of materials but managed to knock up some very artistic dishes which we ate from any receptacle we could find. The space round the fire was hung with muddy shirts and pants steaming with moisture, beneath the empty drum that served as a stove was a heap of boots that never dried out, and all round the hearth lay men in the last stages of exhaustion, very thankful to get close to the blaze. It was rather a homely sort of place and the cook did not seem to mind how many men he had to shove through to get to his billy cans.[9]

•

At Deniki there was no sign of the Japanese and on 31 July Captain Dean sent out several patrols to reconnoitre the immediate area, but all reports came in that the enemy were nowhere to be seen—all remained eerily quiet.[10] Corporal Markham also recorded in his diary: 'At Deniki, we waited until news was brought in from the forward patrols, that the Japs were sitting pat for a while therefore, our defences were made as secure as possible by the main body, while our patrols brought news of movements from time to time. These patrols had minor skirmishes in forward areas, but nothing of great import happened during the days we awaited reinforcements, who were hurried onto us over the range. When, with great relief to us they did arrive, they took over from our forward positions.'[11]

By now, 'A' Company was making its way from Eora Crossing to Isurava. Sergeant Major Mowat recorded in his diary as they approached Isurava, only a few hours from Deniki: 'Hills not so steep, lots of rivers. Tree roots are a trap. Wend way around mountain side, 100-foot [30 metres] fall if you slip. Crawled across 80-foot river on narrow tree trunk. Received Bren guns here.'[12] He then recorded the last three-hour hike to reach Deniki: 'Extra hard climb, 1½ hours to the top, 1-hour descent. Native carriers marvellous. Received instructions to push on with all speed. Things serious at the front. Left packs here. Carried own equipment. Blankets put in bags, sent ahead by carrier . . . Traversed through lovely gullies. A rock gardener's dream; ferns, moss, tiny rivulets, etc. One lovely big waterfall. Weather very much cooler . . . pullovers necessary at night. Reached Deniki, took up position. Everything quiet.'[13]

Signaller Ken Phelan wrote of pushing forward and reaching the front line: 'On to Deniki, that wet, jungle-infested area that scared us all.'[14] Many years later he recalled how the reality of war hit them as they moved up from Isurava to Deniki and came across the exhausted and battle-hardened veterans: 'There we met B Company . . . They had fought these skirmishes around Kokoda. My three signalers . . . they'd all turned grey overnight, incredible. I looked at their faces, they were so distraught with terror and the fact that the Japanese were attacking and killing.'[15]

Phelan also recalled how relieved the men of 'B' Company were with their arrival: 'To have another company there was a tremendous help for them, knowing that they were not the only ones, because the Infantry soldier's most famous sentence is "Who is in front of us?" When someone at the back says "No-one" then of course you brace yourself, but that famous saying, and I used it many times throughout the war, "Who is in front of us?" That is what happened when we picked up with B Company at Deniki.'[16]

Not far behind 'A' Company was 'E' Company which had arrived at Kagi, while the men of 'D' Company had reached Efogi. Also, on the track was Lieutenant Kienzle who was making his way to Isurava from Eora Creek.

> Despite still heavy rain left at 0730 hrs for ISURAVA. Another long day. We moved forward in patrol formation owing to rumours of Jap patrols. We arrived at ISURAVA 1415 hrs ... The 'front' was a perimeter defence of DENIKI. Maj. WATSON C.O. of Maroubra Force, remnants of 'B' Coy 39 Bn and PIB now reinforced with the arrival of 'C' Coy at DENIKI and 'A' Coy at ISURAVA ready to move forward tomorrow, sent word back to me advising not to go forward but to organise the supply line from rear for rations and ammunition as the matter was of extreme urgency owing to the loss of KOKODA supplies and no reserves on hand. Owing to the steep nature of the country along the EORA CREEK valley no suitable dropping ground was close at hand to the scene of operations. I was determined to find an area suitable for dropping supplies somewhere on the main range closer to KAGI ... I advised Maj. WATSON that I know of an area of 'two dry lakes' right on top of main range which I had noted during flights across range between Yodda and Moresby before the War and asked permission to locate these. Permission was granted. Met Capt. VERNON AAMC who was resting at ISURAVA after having gone forward as far as KOKODA earlier and assisted there giving medical aid to troops and natives. Reports from the F.D.L. (Forward Defence Locality) reveal that no action for 3 days with enemy, who was now reinforcing his KOKODA position.[17]

He concluded his report for July:

> The period 2–31 July ended with the fact that I together with my carriers had taken across the Owen Stanley Range 3 Coys 39 Bn safely, who were now in action against a well prepared and equipped enemy who was making a determined effort to press forward to Port Moresby, via the 'Gap'. Our problem of supplying these troops in addition to

carriers in the forward areas with food and ammunition was a real and serious one and had to be overcome by establishing a base closer to our forward defence line. We did not have sufficient carriers for the job to keep supplies flowing along the long and arduous mountain trail from Moresby and the immediate prospects of securing additional carriers were not bright. The period had opened with the prospect of quietly building a road from Moresby to Kokoda with a time factor that was an impossibility from the start but as already stated above, ended with the fact that we were at war and at grips with a determined and ruthless enemy. Road building was a matter that I could not worry about for the time being but had to concentrate on keeping the carriers together and willing to play their part in this struggle and to find a dropping area which could be used closer to the line.[18]

That night Doc Vernon also noted in his diary: 'The sick at Isurava were suffering greatly from rain, cold, and exposure. Some who had been out all night arrived very collapsed.'[19]

•

Japanese 2nd Lieutenant Hirano Kogoro, a candid diarist, commanding No. 3 Platoon, No. 1 Company, I/144th Regiment, had been assigned to bringing up supplies with a few of his men and wrote in his diary the day after the first battle for Kokoda: '30 July: Released from transportation duty. Hurried on over the difficult road, up steep cliffs and across shaky suspension bridges in order to catch up with the main unit. Reached Oivi village and camped.' The next day he wrote of hearing about the battle for the first time: 'Met Major Toyofuku of H.Q. last night and learned that over 20 men, including Coy., Commander, have been killed or wounded. It left me dazed for a while. Hurriedly departed at 0600. Arrived at the Independent Engineer Battalion H.Q., at Advance Unit H.Q. and made report. Reached our Battalion H.Q. at 1100. Returned to the Coy. Prayed for dead and consoled wounded. 1st Lieut, Inouye arrived to be attached to our Coy.'[20]

•

On 1 August, Captain Noel Symington and his men of 'A' Company arrived at Deniki. The young officer recalled his concerns as they made their way across the Owen Stanleys to Deniki: 'When you're on a job like that, going from Moresby to Deniki the first time, and having no information coming to you from any quarter about how Templeton's getting on, you are aware that you don't know whether anybody's much behind you; you don't know where the bloody Japs are; it's raining all the time, every day it rains; its [sic] dreadfully difficult to describe the grotesque situation that exists. You've virtually running a long-range patrol.'[21]

The morale of the men of 'B' Company must have significantly improved with the arrival of 'A' and 'C' companies; they were no longer alone and seemingly forgotten.

Symington was now acting as Watson's 2i/c, taking over temporary command of the 39th Battalion until Major Allan Cameron arrived. Dean and Watson had been trying to construct a strong defence around Deniki and with the arrival of 'A' Company, they could now complete a 'secure' defensive perimeter, enabling the men of 'B' Company to get some well-earned rest. Symington placed his men on the left; with 'C' Company in the centre; McClean's 16 Platoon from 'D' Company on the right; with 'B' Company sent to Isurava as support and to help cover the rear.[22]

Lance Corporal Alexander Lochhead with 'A' company recalled their arrival at Deniki and subsequent patrols: 'The Japanese were down on the airstrip at Kokoda. We could see them from Deniki. We couldn't really dig in; we had no tools. But virtually every second day we went on patrol down towards the airstrip at Kokoda . . . to see what they were doing. They were having a rest . . . Building themselves up, building their stores and supplies.'[23]

The Japanese were also conducting their own forward patrols. Not long after 'A' Company arrived at Deniki, word came in from a patrol that an enemy scout had been seen well forward of Kokoda along the main track, close to Deniki. A soldier from the 1st PIB arrived and reported to Symington and Watson that the Japanese were building a substantial supply depot at Oivi. A request was sent to Port Moresby by radio for Oivi to be bombed.[24]

•

An afternoon trek on 1 August saw Doc Vernon back at Eora Creek where he took over the care of the wounded Australian troops and sick and injured Papuan carriers. He later wrote in his diary:

> It is quite possible I got a reputation for being inattentive to the wounded at Iora [sic] Creek, but this was not the case. Some of them expected the comforts of the base hospital. On arrival of stretcher cases, there was a universal shout for the doctor, half the camp gathered round to see the latest victim's injuries, but as most arrived very exhausted, I generally ordered hot tea, food, and 3 or 4 hours rest instead of changing dressings that had only been on a few hours. This caused disappointment. There were fussy patients who would have liked their wounds dressed half a dozen times a day, and they only felt more injured than ever when told the less interference the better. But on the whole, the . . . troops had a great deal of discomfiture to put up with and they got through . . . very stoically.
>
> I came to two conclusions about the wounds from my work here. One was the comparatively light injury caused by the small calibre bullets used by the Japs which often did not need morphia, and the other number who had escaped dangerous or fatal injury by the merest good luck. Arteries were sometimes almost miraculously missed, and body wounds did not always develop serious symptoms. I remember one lad with a penetrating wound of his neck, with a missile so close to the spine as to make one marvel at the absence of nerve symptoms, who felt no pain and who would have clambered all over the hillsides had I let him. Naturally in the absence of heavy armament on this front, the ghastly wounds seen elsewhere were rarely met with.[25]

29

'It is an Australian Aboriginal name meaning "Dawn of Day"'

During the morning of 2 August, four Allied fighter bombers flew in and bombed Kokoda, focusing on its airstrip.[1] The unknown Japanese signaller with No. 2 Section now based at Kokoda recorded in his diary that day: 'Four enemy planes bombed and strafed our position at Kokoda, forcing us to take shelter in the jungle. Three carbines were damaged, but they are still usable.'[2] Further requests were made for the RAAF to harass the Japanese at Oivi, and along the track between Kokoda and Sangara, with the aim of disrupting communications, as well as seriously hindering supplies and reinforcements being pushed up the line. It was also thought that strafing the main track would make it difficult for the Japanese to recruit local carriers. With this, additional sorties were flown against Kokoda and Oivi.[3]

As Kokoda and Oivi were under attack by Allied airmen, Lieutenant Maurice Whelan, a 23-year-old shoe manufacturer from Brighton in Victoria, and some of his men from 'C' Company were out on patrol towards Kokoda. At the crossing of Faiwani Creek, they saw a similar force of around twenty Japanese approaching from the opposite direction. The Australians moved into ambush position and, within minutes, nine Japanese lay dead on the track, with the remaining falling back across the creek without firing a shot. Whelan now observed a larger number of Japanese forming up behind the creek in support of the patrol just decimated by Australian fire; he wisely fell back to Deniki, concerned that other Japanese were flanking his position.[4]

As Whelan and his men were heading back to Deniki, a local villager approached the radio station south of the village on the track; he failed to respond when challenged and was shot and killed. This was soon followed by a similar incident when Private John Hughes, a 35-year-old labourer from Footscray in Victoria, also failed to respond to three challenges made to him as he came in from a patrol; he was shot and mortally wounded.[5]

•

Corporal Donald Daniels from Caulfield in Victoria with 8 Platoon, 'A' Company, recalled conducting a night patrol shortly after arriving at Deniki: 'We had outstanding patrols ... and we discovered that amongst the foliage was this phosphorous moss. And we thought, "We'd be smart here." Because when you get an outpost out the chap had to be relieved every second hour, so we put down this phosphorous along the track out to the outpost. So that the next bloke could follow this phosphorous track. "Righto, I'm here. You can go back and have a couple of hours sleep." That was very good, smart move until the Japs found the track and they [too] followed it in.'[6]

•

Lieutenant Kienzle left Eora Creek at 8 a.m. on 2 August in search of the dry lakes. The locals knew of the place, but it remained unnamed and was described to Kienzle as 'tarivata—diriva gabuna' ('taboo—a place of ghosts'). At first they refused to go there, but Kienzle was in no mood to argue the point: 'Guv'min I say we find im this place.'[7] Just beyond Eora Creek, where the track topped the range, they headed eastwards cutting through the jungle in search of 'diriva gabuna'. He later wrote in his report to ANGAU of their journey to the forbidden place:

Left EORA CK. At 0800 hrs for the main range to locate the dry lakes for a suitable dropping ground. Heard the bombing of KOKODA and YODDA by our planes about 0900 hrs. There were many loud explosions. At 1200 hrs. I passed the signalers laying down the telephone line right on top of the Main Range and at 1345 hrs. I sighted the dry lake due south by east from the track to KAGI. I descended east through very heavy jungle and followed a native hunting pad, using village policeman SASI and 3 local Koiaris as guides, who were reluctant to show me the area. A Taboo existed on the place except for a few, who used it as a hunting ground at certain periods of the year. The hunting pad had not been used for some time—therefore most difficult to follow, although being flat the country proved good walking.

We made camp at the headwaters of a clear, slow-moving creek which flowed south and proved to be of EFOGI CK. At 1800 hrs erected shelters from Pandanus leaves. There was an abundance of these palms in the area and this proved an advantage in establishing a large camp as a base. Water supply was good. I had to huddle up around fires with my natives that night as it was bitterly cold.[8]

•

The next day—3 August—Lieutenant Stewart Johnston, a 27-year-old farmer from Dardanup in Western Australia, led his men of 15 Platoon, 'C' Company, on a patrol along the right flank towards Kokoda to reach Mambare River. They failed to make it to the river in the allotted time due to thick jungle, but he located a small track that skirted to the right of their position at Deniki. Another patrol from 'A' Company returned with news that a track they had taken, which was supposed to lead towards Kokoda airstrip, seemed to lead 'nowhere', certainly not to Kokoda or the river.[9]

Lieutenant Keith Lovett of 'D' Company, adjutant to Captain Bidstrup, who with his CO had earlier flown to Kokoda only to be forced to turn back without landing, now arrived at Deniki with news that the rest of 'D' Company was just a few days behind. Indeed, Captain Bidstrup and his remaining two platoons of 'D' Company, reinforced with a platoon from No. 2 Anti-aircraft unit, had reached Kagi. The temporary commander of the battalion and Maroubra Force, Major Allan Cameron, had also reached Kagi. Even closer were the men of 'E' Company who had arrived at Eora Crossing.[10]

Allied aircraft continued to bomb and strafe Kokoda and Oivi. The battalion war diary records: 'Six fires were observed in KOKODA as a result. Five of these were identified as buildings by Lieut. BREWER, who had previously resided there as Assistant District Officer. The sixth fire was at the North end of the drome and was thought to be a dump as there was a great deal of heavy black smoke and fourteen explosions.'[11] By early afternoon, Major Cameron had arrived at Eora Crossing— he would arrive at Deniki the next day. That night a soldier from 'A' Company positioned forward of Deniki opened fire against what he thought to be several Japanese; early the next day he and his mates went out and confirmed at least four Japanese had been reconnoitring their position—their footprints embedded in the mud.[12]

Kienzle and his four guides early next morning—3 August—left their bivouac and within 30 minutes emerged from the jungle at the edge of the smaller of two lake beds. They were positioned close together, separated by a low spur, each a distinct shallow depression among the surrounding heights; around 2 kilometres long and about 1 kilometre wide. The ground was flat and treeless and covered with kunai grass— but the smaller of the two was too boggy to be used as an airstrip. The larger lakebed would not be explored for another few weeks, and it would be found to be a suitable location for an airstrip, but by then the Japanese were closing in on Myola. He wrote in his report:

We broke camp at 0700 hrs. and arrived at the first dry lake at 0725 hrs. Only 20 minutes' walk from where we had camped the previous afternoon. It presented a magnificent sight—a large patch of open country right on top of the main range of the Owen Stanleys. It was just the very thing I had been looking for to assist us in beating the Japs. The 'dry lake' is a patch of open ground measuring roughly about 1¼ miles [2 kilometres] long by ⅓-mile-wide, a creek running through the middle a tributary of EFOGI and swampy each side which is covered with sharp reed, the higher ground with short tufts of grass. I saw tracks of Quail and bush pigs. It is an excellent area for dropping supplies—but could also be used by the enemy for landing paratroops. I erected shelters during the afternoon and stayed the night. As no native name was given the area, I named it after a friend—MYOLA—the wife of Major S. Elliott-Smith. It is an Australian aboriginal name meaning 'Dawn of Day'.[13]

It is said when Meryl later heard of this, she was distinctly unhappy that Bert had not named the site after her.[14]

●

Still on the track with 'E' Company was Sergeant Albert Frey, a twenty-year-old student teacher from Ararat in Victoria, who had given up his Vickers machine gun for a Lee-Enfield .303 rifle. He recalled many years later the tenuous conditions of supply and the 'walking' wounded heading back to Port Moresby along the track as they pushed forward.

> The situation was always very unpleasant. You never knew if you were going to have enough ammunition for a particular action and you never knew if you were going to have enough food to sustain people in this sort of thing. It became a real gamble. Without the natives we would have been quite useless after a day or so because we would have had nothing.
>
> Not only did they keep us supplied but they were instrumental in getting so many wounded back and this was a terrible job. It needed eight natives per stretcher to get one man back across the mountains and this was a long journey. So, the turn-around in natives had to be enormous . . . If you were wounded . . . but not bad enough to really warrant a stretcher, you made your own way back across the mountains. A lot of them didn't make it of course . . . A lot of them died and a lot were knocked off by natives and there were some unfriendly natives. A lot of their wounds were just too much . . . Blokes with half an arm shot off, half a foot or half a leg or shot through the head, through the shoulder, through the back. They generally tried to make their own way back. And a lot of them did, but it was the stomach wounds that were the greatest problem . . .
>
> If a man was wounded in the stomach up there and they couldn't get a carrier team or a stretcher, they would normally die. So that was that . . . I saw a bloke on his hands and knees, he went past us and he

crawled all the way back to Moresby, not to Moresby but to the starting off point. That was 7 or 8 days. You can imagine the guts that this takes; God almighty. They never bloody [complained]; they would just say, 'Have you got a cigarette mate?'[15]

Near Buna, the small emergency runway that had been constructed before the war was being expanded by Japanese engineers for use as a fighter base. It was now that nine Zeros landed on the partly completed airstrip. The engineers, assisted by the men of Sasebo No. 5 SNLP, had been working around the clock to complete the airfield. Further recommendations were made to improve the airstrip—it was to be ready by mid-August for full operations; however, the Japanese discovered that drainage problems seriously restricted its ability to serve as a functioning large-scale airbase.[16]

Logistical difficulties continued to seriously impede the ability of the front-line troops to push forward, as recorded in the log of the Sakigawa Transport Unit on 3 August: 'We learned that the frontline infantry BUTAI came to the intermediate dump themselves and carried away their provisions, despite our labour of several days transporting supplies. We can imagine the hardships of the next operation [crossing the Owen Stanleys].'[17]

That day, newspaperman George Johnston concluded that his original assessment of ten days previous, that the Japanese were focusing on constructing airbases for operations against Port Moresby, was incorrect. He reported to his readers in Sydney, Melbourne, London and elsewhere:

It is obvious now that the Japanese mean to do more than establish a beachhead and airfields in the Buna–Gona area. They have advanced half-way into Papua and are now fighting the Australian Militia at Kokoda village, strategic key to control of the Owen Stanleys.

The first land fighting in Papua began a week ago, when a handful of native troops of the Papuan Infantry Battalion, under the command of young Australian officers, attempted to stem the Japanese advance at Awala, 25 miles [40 kilometres] inland, along the Buna–Kokoda–Moresby track. They were outnumbered ten to one and they could do nothing. After a few bloody skirmishes they were forced to retreat, establishing roadblocks as they went.

It's believed now that the Japs have 6000 troops in the area [they had around 3500]—first-class fighting men mainly from specially trained marine landing detachments. That makes the position pretty serious. We have probably less than 1000 men [there were just 400], mostly of a Militia battalion, up in the mountains. They have never been in action before. They are not equipped or supplied as well as the Japanese, and we can't hope to give them the help they need for a considerable time. Their job is to hold the Japs north of the range, while we build up reinforcements, and attempt to cut some sort of supply line through the incredibly wild country of the southern Owen Stanleys.

Four days ago, the Japanese, who have pushed more than 60 miles [100 kilometres] inland in a week, reached Kokoda. Since then the little village sheltering beneath the towering green hills of the main range has been a no-man's-land. It is a tough battlefield, with its green mazes of rubber plantations and humid jungles and snaking tracks through solid walls of bottle-green foliage. But if we can't hold them at Kokoda the battlefield will become infinitely tougher.[18]

Indeed, Kokoda had by this time been in Japanese hands for a week—no-man's-land was defined now by the area between Kokoda and Deniki.

30

'All I can do is make him warm for his last hours'

Next day—4 August—Sergeant Morris Evensen, a 37-year-old plantation manager from Rabaul with the 1st PIB, and his men returned
from a twenty-hour patrol in the Managari area (the next ridge east of
Deniki). He reported that beyond Fila at Kobara, there was a narrow
north-running track which connected with the main Kokoda–Oivi
track before it reached Kokoda, close to the village of Pirivi, and the area
appeared free of enemy troops. The battalion war diary records that
Evensen encountered no enemy troops and was told by the locals
that they refused to stay in their villages overnight from fear of the
Japanese appearing unexpectedly. Tracks running up the valley showed
no signs of having been used by the Japanese nor were they any
indications they had used the main track along the eastern side of the
valley opposite Deniki, which joined the Kokoda–Oivi track at a point
about one hour's march from Kokoda. Warrant Officer Jack McWatters
with the 1st PIB returned from the same area about three hours later
and reported 'having met several native carriers deserting from Port
Moresby. One of these he brought back with him, but the remainder
dispersed into the jungle—on being told that the ENEMY were in
possession of AWALA and KOKODA ... their destinations.'[1]

At around 4 p.m., Brigade Major Allan Cameron, accompanied by
Lieutenant Hugh Kelly, a 23-year-old bank clerk from Colac in Victoria,
arrived at Deniki. Cameron's complete misreading of the situation,
and his determination to stamp his authority, resulted in an appalling

injustice. As recalled by Jack Wilkinson in his diary at the time: 'Major Cameron arrived . . . and took charge of all troops. Very bitter towards men (who fled). Says they were cowards. Must have met up with the few who "shot through". Could have been the canteen and postal blokes who left before the first shot was fired.'[2] However, this was not the case as these men had fought with Corporal Markham in the exposed position just below the Kokoda Plateau and had, like Markham, managed to escape, obviously at some point reaching the Kokoda Track.[3] Cameron considered the men of 'B' Company had failed to provide the required fighting spirit in the loss of Kokoda and its airfield. He chastised the surviving officers and senior NCOs of the company in front of the other officers and informed them that, as far as he was concerned, 'B' Company was finished as a rifle company and the men would be dispersed among other companies in the battalion.[4]

Nothing could be further from the truth, these men, along with their supporting Papuan troops, had done an outstanding job in conducting a fighting withdrawal, while desperately waiting on the promised reinforcements and supplies that were only now arriving—two weeks after the initial Japanese invasion. After Cameron had calmed down, several officers approached him and convinced him not to break up 'B' Company. He agreed that 'B' Company—less 10 Platoon—would replace 'E' Company then located to the rear at Eora Creek while 'E' Company would move forward to Isurava. Major Watson would command 10 Platoon, which would remain at Deniki with battalion headquarters.[5] Understandably, the men were jaded by Cameron's words and actions. Sergeant Major Joseph Dawson recalled with deserved bitterness: 'Cameron took a dislike to B Company, and he stuck us in reserve, which meant we weren't up near the front, which we didn't appreciate either.'[6]

•

Lieutenant Bert Kienzle sent word from Myola to Sergeant Hylton Jarrett at Efogi to move forward to establish a large supply dump there as quickly as possible. Not wasting any time, Kienzle cut a new track back to Eora Creek and in the process suffered an injury to his hip when falling into a deep gully. He remained on the track rather than returning to get medical treatment. His injury became progressively worse and by the time the war ended, he was forced to use a walking stick. At the time he told no one nor did he even record this painful injury in his diary.[7] However, he did write that day—4 August—of establishing a new camp which he named 'Templeton's Crossing'.

I left MYOLA at 0800 hrs for EORA CK and blazed a new trail north-east over the Gap by following a ridge. I sent a report back to majors, Smith, Watson and Cameron (the latter had just arrived in the forward area to take over command of Maroubra Force) regarding the location of the area and my intention of finding a new trail to EORA CK. I also sent instructions for Sgt. Jarrett ex EFOGI to proceed to MYOLA and establish a large camp there as quickly as possible. The blazed trail to first crossing of EORA CREEK was fair going, steep in places, but the trail on from there to the junction of KAGI track was very rough going and needed some attention. The junction of this new trail with the KAGI-EORA CK. track is where I established another camp and named it TEMPLETONS CROSSING in memory of Capt. Sam Templeton who was killed near OIVI. I arrived at EORA CK. at 1720 hrs. tired and hungry and found 'E' Coy 39 Bn. there and 'D' Coy 39 Bn at KAGI ready to move fwd. next day.[8]

•

By now the brigade signallers had managed to lay a telephone cable across the mountains to Deniki. However, the line could not work effectively over long distances, requiring relay stations to be positioned every 10 to 15 kilometres across the Owen Stanleys all the way back to Port Moresby. These were located south to north at: Koitaki, Uberi, Ioribaiwa, Nauro, Menari, Efogi, Kagi, Myola, Templeton's Crossing, Eora Creek and Deniki.[9] Private Halsall with the battalion's Headquarters Company recalled: 'Well we had one phone line, one single strand and for each village . . . There was, must have been about 14 phones on that run and we used to have to relay the messages. It wasn't strong enough to go right through. We had to relay them. That's about all we did. We didn't use much else.'[10] The battalion war diary records: 'Telephone communications with ILOLO was established . . . This was a result of excellent work on the part of Base Sigs. Prior to this, the only means of communication between MAROUBRA and N.G.F. was W/T and there were long delays entailed by wireless blackouts which occurred regularly from 2200 hrs to 0600 hrs approx. The set used was an A.W.A. [established by signallers Clive Turnbull and Bernard Murphy] one of a type used by the civil administration and although too weak to transmit during these periods of blackouts, was generally found to be more satisfactory than the Army 101 set. Many of the messages received were badly mutilated.'[11]

Signaller Phelan recalled: 'At this time a . . . telephone line was laid from Port Moresby to Deniki just before Kokoda. It wasn't laid by the 39th Battalion; it was laid by Brigade Signalers . . . What a fantastic feat. They would have used hundreds of natives, but what a great thing to do, to lay a telephone line, right to the . . . front line.'[12] That said, he recounted with the cable came the responsibility of keeping the line open: 'I was in a native hut for a week looking after this signal station. The line went out once [,] I had to go and patrol it . . . the worst thing that you could have done in the jungle was to go out on your own somewhere without someone to help you, because a lot of people had disappeared and [were] never . . . seen again . . . not only did we have the Japanese [to contend with] . . . also the natives. At times, certain sections of them received the Japanese with open arms as liberators. Some terrible stories were told about . . . the natives giving up Australians to the Japanese, particularly civilians.'[13]

Another problem was noted by 24-year-old signaller Frank Patterson from Box Hill in Victoria, as the cable was 'tied on to trees as it went through and . . . we found the troops trying to get themselves up were pulling themselves by the cable and of course that meant the fellows had to repair that and in the finish they put it up higher, so it wouldn't be grabbed so easily. Originally there was only the one line right across and everything was on that one line.'[14]

Unaware of the escalation of military operations in the area, the Gona mission party members were still hiding out near Siai; hoping against hope that word would reach them that the Japanese had withdrawn. It was on 4 August that May started to first write her long letter to Viola and the next day that Mavis started her letter to her mother. May was unaware that her fiancé, Father Vivian Redlich, had the week before been speared to death by locals not far from Sangara mission.[15]

•

Doc Vernon was still at Eora Creek treating the wounded and sick. Captain William McLaren, a 28-year-old medical practitioner from Chatswood in New South Wales with the militia 14th Field Ambulance, arrived there with five other ranks, on their way to the front line.[16] He asked Vernon if he could stay at Eora Creek to look after the wounded soldiers and the sick carriers until other medical assistance arrived; Vernon was happy to oblige and later wrote of the appalling conditions that the Papuan carriers had to endure, he clearly admired them and was troubled by what he saw and heard.

> The condition of our carriers at Iora [sic] Creek caused me more concern than that of the wounded, none of whom fortunately passed out. Overwork, overloading (principally by soldiers who dumped their packs and even rifles on top of the carriers' own burdens), exposure, cold and underfeeding were the common lot. Every evening scores of carriers came in, slung their loads down, and lay exhausted on the ground; the immediate prospect before them was grim, a meal that consisted only of rice and none too much of that, and a night of shivering discomfort for most as there were only enough blankets to issue one to every two men. For two weeks, these men had had nothing but rice to eat, yet daily they carried hundreds of tins of bully beef for the white troops who never seemed to go short. Such things happen in war time and the difficulty of supplying only the front line was great enough, but the inequality in the scale of rations was too marked to escape notice.

Deprivation of their cherished tin of meat and possibly resentment at seeing others get over plenty had led inevitably to pilfering on the track. On arrival in camp, each carrier had the number of tins entrusted to him checked and shortages became increasingly greater. Some soldiers . . . forcibly opened the carrier's [sic] sacks on the track and recovered what they wanted . . . it takes a long time and a long study of black nature to realize that the white man's ruling is often oppressive where on the surface it appears quite fair. Provided of course that the proper remedy, a more liberal diet, could not be applied, pilfering had to be checked somehow, and some of the methods adopted were no credit to the men who applied them.

Our carriers were not appreciated at their true worth and the time when the Fuzzies were called the Angels of the Owen Stanley Track lay in the future. What the original attitude of our young untrained soldiery to natives generally was I cannot estimate, but in these early days of danger only the most intelligent of the men—and they were not all officers—were beginning to see very dimly that without their help the defending force would have been a much less effective body. Many of the ANGAU men were disgusted at the lack of consideration shown to the natives, and on the rare occasions when Lieut. Kienzle and I met, their lot was a subject of keen discussion and mutual protest. But the base remained unmoved by our representations; the only senior ANGAU officer who relinquished the privileges of Moresby to tackle the Range and the special preoccupations at the war end of it, brought his own team of carriers to handle his own gear—it included a camp bed, a unique specimen in these early days—and he was apparently too occupied to attend to the troubles of his own native force. Under no circumstances could they have [been] given their usual rights, but at least more food and more blankets might have been supplied. They thoroughly deserved both.[17]

Doc Vernon practised what he preached, as demonstrated by the story recalled by 28-year-old Sergeant John 'Jack' Sim from Ballarat in Victoria, with the 39th Battalion signals platoon. At one point he was with Bert Kienzle and Doc Vernon, resting at Efogi:

I shared a hut for a few days with Doc Vernon and Bert Kienzle and in the comfort of the hut during those days we had the luxury of a blanket apiece at night. I remember conversations with the 'Doc' was very difficult because he was so deaf. I also remember how, one night, he disappeared with his blanket to visit the carriers lying on the bare ground below us. After a while he returned without his blanket and lay down on the floor to shiver through the night (at Efogi the nights were as cold as the days were hot). And Bert Kienzle shouted at him [to be heard]: 'Where's your blanket?' to which the Doc replied 'Wrapped a carrier in it. Poor devil, dying of pneumonia. All I can do is make him warm for his last hours.'[18]

•

After a week of slogging over the Owen Stanleys to get help for McKenna's party, Captain Tom Grahamslaw finally reached Amau mission station near Abau on the south coast. He was soon on a launch on his way to Port Moresby.

Amau was established by Reverend Cecil Abel of Kwato, near Samarai. When I arrived the Mission was being run by an ordained native teacher from Kwato. He and his wife were kindness personified. It was lovely to be able to bathe and change into clean clothing, to drink tea and indulge in solid food again. By a stroke of good fortune Cecil Abel arrived at Amau several hours after I reached there. He had come from Kwato on one of his mission craft and had anchored it in a river about two days walk from Amau. When I informed Abel that I proposed to return to McKenna with medicines and food he kindly offered, as an alternative, to dispatch a relief party under the control of one of his Mission teachers. I gladly accepted his offer as I felt it important that I proceed to Port Moresby as quickly as possible so that I could take up duty again. Packs were made up that night and the relief party departed at first light next morning. Months later I learned from McKenna that the Mission party got the wind up after the first day's walk and did not proceed further. Fortunately, however, Lieutenant David Marsh of Abau Station happened to be patrolling inland at the time. When

informed by natives of the existence of McKenna's party and the difficulty they were experiencing because of the two sick and wounded
American airmen, he lost no time in proceeding over the mountains
to their rescue.[19]

Nineteen-year-old Lieutenant David Marsh was Meryl Kienzle's
cousin and had arrived in New Guinea after being offered a job by Bert
before the war and had since joined ANGAU.[20] Grahamslaw recalled
that the leisurely trip onboard the launch was 'just what I needed and
by the time I reached Port Moresby I was fit again . . . the privations
suffered by McKenna and Bitmead resulted in them having to be
sent back to Australia for several months. Captain Peter Bender and
Sergeant Arnold Thompson went back to America to recuperate, where
their experience received much publicity, and Captain Bender was
awarded a decoration.'[21] The war was far from over for Grahamslaw,
within a month, he and a handful of Papuans from the RPC would be
conducting reconnaissance missions along the Kokoda Track, looking
for Japanese infiltration parties.[22]

31

'Gradually we learned that logic was leading us astray'

On 5 August word came in that the Japanese at Kokoda were strengthening the defences around the plateau and airfield, particularly around the south-west corner of the plantation where the track left the plateau heading for Deniki. Cameron was already formulating his plan to retake Kokoda and its airstrip. However, Lieutenant Colonel Tsukamoto, commanding the I/144th Battalion, was now consolidating his force around Kokoda, with plans to take Deniki. Both would launch their respective attacks on 8 August, with Cameron's men moving north to take Kokoda and Tsukamoto's companies marching south to take Deniki—they would collide midway on the Kokoda Track.[1]

•

There were two direct approaches to Kokoda from Deniki. To the west was the main Kokoda Track passing through Pitoki before reaching the Kokoda Plateau; while to the east another track ran to several villages including, Fila, Overa, Kobara and Pirivi before joining the main track between Kokoda and Oivi. However, another narrow path lay between these two tracks, branching off from the Pirivi track close to Overa about 2 kilometres east of Deniki. From here this central track headed north-west before joining the main western track between Deniki and Kokoda just south of the plateau.[2]

Kokoda–Deniki area

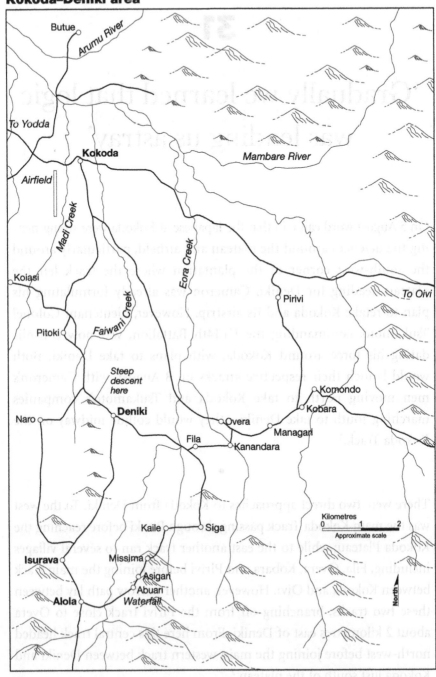

Cameron sent out three patrols during the morning to reconnoitre each of these approaches. The first was led by Captain Brewer and Captain Halford Sorenson, a 25-year-old truck driver from Oakleigh in Victoria, of 'A' Company. With them was the ever-dependable Lance Corporal Sanopa, who had got Templeton's men out of Oivi. They reconnoitred the central track, as no one at this point was sure where it led or whether in parts it was held by the Japanese. As they pushed forward Sanopa was scouting up front carrying his Lee-Enfield. Twenty-three-year-old Sergeant Les Simmons, from Caufield in Victoria with 'A' Company, wrote of Sanopa at the time: 'Over six feet tall he was an impressive figure in his black skirt-tunic edged with red braid, with his rifle swinging in one hand, a grenade in the other, and, in his hair, the leaves he used for camouflage; he inspired our every confidence.'[3]

They found the central track joined the main track near the edge of the Kokoda rubber plantation just south of the station. To their surprise they saw no enemy troops. This track would be used by 'A' Company in their attempt to retake Kokoda.[4] The battalion war diary records that Brewer and Sorenson reported at around 6.30 p.m. that the track led 'along the EORA VALLEY and joined the track OIVI–KOKODA [sic almost certainly the Deniki–Kokoda track] at a point near where it crosses a creek—just before entering KOKODA. They also reported that they had NOT contacted any ENEMY, although they had proceeded to a point from which they were able to see the junction with OIVI-KOKODA [sic]—up to which point it was NOT guarded and did NOT show signs of having been patrolled.'[5]

Another patrol led by Captain Jesser, using the track between Deniki and Kokoda to the west, made its way towards the outskirts of Kokoda to collect intelligence on the Japanese machine-gun positions and other defensive works being constructed there. They succeeded in reaching an observation point which enabled them to see the Japanese at work. Jesser reported back to Cameron at 6 p.m. that he had not seen any enemy troops on the track but, 'had the opportunity of seeing working parties digging defensive posns along the Western side of the rubber plantation' including several machine-gun positions.[6]

The third patrol, led by the battalion's intelligence officer, Lieutenant Richard McNamara, a 35-year-old clerk from Mount Gambier in South Australia, and Sergeant Evensen of the 1st PIB, moved down the eastern track to reach the main track near Pirivi. They were to identify ambush positions along the main track between Kokoda and Oivi. They saw Japanese troops with local carriers moving towards Kokoda from Komondo. They avoided the enemy and pushed down the track heading for Pirivi—the village was occupied by the Japanese. Again, avoiding contact, they moved north finally reaching the Kokoda–Oivi part of the track.[7] They were lucky not to be detected by the Japanese and reported their critical intelligence to Cameron the next morning on their return, as recorded in the battalion war diary.

At 1100 hrs the I.O. with Sgt. EVENSEN (P.I.B.) and a Sec from A Coy returned, having reached a point on the track OIVI-KOKODA, half an hour's march beyond KOMANDO [sic]. He reported friendly natives in the villages en route. The point at which the main track was contacted, he reported as an excellent site for an ambush. While concealed some little distance from the track, he and Sgt. EVENSEN had seen fifty-eight Japanese and five natives carrying stores in the direction of KOKODA. This party also recced a route to by-pass the junction of the track followed—with that to the track KOKODA-OIVI via PIRIVI, which . . . was occupied by the ENEMY. The object of the recce was to obviate the possibility of tps [troops] which might be sent to carry out an ambush being detected before reaching their objective.[8]

Meanwhile, Lieutenant Brewer recorded in his report to ANGAU that 42-year-old Major Sydney Elliott-Smith from Devonport in Tasmania had arrived at Deniki and taken command of all ANGAU men in the area. He also reported that 'many guides were required by outgoing patrols—these were supplied by the R.P.C. and from Village Councillors'.[9]

By 5 August Kienzle had informed the supply officer back at Ilolo of the new drop zone at Myola and of the urgent need for supplies to be dropped there; later that day a lone aircraft dropped the first load of supplies there. He wrote in his report: 'Instructed natives to commence building additional storerooms and latrines etc. The telephone line was completed from PORT MORESBY to DENIKI by this time—the signalers had done a splendid job. I had a telephone conversation with Capt. Kelly at ILOLO and advised him of the acute food position, lack of sufficient carriers, the necessity of plane droppings and the finding of MYOLA. The same day a plane made the first experimental drop at MYOLA. I also had telephone conversation with Maj. Cameron regarding MYOLA. "D" Coy arrived from KAGI.'[10] However, no other drops would be made for another five days, seriously impacting on the defence of Deniki.[11]

Indeed, that day General Morris reported to AAF Headquarters in Australia that the only two transport aircraft available for supply drops to Kanga Force at Wau and Maroubra Force at Deniki had returned to Australia. Morris was notified that at least one transport would soon be made available; Morris understandably signalled a terse reply: 'Kanga and Maroubra personnel cannot be fully maintained by native carriers and latter will desert in large numbers if tracks subjected to [Japanese] air attack. Weather conditions over mountains usually difficult and planes have to stand by for long periods awaiting breaks. Procedure for obtaining transport planes outlined is too slow and has already cost us Kokoda. Consider two machines permanently based here is minimum requirement.'[12]

The war diary of the battalion records in early August the significance of Myola in keeping the battalion supplied: during the previous week experiments had been made in air drops at Efogi and Kagi to help alleviate pressure on the carriers between Uberi and Kagi. These experiments met with only partial success as most stores were 'lost in the jungle. Lieut. KIENZLE of A.N.G.A.U. therefore inspected the dry lakes at MYOLA which is EAST of KAGI—and reported the area as being very satisfactory for dropping of cargo . . . The regular carriage of amm and rations to this point by air and the subsequent comparatively short carry by natives would ensure adequate and regular supplies for the Force.'[13]

Myola would soon be operating as the critical front-line supply base for the men of the 39th Battalion and the few remaining men of the 1st PIB and RPC still at Deniki. However, the supply base was still a good two days' march from the front line. Everything from ammunition, rations and medical supplies to blankets had to be transported over that stage by carrier parties. Kienzle established staging points and dumps at Templeton's Crossing, Eora Creek, Alola and Isurava. At each of these points, the men of ANGAU oversaw the carriers and stores.[14]

To date no effective technique had been developed for dropping supplies from the air in New Guinea. The only guidance was from pre-war days when supplies had sometimes been dropped to isolated individuals or parties, which involved dropping supplies enclosed in two or more sacks to help cushion the impact. While the inner sack would usually burst on impact, the outer thicker hessian bag would usually hold together and help prevent the contents from scattering over a large area. Accuracy in hitting the target area was far from perfect, however, and unless the area was clear and level, much of the cargo would be lost in the jungle and down the rugged deep ravines; those containing equipment that could be recovered were frequently damaged beyond repair.[15]

Newspaperman Geoff Reading later informed his readers in Sydney on witnessing the 'biscuit bombers' in operation at Myola. The C-47 transports would come in low at just 20 metres altitude and a crew member would push out the supplies through the cargo door. Reading recalled: 'Some urgently needed medical supplies were dropped by parachutes, but more than half of these failed to open, and the contents were smashed. Occasionally a food package burst with the impact of landing, and biscuits, tins, dried fruit, or flour went flying in all directions. Each plane made about a dozen sweeps over the dropping-ground, and the whole operation took up to thirty minutes. As soon as it was over ... [natives] and soldiers dashed into the marsh looking for packages that had gone astray.'[16]

David Vaughter, a young American pilot flying one of the C-47 'biscuit bombers', recalled vividly his early missions in supplying the Australian troops at Myola and the problems they encountered before specialised parachutes were issued in 1943.

When we first went to drop supplies, we didn't have any training. I'd never dropped anything in the States. We had dropped some paratroopers but never supplies. Frankly, we didn't have a clue as to what to do. There was no book on the subject, so we wrote our own. At first, we and some of the other early-arrived squadrons went at it wrong. Until Buna [early 1943] we dropped Australian supplies. The Aussies packed it up and wrapped it in beautiful wool blankets covered with burlap. We dropped everything from ammunition to canned fruit.

The first crews given this duty told us to go in as low as possible, and make sure we had enough speed to go over the trees: approximately 150 knots. This was for safety, because we might have to turn to do it again. If you went too slow, you could stall the airplane, which is a bad idea at low altitude. Well, we were actually in there 'skip bombing' supplies at ten to twenty feet [3 to 6 metres] elevation at 130 to 150 miles [210 to 240 kilometres] an hour. We'd kick the stuff out the door and it hit the ground like shrapnel, almost blowing apart. Sometimes the supplies would ricochet off the ground and fly down the hills. We often averaged only 20 per cent recovery. If everything was demolished, we'd have to do it again.

Gradually we learned that logic was leading us astray. It made sense to drop low. However, we learned that the optimum altitude for supply drop was around 300 feet [90 metres]. We flew higher, and also as slow as we could, maybe eighty or ninety miles [130 to 145 kilometres] an hour. The supplies then had the opportunity to lose forward momentum and fell almost straight down. This more than compensated for greater height, and lost material dropped considerably. When they required requisitioned parachutes for this duty, there were times when we had 100 per cent recovery.[17]

All that lay in the future—for now the front-line troops were still very much dependent on the native carriers for ammunition, food and other critical supplies.

•

On 5 August, Lieutenant Alan Hooper with the 1st PIB visited George Chester, a plantation caretaker in the Ioma District. He wrote at the time: 'I learnt that Mavis Parkinson had written Chester from a make-shift shelter at Siai, a long day's walk from Ioma, requesting clothing. Fortunately, amongst personal effects at the plantation were the toweling and other items she and May Hayman needed. They were also given the location of ADO McKenna's cache of food at Riru, on the Opi River. We expressed no concern for PIB or spotters at Ambasi; no news seemed good news, and it was surmised their radio was out of order and that they would soon contact us.'[18] However, Lieutenant Smith and his men of the 1st PIB along with the radio spotters at Ambasi had the week before been forced to fall back when a large Japanese force landed in the area.

32

'. . . all they had to do was enfilade that track'

Next day—6 August—all companies of the 39th Battalion were united in the Deniki–Isurava area with the arrival of 'D' Company.[1] Bidstrup's company was assigned a defensive position on the main track between Deniki and Isurava, to the rear of Cameron's headquarters. Cameron now had a total strength of 31 officers and 433 men. There were also five Australian officers, three Australian NCOs and about 35 men of the 1st PIB, including its commander Major Watson[i]; along with a small number of ANGAU officers and a dozen or so Papuans of the RPC.[2]

Among the former anti-aircraft gunners now attached to 'D' Company was 23-year-old Private Jack Boland from Melbourne who recalled, like many others, of getting their first sight of a Bren gun while on the track: 'It took us eight days to get to Deniki and we spent most of that time climbing up (often on hands and knees) and slipping down (mostly on our backsides) and every time we stopped for a spell we were all sure we would never get up again. At Kagi we had a rest and some of the time was used to show us a Bren for the first time and explain how it worked. But we would have been in trouble later on in action if there was a problem with the gas valve adjustment because hardly any of us would know how to fix it after such a superficial instruction session.'[3] The gas valve could stop the gun from firing

---

i   Major Bill Watson was awarded the Distinguished Service Order for his actions during the Kokoda Campaign; one more medal he could add to the many decorations he had received during the Great War. He would remain in command of the PIB until April 1944.

as carbon built up, and during the early part of the fighting some Brens were discarded as a result.[4]

•

Cameron was defining his plan to retake Kokoda, but he had limited intelligence on the Japanese force he was about to confront; he assessed there were around 500 Japanese at Kokoda with another 150 or so close by in support. The Australians would go into battle with around 300 men. Military logic dictates that any attacking force should outnumber the defenders by at least three to one to have any realistic chance of success. Not only was Cameron's force outnumbered by at least two to one, but he would commit the cardinal sin of dividing his smaller force to attack a larger one.[5]

Two of his company commanders, captains Bidstrup and Symington, were against the plan—the third, Captain Dean, would not survive to recall his opinion, but Bidstrup knew that he too had serious concerns: 'We did not have sufficient information about the positions of the Japs or the size of their force,' recalled Bidstrup, 'no reconnaissance. Remember, our forward troops were kicked out of Kokoda to Deniki. The last time I saw Cyril Dean was on my way down to this Oivi exercise. He didn't survive that day. He knew as well as I knew, that to attack down there on a straight track without sufficient intelligence as to where the enemy was; all they had to do was to enfilade that track, which they did—and that's it!'[6]

Symington also thought the plan was almost certain to fail: 'I questioned the advisability of the whole operation with him, pointed out the lack of patrolling in the area described; the quite unknown numbers and equipment of the enemy in the Yodda Valley, and the complete lack of any information from the rear headquarters, of the number and equipment landed in the Gona area. Was it a battalion, brigade or division or an army? Major Cameron had no answers to these questions. I personally considered that the . . . attack was ill conceived, and highly dangerous bearing in mind the topography of the country.'[7]

Regardless, the attack would go ahead; Cameron was determined to 'bloody' the untried companies of the battalion in an aggressive action—as opposed to a defensive one. He wanted to keep the Japanese off balance, disrupting their plans to attack Deniki. However, in doing so, there was a real possibility of his split force being defeated in detail. Cameron went back to Eora Crossing to ensure the necessary supplies were rushed forward to Isurava and Deniki before launching his attack two days later.[8]

Many have questioned Cameron's decision to attack Kokoda; arguing it was wiser to confront the Japanese at Deniki. The Australian position there has frequently been argued to represent a better position to make a stand against the enemy with a united battalion of four, perhaps five rifle companies. However, Deniki while higher and positioned along the main track, was exposed to a flanking manoeuvre by the Japanese as a track branched off at Hoi well forward of Deniki, heading east and then south for Kaile and Abuari bypassing Deniki, running parallel with the main track beyond Isurava and rejoining the main track at Alola, which would place them well behind the Australians. There was no way that Cameron, even with the five rifle companies, could hope to cover both approaches over such a large area. He would have had to split his forces to cover both approaches or fall back to Alola if he wanted to maintain the integrity of his battalion for battle. However, Kokoda and its airstrip at the time were considered critical to the Australian defence, and Cameron had orders to hold Kokoda, if only to deny it to the Japanese. Dividing his forces in his pincer movement against an unknown enemy force was unwise, but he had little option and tried to make the best of a bad situation. While Kokoda was just as vulnerable as Deniki to flanking manoeuvres, Cameron assessed, rightly or wrongly, if he could retake the airstrip and hold it with his united battalion, reinforcements and supplies could be rapidly flown in.

Doc Vernon was finally able to leave Eora Creek as Captain Douglas Wallman, a 46-year-old physician from Adelaide with the militia 14th Field Ambulance, had arrived there. Doc recalled that the reinforcements who were arriving at Eora Creek were all utterly exhausted from their long trek through the mountains. It was obvious that they had been insufficiently trained to endure the hardships, but even so they were keen to push on to support their mates from 'B' Company. 'One afternoon Capt. Wallman A.A.M.C. with 10 orderlies and a good supply of comforts turned up, swallowed a cup of tea, and with characteristic energy insisted upon pushing on to Isurava though the day was far spent. He left some of his team to look after some of the . . . wounded and I was thus released for work I had long wanted to get to—inspection of our medical posts back to Efogi where I had stationed W.O. Barnes.'[9]

Arriving at Kagi, Vernon came across Warrant Officer John Rae, a 28-year-old field assistant from Gulargambone in New South Wales, now with ANGAU. He noted in his report that Rae was 'one of the best fellows on the line . . . He and I had a long talk over the troubles of the carriers and the upshot was that I sent a message to ANGAU to say that less than half had blankets and none a liberal enough diet. We added that a day of rest once a week was becoming a necessity and that over-work and exposure was playing havoc with the (native) force. Indeed, at this period I thought that our (native) force was rapidly deteriorating.'[10]

•

At Eora Creek, Lieutenant Kienzle was showing the men of 'B' Company their new position, while also trying to organise the urgent movement of supplies to the front line: '"D" Coy moved forward to DENIKI. I showed Capt. Stevenson "B" Coy 39 Bn defensive positions around EORA CK. camp and sent further urgent messages regarding most acute food position in the forward area. The carriers had done an excellent job to date, carrying supplies forward and bringing stores from KAGI which had been used as dropping ground with varied results, chiefly poor recoveries. MYOLA had to be used if we were to continue operations.'[11]

•

In the Philippines, Japanese Lieutenant General Hyakutake Harukichi commanding the XVII Army had ordered the remainder of the Yokoyama Advance Butai, its naval contingent and additional supplies to prepare to leave Rabaul for Buna. On 6 August, three transports the *Kinai Maru*, *Nankai Maru* and *Kenyo Maru*, escorted by the cruiser *Tatsuta*, two destroyers and two submarine chasers, left Rabaul, transporting the 3000 men of the 14th and 15th Naval Construction Units, their equipment, vehicles and army supplies. It would be another two weeks before the remaining two battalions of the 144th Regiment and the II/41st Regiment would land near Gona to commence operations to cross the Owen Stanleys.[12]

On the same day—6 August—the Japanese XVII Army issued the following telegram to Imperial Headquarters concerning their imminent plans:

1. In order to supply by land and reinforce the fighting strength of the South Seas Force, the 41st Infantry Regiment has been summoned. It left Davao on 5 August and is planned to arrive in Rabaul on 15 August.
2. The army intends at all costs to land the main strength of the South Seas Force in the Buna area around 16 August. Consequently, the navy is urged to strive to complete the airfield at Buna.[13]

•

Next day—7 August—saw serious disruption to the Japanese plans with US marines landing at Guadalcanal, which had significant implications for the Japanese fighting in Papua. Japanese pilots reported 21 enemy warships and 30 transports just off the island, indicating a major effort was being made by the Americans to capture their newly constructed airfield on Guadalcanal. Within days, the marines had captured the airstrip and were digging in along the ridges beyond. Allied airmen were soon using the airbase and their ad hoc squadrons were soon christened 'The Cactus Airforce', after the codename for the operation to invade Guadalcanal.[14]

The marines soon christened the captured Japanese airbase 'Henderson Field' in honour of Major Lofton Henderson, who commanded the marine Scout Bombing 241 Squadron. During the

Battle of Midway he was killed leading his squadron in a suicidal attack against the Japanese carrier force. The Japanese were now committed to repulsing the US marines from Guadalcanal, regardless of the cost in men and Japan's dwindling military resources. This meant that the number of Japanese troops and, just as critical, supplies available for the Kokoda Campaign would be significantly reduced.[15]

33

'He and I had a long talk over
the troubles of the carriers'

At Deniki, early on the morning of 7 August, just as the US Marines were storming the beach at Guadalcanal, Major Cameron was finalising his preparations for the second battle for Kokoda, which would place the station and its airstrip back in Australian hands. He issued verbal orders to his company commanders in the early afternoon. Cameron's plan dictated that Captain Symington and his men of 'A' Company would approach Kokoda Plateau using the central track reconnoitred by Captain Brewer just days before, while Captain Dean and 'C' Company on the left were to clear the Deniki–Kokoda part of the main track of Japanese. Bidstrup and 'D' Company would move down the right flank using the track to Pirivi to set up an ambush position east of Kokoda along the Kokoda–Oivi track to target Japanese reinforcements from that direction. Both 'C' and 'D' companies were to converge on Kokoda after completing their original objectives. Captain Kenneth Jacob, a 22-year-old clerk from Unley Park in South Australia, an AIF veteran of the fighting in North Africa with the 2/10th Battalion, would remain at Deniki commanding a small force. Lieutenant Brewer with ANGAU recalled that he was to lead 'A' Company in their advance, while Major Elliott-Smith would lead 'C' Company.[1]

Sergeant Major Mowat with 'A' Company recalled the plan as explained to him at the time: 'Instructions to attack Kokoda. A Coy attack from North [-east]; C Coy from S.East. D Coy to ambush Oivi Road and prevent reinf[orcements] coming to Japs. All amm[unition] possible to be carried. No G[round] sheets, no blankets, no surplus gear. Only rations to be three days emergency rations.'[2] The battalion war diary confirms the lack of intelligence available to Cameron before the attack: 'Patrols so far had NOT been able to estimate strength of ENEMY in KOKODA area owing to their wide dispersal.'[3]

Cameron now ordered Lieutenant Johnston and two of his men from 'C' Company to reconnoitre Kokoda and the airstrip; however, they would not return until the next day. He also ordered 'A' Company to conduct a patrol, likely along the central track that they were to use the next day. These men collided with a Japanese patrol and in the ensuing fight eight Japanese were killed and four wounded, while the Australians got away with one wounded. No definite information could be gathered about Japanese dispositions, other than that they were dispersed over a broad area, with an apparent concentration around Kokoda.[4]

Some of the new arrivals now at Deniki had been equipped with Thompson sub-machine guns. In the 'hands of these young Australians,' wrote Raymond Paull the first historian of the Kokoda Campaign, 'the light automatic weapon proved its superiority for jungle fighting and encouraged them to adopt aggressive tactics against the enemy'.[5] However, not all were provided with sufficient time to train with the weapon, as recalled by 28-year-old Lieutenant Hugh Dalby from Campbelltown in South Australia with 'E' Company: 'The biggest fear I think that I had was that we got issued with Thompson Sub-Machine Guns the day before we left, and my men had never ever fired a Thompson . . . never seen one in their lives. Whenever we had ten minutes to spare at one of these camps [along the track], we'd get the machine-gunners to let off a bit of a burst.'[6]

•

Lieutenant Kienzle and four signallers attempted to lay a telephone cable from the main line beyond Eora Creek to Myola; however, they ran out of cable about 750 metres short of Myola.[7] Not far away, Doc Vernon had finally reached Kagi, just north of Efogi, and later recorded in his diary that the village had 'changed from a solitary hut on a forlorn hill-side to a busy station, and it was now almost uncomfortably crowded.

The Airforce had recently attempted to drop supplies there, but much had been lost on the hillsides and the experiment was not repeated. It was here that I met W.O. McCrae of ANGAU who was one of the best fellows along the line . . . He and I had a long talk over the troubles of the carriers'.[8] Again, it was deemed critical to send another message to ANGAU at Port Moresby stressing the needs of the carriers.[9]

•

Early next morning—8 August—the three companies that were to recapture Kokoda moved out for the attack. Captain Bidstrup and the men of 'D' Company left Deniki at 6.30 a.m. for Pirivi, covering the right flank where they were to ambush and hold back any Japanese reinforcements from Oivi to the east. With Bidstrup was medic Jack Wilkinson and Sergeant Evensen with sixteen Papuan troops from the 1st PIB. Half an hour later, Captain Symington and his men of 'A' Company moved out, with him were Captain Brewer and Lance Corporal Sanopa of the RPC who led the way. Symington's men were to assault Kokoda by the central track reconnoitred the day before, however, they would not divert east to join the central track at Overa but push northward directly from Deniki and join the track midway between Overa and its junction with the main track. Half an hour after they left, Major Elliott-Smith with Captain Dean and his men of 'C' Company, covering the left flank, moved out along the main track. They took with them four Australians and seventeen Papuans of the 1st PIB and a few men of the RPC. Coming up behind them was Cameron and his small Headquarters Company.[10]

Unknown to them, Japanese Lieutenant Colonel Tsukamoto and the bulk of his men of the I/144th Battalion were now also moving up the same track in their planned attack against Deniki. Among these men were 2nd Lieutenant Onogawa and his men of No. 2 Platoon, No. 3 Company, who had moved out at 3.30 a.m., and had by daylight taken up a position on a hill overlooking the main track to the south. He waited there while a three-man reconnaissance patrol was sent out. He was not to know that he and the rest of the column would soon be flanked by the Australian advance against Kokoda.[11] It is likely that

Onogawa and his men were the Japanese that were observed taking up a position on a hill overlooking the Australian positions at Deniki. These men were linked by a telephone cable back to a mountain gun that had been brought forward to assist in the attack against Deniki.[12] The unknown signaller attached to No. 2 Section was also supporting this gun as recorded in his diary for 8 August: 'Left Kokoda at 0750, No. 2 Coy encountered the enemy in the jungle near the Stanley Range. Established a line of communication between the observation post and the gun position. Worked on the communication line between Bn HQ and the Nose Tai [No. 3 Company] which is located on left side of the main road, 100 metres back from a small stream'.[13]

•

Still well behind the Japanese lines were Father Holland and the refugees from Sangara mission. He had decided their presence in the area was endangering the locals who were supporting them. Originally Holland had decided to cross the Owen Stanleys in the Managalas area, where his life-long friend Andrew Unware said the going was easier than the track further south-west at Kokoda and beyond. They arrived at Seapareta village, likely on the night of 8 August, to find that Captain Louis Austen and his small party had relocated to the next village— Sewa. At Seapareta they were fed and provided food for the night by a young married woman who was a friend of Unware's family. The next morning, Reverend Holland tried to recruit some locals as carriers to help them reach Sewa where Austen was waiting for them, but all refused. Indeed, he was told by one, 'that the days of the Europeans were over and that the spirits of dead friends and relatives dressed as soldiers would soon be coming bearing great amounts of valuable cargo'.[14] The cargo cult associated with Melanesia, first recognised in 1945, had clearly already taken root. Holland told the man he was speaking utter rot. For his troubles he was immediately set upon by the man and knocked to the ground. The married woman intervened and, with her husband, they agreed to help carry their supplies to Sewa.[15]

34

'Believe I pinned Jap to ground with bayonet and screamed . . .'

On the right flank, Bidstrup and his men of 'D' Company made good progress until they neared the village of Pirivi where they encountered several snipers, which delayed their advance for over an hour. Bren-gunner Private Leslie Balfour, a 21-year-old labourer from Drouin in Victoria, was killed, while three others were seriously wounded.[1] Sergeant John Manol, a 21-year-old waiter from Prahran in Victoria, a member of the battalion's intelligence section, had been attached to 'D' Company and recalled many years later:

> D Company was approaching its rendezvous on the back track to Oivi, when they struck a Japanese working party. They were foraging for taro in a village called Pirivi. The company killed a few Japanese there, but the Japanese (who) had retreated had left behind snipers . . . They lost Lofty Balfour the Bren gunner, lost Lieutenant Crawford, a South Australian; he was hit in the head and hip. Bill Hoskins was hit in the mouth. Lieutenant McClean, 16 Platoon's commander noticed move-ment. The boys were looking up at the trees for this [one] sniper, but he was laying in the middle of the track with a net over him and Lieutenant McClean killed him with a grenade. Anyway, we had found that the Japanese were waiting for us. Private [Archibald] Skilbeck took Balfour's Bren gun and I can remember that when we ran into that ambush, that poor old 'Skilly' [he was just 21 years old] was screaming at the top of his voice, that he was getting some for Lofty Balfour.[2]

Back again with 'D' Company was Jack Wilkinson, who had volunteered to serve temporarily with 'B' Company as their medic. He wrote in his diary of this encounter: 'Went to Pirivi with D Coy. Shot 2 Japs in village and one in garden. Snipers held us up for 1½ hours. Lost 2 killed 5 wounded. Captured one Rabaul native. Sergeant Evensen talked to him. Japs in gardens getting food and cutting down coconut trees for nuts.'[3] More than 40 years later, 21-year-old Private Jack 'Laurie' Howson from Clayton in Victoria, formerly with No. 2 Anti-aircraft unit, now attached to 'D' Company and carrying a .303 Lee-Enfield, also recalled the fighting at Pirivi and the impact it still had on him.

> We moved off with D Company heading for Kokoda via Pirivi and it was when we reached Pirivi that everything started to happen. If we didn't know before, well we certainly knew then that we were in action. After a few bursts of fire, the order came to fix bayonets, and it was then, for the first time, that I became really frightened. The clash in the village was short and sharp with a few killed and wounded on both sides. One Jap was lying beside the track with both legs chopped from the trunk of his body, and where his legs should have joined the trunk there was just a mass of blood—he had been cut in half by a burst of .45 'Tommy' gun fire! His eyes were still open and had a terrified expression and he was moaning. And then came the beginning of some of the terrible things that happen in combat. Our officer didn't have the stomach to finish off the dying 'Nip'—instead he detailed me to do it, and I have lived to this day with those terrified eyes staring at me.[4]

The twice-wounded commander of 17 Platoon, Lieutenant Hercules Crawford, a 34-year-old waterside worker from Port Adelaide who had served with the 2/10th Battalion in the Middle East, was now ordered by Bidstrup back to Deniki with two of his men to assist. Wilkinson recalled that Crawford was wounded by a bullet, which did not completely penetrate his helmet, but partially drilled a hole through it, driving its jagged edges into his forehead. Wilkinson had a job to get his helmet off without making the wound bigger.[5] One of Crawford's men, Private Arnold Forrester, a 21-year-old textile worker from Eildon in

Victoria, also recalled: 'Lieutenant Crawford got a bullet right in the helmet there and that pinned it to his skull and he had great difficulty getting it off without gouging the hole much larger and anyway Jack Wyld, mate of mine, and one [other] were detailed to take him back to Deniki and he got back along the track and pulled the revolver on these two boys and he said, "I'm right now, you go back to the boys." And reluctantly they left him.'[6]

Sergeant Clifford Pulfer, a 27-year-old machine operator from Footscray in Victoria with the battalion headquarters, had been assigned to lead the rearguard of 'D' Company, which included Private Jack Boland, who witnessed the circumstances of Crawford pulling his revolver on his men—and its consequences.[i]

When the main body of D Company moved on up the track towards Kokoda, they left our group of ten Ack-Ack Platoon [No. 2 Anti-aircraft unit] under Sergeant 'Bunny' Pulfer to protect their rear from any Japs coming up from the direction of Oivi ... While we were waiting there, we heard a lot of firing and sound of exploding grenades coming from the direction of Kokoda, but everything was quiet on the Oivi side. However, Lieutenant Crawford came limping along the track towards us with his head swathed in blood-stained bandages. He had a stick in one hand and a revolver in the other and was escorted by Jack Wyld and someone else. When they came up level with us, he told Jack and the other chap to return to the company. But Jack insisted that they had been ordered to escort him back to Deniki for treatment. Crawford then got very excited. He ordered Jack to return and, to make him obey, pointed his revolver at him. Jack and the other chap went back, and Lieutenant Crawford hobbled on alone. And that was the last time anyone saw him.[7]

Lieutenant Hercules Crawford is listed as KIA on 8 August; the details of his death remain unknown. He was either killed by the Japanese or

---

i The Australian Official History incorrectly states that Sergeant Clifford Pulfer was killed to the west with 'C' Company when trying to bring in a wounded man; it remains unknown who was the man referred to in this heroic act. Sergeant Clifford Pulfer would be killed the next day at Deniki.

possibly fell off one of the numerous small log bridges and was washed away; either way his body was never recovered.

Sergeant Harold Marsh, a 23-year-old grocer from Traralgon in Victoria, took over command of 17 Platoon. The Japanese had delayed 'D' Company's advance—Bidstrup was to be in his ambush position by 11 a.m., close to the junction with the Kokoda–Oivi track just north of the village. They reached the junction and took up their position just as a strong Japanese party from Oivi was advancing westward towards Kokoda. These men belonged to the 15th Naval Pioneers who also acted as combat troops; they had been tasked with transporting supplies to Kokoda and to set up an advance supply depot there.[8]

Lieutenant McClean's 16 Platoon was covering the right flank on the southern side of the junction when they saw the Japanese approaching. He and his men waited for as many of them to appear on the track before opening fire. Sergeant Morrison recalled the Japanese advance, stating that their scouts were, 'almost turning over each separate leaf' as they approached cautiously.[9] Bren-gunner Private Archibald Skilbeck was the first to open fire, sweeping the track and the jungle either side of it with bullets from a full magazine, which he quickly replaced and continued to fire at the Japanese, who were now quickly deployed off the track. His mates were also firing into the enemy, collectively inflicting several casualties. Australians and Japanese fought each other in the thick bush and lowland jungle scrub.[10]

On their left about 100 metres away was Marsh commanding 17 Platoon. He was getting into position just as the fighting broke out to his right. Now his men saw several Japanese quickly deploying on the track coming from the opposite direction, having left Kokoda for Oivi. Marsh and his men were now involved in a firefight with these enemy troops; with the opening shots he suffered four more casualties, two killed and two wounded. Corporal Bailey with Marsh's platoon recalled taking up their position just as the fighting broke out:

> We got onto Oivi Road and we spread out along the road from the track . . . we had a view of Oivi Road. Harold Marsh was our sergeant . . . We had no sooner got there . . . and the Japanese came

along, two files along the road, this was where it was very hard on me. My mate Jack Robinson[ii] ... was only about ten feet [3 metres] away ... and the first shot that was fired went straight through his forehead. I had to leave him, the way it was we started the fighting and we mowed down what we could see in front of us, we fired on and caused a lot of casualties to the Japanese. They fired but they didn't do the damage because they were out in the open and they were a bit of a sitting target. It was only about twenty minutes to half an hour that the heavy fighting took place.[11]

The two Australian platoons were sandwiched between a Japanese force from the east and west. McClean got word from Bidstrup that he was to withdraw his men south, but no one could get through to Marsh and his men. They had been forced into a tight perimeter, cut off from the rest of the company in a fight to the death. Bidstrup tried unsuccessfully to break through to Marsh's stranded platoon. He sent Victorians, privates Thomas Freestone, a 21-year-old turner from Clayton and Erwin Josch, a 24-year-old barman from Toolleen, to try to contact Marsh with orders to withdraw back to the company. Private Forrester recalled: 'The two took off with Lee-Enfield rifles, carried at the ready. They rounded a slight bend in the track; we heard two shots and these men were never seen again.[iii] We were heavily engulfed. All hell broke loose. The enemy was feeling our flanks to get around us.'[12]

Bidstrup had heard no firing from Kokoda and assessed that the attack there had failed. However, Kokoda had already been captured by Symington and his men almost without a shot being fired, as the bulk of the Japanese had left the plateau and were now moving up the main track to the west to assault Deniki. By 4.30 p.m. darkness was approaching; Bidstrup had earlier ordered his platoon commanders to make their own way back to Deniki if they were cut off. He now withdrew 16 Platoon under Lieutenant Doug McClean and 18 Platoon, led

---

ii   Twenty-seven-year-old Private John Robertson from Orbost in Victoria, is listed as KIA on 8 August 1942, with no known grave.

iii Private Thomas Freestone and Private Erwin Josch are listed as KIA on 8 August, with no known graves.

by 23-year-old Lieutenant Jack Hirst from Thornbury in Victoria, back
through Pirivi. These men were harassed all the way by the Japanese,
who attacked their rear and flanks. Jack Wilkinson recalled:

> Left 1630 hours and carried wounded back to village [Pirivi]. Used
> rubber bucket for water and copra bags for stretcher. Estimate Jap
> casualties twenty killed twenty-five wounded on Oivi–Kokoda road.
> Twenty Japs in village ten minutes after we left . . . One man killed on
> road. Bullet struck him on right side of neck and travelled down into
> body. Instant death and rigidity. Still knelt up and held rifle in ready
> position. An awesome sight. I thought he was still alive. Body was quite
> stiff and rigid from moment of bullet impact. Hell of a mess in Pirivi
> village during scrimmage. Believe I pinned Jap to ground with bayonet
> and screamed with laughter. Remember putting field dressing on one of
> our chaps and firing at roof of houses at same time. One of my police
> went back to nature and used rifle as a club.[13]

The battalion war diary records the situation: 'The remainder
of the Coy . . . remained in posn . . . endeavouring to make contact
with 17 Pl and finally withdrew, beating off a determined ENEMY
attack from front and left flank during the retirement.' Before the
action, all had been ordered that if cut off they were to take to the
bush and head for Deniki. As no firing had actually been heard from
the Kokoda area it was deemed 'advisable to return to DENIKI—the
indication being that the KOKODA attack had NOT been carried out
as planned'.[14]

Bidstrup and most of his company—minus 17 Platoon—withdrew
through Pirivi and took up a position north-east of Deniki at Komondo
for the night. Private Forrester recalled at this point how his small party
were carrying the badly wounded Private Bernie Hanlon, a 28-year-old
barber from Albury in New South Wales. They made slow progress with
the 'stretcher . . . we gave Private Hanlon a smoke. A little rain began to
fall, and our wounded man passed out.'[15] Captain Bidstrup's company
had suffered eleven men killed, wounded or missing, but he had no idea
of what had befallen Marsh and his 30 or so men.[16]

With the withdrawal through Pirivi, Private Boland and his mates, in their ten-man section acting as the company's rearguard, were ordered by Bidstrup to advance and try to extract 17 Platoon. He recalled many years later:

When the main body of D Company had passed through our positions, we were detailed to go towards Kokoda to look for 17 Platoon. Our two forward scouts had hardly got around the first bend in the track when they came running back to tell us the Japs were coming by the hundred. We managed to get back into a position near Pirivi village and I set up the Bren gun with a good field of fire along a straight stretch of track ...

Then the Japs came around the corner about eight abreast. I signaled for the spare Bren magazines to be brought up, but Sergeant Pulfer directed that we should not fire as our job was to protect the rear of the company which was handicapped with the wounded. So, we gathered up our weapons and ammo and got out the side of the village to follow the company. It was getting dark by this time and the Japs could not have seen us as they did not follow us. I still have mixed feelings about the decision not to fire. I think we could have got about 20 or more of them, including, perhaps, the one who, next day, shot 'Bunny' Pulfer ...

About an hour after we withdrew from the village it was pitch dark. We had already found the track leading to Deniki, and in our efforts to put as much distance as possible between us and the Japs we had one fellow crawling along and feeling for the track with his hands. We moved along like that for what seemed hours until we were all dog-tired. So we decided to move off the track into the scrub and sleep, hoping we would wake up in time not to be caught by the Japs.[17]

Luckily, they woke the next day to find they were less than 100 metres from the rest of 'D' Company; they were found by a patrol that Bidstrup had sent out at first light to look for them.[18]

35

'Cooked and eat Jap rice'

While Bidstrup's company was engaged, Symington and his men of 'A' Company had pushed through the jungle from Deniki and come up to the central track, approaching their objective partly travelling through Faiwani Creek. They soon reached the junction with the main Kokoda Track just south of the plantation. Leading the way was Lance Corporal Sanopa, as recalled by Sergeant William Guest, a 21-year-old clerk from East Brunswick in Victoria, who was then in charge of 8 Platoon. 'We took off and we had a well-known native corporal by the name of Sanopa and he was a policeman ... Sanopa was out of this world because while we were waiting up there at Deniki, Sanopa would take off on his own down towards the Kokoda airstrip where the Japs were and the next thing you knew about Sanopa is you'd hear a noise and a figure would appear beside you. He would have a piece of jungle vine with ears on it. Two ears represented one Japanese, you divided the number by two and that's how many Japanese that he had killed ... We got down through the jungle and we had to wade up the river to the back of Kokoda, everything was quiet and all, you could hear bird calls, there was no fighting or shooting going on.'[1]

They arrived a few hours after sixteen P-39s, each loaded with a 230-kilogram bomb, had targeted the plateau. After completing their bombing mission each pilot banked his fighter and strafed the plateau and airfield with machine-gun fire, silencing at least one machine-gun position. This sortie had been requested by Cameron the previous day to support their attack against the plateau.[2]

Symington and his men were soon moving through the plantation with 8 Platoon on the right, 7 Platoon on the left and 9 Platoon with Company Headquarters in support. On pushing through to the main station area, they faced little opposition from the dispersed parties of Japanese troops, numbering around 40 men, defending the plateau— most fled. Sergeant Guest recalled many years later his platoon's advance into Kokoda.

> We lay outside Kokoda and one of our Kittyhawks came in and flew over it and [disappeared] and then the company commander said, 'Advance in.' I was on the extreme right-hand side, if you can imagine a big rubber plantation, the troops attacked Kokoda in one straight line, and I was on the extreme right. As I looked down there was a track, a plateau, you looked down on the plateau onto the bottom level and we were on the top. I saw this Japanese standing there like that, staring up with his mouth opened, so I got my rifle up, bang, and I kicked the dirt up between his feet. Of all the greyhounds I had, none of them went faster and he just took off for the jungle. The funny thing about it was, and it would only happen in the Australian Army, the war had stopped, and a voice said, 'Who fired that shot?' and I didn't say it was me. They said, 'Okay, away we go.' We did the final charge in Kokoda and there was no one there, there was absolutely no one there . . .
>
> [There] was . . . a newly dug grave between two huts and it had a little container on it filled with sweets and things and it was sort of decorated and we worked out later on it could have been our Colonel Owen who was killed there with 'B' Company . . . They were the insignia rank . . . seeing that he was a lieutenant colonel and because of his rank they decorated his grave. We saw another heap of rice on a plate and human excreta beside it and we walked further on and there was no Japs.[3]

It is likely that the grave was that of Captain Ogawa Tetsuo commander of No. 1 Company, I/144th Regiment, who had been killed during the first battle for Kokoda. Lieutenant Colonel Bill Owen's body was found the next day, dumped in a slit trench near the former

Australian aid post, and was buried near Graham's house by men of
7 Platoon.[4]

Corporal Donald Daniels recalled their arrival on the plateau: '[We]
went down this disused track and walked up onto the plateau and there
wasn't a soul there. They had all gone up to meet C and D Company.
We walked onto the plateau and we shot one Jap. He was pumping up
his bike tyre. That was it . . . We sat on our backsides or when I say, we
rested there knowing full well that they're going to turn around and
counter-attack or send up another wave from Gona. So we are going to
be caught right in the very middle.' He described the Kokoda Plateau
as being 'only about 500 metres wide by about 1000 metres long . . . it
was all rubber up the top then but all the way around there had a steep
grade down which had steps down which lead out to the airstrip. But it
had a steep cliff all the way around.'[5]

Lance Corporal Lochhead, leading 9 Platoon, who with his men
would soon be in the thick of the fighting to hold the southern part
of the plateau, recalled many years later: 'And "A" Company went
blithely down, and we occupied the plateau because there was no-one
there. Just two of them who were looking after their stores . . . So, we
just moved up and occupied Kokoda. Crikey . . . we realised what had
happened . . . We'd gone on an old track that hadn't been used at all
and they'd gone up the main track, which we didn't go on. But we knew
something was happening, because we could hear the gunfire.'[6]

After the men of 7 and 8 platoons swept the plateau, the men of
7 Platoon moved off its western side and crossed over to the airstrip.
Signaller Ken Phelan recalled a patrol from 7 Platoon was sent to the
Yodda track across the swing bridge spanning Madi Creek. Lieutenant
Sorenson and Staff Sergeant Jim Cowey, a 52-year-old orchardist from
Belgrave in Victoria, went with them to the airstrip to fire a flare using
the Verey pistol, which would indicate to Cameron and others that
Kokoda had been retaken. The flare exploded in the afternoon light,
but no Australians beyond Kokoda saw it. Meanwhile, men from 7
Platoon had found some 'Jap records . . . including a map of the route
to Port Moresby. A set of full marching equipment was found and a
bicycle. There was an ominous silence on the plateau, the company

being aware that the [Japanese] counterattack would soon be launched. Lt Sorenson with 7 Platoon on the west side, the patrol had returned from the Yodda track, 8 Platoon on the north-east side facing the Oivi track and 9 Platoon facing Deniki track on the edge of the plantation.'[7]

Sergeant Major Mowat wrote in his diary on capturing the plateau and anxiously waiting on word from 'C' and 'D' companies: 'Attacked through approx. 400 yds of rubber plantation. Extended order, three waves, no opposition. Few Japs seen. Buzzed off. Platoon went to aerodrome. No opposition. Returned to Kokoda. Consolidated position. No word of C or D Coy. Skipper worried. Collected quantity of enemy gear. Equipment, weapons, food etc . . . Cooked and eat Jap rice.'[8] Lance Corporal Lochhead also recalled: 'They were supposed to send a flare up at night-time or dusk, to say that they had arrived, and everything was all right. Well, they fired the flare, but no-one saw it at all. And we had no wireless there to communicate to say that we had arrived. They were supposed to send an aircraft with ammunition and food.'[9] While the flare had not been seen by any Australians, it is likely that some Japanese strung out along the end of Lieutenant Colonel Tsukamoto's column on the Kokoda–Deniki track saw the flare and passed word up the line to their CO.

Symington placed Lieutenant Frank Trotter, a 29-year-old bank manager from Goomalling in Western Australia, and his men of 7 Platoon along the north-western and western edge of the plateau. Sergeant William Guest and the men of 8 Platoon were positioned along the north-eastern and eastern side of the plateau. Lieutenant Roy Neal, a 22-year-old storekeeper from Caulfield in Victoria, and his men of 9 Platoon were to defend the southern perimeter within the edge of the rubber plantation—these men would face the bulk of Japanese attacks against the plateau.

Symington had achieved his objective of capturing Kokoda Station, which overlooked the airfield—all that he and his men now had to do was hold it. As these men dug in all could clearly hear the fighting of the battles that had broken out to the south-west and east of their position.[10]

36

'The Japs are right behind us'

Covering the western flank, moving north along the main Deniki–Kokoda track was Captain Dean and his men of 'C' Company with Battalion Headquarters in support. It was not long before they ran into Lieutenant Johnston and his two men who had been out all night reconnoitring the western approach and were making their way back to Deniki. Johnston reported that the Japanese were entrenched up ahead, on the other side of Faiwani Creek, including machine-gun and mortar positions, as recorded in the battalion war diary:

> Lieut. JOHNSTON and his patrol were met. This patrol had been out since 0600 hrs on the previous morning. Lieut. JOHNSTON reported ENEMY posns being dug on SW corner of LARGE RUBBER. He estimated that posns would accommodate one Sec. More posns were seen to be situated towards NW corner, but it was NOT possible to obtain detailed information. Further posns were being dug further NORTH. These appeared to include mortar posns. As they moved on to the main track on their return, they encountered an ENEMY patrol of eleven. ENEMY opened fire, but our patrol was able to elude it. It was considered that as this patrol's presence had become known to the ENEMY, the ENEMY patrol already encountered had been sent out to prevent Lieut. JOHNSTON from returning to our lines.[1]

The Japanese were now aware that the Australians were on the track and would be prepared and waiting for them. Indeed, not long after, movement was noticed within nearby vegetation; a burst of fire from a Thompson or Bren gun sprayed the spot, and on investigating, seven Japanese were found dead; but two were seen to get away. Meanwhile the forward elements of Tsukamoto's column had fallen back, and the Australians advanced cautiously towards the creek crossing.[2]

Advanced elements of Arthur Dean's 'C' Company were soon targeted by a well-sited heavy machine gun commanding the Faiwani Creek crossing, which was partly defined by a steep gully. Thirty-five-year-old Lieutenant Alfred Salmon from Poowong in Victoria, commanding 13 Platoon, was ordered to take out the entrenched machine gun. Using fire and movement they forced the Japanese to fall back, allowing Salmon and his men to cross the creek. It was approaching noon; by now they should have been in position to support 'A' Company's attack against the plateau as recorded in the battalion war diary: 'At the river the advance of the Coy was held up by M.G. fire. 13 Pl. (Lieut. SALMON) was ordered around to the right to try to silence the gun, and two secs were sent round to the left to test the possibility of crossing the river there ... the M.G. fire at the river had delayed the advance considerably—so that the river was NOT crossed till 1200 hrs, at which time the Coy had been expected to commence its attack on KOKODA.'[3]

Captain Dean now moved forward to see what was holding up the advance and was immediately targeted by a Japanese sniper as he attempted to cross a log over the creek; he was hit in the stomach. Medical officer John Shera hurried forward but Dean was dead before he got to him. With this, 'like a flame in sun-scorched grass, the words, "the skipper's gone" spread among the men; heedless of snipers and Jukis alike, the Australians rose and swept across the gully at the Japanese'.[4] Major Elliott-Smith was close by and recalled while under fire some of his Papuans of the 1st PIB were burying Dean 'with not the slightest sign of panic'.[i][5]

Major Cameron, who was not far from Dean when he was killed, appointed Lieutenant McNamara as the temporary commander of 'C' Company. Given the confusion created by the sudden rush

i   In 1967 members of the 39th Battalion Association returned to the area and identified Captain Arthur Cyril Dean's unmarked grave. His remains were soon after reinterred in the Bomana War Cemetery near Port Moresby.

forward, a brief halt was called, and the company reorganised with 13 Platoon leading the way, followed by 14 and 15 platoons, and finally Battalion Headquarters. The battalion war diary records: 'The Coy had become dispersed at the crossing and ... after re-forming, the main body ... endeavoured to push forward along the track towards KOKODA, passing the bodies of two of the enemy who had been killed, and some abandoned arms and equipment including a L.M.G. and some rifles.'[6]

The scouts of 13 Platoon advanced to a bend in the track and here heavy machine-gun fire again opened against them. McNamara organised for two sections to flank the machine-gun position in order to find another way forward—they needed to get to Kokoda as quickly as possible and could not afford to waste time getting bogged down in having to take out any number of machine guns covering the main track—nor could they afford the likely casualties that such attacks would entail. It was fast approaching 2 p.m. The battalion war diary records: 'The advance was again held up by M.G. fire at a bend in the track about 400 yards [around 350 metres] from the river. Two Secs were sent out on either flank to recce another route, and if possible, to silence the guns. At 1600 hrs the advance was still held-up—the Secs NOT having succeeded.'[7]

Unknown to Cameron, his force pushing north along the main Deniki–Kokoda track, had collided head on with the main Japanese force moving south, along the same track, to capture Deniki. He was outnumbered by at least three to one, although rear elements of the Japanese force were strung out behind. The company then attacked 'so vigorously that they drove the Japanese out of their most forward positions and killed a number of them'.[8] As they tried to advance further, they came under additional intense fire from other entrenched Japanese, forcing them to ground. Cameron realised his men could advance no further as they were obviously facing a large enemy force. By late afternoon, he ordered his men to fall back with their wounded to Deniki.[9]

Chaplain 'Nobby' Earl, who had moved out with the company at the beginning of the day, had been caring for the wounded at what had been the Japanese forward position near the creek. He gave the wounded several cigarettes that he had scavenged from the dead Japanese lying nearby—he was told to get all wounded back to Deniki 'pronto'. Soon the Australians had withdrawn back across the creek and up the mountain track to Deniki.[10] Lance Corporal William Mahoney with 13 Platoon recalled Father Norbert Earl as, 'one of the greatest people that I have ever known and a very wonderful man ... He was seen frequently in the heat of fire risking his own life and kneeling under trees hearing the confessions of men who could have been dead the next second, he was indeed a wonderful person.'[11] Captain Bidstrup also recalled: 'Father Earl—Nobby to us heretics—and whom he liked to be called by us who were not of his faith; never have I met a man who has made such an impression on me by his absolute, simple faith; and if I was asked to say what my definition of a thoroughly happy man was I would say Nobby Earl. He owned nothing and yet he owned the world.'[12] However, we do know that when he originally signed up with the battalion at Port Moresby he, for a short time at least, had owned four cases of whisky!

Lance Corporal William Bellairs, a 24-year-old bookmaker from St Kilda in Victoria, was a signaller and was laying a telephone line out from Deniki towards Kokoda when the men from 'C' Company began their withdrawal. He recalled many years later, 'we were, me and my two sigs, endeavouring to lay a line. We had a spool of gunfire wire, we were endeavouring to lay a line ... when ... we met a few of the D [sic 'C'] Company coming back. And the first words they said were, "The Japs are right behind us." So it was a case of bring out the pliers, cut the wire, and back.'[13]

The battalion war diary records: 'As it was considered impossible to reach Kokoda before nightfall, orders were given to withdraw. The withdraw took place along the main track, the company resuming its original position at Deniki.'[14]

•

Lieutenant Colonel Tsukamoto now realised his error in leaving Kokoda undefended in his rush to take Deniki. Perhaps word reached him that a flare had been observed being fired from Kokoda Station. He ordered

No. 1 Company to the rear to reoccupy Kokoda, but by now Captain
Symington and his men of 'A' Company were already digging in there.
Second Lieutenant Hirano Kogoro commanding No. 3 Platoon, No. 1
Company, recorded the events of that day:

> The Battalion departed [Kokoda], the Coy bringing up the rear.
> Encountered a considerable number of enemy troops. Attacked them
> with battalion guns and machine guns. Afternoon, No. 2 and No. 3
> Coys pursued the enemy who began to retreat. Occupied a position
> near a bridge. While reconnoitring the enemy position, unconsciously
> advanced too far. At 200 metres in front of Deniki village, two of our
> scouts were killed by automatic rifles. Collected their bodies and
> returned . . . No. 1 Coy was ordered by Battalion to turn back to attack
> the enemy, who had occupied Kokoda.[15]

The bulk of Tsukamoto's battalion had continued their advance not
far behind Cameron's men. Indeed, while the Australian signallers were
rolling up their lines and falling back to Deniki, the Japanese signallers were advancing, laying down cables in their advance as recalled
by the unknown signaller with No. 2 Section who recorded in his
diary: 'At 1600, we crossed over the small stream by a log bridge and
advanced along the main road. Constructed a position near the enemy
barracks [Deniki] in order to watch their movements. Wire communications were maintained by our sec and the leading group of Nose Tai
(Personnel—Okamoto, Eguchi, Sugabe and Taniura). The remaining
personnel established communications with the Yorioka Sec, which is
located 150 metres to the rear.'[16]

By 5.30 p.m., the Japanese were firing into the Australian front-line
positions at Deniki. It was difficult to assess how many Japanese were
present given the thick jungle and encroaching darkness. The firing
continued until about 9 p.m. The front line was held by the men of
'C' Company while the flanks and rear were held by Cameron's HQ staff
and members of the 1st PIB and RPC.[17] Some men from 'E' Company
were positioned further down the eastern track used by Bidstrup and
his men of 'D' Company; here some Japanese managed to penetrate the

line as recalled by Private Stanley Barcham, who was wounded while covering this approach. The then 21-year-old private recalled years later: 'Well we went forward . . . and we just kept an eye [out] to see what movement we could see. And that's the time I got shot through the legs . . . It was just like getting tripped over, you went flat on your back. The velocity from a bullet is unbelievable [,] you wouldn't think that a bullet could tip you up like that. And it wasn't long before they called the medic and took me in and gave me some morphine and along came the fuzzy-wuzzies and raced me down the hill, so the Japanese must have been getting pretty close and that's all I remember of them . . . the morphine was beginning to work.'[18]

The battalion war diary records that just before 6 p.m., the men from 'C' Company were back defending their positions at Deniki. The Japanese were not far behind and were soon targeting the Australian perimeter with rifle and machine-gun fire. Intermittent fire continued until around 9 p.m. It was difficult to assess how many Japanese were present given the thick jungle. With 'C' Company holding the forward positions, Cameron ordered his staff personnel and the officers and men of the 1st PIB and RPC to protect the flanks, along with the canteen staff, including cooks; there was no need for the cooks that night as no fires could be used—all ate dry rations, shivering through the night, anxiously awaiting the dawn.[19]

•

The men of the militia 14th Field Ambulance had established a medical post at Isurava, with elements of the unit pushing forward to Deniki. That night these men helped the wounded, including three stretcher cases, back to Isurava, one of these men would have been Private Barcham.[20] Further south at Myola, Lieutenant Bert Kienzle was waiting in vain for the arrival of the air transports and their vital supplies. He wrote for 8 August: 'At MYOLA we waited all day for planes to drop the much-needed supplies. I had the camp extended for carriers as well as for troops. At 1600 hrs. heard of Japs attacking DENIKI in force. We heard explosions at 2200 hrs. I sent further messages requesting supplies to be dropped [at] MYOLA and not at KAGI.'[21] He did not know that the only two transport aircraft in Papua had just been sent back to Australia. By now he had also heard of the fighting around the plateau on 29 July—unaware that a second battle for Kokoda was now taking place. He wrote to Meryl: 'I am fit but feel the loss of our home very much—I am confident we will recover it [before] long. Wish I could get a few of the yellow blighters, didn't think I'd have to fight for my own home, like this, well, as long as we pull through.'[22]

37

'His main concern was how much trouble he was to us'

Cameron's small divided force was now defending Deniki from a Japanese attack. He had placed Captain Ken Jacob in command of 'C' Company with the death of Dean on his return. The battalion war diary for 9 August records: 'At 0745 hrs, the ENEMY again attacked on our front. It was NOT possible to ascertain the strength of their force owing to the cover which the jungle provided for them. Ample indication of their presence was given by intermittent small arms and M.G. fire, which continued throughout the morning. A and D Coys had NOT yet returned from operations of the previous day and the posn of C Coy and Bn H.Q. appeared to be precarious.'[1] Indeed, during the early hours of 9 August, Symington and 'A' Company had dug in at Kokoda still unmolested by the Japanese; while north-east of Deniki, Bidstrup and his men of 'D' Company—minus Marsh's 17 Platoon—were at Komondo.

•

The men of Marsh's platoon were trying to escape from the road junction north of Pirivi. During the early morning hours, Sergeant Marsh ordered his men to break contact with the enemy; they were to make their way back to Deniki as best as they could.[2] Still in the fight here was Corporal Bailey.

Word came through, but I don't know how it came through, it must've come through one of my men on the left . . . that they were going to withdraw. I had no contact with the rest of the men, the only contact I had was with the four men that were in my area . . . Joe Dwyer from Bairnsdale . . . was with me and we crossed Aurora creek the four of us. Joe said that he was going for a drink back up the creek and I was telling him not to go. Joe was a strange man, he was an individual and Joe wandered away. He walked away and I looked back from where we had walked, and I saw two Japanese . . . We didn't fire on them because we knew if we did, we'd be gone and there were only three of us at this stage, it would have been suicide. Two of them did an encircled movement and came in . . . around where our platoon had been. So, we got out of that area. We were trying to catch up with the other fellows, but we couldn't find them.[3]

•

At around 7 a.m., Bidstrup, who was getting ready to leave Komondo, ordered Sergeant Clifford 'Bunny' Pulfer to lead a patrol into Deniki ahead of the main body of 'D' Company to determine whether it was still in Australian hands, and if so, to inform Cameron that the rest of 'D' Company would be there by noon. He also sent another patrol, led by Lieutenant Bevan French, a 24-year-old dairy farmer from Malvern Hill in Victoria, further south to reconnoitre Eora Creek to make sure the rear of Deniki was clear of Japanese.[4]

Bidstrup allowed Pulfer to pick the men who would accompany him, among them was Private Laurie Howson: '"Bunny" naturally picked chaps he knew to go with him. I remember Dudley Beulke [sic Beuike] was with us and about four others. A native police boy led us across country'.[5] Not long after Bidstrup heard intense fire coming from the direction of Deniki; he was concerned that Pulfer and his men had been ambushed, he picked up the pace towards the sound of the firing. However, one of his men, 33-year-old Private Reginald Tierney from Morwell Bridge in Victoria—one of the older men of the battalion— could not keep pace and sat on a log, telling the others to push on, he would catch up as soon as he had regained his breath. Not long after his mates heard him yelling in agony, it was distressing for these men as they knew he was being slowly tortured by the Japanese, who were trying to draw them back to rescue him. Private Reginald Tierney's remains were never found.[6]

•

Pulfer and his men came out of the jungle onto the main track right to Deniki as recalled by Private Howson: 'So, a message was sent back to "Biddy" [Bidstrup] that C Company was holding Deniki and we were absorbed into C Company's strength.'[7] At Deniki, the Japanese were conducting several ad hoc attacks; continually sweeping the Australian positions with heavy machine-gun fire. It was difficult to see the well-camouflaged Japanese, who garnished their helmets and clothing with jungle vegetation. There was a real danger that Deniki was about to be overrun; all anxiously looked for the men of 'A' and 'D' companies to reinforce them. During one of the first assaults made, Sergeant Pulfer was killed as recalled by Private Howson:

> Captain Jacob was expecting that the 'Nips' wouldn't lose any time
> having a go at us after everything that had happened the day before.
> He made me a corporal and put me in charge of a section. Then
> he sent Bunny's section and mine forward of the company's main
> position. There was a long ridge sloping down about a hundred
> yards in front of us ... all of a sudden, a column of 'Nip' soldiers
> appeared moving along the ridge and we opened up with everything
> we had. Then one of Pulfer's section yelled out, 'They've got Bunny!'
> That gave me a shock. Bunny was one of the older chaps in the unit
> and he meant a lot to me. Things were grim at that stage and your
> comrade alongside you became your mother, father and God all
> rolled into one.[8]

About this time, news arrived at Deniki from 'A' Company, brought in by the indefatigable Lance Corporal Sanopa and one of his men, who had made their way through the Japanese lines and reached Deniki with the captured documents and maps. These were the first Japanese documents to be captured during the Kokoda Campaign. They also brought a note from Symington requesting reinforcements and an airdrop of food and ammunition as each man had only gone into battle with two days' rations, 100 rounds of ammunition and just two grenades.

As if he hadn't done enough, Sanopa now requested that he be allowed to return to 'A' Company with a supply of sugar and tea for the troops at Kokoda. Soon he and his mate were heading back down the mountain slopes avoiding the Japanese with their self-appointed mission of providing tea and sugar to the Australians entrenching at Kokoda—no one should trivialise the beneficial effect of a good hot cup of tea on troop morale.[9]

During the early afternoon at Deniki, Captain Jesser was wounded in the arm when standing to fire at a Papuan who was attempting to guide a party of Japanese into the battalion's perimeter—Jesser shot and killed the man. Under covering fire from Jesser's men of the 1st PIB, privates Paul Lafe and Gabriel Ehave carried Jesser to the aid post. Shortly after, the Japanese attacks ceased as did much of their machine-gun and rifle fire; it became evident that they were withdrawing back towards Kokoda. Bidstrup, with advance elements of 'D' Company, had arrived at Deniki at around 1.30 p.m., while those further back, including those helping the wounded, arrived many hours later. All hoped that Marsh and his men of 17 Platoon would be at Deniki—they weren't. The survivors of this platoon would not arrive at Deniki until the next day bringing in two of their wounded.[10]

Jack Wilkinson with 'D' Company was still looking after the wounded and wrote in his diary after returning to Deniki: 'Sat up all [previous] night putting hot stones around stretcher case (Hanlon). Sucking wound of back. Holding rosary and crucifix all the time. No rations at all. Made Deniki 1700 hrs very wet and tired. Completely buggered but felt better after a meal. Cameron chewing his whiskers.'[11] Private Boland also recalled the journey: 'It took us most of the day to get to Deniki with our wounded. All who could had to take a turn carrying Bernie Hanlon's stretcher. He wasn't a very big chap, but after you had carried his stretcher for about 20 minutes you were almost exhausted (since then I have often wondered how those New Guinea natives managed to carry a stretcher case for 6–7 days). Hanlon had been shot through the lung, but his main concern was how much trouble he was to us.'[12] By now the only sound of battle that could be heard was coming from Kokoda, the fighting there had broken out around 11 a.m.[13]

38

'My bloody brains are running out'

Symington and his men of 'A' Company had dug in along the old Australian positions held during the first battle for Kokoda almost two weeks before as well as those dug by the Japanese after its capture. It had been a quiet night and at first light—9 August—there was still no sign of the Japanese and a patrol was sent out led by the company 2i/c, Lieutenant Sorenson. Among them was Lance Corporal Alexander Lochhead and his men of 9 Platoon who recalled: 'At daybreak, after a quick "breakfast" we cleaned our weapons and then joined a patrol by Lieutenant Sorenson. We passed through the rubber towards the foothills of the Owen Stanleys along the Deniki–Kokoda track axis, but there was no enemy contact and we returned to our position about 10 a.m.'[1] He was soon back taking up his position along the southern end, close to the plantation. He was not to know that the Japanese had followed close behind them to break into the southern perimeter under the cover of their return. The men of 9 Platoon would be the focus of Japanese attempts to break through the Australian perimeter as they pushed north from Deniki along the main track to retake Kokoda.[2]

At around 11 a.m., Lieutenant Neal commanding 9 Platoon spotted around 100 men camouflaged with vegetation and covered in mud moving cautiously towards his position through the southern part of the rubber plantation. At first some of Neal's men thought these were the men of 'C' Company, as recalled by Acting Sergeant Lawrence 'Laurie' Downes, a 23-year-old tram conductor from Melbourne with

9 Platoon: 'Someone yelled out, "Here comes C Company" from down here. They're running from tree to tree, but it wasn't C Company ... C Company got knocked out at the crossing and the Japs were coming. So the Japs were coming up here.'[3] Lochhead also recalled: 'We had just settled down and organised sentry duty when someone called out: "Here comes C Company through the rubber!" We all stood up for a good look, but it was difficult to distinguish just who was moving through the trees. Then when they were about 200 yards away, the matter was settled by a shot. Obviously, our patrol had been followed in, although we had not sighted any enemy.'[4]

The Japanese of No. 1 Company, supported with a heavy machine-gun platoon and mortars, launched their attack—Neal's men drove them back. Around noon the Japanese launched another attack against his position—again the Japanese were forced to retire, now heading for the rear of the plantation. It was now that Neal's platoon was reinforced with No. 1 Section, 7 Platoon, led by nineteen-year-old Corporal 'JD' John McKay from Mordialloc in Victoria.[5]

Earlier, McKay's No. 1 Section had been out on standing patrol near the northern end of the airstrip along the track leading to Yodda. On hearing the attack, 28-year-old Sergeant William 'Ted' Murray, from Rainbow in Victoria, who was with McKay, ordered their return to the plateau. Soon after arriving, McKay and his section were sent by Lieutenant Trotter to reinforce 9 Platoon who were hard-pressed. He and his men at one point had to crawl across the plateau to reach 9 Platoon, as the Japanese were sweeping the immediate area with machine-gun and mortar fire. The young NCO recalled:

We left the track and hooked our way onto the escarpment in rear of Kokoda village and, as we came out of the scrub, we were met by the smiling face of Ser-Major George Mowat. When we got back to our platoon position Frank Trotter called me over and said, '9 Platoon will have to be reinforced and I want you to take your section up to them. If you leave quickly in extended line, you'll get there without trouble.' So away we went. We had no casualties going up, although the Japs threw everything they had at us—mortar, heavy MG and rifle fire. We went to ground and crawled the last 30 yards on our stomachs. When we got up to the rubber Roy Neal and Laurie Downes put us in position.[6]

About an hour later the Japanese launched a third attack against Neal's position and the south-western flank, and while they were again repulsed, they managed in some places to dig in just 50 metres from the Australian perimeter, conducting intermittent rifle and machine-gun fire into the Australian positions, forcing them to keep their heads down.[7] Sergeant Downes recalled the Japanese attacks.

I was kneeling behind a rubber tree ... [Private Arthur] 'Bluey' Williams come running up on my right. [Lance Corporal] Frank McLeod was on my left. There was a shot and I looked and Bluey Williams rolled over ... lying on the ground. The next shot I said, 'They're behind us.' And I was looking back ... [a bullet] went passed [*sic*] my ear, he just missed me. There was one more shot and Frank McLeod rolls over and he was down ... and the only mark on them, a little trickle of blood running down the side of their faces ...[i] I was pinned there. Every time I tried to move, there was a shot ... I was lying behind the rubber tree ...

I had troops on the right and the rest of them were spread out ... But it was just that they [Japanese] came down through the rubber trees ... and the one that was doing the damage was a bloke up a tree ... The bullets were coming down on an angle and I was laying there, and something flopped on the back of my head and I put my hand up ... Christ! It was all sticky. So, I pulled my hand down slow. And I looked at my hand and it was white. It wasn't blood. I looked at it and I said, 'My bloody brains are running out.' It was rubber coming out of the rubber tree, latex ... there was all this bloody rubber. I had it in my hair. It was a relief quietly ... So, then they put on an attack. They'd charge, and they would get within twenty yards [about 20 metres] of you and a whistle [would] blow and they'd go back. They had the greater numbers.[8]

---

i   Twenty-year-old Private Arthur Williams from East Coburg, Victoria, and 25-year-old Lance Corporal Frank McLeod from Rutherglen, Victoria, are listed as KIA on 9 August, with no known graves.

Nearby Corporal McKay and his men had taken up a position in a drain near the edge of the plantation, thinking it would offer some protection. However, he recalled the ongoing work of the deadly Japanese snipers in the trees: 'Every time we tried to move in this drain the snipers got at us and the sniping continued all day. It was at this stage we realised they'd climbed trees and that was why they could see us in the ditch. It was then I lost the first of my section—Jack Stormont. They shot him through the back.'[9]

Sergeant Guest with 8 Platoon, along the eastern edge of the plateau, also recalled these attacks: 'The Japanese attacked us, they mortared us, they shelled us and they did everything. They attacked through the rubber, but 9 Platoon held them back...we were around the top of the escarpment and if we heard a noise, we would roll a grenade down because there was no other troops except the Japanese.'[10] Corporal Donald Daniels, with 8 Platoon, recalled his first experience of combat.

> You go numb. You go beyond being frightened. We first went into ... action ... at Kokoda proper, it was numbness. Secondly, the fact that you were there on the plateau and you more or less had no alternative ... You learn very, very quickly just how dangerous war is when the bullets start coming around ... The officers said you had better [start] digging, start scraping a bit of a hole and get down under ground level. But we had no shovels, we had no spades, we had nothing. All we had was the clothes that we stood up in and a groundsheet and that's all because all our gear we left up at Deniki ... when the first shots came over it's amazing how quickly you can dig a hole with your fingernails ... You got the heel of your boot to loosen the ground and scrape it out with your hand. Just enough to get down as low as you can into an indentation.[11]

•

Japanese 2nd Lieutenant Hirano Kogoro and his men of No. 3 Platoon, along with the rest of No. 1 Company, had earlier been ordered to retake Kokoda. He would survive the fighting and after the battle wrote in his

Australian defence and Japanese attacks against Kokoda Plateau, 9 August 1942

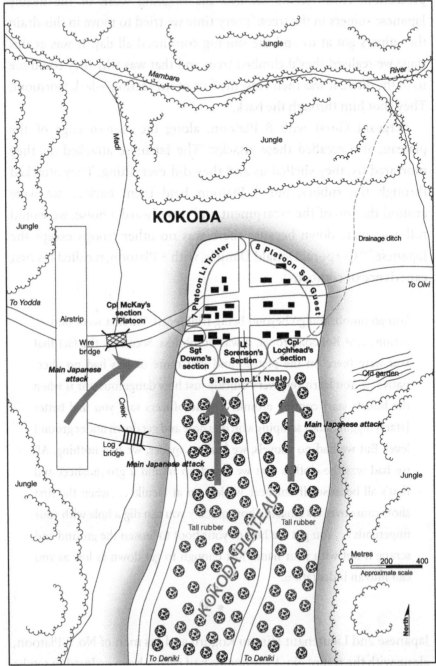

diary: 'Reached a rubber plantation at 1000. After reconnaissance, the Coy carried out a deployed attack with an additional machine-gun. The attack did not progress as desired because of the enemy's intense firing power and the pouring rain. We were unable to communicate with the Coy Commander or No. 1 Platoon leader. Decided to carry out a charge independently at dusk. Reported this decision to the Coy, and gradually closed in on the enemy.'[12]

At 2 p.m. another assault was launched against the Australian southern perimeter held by 9 Platoon, with this attack focused on Lance Corporal Lochhead's section. As he looked out from the firing line, he suddenly realised that a fern next to a tree just 50 metres away had suddenly sprouted from nowhere—he fired into it—the bush rolled over and died. His Bren gun team consisted of Victorians, twenty-year-old Private Frank 'Ron' Dridan from Amphitheatre and Private Albert 'Vic' Smythe, a 28-year-old labourer from Merbein West. In seven assaults against this section over a 24-hour period, all members were either killed or wounded, but the wounded tenaciously clung to their positions. While Dridan was wounded in the head and Smythe in the right arm, they continued to pour fire from their machine gun into the enemy, forcing the Japanese to ground. These men were lucky to survive; Lance Corporal Lochhead recalled the fighting.[13]

> During the rest of daylight, the Japs put in four or five attacks, but all were repulsed. They were obviously moving across our front to draw fire (we still hadn't learnt Tactical Lesson No. 1—NOT to give away positions by firing!). My section was pinned down by fire from a LMG and two snipers who succeeded in wounding both my Bren crew. Vic Smythe and Ron Dridan. As soon as it was dark, I moved back to Smythe and Dridan. The rest of the section were behind rubber trees to our rear. During the night there was a lot of movement. The Japs had pinpointed our positions and came in amongst us. It was pitch dark and they must have been guessing, but they guessed pretty well. My section must have done a lot of damage and annoyed them. We had no sleep that night.[14]

Privates Frank Dridan and Albert Smythe were each awarded the Military Medal for their actions over the next few days. Their section commander, Lance Corporal Alexander Lochhead, was also awarded the Military Medal for his leadership and coolness under pressure, keeping his men together over an extended period of combat, isolated from the main Australian perimeter—not giving an inch of ground.[15] Sergeant Downes nominated these men for their well-deserved awards, but many questioned why the sergeant himself was not nominated by his platoon commander for the same decoration, by all accounts he led from the front and remained cool throughout.

•

At around 4 p.m. the western perimeter of the Australian line held by 7 Platoon was assaulted in strength with around 200 Japanese charging the perimeter. This attack was supported with heavy machine-gun and mortar fire, but it was repulsed with the Japanese forced to withdraw to their positions leaving behind their dead and wounded. During the fighting Corporal McKay, who had earlier reinforced 9 Platoon, led his men under heavy fire forward to support 7 Platoon with flanking fire, placing his men in three forward positions, which greatly assisted in repelling the attack. It was not long before only three of his men were able to fire their weapons, the remaining men either dead or seriously wounded, but McKay continued to move between these posts encouraging his men to hang on—and hang on they did. Corporal John McKay would also be awarded the Military Medal for his gallant actions during the fighting.[16]

Having been unable to break through the Australian southern and western perimeters, the Japanese launched several attacks in the late afternoon against the northern and eastern parts of the line, but again failed and were forced to fall back. These attacks would continue into the night along the whole line. Just before darkness, Symington saw a Japanese force, estimated at around 200 men, massing near Neal's position at the rubber plantation. His men, however, had also seen them and were ready. In the early evening, 'quiet figures crept towards the defence and there was close fighting with grenades and bayonets. Going up to Neal's position later in the night Sorenson found two of his men lying in a forward position with their throats cut.'[17]

Leading the attacks was 2nd Lieutenant Hirano Kogoro, who had earlier told his company commander that he would launch a charge against the Australian perimeter just on darkness. He wrote in his diary: 'As dusk approached, we advanced to within 70 metres of the enemy, who concentrated an intense fire on the No. 1 Platoon. Because of our faulty formation and the hindering rain, we were unable to carry out a charge. Decided to attack at night, but men were not properly assembled. Valuable time was wasted in the torrential rain and darkness. Even the section leaders could not be lined up.'[18] Hirano eventually got his platoon organised and in the moonlight launched his attack just before 10.30 p.m., as recorded in his diary:

> Advanced stealthily on hands and knees and gradually moved in closer to the enemy. Suddenly encountered enemy guards in the ... large rubber trees. Corporal Hamada killed one of them with the bayonet and engaged the others, but the enemy's fire finally compelled us to withdraw. The platoon was scattered, and it was impossible to repeat our charge. 1st Class Pte Hirose was killed by an enemy bullet. The soldier I tangled with was wounded in the leg by a grenade thrown by Corp. Hamada. The latter was unable, due to the darkness, to assemble the men remaining. I went to the rear and tried to assemble the men by myself, but because of darkness two men and I took the wrong direction. We suddenly realised that we were within 40 metres of the enemy lines. Hand grenades were thrown at us. The night attack ended in failure. No. 1 Platoon also carried out an attack at about 0300, but it was unsuccessful also. Every day I am losing my men, and I could not repress tears of bitterness. Rested, waiting for tomorrow and struggled against the cold and hunger.[19]

In the darkness it was almost impossible to see the Japanese, and to make matters worse it began to rain heavily. Firing continued, and the Australians were now low on ammunition, grenades and food. All through the afternoon, Symington had anxiously awaited in vain for the dropping of supplies that he had requested and the arrival of reinforcements. The battalion war diary concluded for the day's fighting at Kokoda Plateau: 'Persistent attacks ... continued until dark but were unsuccessful. At 1900 hrs endeavours to infiltrate with aid of grenades was [sic] made by the ENEMY. Unsuccessful attempts at these tactics continued until 2130 hrs. After this, intermittent exchange of shots continued throughout the night.'[20]

•

Second Lieutenant Onogawa and his men of No. 2 Platoon, No. 3 Company, were heading back to Kokoda along the main track from Deniki to help the rest of the I/144th Regiment retake Kokoda. As they marched north towards the plateau, he heard that the Australians had inflicted around twenty casualties the day before against the engineers of the 15th Naval Pioneers around Pirivi; up ahead all could hear the fighting at Kokoda. Further north, Private Teruoka Akira and his comrades of the Tanaka Medical Unit were still advancing towards Kokoda from the east and had reached the Kumusi River and crossed the rebuilt suspension bridge at Wairopi. Here they set up a bivouac as the clouds opened with a massive tropical downpour.[21]

At Buna, the unwelcome news arrived that the Allied air attacks were seriously disrupting the Japanese navy's ability to supply them and that rations for the remaining weeks of August would need to be reduced. It is also likely that the marines landing at Guadalcanal necessitated the redistribution of men and supplies. At the time a local villager stated: 'The Japanese finished the food in the gardens ... Defecating and urinating, they spoiled the church. Calling out, "buta, buta", or "pig, pig", they killed and ate our pigs.'[22]

To make matters worse for the Japanese in terms of recruiting labour, 22-year-old Captain Geoffrey Lyon from Brighton in Victoria, with the 2/14th Battalion, recalled that the Japanese had, 'blotted their copybooks the moment they arrived with improper treatment of native women. That turned the natives against them which was fortunate for our side.'[23] Even worse, when retreating in the later parts of 1942, it became known that the Japanese would kill 'scores' of local labourers from fear that they might provide critical intelligence to the advancing Australians—as payback, small groups of Japanese who were forced into the jungle and bush would often disappear never to be seen again by their comrades.[24]

Further bad news arrived soon after that the convoy that had left Rabaul on 6 August for Buna carrying the construction units and desperately needed supplies had turned back for Rabaul as they had been spotted by Allied aerial reconnaissance. The landing of the US marines at Guadalcanal had sowed seeds of hesitation into the Japanese high command—they were now debating where the remaining battalions of the 144th and 41st regiments should be committed: Papua or Guadalcanal?[25]

As the battle for Kokoda raged, May Hayman along with Mavis Parkinson and Father James Benson were still at Siai. May put pencil to paper to continue her letter to Viola. Little did she know at the time that events would soon overtake them and within days they would be forced to leave their idyllic hideout.

It's just a fortnight since we came to Siai and found friends, food and peace. No not quiet for the noises of the bush have been almost as nerve racking as those of the battle zone: and of course, being shut in and not knowing anything of what is happening between our forces and the Japanese has made this fortnight almost unbearable. Yet we feel sure we are doing the right thing by waiting in the retreat because everything for our need has been so wonderfully provided.

I'll tell you of our blessings before I introduce you to the so-called quiet of the Papuan forest. In response to our letter to Ioma, overcame a tin of tea, a suitcase of Mrs. Durcher's clothes, towels etc., put together by the bachelor now resident there (both Mr. and Mrs. Durcher evacuating back in December and leaving most of their things as did all other evacuees). Also, we were told we could help ourselves to a hidden store of food stuffs just over the Kurnusi [*sic*] River. Sister and I visited this place and brought back a few tins of fish, meat and fruit also some writing material and some [condensed] milk and wheat meal. A few days later Father John got word that this store was being raided by the natives because they had heard that the Government had left Ioma, setting fire to everything there first. Father John managed to rescue more flour for us, almost a whole bag of sugar, several tins of sunshine milk, lots of tinned peaches, a few tins each of meat and veg and bacon, some jam and a case of baked beans, and several tins of coffee, so our diet these days is most nourishing and quite variable, for we have plenty of corn, yams, potatoes and papaws brought to us by our village friends.

But if we could only get some news of what is going on—all is so quiet, we rarely hear any bombs or shelling, and planes pass up very infrequently. Of course, we hear many native rumours and we find that despite our resolve to believe only firsthand information, we try to construct what seems to us a reasonable cause for the lack of air activity and sound of bombs etc.[26]

•

Back at Myola, Lieutenant Kienzle was still anxiously waiting for supplies to be dropped—it had been days now without the appearance of any aircraft—he was still unaware that Moresby had no transport planes. He wrote of his frustrations in his report to ANGAU: 'The weather was good all day but still no planes. Capt. Vernon arrived from EFOGI to inspect the medical side of the carrier line. I ordered some carriers and [a] few local village people to clean and widen the track to EFOGI.'[27] Indeed, Doc Vernon recalled his visit to Myola:

In company with Pte Small ANGAU and a guide, we broke a new trail to Myola on Sunday 9th August. It was rough going at first but when we reached the top of the range, we got onto a long strip of level ground, an unusual formation in the topsy turvy of the Owen Stanley Area. Just before reaching Myola, we met Kienzle who told us that our troops had gone back to Kokoda . . . Myola was tough; bitterly cold, wrapped

in mountain mist ... persistent every day after 11 a.m. I visited the
new landing ground, a wide-spreading grassy depression surrounded
by low hills. It stood there true to its description of a dried-up mountain lake, except that it was not particularly dry, being ... swampy in
places ... A single native sentry was guarding the area from unauthor-
ized visitors so that no sign of our occupation should be visible to
passing Japanese planes. The guard had orders to throw himself down
on the ground if he heard an aeroplane, and the huts and personnel
were safely hidden under the thick forest that surrounded the meadow.
Sgt. Jarrett was in command here and was just off on one of his reconnaissance trips into the invaded area. We sat round the fire and ate hot
scones that a certain young native policeman who I've always known as
'Little Rigo' was cooking in batches in a dixie [,] the greatest delicacy I
had had for weeks, and otherwise we spent the day warming our fronts
and sterns alternatively before the blaze. I told Kienzle of my signal to
ANGAU reporting the needs of the carriers; he was always most keen
to improve their conditions, and his representations no doubt counted
greatly in our final success on this point. Desertions from the force
were frequent, but wherever Kienzle happened to be they died down;
on his arrival in a camp, the boys bucked up and went about their work
as if General McArthur [sic] himself were among them.[28]

39

'Just on dusk the attack came in . . .'

Early next day—10 August—medic Jack Wilkinson at Deniki, who had been caring for the badly wounded Private Bernie Hanlon, wrote in his diary: 'Stretcher case (Hanlon) died in night after dressing wound. Had hoped he would pull through; would have if transfusion gear had been available. When shooting started yesterday all gear sent back to Isurava. A Coy holding Kokoda; C Coy Deniki village; and D Coy rear lines. Japs at creek crossing below Deniki. Position very involved and obscure.'[1]

Major Cameron had sent out several patrols to try to break through to 'A' Company at Kokoda, but none could get through. The first encountered a Japanese patrol, resulting in a brisk but furious firefight and the death of one enemy soldier. Another patrol was sent out to the east to determine whether the Japanese had occupied the valley and if there was a way of reaching Kokoda from that direction. A third patrol was sent out under the leadership of Lieutenant Hugh Dalby who backtracked to Isurava and swept the area with men from 'E' Company to make sure no Japanese troops were in their rear—they came back having encountered no Japanese.[2]

All at Deniki were anxious with the ongoing sound of fighting in the Kokoda area, including the distinct burst of heavy machine-gun fire, and exploding mortar bombs and artillery shells. Cameron requested the RAAF conduct a sweep over the area to confirm the exact location of 'A' Company. One aircraft was sent up to conduct a reconnaissance flight but returned with no definite information. Another request was made for the RAAF to bomb and strafe the Japanese around Kokoda, but this never happened; likely from fear of inflicting casualties against Symington's men from friendly fire.[3]

•

At Kokoda, the fighting had raged intermittently throughout the night and early morning hours. Lance Corporal Lochhead and the men of 9 Platoon were still in the thick of it: 'That night it was raining very heavily, and they snuck in amongst us. We knew they were there; we couldn't do anything about it, because you can't see anything at all. It's just black. We'd heard them go past.'[4] Indeed, with dawn he looked out and saw, 'the bodies of two of my men lying on the ground but couldn't distinguish who they were ... I tried to go to them but was fired on so gave up the idea. Then I called out to Roy Baxter who said he had two killed and one wounded and thought that Les Skinner had been killed too.'[5] His section was now reduced to just three men; one of his worst memories of the fighting was having to collect ammunition and weapons from his dead men.

Just before 10 a.m., the Japanese launched another assault against Symington's men at Kokoda with over 200 Japanese breaking out of the jungle. Using fire and movement, and taking advantage of available cover, they skilfully attacked the Australian perimeter. It was touch and go for a time, with some bitter hand-to-hand fighting, but the Japanese were again repulsed. At noon another similar attack was launched, the heavily reinforced Japanese were desperate to retake their lost position— Symington and his men were equally determined to hold it—this attack was also repulsed.[6]

At some point in the morning all saw the lone P-39 Airacobra fighter circle Kokoda on its reconnaissance flight. The Australians tried to gain the pilot's attention by waving their slouch hats, few had helmets. They wanted the pilot to report their presence, which would surely result in Cameron sending reinforcements and the RAAF dropping supplies—they had already requested this in the message delivered by Lance Corporal Sanopa the previous morning. At the very least the pilot could strafe the Japanese that were below the plateau around the airstrip. Sergeant Laurie Downes recalled with dismay many years later: 'All the pilot did was give a bit of a waggle with his wings and fly off again.' Sergeant Major George Mowat also recalled: 'Men repulsed every attack; some casualties. Air Force Plane recce position—no food or amm[unition] dropped. Amm getting very short. Guns seizing for want of oil. No sign of reinf[orcements].'[7]

For most of the afternoon the Japanese appeared to be content to fire into the Australian position—apparently licking their wounds. Lochhead recalled at this point: 'There were a few more half-hearted attacks and then it rained. About six mortar bombs fell just behind us. None went off and all thought they were gas bombs. A voice down the side of the plateau kept calling out: "Help me! Help me!" It was very disconcerting as we didn't know if the voice belonged to one of us or to a Jap trying to trick us. Every time I made a move to see who it was calling out that LMG opened up.'[8]

•

Lieutenant Colonel Tsukamoto was concerned about the appearance of the enemy fighter plane. Did this mean the enemy was preparing to reinforce Kokoda? It increased his urgency to retake the plateau. He was determined to force the issue. By now his battalion had regrouped at Kokoda and he would launch an all-out attack on dusk—timed for 5.30 p.m. Private Watanabe Toshi with No. 1 Company, who had survived the first battle for Kokoda, wrote of the battle to retake the plateau before his commander launched his assault later that day: 'We went back to Kokoda in order to recapture it . . . We fought all day and night. We had still not captured it by midday of the 10th.'[9]

Sometime in the mid-afternoon, Private Teruoka Akira and his comrades of the Tanaka Medical Unit reached Kokoda and were put to work in a field hospital that had been set up near the airfield, just west of the plateau. There was no shortage of wounded to treat. At dusk those in the aid post heard fighting breaking out in earnest about a kilometre from their position.[10]

Second Lieutenant Onogawa and his men of No. 2 Platoon, No. 3 Company, had arrived the previous day and he wrote on 10 August how the Australians were 'resisting desperately from AA [anti-aircraft] trenches we built there. Although the Australians are our enemy, their bravery must be admired . . . A general attack will be carried out this evening.'[11]

Also preparing for this imminent attack was 2nd Lieutenant Hirano Kogoro leading No. 3 Platoon, No. 1 Company, who was organising his men for the attack. Hours later he recorded in his diary: 'Assembled the men at our rear and rested. Only the sound of occasional sniping was heard. The Coy Commander ordered an attack at dusk. Made preparations in good spirit. Superior Pvt Miyabe was fatally wounded in the head by an enemy sniper. At 1430 , passed on the order to every section leader to carry out an attack at dusk.'[12] Their attack would be supported by Lieutenant Shimomura commanding No. 1 Platoon, No. 1 Machine Gun Company. Hirano recorded that he was confident of success as they were going to launch an attack that they had perfected during their fighting in China—a night attack. He wrote in his diary: 'No enemy can withstand such an attack.'[13]

•

During the latter part of the afternoon, the Australians on the plateau witnessed increased Japanese activity. Not only could they see it, but they could hear it, as recalled by Lance Corporal Lochhead: 'They kept probing and probing all day . . . Mid-afternoon we could hear orders being passed back and forth—the Jap company commander had a voice like a bull. So, we knew the final attack was due to come soon.'[14] Just before 5.30 p.m., all heard the loud chanting of the Japanese and as it died down a Japanese soldier called out in perfect English: 'You don't fancy that, do you?' The Australian obscenities in reply were not recorded; but Raymond Paull wrote: 'He must have been momentarily appalled by their irreverent response.'[15]

Shortly after, Lieutenant Colonel Tsukamoto launched his attack— the most ferocious yet against the thinly manned lines. Around 300 Japanese assaulted the southern and south-west perimeter, with additional smaller feints launched to the north and east; the Japanese commander was throwing everything he had into the fight. The plateau was swept with heavy machine-gun fire and exploding mortar bombs. Mountain guns were also firing high-explosive and smoke shells onto the plateau, which created confusion among the defenders as men could not see what was happening either side of them—a horrifying situation.[16]

Lance Corporal Lochhead recalled many years later ordering the wounded Smythe and Dridan to 'fall back to where Company Headquarters should have been. [Their] Bren was out of action, no ammunition and gas cylinder carboned up'. As they left their position the Japanese attacked, as recalled by Lochhead: 'Just on dusk the attack came in I . . . covered them with my Thompson. When I saw Roy Baxter fall back, I emptied a drum magazine at the advancing Japs and moved back through the rubber myself.' Covering the right flank here was Sergeant Laurie Downes and his men, and the sergeant recalled: 'The closest they'd got to us until then was about 5 yards [or 5 metres]—the distance to the next row of rubber trees. That was pretty close. Then one of them would blow a whistle and they'd all go back again. They couldn't get through and that's why they were so frustrated. They never would have got through if we'd had enough ammunition. They would have had to kill every one of us, but you can't fight without ammunition.'[17]

•

In this attack, 2nd Lieutenant Hirano Kogoro and his men of No. 3 Platoon were advancing using stealth and smoke candles to help cover their advance:

Completed our preparations, and started to advance . . . The enemy's sniping was intense. Heard the sound of bullets passing us. At 1620, our grenade discharger began to roar. 2nd Lt. Shimomura aided us with M.G.'s. We advanced to within 70 metres of the enemy. It began to drizzle. At 1700, fired a smoke candle with excellent results. Pressed closer and closer to the enemy. At 1720, finished our preparation for a charge and discharged 2 smoke candles, one of which failed to explode because of dampness. Nevertheless, the entire platoon carried out a determined charge. During this assault, as I jumped over a fallen tree, my foot caught in something and I fell flat. The platoon instantly lined up alongside me and charged again. We encountered no enemy. Believing they had retired and taken up another position, we approached on our hands and knees. Enemy violently resisted with hand grenades and rifle-fire.'[18]

•

Somehow the Australians managed to check the Japanese advance, but the fighting continued in earnest. Australian wounded remained at their positions firing into the enemy as the Japanese tried to encircle them. Private William 'Ken' Troeth, an eighteen-year-old labourer from Coleraine in Victoria, passed out after being hit three times, in the shoulder, in the jaw and the hand. When he regained consciousness, he made his way to the aid post and was given a blood transfusion to survive shock and loss of blood. Shortly after, he returned to his position to the admiration of his mates.[19]

Symington knew that his company's time was up—he had suffered numerous casualties and his ammunition and food supplies were almost exhausted—and there was no word that he was about to be reinforced or resupplied anytime soon. He and his men had done well to hold their position for two and a half days—the Japanese had not gained an inch of ground—he would later be awarded the Military Cross (MC) for his leadership during the fighting. In later life when asked about his MC he would proudly state it was awarded to him on behalf of 'A' Company—it was not his award; it was 'A' Company's.[20]

He and his men were totally cut off from the rest of Maroubra Force, which was now behind them at Deniki. The Australian wounded were lying at the medical aid post where the company clerk, Corporal Alan Smith, a 21-year-old clerk from Kilsyth in Victoria, was caring for them, cooking what food he could find, including Japanese rice and 'doing his best to keep up the strength and spirits of his companions with "something hot". But the most he could gather was all too little.'[21] Sergeant Simmons also recalled: 'Our only food now was unpolished Japanese rice that Corporal Smith cooked and brought up to us under enemy fire.'[22] Smith and 28-year-old Corporal Albert Bull from Myrtleford in

Victoria now delivered the last reserves of ammunition from Company Headquarters to the platoons. This included .303 bullets removed from Lewis gun drum magazines left behind by the men of 'B' Company the week before; these were sparingly handed out to the riflemen.

Captain Symington decided if they received no supplies of food and ammunition by dusk, then they would have to fall back to Deniki—to remain was suicide. With dusk, and no supplies being dropped and the Japanese continuing their attack, orders were given that they would break out for Deniki at 7 p.m. Symington tasked Staff Sergeant Guest with informing the isolated men of 9 Platoon to the south of his orders to fall back to Deniki. Symington told him: 'I want you to crawl around the perimeter and try and contact 9 Platoon and tell them we are getting out at seven o'clock tonight.'[23] As ordered, Guest moved out, recalling:

I crawled round, and I was undercover more or less until I got to the corner . . . When I looked down on the road, I saw three figures standing beside an old bridge [swing bridge over Madi Creek]. One of them was pointing up, obviously at me because I would have been in full view. Then the next minute the lead started to go past my ears because they didn't like me, so they started to shoot. I went down to the ground and I crawled up on my hands and knees to where the rubber started, and I called out, 'Can anybody hear me [?]' and a voice said, 'Yes.' I said, 'We are getting out at seven o'clock tonight, pass the word along' and the voice said 'Okay.' I turned around and crawled back around to my hole. They started to shell the plateau, a big clear plateau, away from where the huts were, and you couldn't walk across there. The Japanese fire was coming up through the rubber, across this clear space, and you couldn't stand up, so you had to lay down because you would have been shot.[24]

Sergeant Major Mowat scribbled in his diary: '1800 hrs. Tension great. No food or Amm arrived. Time of withdrawal getting near, 1845. Jap attacks heavier. Heavy Mortar bombardments: 1900. Withdrawal commences. Japs swarm through. In darkness probably fight own men.'[25] The battalion war diary records of this final attack: 'This time the ENEMY force was estimated at three hundred, and mortars firing smoke and H.E. bombs, heavy and L.M.G.'s, grenades and rifles were brought into action. This attack was held off until 1930 hrs.'[26]

•

Earlier that day at Myola, the aircraft and supplies were still a no-show. Kienzle reported leaving Myola at around 8 a.m. for Eora Creek via a new track he was cutting. With him was Corporal Irvine with the engineers who would improve those parts of the track which remained difficult to negotiate. They arrived at Eora Creek just after 4 p.m., where Kienzle discussed the situation with Major Elliott-Smith, who had 'been "up at the front" and brought back first captured Jap documents, arms and ammunition.' The carriers arrived well after dark from Kagi and Kienzle ordered the establishment of a new camp at Templeton's Crossing, as the lines between Kagi to Eora Creek and/or Myola to Eora Creek were too far for a one-day journey for the heavily loaded carriers. However, he reported the 'boys were still doing a marvellous job but were now beginning to feel the strain of continuous carrying without a break.'[27]

They were not the only ones feeling the stress—the 60-year-old Gallipoli veteran, Doc Vernon, had been up and down different legs of the track and was now fighting a bad case of malaria, recording in his diary for 10 August:

One of the worst days I spent on the Owen Stanley track . . . Kienzle was going to cut a new and shortened track to Templeton's Crossing and offered to take me but fortunately I decided to stick to the old Kage [sic] road over the gap and not try any experiments over new ground. Two signalers and my team went forward with me to Iora [sic Eora] . . . I gradually developed a temperature due to an attack of fever, my first on the track. I don't quite know how I eventually managed to reach Iora [sic], but I do know it was a rotten trip, and had it not been for one of my boys I might not have accomplished it before dark. But the walk did come to an end and I staggered into the hut, needing nothing else but some hot tea and a place to lie down. Fortunately, my old sack bed was still on the verandah and someone very kindly gave it up to me. Kienzle arrived [at] . . . dusk after cutting his way through the upper gorge of Iora [sic] Creek, looking more tired than I had ever seen him.

Of my short stay at Iora [sic] there is little to say; most of my old wounded had gone back but were replaced by others, none of whom were very serious cases. There were then several competent orderlies to attend to them, and there was really little need for me to be there except that it gave me an opportunity to doctor up our carriers. Capt. Stevenson and Lt. Brewer were both there, really ill with malaria, and Capt. Jesser, first P.I.B., was nursing a slight wound to his arm; he had done first class work with his regiment round Oivi . . . One evening a decrepit old native who had been storeman at BP's in Moresby tottered in and collapsed on the ground. I was shocked when I tested the weight of his load. An officer standing by told me he was only shamming, but I could see that a few more days of overwork and exposure like this and he would have left his bones in the mountains. The age of this old chap showed me how disparate was the call for carriers, he was far too old and weak for such work. I put him off duty.[28]

On his next return to Port Moresby, Doc Vernon called in at Eora where this man was still working, and both made their way to Moresby where Doc found him a more suitable job. Indeed, a week later Doc came across the man 'happily and usefully employed at Gemo, safe in the bosom of his family of eight youngsters'.[29]

40

'. . . he'd stayed to get us out'

Back at Kokoda, under the cover of heavy rain and darkness Symington began the withdrawal of his men from the western edge of the plateau. It was here that the Japanese appeared to be weakest and, for whatever reason, they were not attacking this part of the line in any great numbers. If they had, the men of 'A' Company would never have made it off the plateau alive. The plan was to cross Madi Creek and the airstrip and then move into the jungle 800 metres beyond. The men of 7 Platoon, covering the western part of the line, would lead the breakout. These men would be covered by Company Headquarters and 8 Platoon, which would follow them off the plateau, bringing out the bulk of the wounded. The already hard-pressed men of 9 Platoon would remain behind for as long as possible as the rearguard to cover the withdrawal.[1] Staff Sergeant Guest leading 8 Platoon recalled the withdrawal:

> Captain Symington called me across to his dugout under the Assistant District Magistrate's house and said: 'Your platoon will follow Company Headquarters out and bring the wounded.' The most seriously wounded in the dugout were Privates John Stormont, who was breathing through a large hole in the back, and Les Skinner who had one of his thighs almost torn away by a grenade, or a machine-gun burst. At 6.45 p.m., dusk had already fallen, and I sent word around to 8 Platoon to leave their holes and close in on Company Headquarters by skirting around the edge of the plateau. The firing in the rubber was now at its most intense as 9 Platoon and McKay's section tried to stem the final attack. It was about 7 pm when Symington said:

'Get the wounded and follow us out.' He then moved off accompanied by Sanopa and Lieutenant Brewer. I saw 7 Platoon start to leave their positions and . . . Company Headquarters [followed] down the western edge of the plateau heading for the swing bridge over Madi Creek. Johnny Stormont was dying, and we couldn't move him, but we managed to get Les Skinner onto a blanket stretcher. I took one end of the stretcher and Ted Mitchell took the other. It was pouring rain as we struggled down the edge of the plateau, but the firing was still intense

In the darkness, we found ourselves in the waters of Madi Creek. Luckily, 'Bluey' Murray . . . [took] my end of the stretcher just as I was swept off my feet by the current to land on the creek bed held down by a haversack full of .45 Tommy gun [ammunition]. I managed to get rid of the haversack and reach the far bank of the creek. We were now some distance from the plateau itself and no shots were coming in our direction. It was then that Ted Mitchell said to me: 'Les Skinner is dead' (the shock of being plunged into the water had put an end to his agony). So, we left him there in the pouring rain, and by now [it was] almost pitch darkness . . . it was a case of the blind staggering after the blind. The firing had died away except for an occasional rifle shot and I decided it would be best to remain where we were until dawn. I told the men nearest me to pass the word to the front and rear to halt. There were sounds of shouting coming from the plateau, but I couldn't understand anything because of the pouring rain.[2]

Corporal Daniels with Guest's 8 Platoon also recalled: 'We had gone off down the steps and along the track and there is a Jap setting up a machine gun right on the corner. He'd only have to look around to his left and seen us down below. He could have wiped the bloody lot of us out. He didn't. He stood up there and he is looking to his front.'[3] They managed to bypass the Japanese machine-gun position unseen.

•

Lieutenant Neal and his men of 9 Platoon were still defending the southern perimeter as the rearguard. These men were heavily engaged as the Japanese continued to probe the line looking for a weakness.

The tall, lean and tanned Staff Sergeant James Cowey was a veteran of Gallipoli and the Western Front where he had risen from the ranks to command an infantry company. During that war he had been awarded the Military Cross. He was an expert marksman, outspoken and not afraid to call a spade a spade, regardless of rank—his men worshipped him. It was said that no Australian 'Company Commander ever had a better, or more critical, Sergeant-Major'.[4]

True to form, Cowey had volunteered to remain behind with two sub-machine gunners to help Neal's men withdraw while the rest of the company evacuated the plateau. As Neal and his men tried to disengage, the Japanese followed up closely behind, but the covering fire from Cowey and his men enabled them to fall back. Corporal McKay and his men of No. 1 Section, 7 Platoon, were still manning the southwestern perimeter in support of 9 Platoon. McKay recalled many years later:

> Just on dusk there was a nice little shower of rain and the first assault wave came in and we stopped 'em. My Bren gun group, Bill Drummond and Bill Spriggs, were firing and I can see the gun firing now—no kidding, you could see the bullets going up the barrel and it ran red-hot. Vern Scattergood had a Bren too and he was firing wildly. We topped 'em again. Then there was a bit of a pause before the next wave came in and overran us. So we said: 'We'd better get out because they've gone past us.' Well old Scattergood (or should I say young Scattergood—he was younger than me) he got excited. He was standing up firing the Bren gun from the hip and that was the last I saw of young Scattergood. He must have been hit. We couldn't find him in the dark and we moved back.[i]
>
> After we came out of the rubber, we found Johnny Stormont in the Company Headquarters dugout. We tried to put a shell dressing on him, but the hole was too big, and he was dying. We had to leave him.[ii]

---

i   Private Vernon Scattergood, a twenty-year-old clerk from Elwood in Victoria, is listed as KIA on 10 August, with no known grave.

ii Nineteen-year-old Private John Stormont from Northcote in Victoria, is listed as KIA on 10 August, with no known grave.

We only moved a few more yards and we were challenged! It was old Jim Cowey, the coolest, bravest man I have ever known. There he was, in a kneeling position, with his rifle pointing at us. Jim's motto was if you were a 'digger' he had to get you out. The rest of the company had gone, but he'd stayed to get us out because he knew we'd been left behind.[5]

Lance Corporal Lochhead and his men were now also withdrawing from the southern perimeter: 'When I got back to the clearing Jim Cowey was waiting there. He grabbed me and said: "Wait with me and we'll pick up a few more as they come out". The main attack had died down, but there was still some small-arms fire and grenade explosions on the right [eastern] flank.'[6]

Another who recalled the actions of the Gallipoli veteran was Sergeant Downes: 'It got dark. Seven and 8 platoons got withdrawn to leave us there to get them out and that was the hardest part. Old Jim Cowey was a First War man and he come up and he said, "Get whatever boys you've got still alive and get out"; and if it hadn't been for him, I wouldn't be talking to you now.'[7]

Many years later, McKay who was among the last to leave the plateau, remembered vividly with gratitude and admiration the actions of Staff Sergeant James Cowey, who was largely responsible for getting the men of 9 Platoon and numerous others off the plateau that night: 'Old Jim had picked up about three or four of us by now and he said: "Just stay quietly", and he dispersed us a bit. And then he got Roy Neal and Laurie Downes, and I think that was about all of us. You know most were dead [by] then. There were no wounded in our group.' The young lieutenant must have been relieved to have the old warrior with him. When sure that all of the men were accounted for, Cowey organised their with-drawal off the plateau as recalled by McKay:

Jim said: 'Good! We'll walk out.' I was all for running out but there were Japs everywhere. They were throwing grenades into weapon-pits, they were searching under the huts, and Jim said: 'We'll walk out. They don't know who we are,' and, if you don't mind, [he] casually got up, put us into single file and walked us out over the bloody bridge. We walked across the airstrip into the dense scrub and then Jim said: 'Good! We'll rest here till daylight.' So, he puts us down and then 'clunk', being a youth and mentally and physically exhausted, I fell straight asleep. But I suppose old Jim Cowey, being the amazing soldier that he was, stayed awake all night.[8]

Among the Japanese soldiers now on the plateau was 2nd Lieutenant Hirano Kogoro and his men of No. 3 Platoon, who, by 9 p.m., had taken over one of the houses of the station; he considered himself lucky as that night his platoon had suffered just four casualties. He wrote in his diary: 'The bloody fighting in the rain during the last few days seems like a nightmare. I swore to the souls of the warriors who died that I would carry on their aspirations.'[9]

Earlier, Captain Symington had crossed the airstrip and was with his men in the jungle scrub beyond. On reorganising his men he realised that Sergeant William Guest and twenty men from 8 Platoon were missing, along with Staff Sergeant Jim Cowey and most of 9 Platoon. There was no way of going back as the Japanese were all around and the missing men knew the plan of escape; they were to head for Deniki.[10]

Just east of Kokoda, Corporal Bailey and three of his men from Marsh's 17 Platoon, 'D' Company, were still trying to make their way back to Deniki from their ambush position along the Oivi–Kokoda part of the main track.

There was a lot of firing going on at Kokoda, so we knew where we were. Twice we were cut off, and we saw Japanese and we evaded them . . . just having three there was no sense in doing anything about it because you are only asking for trouble and letting them know your position, so we had to work our way back to Deniki and that only took a day and a half... It's rather strange, you'd head in one direction and you'd hear the heavy fire [and] you knew where Kokoda was because you could tell by the fighting. We didn't strike any Australian soldiers...

We got to a certain spot and we were resting, this was the next morning. I heard this noise and I thought the bloody Japanese were coming back again. We all got behind trees and got ready to fight them. In came two of the most glorious dressed up men you have ever seen, they were two Kukukuku head hunters from the Fly River. What they were doing down there I would not know. They would have been six foot six both of them, if you judged their ages, I'd say about twenty-eight to thirty. They had all their war gear on, all bright feathers, they were really something, I don't know that anybody else would have seen them. I said 'Ararnoo' which was water, because we hadn't been near a stream and he just pointed, and we just let them go, but they were heading toward Kokoda.

There was a big story that they [Australian commanders] were hoping if the Japanese did attack Moresby they would... come down from the north; and... would've struck these men who are pretty tough guys and they would have had a hell of a lot of trouble. That was the last we saw of those guys... We got back to Deniki, the three of us. Joe Dwyer he was gone, there was no doubt about that, because when he went back to that creek there was no way he was going to be able to get away from there[iii]... Most of my section were OK, I think I lost two...[11]

•

As the battle for Kokoda raged on 10 August, Japanese Army Chief of Staff, Lieutenant General Sugiyama Hajime, and Admiral Nagano Osami of the high command issued a new directive outlining future operations for Papua and the Solomons, 'in accordance with the changed situation'.[12] Lieutenant General Hyakutake commanding the XVII Army was to focus on capturing Henderson Field from the

---

iii Private Joseph Dwyer, a 32-year-old farmer from East Bairnsdale in Victoria, is listed as KIA on
8 August, with no known grave.

marines on Guadalcanal and then annihilate the remaining American forces there. He was to do so using the forces already assigned him, including Major General Horii's force now in Papua, tasked with crossing the Owen Stanleys to capture Port Moresby. This was in line with the statement Sugiyama had made the month before: 'We must hold the fronts in eastern New Guinea and Rabaul to the end. If they fall, not only will the Pacific Ocean be in peril, but it will allow the Western advance of MacArthur's counter-attack through New Guinea and herald the fall of our dominion in the southern area.'[13]

•

Sister Mavis Parkinson of the Gona mission sat down to continue what would turn out to be the last few paragraphs of her long letter to her mother: 'I wish you could see us—our house in the heart of the bush. It is covered with leaves and the people have made May and me a double bed at one end of the house and another for Father at the other end. These beds are quite a success and are made of Sirl (a vine that grows in the bush woven and fastened onto the timber frame) and on them we put native sleeping mates [sic] and our ground sheets.' As in May's letter to her sister she described the much-needed and appreciated supplies sent to them from George Chester and, unknown to her, Lieutenant Alan Hooper with the 1st PIB based in Ioma District. 'Mr. Chester rose to the occasion beautifully and sent May and me some clothes belonging to a friend, who evacuated in January, dresses and a few towels and two nightgowns, so we are beautifully fitted out. He also gave us permission to use some supplies he had stored near here.' Mavis was also frustrated by the lack of news and was feeding off the rumours that were spreading throughout the region. She concludes her letter to her mother: 'The inactivity and lack of news is hard to bear, but we are hoping we shan't be here very long. We've simply no idea as to what is happening, though we do know that the bombing of Gona has stopped. Of course, we hear all sorts of rumours—we heard of fighting for Kokoda . . . and now we hear of fighting on the Moresby road [Kokoda Track]. We hear that the Jap's cartridges are finished, and the fighting is now hand-to-hand.'[14]

The next day, as Symington and his men were trying to fall back to Deniki, May Hayman unknowingly concluded her letter to Viola.

Three weeks today since we left Gona, and still no authentic news; however, all rumours put together, it seems that we might conclude that the Japs are about half way to Port [Moresby], but being killed by the thousands . . . that they have moved their headquarters from Gona to Buna and two more ships have brought men and equipment which are daily on the move along the better Kokoda road. One big boat is still burning off Gona and another was seen to go down there.

Enough of conjectures and the repeating of native stories. Our letter to Father Gill evidently did not reach him, so tomorrow Father John goes in person and should be back with some definite news within a week. Meanwhile we live comfortably and without fear. Father B. has been rather nervous, for he fears what might befall us girls if an irresponsible patrol of Japs should find us, but Mavis and I are not worrying and even the noises of the night fail to disturb our slumbers now.

Father sleeps badly, rises early, attends the fire (which he keeps in all night to save matches), has his swim and makes the coffee. Then when he sees us stir, he announces 'time for early morning prayers' which he says, then he brings our coffee in bed to us, after which, still being beneath our nets, we join him in saying Mattins. He then absents himself while we rise and dress. Porridge of wheat meal with rice rich milk and sugar constitutes our breakfast. We have some enamel plates, 3 spoons, another billy and some enamel wash basins, also 3 cups; so we manage very well. Next, with some soap which Iona [*sic* Ioma] sent us, we do a spot of washing and go with it up the stream to a place where the sunshine penetrates and leave it there to dry. Oh, the joy of that little open space, for we have felt so dreadfully shut in here beneath the tall timbers where never a breeze stirs even, although we can hear it at times far above us and of course the result of its movements frequently caused us much alarm during those first days and nights as dead sticks and limbs came suddenly crashing down: even dead leaves caused a disturbance down here and when occasionally a whole tree has crashed our nerves have jumped I can tell you. Added to these noises are those of the crickets, frogs and birds. Oh. How incessant are the crickets and the frogs and what queer calls the night birds make, but the flying foxes will not let them have it all their own way, for most nights they come flap flapping about causing such a commotion.

Three weeks, and still we hide out, knowing nothing of the outside affairs—indeed we feel for all the world like Laurel as we pile up our Pork and Bean tins day by day. Did you ever see that picture? A Laurel and Hardy one set in the last war and Laurel was found months after the Armistice, still marching up and down his trench which was by this time surrounded for miles around by his empty P&B tins.

We have worked out quite a routine for ourselves now. While our porridge is cooking Sister and I do our daily dozen. Breakfast and washing up are soon over, then most days we wash out a few articles of clothing or towels (there were some lovely towels, a pair of sheets and two quilts amongst Mrs. Durcher's things). Sister and I having folded our sheets and quilts, mostly get back under our net at this stage where we write, read or do fancy work (Mrs. Durcher's again), or mend Father's few clothes, for his wardrobe is very scant, comprising an old white cassock which he has to wear while his only pair of trousers are washed and mended. A Siai native lent him two shirts, but like us he only has the one pair of old shoes, so none of us do much walking about. While Sister and I prepare the native veg for lunch, Father scrapes the coconut: sometimes we have some meat—we had 10 or 12 tins of meat, so do not eat meat every day. After dinner, Sister and I again crawl under nets—flies, mosquitoes and other insects give us a bad time otherwise. Father usually steps up 'on guard'. About 4pm., say Evensong then after making our bed Sister and I take it in turns getting tea ready while the other has a hot bath in a big enamel basin—we put on nighties and pop under our net again. Father brings us our tea, mostly P&B with [coconut] milk added to it, and fruit of some sort, then he sits at the top of our bed in a deck chair (supplied from Siai) and we tell stories, after of course many speculations as to what is happening along the road to Port, and out at sea. Our beds are very comfortable being made of interwoven split cane and covered first with a native mat, next our canvas, then our blanket because a sheet and quilt is quite enough for coverage.

Our three books are finished and note paper almost, but we spend a good deal of time doing nothing, singing or making up new words to old tunes—and haven't had a fight yet.[15]

Then came the Japanese and threats of murder from an old native sorcerer.

•

In Melbourne that night, Australian General Thomas Blamey was preparing for dinner. He had spent a 'tiring' day at the Australian Prime Minister's War Conference. They had discussed the war and the numerous theatres of Australian operations. When discussing the fighting around Kokoda, Blamey merely mentioned that not much was happening there and overall, 'it was not of great importance'.[16]

PART FIVE

LINES OF ESCAPE

41

'Throw that bloody thing away!'

In the early morning hours of 11 August, Symington's party, numbering just 46 men, climbed the foothills west of the Kokoda airstrip and by the late afternoon had made their way to the village of Naro, south-west of Kokoda. Unknown to them they were almost directly west of Deniki; separated by a deep, broad, rugged valley.

Back at Kokoda, Sergeant Guest and his men of 8 Platoon and the wounded were just beyond Madi Creek, close to the airstrip shrouded in early morning fog. Guest recalled many years later:

As dawn started to come through, I thought, 'We have got to get out of here'. These wounded blokes were terrific all night, there was a bloke called [Robert] McCorkelle and he had a big hole in his back and he just laid there in the mud without making a noise. I looked to my left and I saw somebody laying there and I called him over and I said, 'Pass the word along to the left and find out how many of our fellows are to the left,' and [to] the bloke on the right I said, 'Pass the word along as far as you can about how many,' and when the two figures came back I found out that there were twenty-one of us . . . it was starting to get light and we were getting a bit worried.

We must have gone around in a circle because we ended up back at the same place that we started from. Then . . . Ted Murray . . . said, 'Bill, I think I can get us to the airstrip' . . . We followed him, crawling along dragging the wounded blokes with us, some had leg and arm wounds. All of a sudden, I'm beside the Kokoda strip . . . I remember looking back up at the Kokoda plateau and it was covered in a mist and I remember thinking to myself. 'We are out so far and if we can get across the strip, we might be lucky.' Just down to the left I saw a native hut and we found out later that it was used by the air travellers . . . waiting for planes, it was just native material. Alan Smith, he was the lance corporal and he had the Tommy gun and it had twenty rounds in it and that's all the ammunition that we had, and he said, 'I'll go out and check out the hut' . . . He came back, and he said, 'There's nothing there' . . .

All this time it was getting lighter, but the mist was still over Kokoda and I said, 'It's no good trying to go across one or two at a time, when I say, "Go" grab all these wounded blokes and go across as fast as you can on the other side of the strip' . . . I expected to be mowed down, we were in full view, the airstrip was in full view of Kokoda, but nothing happened.[1]

When Guest gave the word, all moved out carrying and assisting their wounded across the open ground of the airstrip, no doubt fearful of being swept with machine-gun fire, however, the fog covered their retreat into the jungle scrub–covered hillside beyond. Guest continues:

We laid there panting . . . and then one of our boys said, 'There's a bit of a track leading up to the grass,' so we followed that, and we started to climb. We were dragging these wounded blokes or helping them along and I had my corporal with me, and he had a field dressing on his shoulder, and he was a very brave man. He carried his rifle and it was still on his shoulder, you can't believe it.

We kept going . . . and then all of a sudden, we came to this bit of a road, which widened out and it was in a native village. Alan Smith went ahead again with the Tommy gun and checked out all the huts and there was no one there so we all just collapsed under the huts and laid there. I remember thinking to myself at the time: 'The Japs have got to follow us because they must've captured the place.' We didn't know what happened to 9 Platoon . . .

We sat around and we had these two Bren guns, the boys were only young fellows like myself and they said, 'What's the good of the Brens because we can't shoot them' and I said, 'Right, take the grease box out and hide the Brens under a hut, under some banana leaves.'[2]

The men suggested to Guest that they should divide into two groups, with the sergeant leading one team, with the wounded and married men. 'I had about seven and the idea was for us to go ahead and follow the track out of the village and cutting trees as we went to let the mob coming behind us know which way we went.' Their cook, Private Ted Mitchell from South Yarra in Victoria, was with them carrying a 'haversack full of Jap rice so we divided it up before we left'.[3] The second group would fight off any pursuing Japanese as the leading element made their way towards Deniki. Somewhere along the way, Corporal Alan Smith and five others, one wounded, had become separated and would remain lost for over a week, turning up at Isurava on 19 August.

•

Great War veteran Staff Sergeant Cowey and his party had moved out from the lowland jungle scrub above the airstrip. Lance Corporal Lochhead recalled:

We were off at daybreak next morning (11 August) and kept moving. Old Jim organised us as a section with himself as point scout and me as rearguard, and every time we halted, he would give us a lesson in tactical movement ... He was a remarkable old fellow—calm and cool and collected, and he passed it on to us. As we were moving back, he was giving us little lessons the whole time. At the end of the First World War, of course, fellows like that just disappeared back into civilian life and when the Second World War came on, a lot enlisted. They became NCOs, and luckily, we had people like him. I think he would have been approaching fifty ... We kept to streams and waded up them to throw any Jap pursuit off our track (we thought we'd heard them following us that morning). On our way we picked up Harry [Henry] Barkla.[4]

Corporal McKay also recalled:

Some time that morning we blundered onto the main Kokoda–Deniki track and started to walk up it with comments to Jim Cowey from 'old soldiers' like myself such as: 'Do you think we'd better . . . ?' And it was while going along that track that we realised [what] C Company had run into on the morning of the attack—there were trees . . . with Japanese writing on them and hitching wires and Jap supplies stacked up at the foot of trees! But Jim continued up the track (I can remember Roy Neal saying then: 'Do you think we'd . . . ?' 'No,' says Jim, 'we'll keep on going for a while'). And it was about then that Bill Drummond and Bill Spriggs [McKay's Bren gun team] walk out of the scrub onto the track with their Bren which . . . had seized up, and apart from that they only had one magazine left with three rounds in it.

At that stage we took stock. Alex Lochhead and I had 'Tommy' guns (I had one box magazine left) and I think the rest were rifles. I also had a grenade that I'd saved, and Roy Neal had a couple too. We'd all just about run out of ammo. So, we pressed on. There were about eight or nine of us now—I think there was Roy Neal, Laurie Downes, Alex Lochhead, Harry Barkla, Tony [Leslie] Ruwolt, old Jim Cowey and myself and, of course, Bill Drummond and Bill Spriggs who'd just sort of walked out of the scrub still grinning.

So, we continued the 'advance' (as I call it) when all of a sudden, a burst from a 'Juki' MG chops a billet of wood from a tree above Jim Cowey's head. Jim didn't even grunt—he just carefully leans against the tree, restrains the breathing slightly, and shoots the No 1 on the 'Juki'. Then the No 2 rolls in and takes his place. Jim restrains the breathing again after reloading at the shoulder and shoots the No 2. Talk about coolness! Of course, by this time there's Japs running everywhere and every time one of 'em jumps down behind the 'Juki' Jim shoots him. I remember I fired a burst of 'Tommy' gun and the damn thing jams, and old Jim still firing from the shoulder, says: 'Throw that bloody thing away!' You know, they couldn't even ruffle him! And then he says: 'I think we'll withdraw,' and he just casually moves off the track into the scrub. So, we withdraw—went around the back of 'em. And then we bump into another outpost—a listening post, I think. We see them first (otherwise we would have been sitting ducks) and Roy Neal lobs a grenade into their hole and that finishes them.[5]

Cowey had earlier noted that the Japanese seemed to overestimate the safety provided by the large tree roots that projected well above ground level from the main tree trunk. The Japanese frequently used these as cover and Cowey directed his men to fire into the roots; the velocity and impact of the .303 bullet (travelling at around 750 metres per second) easily penetrated this cover, killing or wounding anyone seeking cover behind it.[6]

•

Captain Symington and his men were patrolling close to Naro in the late afternoon when they heard fighting breaking out well below the village—the firing from Cowey's party. Symington decided to head back to the village. Not long after, Cowey and his men were approaching Naro from the opposite direction as recalled by Corporal McKay.

Just on dusk we're climbing a mountain when we come to this village called Naro (we were sort of hooking to the ... [west] of Deniki coming from Kokoda). So, we lie there quietly for a while and have a look at it. Then old Jim (who was obviously in charge) says: 'Well, I think we'll go in and have a look.' And Roy Neal and Laurie Downes go into the village with Jim while we sort of gave 'em covering whatever we could (we were going to throw bricks at 'em I think!). So, Jim and the other two go into the village and then wave to us to follow them, and the natives wave us in too, and we go. It was just getting dark and we could see their fire-glows. And then bloody A Company walks in from the other side of the village with Symington—they had arrived there a few hours earlier and had been having a scout around.[7]

From the village, Symington and Cowey could see Japanese troops in a small village about 200 metres below, but the Australians were tired and remained largely unconcerned. As night fell, they lit a fire, with the flames and smoke lost in the mist. They raided the garden, cooking bananas, pumpkins and sugar cane, turning them into stew. McKay recalled Symington said: "'These fellas (our party) will sleep the night. Everybody else except the wounded will stand to." So, they put us in a hut and of course we were starving and the "marys" [native women] were cooking this pumpkin . . . and I can still taste it—it was delicious you know! But it was cold and dark in the hut and I remember rolling over and a bloke said: "Watch my arm!" and I said: "What's the matter?" and he said: "It's got a bullet in it." And it was Vic Smythe who'd come out with Company Headquarters with some other walking wounded.'[8]

•

Major Cameron at Deniki finally got the first word from 'A' Company since Lance Corporal Sanopa had turned up during the morning of 9 August. Twenty-one-year-old Corporal Roy Baxter from Barnawartha in Victoria with 9 Platoon, had become isolated from the company during the late afternoon fighting on 10 August. Somehow, he'd managed to break through the Japanese lines along the southern perimeter of Kokoda and made his way to Deniki. He had been separated just before the order was given by Symington to evacuate Kokoda, and as far as he knew 'A' Company was still holding out on the plateau. He told Cameron they were in urgent need of food and ammunition, and Cameron put in another request for an urgent airdrop; bad weather prevented the drop from happening that day, but they agreed to drop supplies first thing the next morning, weather permitting. Cameron continued to send out patrols to try to contact Symington who he believed was still at Kokoda, but all returned unable to reach the plateau—all knew that Symington and his men must be in dire straits. The deathly silence that had broken out from that direction since dawn must have been disconcerting to many.[9]

•

Doc Vernon was still at Eora Creek tending to the sick and wounded, but soon he pushed onto Isurava. He wrote in his diary of coming across Captain McLaren, with the militia 14th Field Ambulance, who had moved forward to assist: 'Attended to sick and wounded white troops and obtaining the release of a few carriers on the grounds of broken health. Went forward one day to Isurava and met Capt. McLaren there.'[10]

●

That day—11 August—the new commander of New Guinea Force, Lieutenant General Sydney Rowell, landed at Port Moresby. General Morris was waiting for him; Rowell was to replace him as head of NGF. Rowell recalled:

I left Brisbane on 10 August to fly to Port Moresby, together with Cyril Clowes and Brigadier Henry Rourke, my senior operations staff officer. I fondly expected some high United States officer's plane, but we went to Townsville by civil airline and the next day flew on to Port Moresby in a United States Air Force DC-3 flown by a young civil pilot under contract, [we sat] on mail bags or tin seats. Half way between Cooktown and Port Moresby the pilot started flying low in a series of loops, apparently trying to see how close he could get to the tops of the waves without actually hitting them. I told Rourke to stop him and he came back from the cockpit grinning, saying that the second pilot had already told his No. 1 not to be a bloody fool. I asked what the procedure was to fly into Port Moresby and was told that it was to circle twice [around] the anti-aircraft [batteries] on the hill overlooking the harbour, and then fly along the corridor to the seven-mile airfield . . . at 1000 feet [300 metres]. Not a bit of it. The pilot made a half turn around the hill at 500 feet and one could almost read the fuse settings on the anti-aircraft shells. Fortunately, no one fired at us and we duly landed to be met by Major-General B.M. Morris and two senior United States Air Force officers. The only advice Morris had received from Australia was a cryptic signal from [Major General George] Vasey saying 'Syd is coming' but he understood. I took over operational command from Morris when I arrived, and he became general officer commanding Australian New Guinea Administrative Unit (ANGAU) which was responsible for the government of the native civil population.[11]

42

'That's our biggest hurdle crossed'

Father James Benson, and Sisters May Hayman and Mavis Parkinson were now forced to leave the relative safety of their hideout at Siai. Father Benson recalled: 'We went to the village Church for Mass on Sundays and Holy Days; at other times being content with Mattins, Evensong and Angelus at home. Each time we went to the village . . . there were rumours of Japanese doings growing daily nearer.'[1]

Benson had also just days before been told by a native lay preacher that an older sorcerer at the nearby village of Oitanandi wanted to kill the missionaries in fear that they would be punished by the approaching Japanese:

> My fears reached their height—or depth—when one day good father John Livingstone came and took me aside to tell me that he had been to Oitanandi the day before, and that the old 'Ferryman' there, who is also one of the greatest sorcerers in this sorcery-ridden country, and therefore perhaps the most powerful man in the district, had said to him: 'Why are you looking after the white people there at Siai? Much better you should kill them. Soon the Japanese will be here looking for them, and they will kill us if we do not give them up. If you do not kill them soon, then I shall come and kill them.' In vain John Livingstone had reminded the old man of how Sister Hayman had undoubtedly saved the life of one of his wives a few months before and how the old man had formerly tried to make himself out as my friend. A young

man, a Catechumen, of Oitanandi had undertaken to keep an eye on the old man and let us know immediately if he made any move, but I fear I slept but little after that.[2]

•

Not far away was Lieutenant Arthur Smith's party of men from 1st PIB, with the Australian spotters and five American airmen, who were all fleeing from Ambasi. On hearing of the stranded missionaries, he sent Sergeant Robert Hanna and Corporal Harry Palmer to collect them.[3] Benson, May and Mavis must have been surprised to see Corporal Palmer, as the last time they had seen him, he had been on the beach at Gona with Sergeant Lyle Hewitt, both about to take on the whole Japanese invasion force with a Tommy gun and Lee-Enfield rifle. Benson recalled in 1945 how Hanna and Palmer walked into their camp, guided by former policeman and now local evangelist, Stanley Tago.[4]

They explained that there were three other Australians and five Americans—two wounded—five boys of the Papuan Native Infantry [1st PIB] down the river at Deunia, and that they intended to work east and south, crossing the Japanese lines on the Kokoda road, and then making over the lower height of the Owen Stanleys behind Cape Nelson, and so coming down on the west coast at Rigo, where [there] is a good coastal road to Port Moresby. In this way they would avoid the strain of the terrible high mountain track via Ioma, for the wounded. The Deunia people had told them we were at Siai and so these two came on to invite us to join them, if we felt that way.

The two sisters thought it a Heaven-sent opportunity, but I warned them that the number of men who have walked across Papua is probably less than a dozen, and I knew of only one woman. Moreover, in each case these people were members of well-founded expeditions with plenty of guides and carriers, while we already had our poor boots bound to our feet with strips of bark and very soon we should be reduced to bark only. On the other hand, I realised the immense value of being part of a fairly large party, in any such venture, and I confess I was not unmindful of the fact that these brave fellows would in this way share, and so greatly ease, the by now almost too great a burden of my responsibilities for my two gallant companions. So, though I pointed out the difficulties, I did nothing to dissuade the sisters. The fact that it would take a month at least and probably six weeks to get across was itself sufficient to make the strongest heart quail. In retrospect I have always considered that my greatest mistake was in not insisting upon our waiting the five days or so for Father John to return; the five days' wait at Deunia would have been good for those two wounded men. Then we could all have gone over to the Mamba and, if necessary, lived out the war in the Ioma district. But the soldiers were insistent that it was their duty to report to Port Moresby as soon as possible. I remember as we discussed it, in the end Sister Hayman said, 'Father don't try to persuade them. It is a soldier's job and we should leave it to them.' 'But,' I said, 'we know the country and it is true we could live for years up around Ioma. The Japs will not go there.' Now I see I should have insisted more strongly on that, but it is easy to be wise after the event . . . So with the two soldiers we packed what we thought we could carry and what would be most useful; and that night . . . we slept in the village. At 4.30 next morning . . . while it was just breaking dawn, we slipped down the river in two canoes.[5]

They arrived at the lower Kumusi River at Deunia and joined Lieutenant Smith, Sergeant Hewitt, Private Holyoak and the five American airmen from Major Floyd Rogers' near suicidal attack against the Japanese convoy anchored off Buna; lieutenants Dean, Parker and Cassels, and Sergeant LeBoeuf and Corporal Hoppe. Most of Smith's men of the 1st PIB had already slipped into the jungle heading back to their villages.[6] Benson recalled:

We drifted downriver to Deunia, arriving without incident at the pretty waterside village after almost six hours. The soldiers were expecting us and were ready to start at once, Sister Hayman suggested making a better pair of crutches for the American pilot, who had a nasty leg wound, and this took most of the afternoon. The other wounded man, a machine gunner, had splinters from a bursting 'pom pom' in both hands, but, apart from needing help in dressing and feeding he was able to get along splendidly; he was a tall young corn stalk from Virginia, with hair and embryo whiskers of appropriately corn-like colour and texture; his speech was slow, soft and deliciously droll, with the right reply to every attempt to score off him. The other member of this particular crew was a short, stocky lieutenant, who had developed a fine Captain Kettle beard; he was as strong as a horse and had a great sense of humour. I remember him saying: 'If my old mother could see me now, she would say: "Son this is no place for you. You had best come home." And I reckon I'll take her advice!'[7]

Smith, now in charge of the expanded party, set off towards Popondetta, planning to cross the Kokoda Track and then make their way around Sangara and then over the shoulder of Mount Lamington. From there, they would cross the lower parts of the Owen Stanleys to Rigo and then on to Port Moresby.[8]

All now moved out, with Benson wearing a pair of civilian shoes from Smith with the toes cut out. Mavis wore thin shoes quite unsuited for walking, while May was almost barefoot and, after crossing the next river, they planned to make a rudimentary chair to carry her, 'Army boots being out of the question for such tiny feet'. However, Benson recalled her reply to this proposition: '"Sister will walk in her bare feet, just as far as any of you" and I believe she would have.'[9] After a few days of an exhausting slog through lowland jungle and scrub they reached the vicinity of Popondetta, still well behind enemy lines. Benson recalled:

Two of our Papuan Infantry boys acted as guides; but when we neared the Jap [front] lines three men from a local village were persuaded to join us; somebody said that one of them was the local village constable. We reached the Jap lines, near Popondetta, on the fourth evening. It was turning dark as we crouched down on the edge of the deserted village. Suddenly our erstwhile village constable rose to his feet.

'You stop here,' he whispered. 'Me go Popondetta, look see Japan he stop' and before we could prevent him he was away.

One of the other local men went straight to Lieutenant Smith. 'Taubada,' he said excitedly, 'you not let that man go, he take us to Japan.'

But it was too late. Two soldiers ran after him, but he had disappeared like a shadow into the darkness of the great trees.

We clustered together questioning the two remaining guides. It seemed more than likely that they had grounds for their fears about the village constable; so, we decided to double back on our tracks and came on to the road at another point nearer the sea.[10]

During the early afternoon of the next day one of their Papuan scouts came running up gasping for breath, 'Japs! Coming up from behind.'[11] American pilot 'Big Joe' Parker lay prone on the ground covering the Japanese approach with a Tommy gun, while kneeling behind and on either side of him were the Australian soldiers and another American airman all with rifles. May, Mavis and James Benson took cover in the nearby scrub, while Smith with his revolver and the remaining Americans covered the flanks of the track. Benson recalled at this point that Smith 'whispered to us that, if there was any shooting, we were to slip away to the right, through the trees and across the road, while they would fight a rearguard action, and—if they could—join us later. So, we waited tense and silent for what seemed to me a terribly long time. At last Smith whispered to one of the scouts to crawl out and have a look.'[12] At this point, there were three Papuan troops still with the party, and one of them moved out quietly and circled around their position; he returned ten minutes later with the welcomed news that the Japanese were nowhere to be seen. Another soldier was sent forward, and soon reported they were close to the main Kokoda–Buna track where it meets with another track leading back to Sanananda Point; he also reported the all-clear. They succeeded in crossing the main track as recalled by a very relieved Father Benson:

I remember shaking Smith by the hand and saying, 'That's our biggest hurdle crossed.' I remember, out of the corner of my eye, seeing the happy smiles of the Sisters as they chatted gaily to Joe. Then came the stutter of rifle fire. We span round and before I dived headlong into the bush my mind registered the scene in exact detail; the eighteen or twenty Japanese, with rifles to their shoulders, ranged along the edge of a clearing less than fifty yards away. I remember Miss Hayman crying out; I remember her starting to run, then she seemed to spin round and fell. I dived into the bush. I was still clutching my blue canvas bag, but I had lost my hat, and I remember that this, for some peculiar reason, disturbed me. I crouched down low and began to work my way sideways towards the place where I thought Miss Hayman had fallen. I heard more rifle-fire away to my right; but of the others I saw nothing. It was growing dark now. I called out softly, but there was no reply. I wondered if the Japs would find me; and if they did, would they finish me off with a bullet or a bayonet? I was very much afraid.

After a little while I was too afraid to move, so I simply lay there, in the damp grass while darkness came softly and silently, blurring the outline of grass and trees. After about a minute I heard more firing, again over to the right. Then several times I heard Joe's tommy [*sic*] gun roar out, each time getting farther and farther away. I tried to work my way towards the firing, but soon I became hopelessly lost. So I consoled myself with the thought that I had been the only non-combatant man in the party, and by far the oldest member; I could never have been much of an asset to them; before they reached Port Moresby I should probably have been a terrible liability; if somebody had to fall by the wayside, it was only right it should be me. I told myself too that I had a special duty to the New Guinea natives; by far the best thing for me to do now was to find the Japanese and give myself up; perhaps I would then be able to help my Gona people in their relations with their new masters. So, I lay there, while the periodic shooting grew fainter and more intermittent, until, at about nine o'clock, it faded utterly away. I hoped that some at least had managed to escape.[13]

●

After wandering around lost in the jungle for five days, Father Benson came across a clearing and soon found himself on the main Kokoda Track. He was determined to surrender to the first enemy troops he came across, he didn't have long to wait—but surrendering was more difficult than he thought.

I was passing now through fairly open country—open that is for this part of the world—and eventually I came to a little clearing, where I could see that trees had been felled recently. Opposite the clearing was the usual wall of green; as there seemed no way round it I crossed the clearing and pushed forward through the dense jungle for perhaps five or ten minutes, when suddenly, and quite unexpectedly, there at my feet was the road. I thanked God as I stepped on to it. To the right, I thought, was Buna and the sea; somewhere in that direction I would find the Japanese. I stepped out seaward with as brave an air as I could muster.

About a mile along the road I passed a motor-cycle lying on its side at the edge of a small swamp; there was no sign of its rider, but the red star on its number plate confirmed that it was Japanese. A little farther on, the road forked, and as the left-hand road was the newer, I followed it. Soon I was climbing a fairly steep hill and I was puzzled; roads should descend to the sea. Then, through a break in the bush, I saw men moving about in the sunlight; the Japanese army. I took my ragged old cassock out of the bag and put it on; I wanted them to know me as the priest of Gona; and even if they didn't understand the significance of the cassock, it should at least be proof that I was no soldier. So, commending myself to God's care, I walked up the remaining stretch of road and into the middle of some three or four hundred Japanese soldiers. I walked among them for several minutes repeating:

'Is there anybody here who speaks English?'

Each group of men waved me away with a grunt and went on eating their rice.

Puzzled, I stood and looked carefully around. I saw some half-dozen small mountain guns, and beside them what appeared to be a group of officers, eating their rice at a low table, and next to them, in the middle of the camp, and set apart from the rest, sat a man who looked as if he might be the officer commanding. I walked over to him and said:

'Do you speak English, please? I am the priest from Gona.'

He pointed a finger at me and said: 'Spy!'

Then he waved me away.

'If I am a spy,' I said, 'why do you wave me away?'

Again, he said 'Spy!' as though he were spitting at me and waved me off; evidently that was the only English he had.[14]

After getting a beating from a different Japanese officer, he walked away, but he soon realised that two Japanese soldiers were chasing after him, carrying their rifles with bayonets fixed. He turned to face them and made the sign of the cross, expecting to be killed, but the two men took him by the arm and led him to another officer. He collapsed before making his way there and expected to be executed on the spot, but instead he was dragged off the track and the officer gave him some rice and tinned fish. He was soon shipped to Rabaul where he would survive the war as a POW.[15]

43

'. . . it looks like you won't see your family again'

The rest of the Gona party had managed to evade the Japanese and regroup; two of the three Papuan troops had disappeared into the jungle scrub, only Sergeant Haria remained with them. The next day they headed for Dobodura and reached it just on dusk. Cautiously they entered the village, unsure of their reception. While the villagers were hesitant about their appearance, all seemed relatively safe; however, one man had bolted into the jungle heading for the Japanese at Popondetta, just 4 kilometres away. The refugees slept just outside the village and, early the next morning, they moved out, heading for the village of Managalasi.

They had only gone a short distance when they heard behind them some commotion and, turning, they saw around twenty Japanese who now opened fire; among the Japanese was the villager who had betrayed them. Smith, Mavis and May were able to quickly disappear into the bush, while the remaining Australians and Americans confronted the enemy, conducting a one-sided firefight—they had no chance and the few wounded survivors were quickly bayoneted by the Japanese, while three of the American airmen managed to escape into the bush.[1]

•

At the time, Sergeant Katue with the 1st PIB was still behind enemy lines collecting intelligence and killing any Japanese he came across. He entered Dobodura a few weeks after the killings and was given a version

of what happened. On returning to the Australian lines in October
he informed his superiors who wrote down his story: 'Village councillor BODUE of DOMBADA [sic] who was wearing a big Jap medal
informed Katue that Lieut. SMITH and party who were quartered
at DOMBADA [sic] had mounted guards on the road, but these had
deserted on the approach of the Japs without notifying Mr. SMITH.
Village natives [helped] the Jap patrol. Lieut. SMITH, Sgt HEWITT,
TWO WHITE WOMEN and FIVE AMERICANS were taken prisoner
by the Japs. Sgt HARIA (PIB native Sgt) and one PIB native were killed.
Sgt Katue was shown the grave of these two.'[2]

•

Sergeant Haria had not been killed, nor had Lieutenant Smith, Mavis or
May been captured. Haria managed to escape and from his hiding place
he witnessed the murder of the wounded Australians and Americans.
He later recalled: 'We were going up the creek for about a quarter of a
mile [400 metres] when firing began behind us ... I ran about 20 yards
and laid down and put some leaves on top of my body. I saw the Japs
bayoneting something on the ground on the other side of the creek.'[3]

After a few hours he took off his uniform and buried it and, on
approaching where the party had been attacked, found six bodies.
He then walked around Dobodura, but rather than escaping further
into the jungle he returned to the village from the approach they had
made the previous day, pretending to be a villager from Sanananda.
He planned to stay in the village in case Smith, May and Mavis were
captured and brought back to Dobodura; he would then help them
escape. However, the villager who had previously reported the party's
presence to the Japanese and who had been promoted to 'Captain' as a
reward recognised Haria and he took off again to inform the Japanese;
Sergeant Haria was soon in Japanese hands. However, the next day he
managed to escape and later reported to Australian troops on their
return to the area in late 1942.[4]

The three American airmen who had escaped would only have a
momentary reprieve. The next day they stumbled into the village of
Jegirata where they were able to hole up for a few hours and regain some

of their strength. After trading for food, they set out again, but it was not long before they were ambushed by locals. Two of the airmen were killed outright—speared and clubbed to death. The third, even though wounded by a spear, disappeared off the track, however, his luck was not to last as, within hours, two locals, one named Kirari, hunted him down and clubbed him to death.[5]

•

Mavis and May, after escaping into the jungle from the Japanese attack, had lost contact with Lieutenant Smith. They were soon completely lost and two days later found themselves back at Dobodura. Unknown to them Sergeant Haria had already been captured by the Japanese while staying at the village. However, a friendly villager, likely aware of their pending betrayal by the recently promoted captain, hid them and told them that he would pass them along to a loyal village; from there they would make their way cross the Owen Stanleys via a chain of friendly villages. Both women were relieved to see a friendly face and eagerly the next day, with two guides, made their way towards the next 'friendly' village—the village of Jegirata—the same village that the American airmen had stayed in for a short time, before being speared and clubbed to death.

Before reaching Jegirata they spent the night in the hut of a friendly villager, Michael Tigasepa Akute (also known as Aikere), in the small village of Kakendetta. The next morning the two guides were replaced with two others who soon delivered May and Mavis to the Jegirata village councillor, named Aramipa, who told them that he would take them himself onto the next friendly village of Managalasi. However, instead he led them to Popondetta and the Japanese.[6]

On hearing of their betrayal, Michael Akute raced to Popondetta to see if he could help them. He arrived at 7 a.m. the next morning and heard that the two women were being held by the Japanese in a nearby small coffee mill. He approached the mill, which was near a creek, and found a large group of Japanese taunting the two women, giving them a biscuit each, and snatching it away before they could eat it; all were laughing. Akute watched as the women went to the creek to get a drink under heavy guard. It was now that May and Mavis recognised their friend and waved him away, fearful for his safety; even so he refused to leave and stayed as close to them as he dared. He stayed close to the hut seeking an opportunity to help them escape, but Japanese soldiers were all around, with some entering and leaving the hut throughout the night. At around 3 p.m. the next day there was a commotion among the Japanese, and soon four soldiers approached the mill and took the two women to the nearby coffee plantation called Haruru. Michael Akute followed closely behind, avoiding the Japanese, and later recalled that Mavis was wearing a red, white and yellow dress, while May was wearing a green dress.[7]

May Hayman and Mavis Parkinson must have known their fate as two of the four soldiers were carrying shovels, while two had bayonets, but surprisingly no rifles. Three hundred metres into the plantation, the Japanese ordered a halt; the two men with the shovels went about 10 metres off the track into the trees and began digging a hole while the other two guarded the two women. A one-metre deep hole was all too soon dug. Michael Akute later told Captain Thomas Grahamslaw what happened next. Mavis was the first to be murdered. A Japanese soldier grasped her from behind and attempted to embrace her, but Mavis struggled and almost managed to break free, the soldier plunged his bayonet into her side. She screamed and sank to the ground; 'her spectacles incongruously still in place'.[8] May was ordered to cover her face with a towel and as she did so, she was bayoneted in the throat. The four soldiers dragged the bodies and threw them unceremoniously into the shallow grave; one on top of the other and covered them with a little dirt. As soon as the Japanese left, Michael Akute, at great personal risk, approached; both May and Mavis were dead. He covered the bodies with tapa cloth and filled in the grave. He reported its location to the Australians in early 1943, leading Doc Vernon to the site.[9]

●

Lieutenant Arthur Smith spent several days searching for May and Mavis. He came across two boys who encouraged him to follow them to a friendly village. The starving officer was eating sweet potatoes from a local garden when two locals, one named Diperembo, armed with a rifle, bailed him up. Diperembo took Smith's empty revolver and belt and handed him over to the local village headman—Embogi. Smith was kept prisoner for three days. On the third day, Embogi, the Japanese collaborator and local sorcerer who had earlier informed on Reverend Redlich and Harry Bitmead near Sangara, unsurprisingly decided to hand Smith over to the Japanese at Buna.

As the locals headed for Buna with their prisoner, they passed through the village of Inonda where another leading collaborator with the Japanese, named Ururje, decided to get in on the act and handcuffed Smith for the last part of his journey to Buna. Smith was soon passing through Dobodura and here a villager named Aintapa became agitated at seeing Smith in handcuffs and learning that he was being handed over to the Japanese. Aintapa tried to remove the handcuffs but Embogi ordered Aintapa to stop, the villager ignored him. It was only when Embogi threatened to shoot him—possibly with Smith's own revolver—that Aintapa was forced to back off. Smith asked Aintapa to tell the Australians what had happened to him, knowing he would almost certainly be executed on being handed over to the Japanese.[10]

Twenty-one-year-old Lieutenant Arthur Smith, arrived at Buna on 28 August and was brutally interrogated by the Japanese. Witnesses later said that a Japanese interpreter named Sato Toshio had asked him several questions about the defences of Port Moresby, but Smith replied he had no information to provide. Sato continued: 'We will give you another chance. If you will tell us, we will treat you as a prisoner of war. If you don't, it looks like you won't see your family again. If you will think about your children and your wife at home, it is far better for you to talk.'[11] Smith refused to provide any information and he was soon handed over to the Medical Officer of the 14th Pioneer Regiment, Captain Kato Ginjero, who beheaded him.[12] Lieutenant Arthur Smith has no known grave and is commemorated on the Port Moresby Memorial.

44

'It sickens me every time I think about it'

Father Henry Holland and his group arrived at Sewa village on the day that Kokoda finally fell to the Japanese—10 August. Here, they joined up with Captain Louis Austen and his small party. It was now decided that, rather than crossing the mountains, it was preferable to make their way to Oro Bay and await the arrival of an escape vessel. The group now consisted of ten people; Austen, Holland, Sisters Margery Brenchley and Lilla Lashmar, lay preacher John Duffill, evangelist Lucian Tapiedi, native plantation manager Anthony Gors, his wife and seven-year-old son, and Louise Artango, a sixteen-year-old Papuan/Filipino girl.

Later that day, the expanded party made their way to Perumbata village and stayed there for a few nights. Shortly after arriving, Austen scribbled in the village constable's notebook: 'Food was scarce and the villagers unhelpful or willing to carry.'[1] While there, however, one man offered to take them to the headwaters of Eroro Creek and from there it was a relatively safe and easy trip to Oro Bay. Meanwhile, news of their arrival at Perumbata had spread through the area, including those at Embi village. The villagers there were warned by a local named Pauembo that the Japanese would punish them if they did not turn the white people in.[2]

A few days later Austen's group left the village at around 8 a.m. for Oro Bay. All looked forward to reaching the coast and waiting for the boat that would soon arrive to take them to the safety of Port Moresby. They crossed Jewain Creek and, after travelling a short distance, they realised that an important box had been left at the creek by their guides and reluctant carriers. Lucian Tapiedi, by far the fittest of the group, volunteered to go back and collect the package. Some think that the locals left the package behind intentionally so that he would go back alone to retrieve it, separating him from the group. Lucian was never seen again by the rest of the party—he was killed with an axe by an Orokaiva man named Hivijapa and his body buried nearby. His body was later exhumed and buried next to May Hayman and Mavis Parkinson whose bodies had been reinterred and reburied by Australian troops at the Sangara mission station.[3]

The group pushed on, arriving at Kurumbo and from there heading to Hanakiro. One of the women became ill and had to be carried to Embi village, where they stayed for the night. All were concerned that Lucian had not yet caught up with them. It was at Embi that the men from Perumbata left the group, and some men from Boro volunteered to lead the way on the next leg of their journey. The next morning the party left for Eroro, but towards Dobodura; soon after leaving the party's baggage disappeared—all must have been concerned as Lucian had still not made his appearance.

They soon came to Kurumbo Creek; it was here that they were attacked by their guides. They were dragged out of the creek and the ringleader of the group, a man named Esega, ordered all to be tied up, using chains, bush rope and handcuffs. They were then taken to the village of Embi and thrown into the government rest house where the women were raped by villagers. The next morning—12 August—Esega and his followers proudly escorted their prisoners through Dobodura village and then took them to Giropi plantation near Buna. Here they were delivered to the Japanese.[4]

Outside the headquarters of the Sasebo No. 5 SNLP, they were interrogated; Sato Toshio, who had been present during the interrogation of Lieutenant Smith, was also present during these interrogations. As recorded by historians Dorothea Tomkins and Brian Hughes: 'At the camp at Buna the party was questioned. Why did they run away if they really were missionaries? Margery Brenchley answered, "We did not run away from you, but as we heard the shooting getting nearer we went away to be safe from that."[5]

The next morning the prisoners were taken by truck to the beach where all were forced to kneel and one by one they were beheaded or shot. A captured Japanese diary, belonging to 1st Class Seaman Shin Shunji with Sasebo No, 5 SNLP, records for 13 August: 'Natives brought Australian prisoners—5 men and 3 women and child.' Next day he records: 'About 8.00 decapitated or shot the 9 prisoners.'[6]

The execution of Louise Artango was bungled. She was forced to her knees in terror and suffered several sword strikes. Sato Toshio recorded in his diary a few weeks later—entry 8 September 1942: 'A soldier told me that the Tsukioka Butai (Sasebo No 5, SNLP) which occupied Buna caught 6–7 Australian men and women and cut their heads off one by one on the beach. There was a young girl of 16. She yelled and cried as they missed her head, but they cut off her head in force. He said it was a dreadful sight. The heads and bodies were thrown into the sea.'[7] Another recorded in his diary that he was so 'sickened by the spectacle especially the killing of [Louise Artango] who was very beautiful and who struggled until forcibly held, that he could not stand it and turned away'.[8] Anthony Gors' wife and seven-year-old son were the last to be killed. The little boy buried his face in his mother's body, obviously terrified; perhaps to 'spare' them the horror, they were both shot in the head.

The executioner of the Sangara missionary group was company commander Sub-Lieutenant Komai Uichi, who volunteered to do the killings. He would later also become infamous in the beheading of 23-year-old Flight Lieutenant William Newton VC (Victoria Cross) from Melbourne in March 1943 and later 27-year-old Sergeant Leonard 'Len' Siffleet from Gunnedah in New South Wales, who was with Australian special operations and was beheaded in October 1943.[9] A photograph of Komai about to behead Sergeant Siffleet was found by American soldiers in April 1944, and remains one of the most poignant and best-known images of the Pacific War. An Australian War Crimes investigation team traced down Komai and confirmed he was killed in the war.

•

Alan Champion later recalled the fate of those attached to the Sangara missionary party with sorrow and anger: 'This episode has haunted me all my life. I knew all the unfortunate ones who were executed. One was a small boy seven years of age. It sickens me every time I think about it.'[10]

45

'A very gallant soldier was Jim!'

On 12 August, the RAAF was able to finally conduct airdrops at Kokoda during the early morning hours, but by then they were merely supplying the Japanese as Symington and his men were long gone. Instead, 2nd Lieutenant Hirano Kogoro and his men of No. 3 Platoon were finally getting their first good feed in days. Hirano wrote in his diary: 'The day was beautiful, and the birds sang gaily. It was like spring. Cooked sufficient rice for three meals.'[1] It is also likely that many of the Japanese troops at Kokoda were enjoying the food and cigarettes dropped to them care of the RAAF. Within hours Hirano and his men, along with the rest of the I/144th Regiment, would be advancing towards Deniki along with the signallers attached to No. 2 Section to launch another assault against the Australian position, as recalled by its unknown diarist: 'To support the attack, Shitamoto, Shiraki, Sugabe and Nyudo advanced towards the ridge [Deniki] with the MG detachment, followed by Okamoto, Taniura, Kubo, and the Nose Tai.'[2]

•

To the great relief of Lieutenant Bert Kienzle, the morning of 12 August finally brought with it the appearance of the 'biscuit bombers' over Myola. He wrote in his report: 'The planes had now commenced drop-ping supplies at MYOLA. I was still at EORA CK. I spelled [rested] half the carriers force owing to their exhausted state.'[3] He had also just heard of renewed fighting around the Kokoda Plateau and wrote to Meryl: 'What a wicked thing war is. To think that twice in my life I have had to feel the effects of war in no mean way. I have a wild desire to go right into it and get even with a few Japs but have to hold myself back as there is a much bigger job depending on me in supplying even though it is right up to the front.'[4]

•

At Naro, Captain Symington assessed his losses so far at ten killed and eleven wounded, but he still had not heard from Sergeant Guest and his twenty men of 8 Platoon. Symington had sent a runner to Deniki with a note to Major Cameron—the runner arrived at around 9.30 a.m. The note informed Cameron that he had been forced to withdraw from Kokoda and was making his way back to Deniki, being led by a friendly local. He also wrote that 'A' Company had split into two groups; he was leading a party of four officers and around 50 other ranks, while a smaller group of around twenty men was being led by Sergeant Guest—the sick and wounded were dispersed among both groups. He requested help be sent for the wounded and estimated that the Yodda Valley was now occupied with between 1000 and 2000 enemy troops. Cameron must have been greatly concerned as his force at Deniki was fewer than 200 men at best.[i]

Cameron reported to Port Moresby that he was expecting an attack from a force of up to 2000 Japanese who were massing in the Yodda Valley. With this news, officers and men of the battalion and 1st PIB at Deniki went out in patrols to further identify enemy numbers and their location. These patrols focused on the area around Kokoda and Pirivi in the Managari area, while Captain Jesser, who had been sent back to Isurava because of his wounding, sent out additional patrols from there to the far side of Eora Creek.[5]

Sergeant David Irvine, a 26-year-old truck driver from Warrawong in New South Wales, with two of his men of the 1st PIB, as well as Jack Wilkinson and two men of the 39th Battalion, conducted a patrol towards Kokoda—it was to be a busy day for Wilkinson. Irvine reported that they killed six Japanese soldiers. However, Wilkinson said

---

i   The nominal roll for the 39th Battalion indicates that Cameron's force suffered 43 casualties during the fighting from 8 to 10 August with 23 killed and 20 wounded—casualties for the 1st PIB and RPC are unknown.

that Irvine had shot them all himself with a sub-machine gun. Other reports came in of increased Japanese activity and the Japanese were seen marching out from Kokoda in strength.

Cameron ordered Captain Edward Merritt, a 31-year-old assurance agent from Dandenong in Victoria with 'E' Company, to move forward with his men from Isurava, where they had been for about a week. He also ordered 'B' Company to move forward to Isurava from Eora Creek. Additional reports soon came in that the Japanese were moving along the main track towards Deniki—all troops were ordered to stand to.[6]

The battalion war diary records that the men of 'E' Company 'did NOT arrive at Deniki till after 1700 hrs and consequently, many of their posns were taken up in the dark and no recces could be made of their area. Careful watch was kept throughout the night, but the ENEMY remained quiet and NO attack materialised. Heavy rain fell during the night and very few of the tps were able to keep dry.'[7] Cameron and his men would not have long to wait for the Japanese attack.

During the late afternoon, Jack Wilkinson had returned to Deniki and heard that 'A' Company had been located; among them were several wounded. He volunteered to go to Naro to help bring them in. He, along with a few men of the 1st PIB and the local villager who had delivered the note from Symington, headed for Naro at dusk in a heavy downpour. In the darkness and rain, they pushed through the jungle— they observed that the Japanese had taken up several positions close to Deniki. It was so dark that they had difficulty in keeping together. Wilkinson wrote in his diary:

Word from A Coy that they are in the hills west of Deniki with wounded. Volunteered to go for them and left 1715 hrs with guide and P.I.B. natives as carriers. Deniki expecting attack when I left. Sighted Japs on track to A Coy but we sneaked through long grass. Held my breath for nearly half an hour or it seemed like it. Worst trip I have ever made. Jap coughed about ten feet [3 metres] away and I shriveled up into almost nothing. P.I.B. lads stuck and we had to hold onto each other to keep on path. In the forest luminous fungi took on all sorts of shapes and made weird effects. All fell off track at times. Eventually lighted fire and used fire sticks for guides.

Came into old garden in light rain. Too black to see six feet. Could see Naro village outline on top of hill. Was told troops were there. Five of us fell into deep ravine from a log we were crawling across. Heard voices faintly on hilltop and got scared troops would fire on us and I would lose carriers. Swore loudly and long to let them know it was an Australian there (also because I had fallen on top of one native but three had fallen on me). Heard someone say: 'That's Wilkinson down there. I recognize the way he swears.' Reached Naro village by 2320 hrs . . . Several wounded. Peter Brewer very weak with dysentery but still able to smile. All food air-dropped to troops (thought to be) in Kokoda fell in Jap lines. Symington very annoyed.[8]

•

As dawn broke the next day—13 August—Wilkinson, Symington, Cowey and their men of 'A' Company moved out of Naro on their way back to Deniki. Wilkinson had informed Symington that it looked like Deniki was about to be attacked and he wasn't sure whether the Australians would be able to hold the village given the reported large numbers of Japanese now in and around Kokoda. Wilkinson wrote in his diary: 'Left Naro 0600 hrs. Arrived old WT Station 1200 hrs. Still no food. Heavy firing from Deniki from 1000 hrs. Led troops back by another track to avoid Japs on road. Cowey took up place as rearguard. Good bloke. Brewer still able to move feet but cannot stand up unaided. Most troops tired but still fighting force. Very little ammo. Symington considered patrol to test Jap strength but decided against it for lack of ammo. Moved off towards Isurava.'[9]

They soon reached the junction with the main Kokoda Track behind Isurava and not long after they came up behind Reverend Earl who was in charge of some carriers. Just moments before, he had heard what he believed to be a short but heavy firefight up ahead. Indeed, Earl and his men were lucky as some Australians had come across some Japanese who were preparing an ambush position with a Juki machine gun—they had penetrated behind the Australian lines. Twenty-four-year-old Sergeant William Auchettl from East Brunswick in Victoria with the Battalion Headquarters Company was usually posted at the aid post at Isurava caring for the sick and wounded, but now he was armed with a rifle and grenades. He told Father Earl: 'There's been some fairly heavy fighting at Deniki. The Nips broke through here, too, and planted a woodpecker [machine gun] on the track. Lucky you weren't a few minutes earlier.'[10]

Now coming up behind the supply column, Wilkinson wrote they were soon among the supplies: '"Nobby" Earl bringing up natives with supplies as men in charge of carrier line had "shot through" as soon as firing started at Deniki. Raided [carrier] line and shared a tin of salmon to every two men. Cut my tongue licking tin. Hell I was hungry! Reached Isurava 1530 hrs absolutely done in.'[11]

At Isurava the men of 'A' Company were finally provided with a decent hot meal, the first in days, as recalled by Sergeant Major George Mowat: 'Arrived Isurava about 1700 hrs. Wounded received attention from MO. Poured rain immediately on arrival. Bumper hot meal ready—delicious. First hot meal for 7 days. Issued with one blanket to 3 men. Slept on two bags of boots.'[12] Corporal McKay also recalled: 'They were cooking dehydrated mutton at Isurava at the "Rest House" when we got there. Ken Phelan and a few other "sigs" were looking after the telephone line and they were doubling as cooks to feed us poor buggers. We were starving, and we ate that dehydrated mutton like it was caviar. When the food was dished out, I sat down beside old Jim Cowey and now we knew how hard it must have been for him because he could hardly eat. And I said: "What's the matter Jim?" and he said: "J.D. I am absolutely buggered!" And he was (You can imagine the physical and mental strain of what we had just been through for a man of his age). A very gallant soldier was Jim!'[13] The Great War veteran, Staff Sergeant James Cowey, had not just endured ongoing days of physical and mental strain, but he had taken charge of the small group and accepted the daunting responsibility of getting them all out, which he did.

•

Lieutenant Brewer later wrote in his official report to ANGAU: 'Rested and fed on the native gardens in the Hills south of KOKODA and later returned to ISURAVA—I had been delirious for 3 days and was evacuated to EURO [sic] CREEK and there remained for 15 days'. He concluded his report: 'I must commend the work carried out by Signalers: W.O. MASON; CPL. SKINNER; PTE [sic] CRADDOCK and by W.O. [Gerald] BROWN on the carrier line, for although W.O. BROWN had fever very badly, he stuck to his jobs until he was no longer able to walk.'[14]

•

Newspaperman George Johnston based at Port Moresby reported on the second battle for Kokoda for his readers in Australia:

> On Saturday they counter-attacked . . . and drove the Japanese out of the village . . . Major Watson, [sic Cameron] the new commander, had only one order for his men: 'Stand and fight!' Near the torn, bomb-blasted plateau they found the body of Colonel Owen, tossed into a ditch. He was buried with full military honours near a line of Japanese graves marked with wooden sticks covered with ideographs, and with a bowl of food before every grave . . . We held Kokoda, against furious Japanese attacks. The government buildings were shattered, the village almost demolished in those fierce exchanges. But men cannot do the impossible [and they] . . . were hurled out of the tiny village in the foothills. But we are standing firm in the hills behind, guarding the villages of Deniki and Isurava that lead to the vital pass through the range.[15]

•

Meanwhile, Sergeant William Guest and his men of 8 Platoon, who had brought most of the wounded out of Kokoda, were still trying to reach Deniki.

> We found another path leading away to our left and we followed that. Then I heard a roaring, then all of a sudden, we came out of the jungle into the open and it was the most amazing sight, this huge waterfall was coming down over a cliff with tons and tons of water crashing

down into a deep gorge and you couldn't see the bottom of it. Across it was a swinging native bridge made from native materials which consisted of two ropes that went across on either side to hold onto and the base of it was just wooden slats.

I remember we stood there and looked, and I remember thinking to myself, 'this is the end of it'. We were hungry and starving, and then McCorkelle, he said, 'I didn't come this far to die here,' and . . . [when] he stepped on the bridge his rifle fell off . . . it disappeared right down into the depths somewhere, we don't know. He had a big hole in his shoulder, and he started very slowly to get across this swinging bridge. I remember saying to myself, 'Here's this man the way he is and here's me,' and I said to the others, 'Come on, let's get across.' Eventually we got across and we laid on the other side. We only had a field dressing and that's all we could do for McCorkelle[ii] was change the dressing, we couldn't do anything else for him . . .

We struggled on that day and we came to a big palisade, the wall of a native village, with logs leading up to cross it to get to the top. I said, 'I'll go up and have a look.' I had a look over the top and I saw an Australian soldier standing there trembling with his rifle and bayonet pointing up. He was a bloke called Bernie Fleming and we found out later that he got out of Kokoda and got lost and he got to this village and heard us coming and thought we were Japs. So, we took Bernie Fleming under our wing. We started off on what was going to be the second last day . . . All of a sudden, we heard voices, so we stopped, it could only be the Japanese or the natives. I said to the boys, 'You wait here . . . I'll go across the gully and see what this is.' So, I crawled across the gully and . . . there were all these native kids, it was a village.

As soon as they saw me, they panicked, and they started to run, and I yelled after them, 'Australia, Australia,' and they came back, and they pulled me in. The natives come up with 'cow cow' the first feed in bloody days, and I started to eat it and there was a voice floated from the gully, 'Bill what are you bloody doing?' I said, 'Come over boys, we are in good hands.' They struggled across into the village and they

---

ii   Private Robert McCorkelle, 26 years old from Mount Macedon in Victoria, would survive and
      serve throughout the war.

sat down and had a big feed. Then I saw what I took to be the chief of the village ... He couldn't talk English ... I put my hand up and point away like that, pointing to us and put my finger up and pointed to the natives, two to go, he got the message that I was asking for guides. We watched him call two of the native boys across and 'yakka, yakka, yakka' in their dialect. Then these two natives started to move, and ... I said, 'Right, follow them and don't let them out of your sight,' so away we went behind them.

We followed them and went over the mountains and then we heard the shooting start, and I thought, 'They are leading us into a trap' and I pushed my rifle into one of their backs which I didn't want to do but [did] just to give them the right idea, and they changed direction and started to go the other way ... What we didn't know was the Japanese had attacked Deniki and if we had gone down there, we would have been gone. We continued on for the rest of that day and then all of a sudden, we found ourselves coming down through a native garden and we followed these two natives down and the next minute we were on the Kokoda track ... I remember thinking, 'God, where are we?'

The two natives turned around and went straight back up through the garden, they disappeared and there we were panting on the track. Almost immediately around the corner came this patrol who were PIB ... They were native troops and they wore a jacket and a lap flap with blue piping on it and rifles and fuzzy hair and they had a white man with them. He was an Australian lieutenant and he said, 'What happened, where did you blokes come from?' and I told him the story. He got two of his fellows, a sergeant and one other, to go back and follow our track back up to try and see what happened to the rest of our blokes and I said, 'Where are we?' and he said, 'You are half an hour out of Isurava, the 39th are back at Isurava,' and he said, 'we have got kicked out of Deniki and they are back there,' and I said, 'Good.' We struggled on back down for half an hour and all of a sudden, we are back amongst our boys, back home, and they came up and shook us by the hand and were glad to see us.[16]

Cameron had earlier issued his orders for 'E' Company to move forward to Deniki to take over the position formerly held by 'A' Company, and for 'B' Company to move forward to Isurava. He now ordered the badly mauled 'A' Company to fall back to Eora Creek to recover. Cameron had also been informed that Lieutenant Colonel Ralph Honner, a 38-year-old lawyer from Nedlands in Western Australia, had taken over command of the 39th Battalion (he had been appointed on 1 August). Honner had been a captain and then major with the 2/11th Battalion and had fought with great distinction during the Greek Campaign. On his return to Australia he was promoted to command the 39th Battalion and on 12 August he set out from Ilolo for Deniki. However, he would not arrive in time to command the battalion's defence there, by the time he reached Isurava, he would find the battalion digging in—it was here that Honner and his men would make their gallant stand.[17]

Indeed, Colonel Eustace Keogh, a Great War veteran and now a member of the Australian general staff, wrote of the men of the 39th Battalion: 'Always wet, cold and hungry, always faced by superior numbers, the young soldiers of the 39th had yield[ed] ground grudgingly and counter-attacked whenever they got the chance. If they were not all as brave as lions, if they were not particularly skilful, they inflicted on the enemy a credible toll of casualties and they made him fight hard for his success. When their new commanding officer, Lieutenant Colonel R. Honner, took over at Isurava on 16 August he found the first fruits of confidence and regimental esprit-de-corps beginning to take effect.'[18]

•

At this point Lieutenant Bert Kienzle wrote to Meryl; he knew that the campaign hung in the balance—the next few weeks would determine whether the Japanese advance could be stopped and pushed back.

> Am still within a day's walk from home. [Peter] Brewer has just come in worn out and fever-ridden—just done in and tells me he saw huge fires at our house, everything destroyed, also at Kokoda not a thing left standing not even coconut trees. So far, the weather has been

shocking and not at all an easy matter. The yellow curse is a determined swine and certainly has the numbers. I wonder when we will
have him worried and chased out of his ill-gotten domains . . . Peter
did a good job of work—is very tired and ill. Some even do just as big
a job—if not bigger and get through—others can't take it physically. It
is worrying to see some of our chaps perforated and hurt—but that is
war. We have inflicted heavy casualties on the rising sun but not nearly
enough to stop them . . .[19]

•

By 12 August, the Yokoyama Advance Butai had accomplished its core
objective, the capture of Kokoda Plateau and the station's airstrip—
the gateway to the Owen Stanleys appeared to be open. The task of
conducting a reconnaissance in strength to determine the viability
of attacking Port Moresby from the north had already been super-
seded—the advance across the mountain barrier had been approved
two weeks previously. The next objective was Deniki about 8 kilometres
south of Kokoda, where the Australians were known to be digging
in—400 metres above Kokoda Plateau.

Meanwhile, the remaining Japanese of the South Seas Force were
due to land at Buna on 18 August. With this, Colonel Yokoyama, would
hand over command of the Yokoyama Advance Butai, which was part
of the South Seas Force, to Major General Horii Tomitarô. Those
landing with Horii would include the men of the II and III battalions,
144th Regiment, and the II Battalion, 41st Regiment. These men, along
with supporting elements, would be rushed forward to reinforce their
comrades of the I Battalion who had been fighting since the invasion
almost four weeks before. The 144th Regiment, when united, along
with supporting elements, would begin their advance along the Kokoda
Track through the mountains.

However, it was also now that the Australians of the 39th Battalion
were being reinforced with the militia men of the 53rd Battalion,
and two tried and battle-hardened units of the AIF—the 2/14th
and 2/16th battalions. These men were now either moving up, or
preparing to move up, the track from Port Moresby towards Deniki,

with Maroubra Force's new temporary commander, Lieutenant Colonel Ralph Honner.

Japanese Lieutenant Colonel Tsukamoto launched his attack against Deniki just before 10 a.m., 13 August 1942. More bloody and exhausting battles for the Kokoda Track in the cloud- and jungle-covered mountains of the Owen Stanleys were about to begin.

Epilogue

The massacre at the Tol/Waitavalo plantations was one of the first cases to be listed by Australia with the United Nations War Crimes Commission (UNWCC) in London in October 1942. The testimony of Private William Cook and other survivors provided critical evidence which was collated by Australian Brigadier Arthur 'Tubby' Allen. In January 1943 orders were issued for the collection of further evidence relating to the identification of the Japanese involved. In March 1943 the Minister for the Army wrote to the Australian Prime Minister, John Curtin, requesting 'the appointment of a judicial authority who would take the evidence and submit a full report on this matter'.[1]

Subsequently a commission was organised to examine Japanese war crimes against civilians and prisoners of war in Papua, which included an investigation into the murder of the Gona and Sangara missionary parties in 1942. The commission was later authorised to investigate war crimes committed against Australians regardless of location. In all, the UNWCC would investigate around 25,000 Japanese army and navy personnel for war crimes, but fewer than 6000 were actually charged and far fewer sentenced. The commission's chairman went to the heart of the matter stating 'the majority of war criminals will find safety in their numbers'.[2]

Among those who escaped justice were those considered responsible for the Tol and Waitavalo massacres. Major General Horii Tomitarô, commanding the South Seas Force, drowned when the Japanese withdrew down the Kumusi River on 19 November 1942; while Lieutenant Colonel Kuwada Gen'ichirô, who commanded III/144th Regiment, was killed in action near Giruwa on 22 November 1942. Lieutenant Colonel

Kusunose Masao, the commander of the 144th Infantry Regiment, survived the war and was charged with war crimes but committed suicide in 1946 before he could stand trial.[3]

•

Others who escaped justice were those Japanese considered responsible for the murder of the Gona and Sangara parties, including the commander of No. 5 SNLP, Commander Tsukioka Toroshige, who was killed in an air-raid at Salamaua in August 1943, while others were assessed to have been killed during the ferocious fighting for Buna and Gona in late 1942 and early 1943.[4]

Doc Vernon recalled visiting the Sangara mission shortly after its recapture by Australian troops: 'We found a handful of signalers and A.M.C., men who gave us some food. The Mission was a sad sight, the church was only a heap of cinders with a rough home-made font rising from the ruins, and the house where we had been made so welcome destroyed beyond repair. Only the Sisters' roses were still flowering in their garden.'[5]

The letters of May Hayman and Mavis Parkinson eventually made their way to their families. The letters were given to Australian soldiers when they reoccupied the area in late 1942. It is difficult to imagine the pain these family members felt on reading the women's accounts—full of hope and faith that they and the others would escape.

Earlier in October 1942, May's sister Viola received a letter from Bishop Strong informing her that May appeared to have been killed in September while trying to escape from the Japanese. The bishop had encouraged all the Anglican missionaries to remain on the northern side of the Owen Stanleys despite the very real risk of a Japanese invasion, and even though Australian officials were trying to get them to leave. The bishop wrote to Viola:

> Dear Mrs Waterman,
> You will, by now, have received the grievous news which has come
> through about your sister, May Hayman ... The reports, as you will
> have heard, are that May together with Mavis Parkinson and Fr Benson

and some Americans and Australians who were with them were annihilated on September 1st. Nothing further is known ...

I feel most deeply for you and your family in the sorrow and anguish which will be yours on account of this news and I pray that God will comfort and sustain you, and give you strength to bear this blow ... I cannot possibly speak too highly of May. Her strong faith, her absolute confidence in God, her firm resolve to stand by her vocation whatever its cost, and her devotion to the work to which she had been called and sent, and her love for the people whom she served—the memory of all this will ever be an inspiration to me, and, I am sure, to many others as well. She always seemed so bright and cheerful, so sensible in her outlook, and to be animated by the highest ideals in her life, and in these days of fear she seemed to have no fear. Her whole heart and soul was in the work at Gona, and there was no doubt but that she was tremendously happy there. It was a lovely station, and I always felt, when I went there, the wonder of the atmosphere... As it is—her life though short (if it has gone from us) has been gloriously lived and gloriously given up in the noblest and highest service possible, and the light kindled in that short span will never be extinguished.

I know that May was fully aware of all that her resolve might involve in the way of suffering ... we can and do hope that their bodily sufferings may not have been great ... but even if the future should reveal them to have been as terrible as some others have had to endure—they will but have been a passing phase in a life marked out for an eternal destiny ... If the sad news should eventually be confirmed, then I hope you may be able to mingle with your sorrow joy and thankfulness that your sister has been faithful unto death and counted worthy to be numbered among the glorious band of martyrs.[6]

If Viola, Mavis's parents, and others who undoubtedly received a similar letter, had known that Strong had encouraged their loved ones to stay in northern Papua, their reaction to these self-serving letters would have been devastation.

At about the time that both families were receiving the final letters of May and Mavis, the women's shallow grave near Popondetta had been identified, as recalled sadly by Doc Vernon, who accompanied the District Medical Officer to the burial site: 'I accompanied him to the exhumation of two Anglican Mission sisters whose grave ... [which] had been found near the original Popondetta [destroyed in the recent fighting]. This very necessary piece of work was perhaps the saddest I have ever taken part in, the only consolation about it being that it permitted these martyred girls to be laid at rest alongside the site of the burnt-out church of St. James at Sangara. So far as I know, these were the only bodies of the little band of sufferers that were found.'[7]

A few years later Viola was introduced to Bishop Philip Strong; she refused to shake his hand and accused him of contributing to the death of May, the other missionaries and some of their parishioners. Strong denied any responsibility stating that the missionaries had been free to leave but had chosen to stay. Fifty years after May's murder, Viola was invited to attend a memorial service at May and Mavis's grave-side in 1992; also present was a Japanese Anglican bishop along with some of his Japanese parishioners. The bishop tried to embrace Viola immediately after she had laid flowers on the graves—she pushed him away. If that was not bad enough, soon after the Japanese bishop gave a sermon stating in part: 'We are gathered here to honour the brave missionary women who were unfortunately killed by Japanese bomb-ing.'[8] Viola confronted the bishop and told him some home truths, including the fact that May and Mavis had been repeatedly raped and then murdered by Japanese soldiers. The bishop claimed ignorance of these circumstances but said he would let the truth be known on his return to Japan.[9]

Father James Benson was again destined to be a lone survivor of a personal tragedy; first he had survived the death of his wife and children in Australia, and now he was the only missionary to survive capture by the Japanese in Papua.

In 1945 while still a prisoner of the Japanese, he recalled someone yelling a 'coo-ee!' as, 'big men in khaki, many of them stripped to the waist, came striding down our zigzag precipice track'.[10] Standing beside him was another prisoner, Father Zeeland—a huge Dutchman. Benson was soon replying in kind and wrote:

'Vat is dot noise you make?' he yelled in my ear. 'I do not like it.'

'That's an Australian coo-ee.' I shouted, 'and you're going to hear it again, whether you like it or not!'

Presently we were a surging mob around the troops, three hundred people all clamouring for news at once. I managed to work near one of the two officers, a Major Fairfax Ross, and asked him if he had news of the Sisters from Gona. He caught my question and its urgency and replied quietly and with real sorrow:

'The Mission Sisters from Gona? I'm afraid they are dead—murdered by the Japanese.'

I turned away with all the joy drained out of me. Later when I found the major not so pressed, I asked him for details. He said he did not know the full story, but that it was quite certain the Sisters were dead.

'But,' he said, 'who are you?'

And when I told him he cried in amazement:

'Benson! But, Good God, you are dead too!'

That night we went over the events of the last three years and I had to face the sorrowful fact that not only had my two dear Sisters perished, but that, of all the priests, Brothers, Sisters and Lay Teachers from north-eastern Papua, I, unworthy that I am, was the sole survivor; the flotsam after the deluge.[11]

Father James Benson returned to New Guinea in 1946 to continue his work at Gona. He died in 1956 on a return visit to England shortly after completing his manuscript about his time in New Guinea and as a prisoner of the Japanese. It was published posthumously in 1957 under the title: *Prisoner's Base and Home Again: The Story of a Missionary POW*. In 1972 his ashes were installed in the Gona church, interred in a brass Japanese shell case which was placed near the pulpit.[12]

•

Several investigations were conducted by Australian authorities to identify Papuans who had collaborated with the Japanese, resulting in the murder of civilians and POWs. In 1943 Captain Thomas Grahamslaw and the newly promoted Captain Bert Kienzle accompanied several Papuan witnesses to Mareeba in northern Queensland to attend the War Atrocities Commission.[13] Among those who testified was Michael Akute; Grahamslaw many years later recalled:

> Kienzle and I took it in turns to translate the evidence given by the native members of our party. We had to be particular with our rendition, as the only evidence admissible was what actually had been seen by the witness.
>
> Perhaps the most harrowing evidence was that given by a native [Michael Akute] from Kakendatta [sic] (near Popondetta) concerning the killings of Miss Hayman and Miss Parkinson. This man was lying in the undergrowth near the coffee buildings at Popondetta observing the movements of Japanese troops stationed there . . . when he saw the two European women being led out from one of the coffee buildings. As I recall it, the witness said that the women had been incarcerated in the building for a full day and night. He was unable to describe what happened in the building but saw a number of Japanese enter and depart.
>
> When the women came out a Japanese stepped forward and seized Miss Parkinson and started to hug her. She pushed him away. He thereupon drew a bayonet or dagger and stabbed her in the throat. She gave a slight scream and dropped dead.
>
> Another Japanese, who was standing near Miss Hayman, drew a handkerchief from his pocket and handed it to her indicating at the same time to blindfold herself. She did so and then stood with head upright facing the Jap, and without speaking. The Jap then bayoneted her, and she fell dead. The bodies were buried in a shallow grave at Popondetta. This, to the best of my knowledge, was the only factual eyewitness account of the death of those two dedicated and courageous Australian women. Incidentally, the Kakendetta witness had

previously reported the matter to ANGAU and he led Dr Vernon to
the place where the bodies were buried.[14]

•

In September 1943 a total of 22 Papuans were arrested and found
guilty of betraying missionaries, civilians, soldiers and airmen to the
Japanese, resulting in their murder and execution. All were sentenced
to death, among them the notorious Embogi. Grahamslaw was again
district officer for the area and recalled the hangings of these men; a
group of five men were first hung and a month later another seventeen
were executed.

> Shortly after restoration of native administration ANGAU officials
> arrested an ex Village Constable named Embogi and a number of
> his compatriots for the betrayal and killing of the Ambasi spotters
> named Hanna and Holyoak, the Gona Mission teachers Miss Hayman
> and Miss Parkinson, two European members of the PIB and several
> American airmen. Embogi and four other natives from the Sangara
> area were sentenced to death.
>
> One morning the ADO, Captain Frank Moy, and myself, were in our
> newly constructed office at Higaturu preparing reports for Headquarters,
> when a jeep arrived from the airstrip at Popondetta carrying a passenger
> with the rank of Captain. The back of the jeep was piled high with rope.
> Frank looked at me and called out 'Here comes Neck Ketch'. It took
> me a moment before the significance of his remark sank in. The new
> arrival introduced himself as Ron Hicks of RPC ... Headquarters. He
> produced copies of warrants for the execution by hanging of Embogi
> and the four other condemned men. Hick wanted to know if we had
> gallows? I replied 'No' and at the same time pointed out that one could
> not be constructed at short notice as the only tools on the station were
> one hammer and one saw. We had no nails. Hicks then announced that a
> tree would have to do. Accompanied by Captain Humphries, who was at
> the time conducting investigations into major crimes committed during
> the period of enemy occupation, he went in search of a suitable tree.
> They arrived back a couple of hours later sweating but successful. Hicks

was anxious to get the job over and done with. However, I informed him that, firstly, I would not act until the originals of the warrants had been received and secondly, the condemned men would have to be given the opportunity to bid farewell to their relatives.

The hangings took place several days later in the presence of thousands of people from nearby villages. I addressed the multitude in Motu . . . explaining fully why the men were being executed. To make sure that the words sank in, the Station interpreter repeated what I said. It was a grim experience, which I shall never forget. Each man was given a chance to speak and each elected to do so. Embogi's speech had a profound effect on all present. He had a sonorous voice and was obviously a gifted orator. The gist of his speech was that he went wrong because he was uneducated and did not know better. He freely admitted his crimes and said that the punishment he was about to receive was just. He concluded by enjoining his people to heed what the Government said and to obey its laws.

Embogi was one of the first people to report to me after our troops entered the Buna area and I had taken a liking to him. However, it was not long before I heard whispers that he had been on friendly terms with the Japanese, had played a major part in the betrayal of the Europeans and had actually participated in the killing of the PIB Lieutenant [Arthur Smith] and others. He was obviously a bloodthirsty type, but he met his end like a man. The other four also spoke up like men. They freely admitted their guilt and said they were prepared to pay with their lives. I lay awake most of that night listening to the drums beating and the wailing of the mourners in the villages adjacent to Higaturu and re-living the events of the day. I had seen death in various forms during the preceding twelve months, but nothing affected me as deeply as the hangings of Embogi and his fellow murderers. Perhaps it was the courage they displayed when the time came for them to die. Be that as it may, the punishment meted out to them was in accordance with their own tribal code of 'an eye for an eye'.[15]

Grahamslaw soon received news that seventeen other Papuans had been found guilty and sentenced to death for assisting the Japanese in rounding up civilians, soldiers and airmen and/or involved in the killings themselves. He recalled:

> I set out on a patrol and was about two days inland when a messenger
> arrived from Claude Champion at Higaturu advising that instructions
> had been received from Port Moresby to construct a gallows. Claude
> also advised the receipt of warrants for the execution of seventeen
> natives convicted of wilful murder. I replied telling Claude to go ahead
> with the gallows and at the same time I fixed a date for the executions
> which would allow sufficient time for the relatives and fellow
> villagers of the condemned men to reach Higaturu. By the time I
> returned to Higaturu, Claude, with the able assistance of the station
> clerk, Nansen Kaisa, had constructed a gallows with two trapdoors
> from bush materials in accordance with specifications received from
> Headquarters . . . The gallows were situated in the centre of what could
> be described as a natural amphitheatre several miles below Higaturu . . .
>
> The day before the hangings relatives and friends of the condemned
> men trooped through Higaturu wailing and beating drums. These
> groups included women who had gashed their foreheads and cheeks
> until the blood welled. As a group reached the flagpole near the office
> their wailing would suddenly cease, and they would pound the earth
> in unison with their feet. These expressions of grief accentuated the
> feeling of depression, which permeated Station personnel, Europeans
> and Native alike. On the morning of the executions the hillsides
> surrounding the gallows were packed with thousands of natives and
> there was a hushed silence as we appeared.
>
> The procedure was as follows: The condemned men would be led
> two at a time from the station to the gallows. I would then mount
> the gallows and inform the multitude of the crimes they were being
> punished for. The men would then be asked if they wished to speak.
> With but two exceptions they elected to do so. On conclusion of the
> speeches the men would mount the gallows where they would be
> blindfolded before being led on to the trapdoors. These would then
> be released, and the bodies would disappear. I might explain that the
> gallows were built on posts about 10 feet [3 metres] high. These posts

were surrounded by hessian to ensure that the dangling bodies could not be seen. The detailed instructions from Headquarters, based on old English rules, provided that each body had to hang for 30 minutes after which it was examined by a medical officer who had to declare that life was extinct before it was cut down. The bodies would be moved out of sight before the next lot of two condemned men were led down. In some instances, where the relatives so desired, the bodies were handed to them for burial. Otherwise, they were buried in the station cemetery. With but one exception the condemned men who spoke recanted their evil ways when addressing their people . . . The exception was a man who had been a Village Constable. His speech was short and to the point. He said, 'The Government is about to kill me. My wives must follow me.'

The whole grisly job lasted from about 8 a.m. until the late afternoon. When it was over, Jack McKenna and I moved around the people. 'Do you agree that everything is square now?' we inquired. 'Yes, we agree,' they replied. I spoke to the two wives who had been instructed by their husband to kill themselves. One was elderly, the other quite young. 'He was a bad man who has been made to pay for his crimes and you should take no notice of his talk,' I said. I then spoke to the Village Constable and to the village elders and requested them to watch the women to make sure they did not kill themselves. Sometime later I received word that the young woman had hanged herself. The village elders had kept an eye on her for about a week and then relaxed in the belief that the danger period was over. It transpired that there was no need for concern about the older woman. She made it clear that she regarded his execution as good riddance.[16]

•

Doris Templeton had no idea about the fate of her husband, Sam. Originally, she received word that he was posted as missing in action, but soon after she was informed that Sam had probably been killed in action. Later, she was told there was a possibility that he had been captured and may be a prisoner of war. It was not until 17 April 1946—four years after his actions at Oivi—that she received correspondence that the Australian Army had concluded that Captain Sam Templeton had been killed in action on 26 July 1942. A copy of this letter is held in his service records at the National Archives of Australia.

Dear Madam,

It is with deep regret I have to inform you that the death of your husband, V50190, Capt. S.V. Templeton, has now been officially presumed, and his records have been endorsed 'Because missing on 26/7/1942 and is for official purposes presumed to be dead'.

Investigations have been proceeding for some time past in an endeavour to trace and interrogate individual members of the Japanese forces which opposed your late husband's unit at the time he is believed to have been captured, but up to date the investigations have not been successful.

These investigations will, however, not cease because death has now been presumed, but in view of the fact that the Japanese survivors from the campaign in Papua are thought to have been few in number, it cannot confidently be expected that any further information will be ascertained concerning the fate of your late husband.

In the circumstances it is not desired to further pro-long [sic] your anxiety by awaiting information which may never be obtained, and action has been taken as above mentioned.

In view of the special circumstances of the case it is thought desirable to notify you by this memo rather than by the usual telegraphic communication.

With the profound sympathy of the Minister for the Army and the Military Board . . .[17]

In late 1947 Doris Templeton received further correspondence from the Australian Army—the investigation into Captain Samuel Templeton's disappearance was now officially closed. Doris would never know the details of her husband's death, nor would his children Malcolm or Margarette live long enough to hear the details of their father's death; only Reggie would get to hear the details. It was not until 2009 that Reggie, aged in his eighties, was informed that his father had been

wounded and interrogated—providing critical *misinformation* to the
enemy, greatly inflating Australian numbers, not only on the track, but
also at Port Moresby—helping to sow seeds of serious doubt into the
Japanese commanders and helping to stall their advance for a precious
two weeks. Reggie was finally told that, during his interrogation, his
father was executed by Lieutenant Colonel Tsukamoto.

Acknowledgements

I am indebted to the men and women mentioned in this book who wrote down and/or recorded their experiences. Without these critical historical records this narrative could never have been told in any meaningful detail. It has always been important for this author to tell the story using the words of those who were there—it brings the narrative into a whole new light as many voices are heard as opposed to the monotone of a single writer. Like all researchers, I am also indebted to these individuals for unselfishly donating their precious documents, writings and 'curios' to numerous research institutions for others to study. This also applies to relatives who have provided similar valuable records. For any copyright holders I was unable to locate or who did not reply to my request to use quoted material in this book, I trust that the material quoted meets with your approval.

I would also like to thank the 39th Battalion Association, specifically David Howell, who has been a great supporter of this book. As the Managing Director of Kokoda Historical he has conducted countless treks across the track and probably knows more about the Kokoda Campaign than anyone. David also provided details of Captain Sam Templeton's early life—I'm keenly waiting for David's biography of Sam Templeton to be published. A big thank you to the association for allowing me to quote from Vic Austin's book *To Kokoda and Beyond: The story of the 39th Battalion 1921–1943*; 'Doc' Geoffrey Vernon's diary, published by the Association; and stories from the diggers themselves published in the battalion's journal, *The Good Guts*. The author did not have access to the journal issues themselves but has used Carl

Johnson's book *Blood over Mud* which has reproduced these stories first published in the battalion's journal to tell the story of the digger's in their own words.

I would also like to thank the following authors/publishers for allowing me to quote from their books: much thanks to Lex McAulay for allowing me to quote from his groundbreaking book *Blood and Iron: The battle for Kokoda 1942* (Hutchinson Australia); the Papua New Guinea Church Partnership for allowing me to quote from Patrick Redlich's book, *My Brother Vivian ... and the Christian Martyrs of Papua New Guinea*; a big thanks to Robyn Kienzle for allowing me to quote from her excellent book *The Architect of Kokoda: Bert Kienzle— the man who made the Kokoda Trail* (Hachette Australia, Sydney); and Allen & Unwin for allowing me to quote from the grand master of all things Kokoda, Peter Brune, and his books *Those Ragged Bloody Heroes: From the Kokoda Trail to Gona Beach, 1942* and *A Bastard of a Place: The Australians in Papua*; and thanks again to Allen & Unwin for allowing me to quote from the book by Craig Collie and Hajime Marutani, *The Path of Infinite Sorrow: The Japanese on the Kokoda Track*. I would also like to thank the Australian War Memorial for granting access and permission to quote from their holdings.

Thanks to historian Peter Williams for reading and commenting on an early manuscript draft—his constructive criticisms did much to improve the final manuscript. A big thanks to my literary agent Rick Raftos for his ongoing help and support. At Allen & Unwin I would like to thank my publisher Rebecca Kaiser for believing in this book, when all too often others incorrectly stated there was nothing more to be said about the Kokoda Campaign—we still have much to learn. Thanks also to Tom Bailey-Smith, the senior editor at Allen & Unwin who took on the manuscript and quickly and efficiently had it ready for publication; similarly, to Deonie Fiford who went through the manuscript correcting numerous errors. It goes without saying that any remaining errors are those of the author alone.

My biggest thanks are to my three wonderful children, Emma, Anita and Lloyd, and my precious little granddaughter, Naomi.

Bibliography

Australian War Memorial (AWM), Canberra

PERSONAL RECORDS

Benson, James—manuscript, *Gona and After*, AWM MSS 0768
Cook, Private William—statement, AWM PR90/053
Hayman, May—letter, AWM 3DRL/5092
Markham, Corporal Reginald—diary, AWM PR89/087
Porter, Brigadier Selwyn—papers, AWM PR00527
Strong, Bishop Philip—letter, AWM 3DRL/5092
Vernon, Captain Geoffrey—diary, AWM PR00787 (original of AWM 54 253/5/8).

UNIT WAR DIARIES

21st Brigade War Diary: August to October 1942, AWM 52 8/2/21
30th Brigade War Diary: July to August 1942, AWM 52 8/2/30
39th Battalion War Diary: July to December 1942, AWM 52 8/3/78
ANGAU Headquarters War Diary: May to June 1942, AWM 52 1/10/1 002
ANGAU Headquarters War Diary: July to August 1942, AWM 52 1/10/1 003
ANGAU Headquarters War Diary: September 1942, AWM 52 1/10/1 004
ANGAU Headquarters War Diary: October 1942, AWM 52 1/10/1 005
ANGAU Headquarters War Diary: April 1943, AWM 52 1/10/1 010

WRITTEN RECORDS, 1939–1945 WAR

'I'll remember Rabaul' (The Toll Massacre), story told by Mr Cook, 2/10 Field Ambulance, AWM 54 607/9/1
Kienzle Report, AWM 54 577/6/8
Notebook no. 32, Lieutenant Noda Hidetaka diary, AWM 54 577/7/26
Vernon War Diary, Part 1, July–November 1942, AWM 54 253/5/8

ATIS RECORDS OF POW INTERROGATIONS AND CAPTURED DOCUMENTS

Diary of unknown leader of signals unit with No. 2 Infantry Section, No. 1 Company, I/144th Regiment, AWM 55 Current Translation 3/2 No. 266
Field Log of *Sakigawa Tai*, AWM 55 Enemy Publication No. 27

Intelligence Reports Issued by *Yazawa Butai HQ*, AWM 55 Enemy Publication
No. 28
2nd Lieutenant Hirano diary, AWM 55 Current Translation 3/2 No. 218
Lieutenant Nose diary, AWM 55 Current Translation 3/2 No. 210
Private Watanabe Toshio diary, AWM 55 Current Translation 3/2 No. 87

University of New South Wales (UNSW)

AUSTRALIANS AT WAR FILM ARCHIVE (AWFA)

Bailey, Gordon: Archive number 1407, interviewed 20 January 2004
Barcham, Stanley: Archive number 1287, interviewed 11 December 2003
Bellairs, William: Archive number 1324, interviewed 2 February 2004
Daniels, Donald: Archive number 230, interviewed 10 June 2003
Dawson, Joseph: Archive number 1592, interviewed 16 March 2004
Downes, Lawrence: Archive number 1238, interviewed 5 December 2003
Forrester, Arnold: Archive number 1805, interviewed 26 March 2004
Fry, Albert: Archive number 1234, interviewed 4 December 2003
Garland, Arthur: Archive number 458, interviewed 11 June 2003
Guest, William: Archive number 588, interviewed 13 August 2003
Halsall, Ronald: Archive number 574, interviewed 22 August 2003
McClean, Douglas: Archive number 235, interviewed 30 May 2003
Mahoney, William: Archive number 742, interviewed 13 July 2004
Markham, Reginald: Archive number 704, interviewed 17 September 2003
Patterson, Frank: Archive number 193, interviewed 22 May 2003
Phelan, Kenneth: Archive number 509, interviewed 17 June 2003

National Archives Australia

B2455—Samuel Victor Templeton: Service Number—5757
J1889, BL43895/13—*A Report by Sir William Webb on Japanese Atrocities.
Depositions re Japanese Atrocities—1943. I 11 Treatment of the Inhabitants and
the Murders of Four White Female Missionaries and Others.*
Note: most basic biographical details of Australian military personnel discussed
are checked against the online electronic files of the NAA using identified
army SX, V or VX serial; most serial numbers taken from Johnson, 2006 or
McCarthy, 1959.

National Library of Australia

Sissons, D.C.S., 2006, The Australian War Crimes Trials and Investigations
(1942–51), MS 3092 (Sissons papers—File 24)

Official Histories

Bullard, S., 2007, *Japanese Army Operations in the South Pacific Area: New Britain and Papua Campaigns, 1942–43*, Australian War Memorial (English translation of the Japanese Official History)

Gillison, D., 1962, *Royal Australian Air Force 1939–1942, Australia in the War of 1939–1945*, (Air Series) Australian War Memorial, Canberra

McCarthy, D., 1959, *South-West Pacific Area First Year, Kokoda to Wau, Australia in the War of 1939–1945*, (Army Series) Australian War Memorial, Canberra

Milner, S., 1955, *The War in the Pacific: Victory in Papua, United States Army in World War II*, Center of Military History United States Army, Washington, D.C.

Walker, A.S., 1957, *The Island Campaigns: Australia in the War of 1939–1945*, (Medical Series) Australian War Memorial, Canberra

Wigmore, L., 1957, *The Japanese Thrust, Australia in the War of 1939–1945*, (Army Series) Australian War Memorial, Canberra

Unit History

Austin, V., 2007, *To Kokoda and Beyond: The story of the 39th Battalion 1941–1943*, Australian Military History Publications, Australia

Budden, F.M., 1987, *The Chocos: The story of the Militia Infantry Battalions in the South West Pacific Area 1941–1945*, Summer Hill, NSW

Byrnes, G.M., 1989, *Green Shadows: A History of the Papuan Infantry Battalion*, Queensland Corrective Services Commission

Downs, I., 1999, *The New Guinea Volunteer Rifles (NGVR): 1939–1943—A History*, Pacific House Books, Queensland

James, C., 1999, *ANGAU One Man Law: Australian New Guinea Administrative Unit*, Australian Military History Press, Loftus, NSW

Oakes, B., 2002, *Muzzle Blast: Six years of war with the 2/2 Australian Machine Gun Battalion*, AIF, Australian Military History Publications, Loftus

Perrin, A.E., 1990, *The Private War of the Spotters: A History of the New Guinea Air Warning Wireless Company February 1942–April 1945*, NGAWW Publication Committee Victoria

Powell, A., 2003, *The Third Force: ANGAU's New Guinea War, 1942–46*, Oxford University Press, Melbourne

Sinclair, J., 1990, *To Find a Path: The Life and Times of the Royal Pacific Islands Regiment, Volume 1—Yesterday's Heroes 1885–1950*, Boolarong Publications, Brisbane

Academic Dissertations

Harwood, J.M., 1979, 'The Australian Militia in New Guinea 1940–1945', MA dissertation, Macquarie University

Williams, P., 2008, 'The Kokoda Campaign, July–November 1942, An Analysis', Ph.D. dissertation, Charles Darwin University

Books/Book Chapters

Alpin, D., 1980, *Rabaul 1942*, the 2/22nd Battalion A.I.F., Lark Force Association, Melbourne

Anderson, N., 2014, 'To Kokoda', *Australian Army Campaign Series No. 14*, Australian Army History Unit, Canberra

Anderson, N., 2018, 'The Battle of Milne Bay, 1942', *Australian Army Campaign Series No. 24*, Australian Army History Unit, Canberra

Barrett, J., 1987, *We Were There: Australian soldiers of World War II tell their stories*, Allen & Unwin, Sydney

Barter, M., 1994, *Far Above Battle: The Experience and Memory of Australian Soldiers at War 1939–1945*, Allen & Unwin, Sydney

Benson, J., 1957, *Prisoner's Base and Home Again: The Story of a Missionary POW*, Robert Hale, London

Bergerud, E., 1996, *Touched with Fire: The land war in the South Pacific*, Penguin Books, New York

Blake, G., 2019, *Jungle Cavalry: Australian Independent Companies and Commandos 1941–1945*, Helion & Company, Warwick, United Kingdom

Borneman, W.R., 2016, *MacArthur at War: World War II in the Pacific*, Little Brown and Company, New York

Bradley, P., 2008, *The Battle for Wau: New Guinea's Frontline 1942–43*, Cambridge University Press, Melbourne

Bradley, P., 2010, *To Salamaua*, Cambridge University Press, Melbourne

Bradley, P., 2012, *Hell's Battlefield: The Australians in New Guinea in World War II*, Allen & Unwin, Sydney

Braga, S., 2004, *Kokoda Commander: A Life of Major-General 'Tubby' Allen*, Oxford University Press, Melbourne

Bride, M., undated, *I Wait For The Lord, My Soul Waits For Jim: And In His Words is My Hope. A resource book of the Martyrs of Papua New Guinea and Melanesia*, Anglican Board of Mission, Australia

Brune, P., 1991, *Those Ragged Bloody Heroes: From the Kokoda Trail to Gona Beach, 1942*, Allen & Unwin, Sydney

Brune, P., 1994, *Gona's Gone: The battle for the beach-head 1942*, Allen & Unwin, Sydney

Brune, P., 2003, *A Bastard of a Place: The Australians in Papua: Kokoda, Milne Bay, Gona, Buna and Sanananda*, Allen & Unwin, Sydney

Brune, P., 2007, *Ralph Honner: Kokoda Hero*, Allen & Unwin, Sydney

Cameron, D.W., 2007, *25 April 1915: The Day the Anzac Legend was Born*, Allen & Unwin, Sydney

Cameron, D.W., 2014, *Our Friend the Enemy: Anzac from both sides of the wire*, Big Sky Publishing, Sydney

Cameron, D.W., 2017, *The Charge: The Australian Light Horse victory at Beersheba*, Penguin Books Australia, Melbourne

Cameron, D.W., 2018a, *Australians on the Western Front Vol 1: Resisting the Great German Offensive*, Penguin Books Australia, Melbourne

Cameron, D.W., 2018b, *Australians on the Western Front Vol 2: Spearheading the Great British Offensive*, Penguin Books Australia, Melbourne

Campbell, J., 2007, *The Ghost Mountain Boys: Their Epic March and the Terrifying Battle for New Guinea—The Forgotten War of the South Pacific*, Crown Publishers, New York

Chan, G., 2003, *War on Our Doorstep: Diaries of Australians at the frontline in 1942*, Hardie Grant Books, South Yarra

Claringbould, M. & Ingham, P., 2017, *South Pacific Air War Volume 1: The Fall of Rabaul December 1941–March 1942*, Avonmore Books, South Australia

Claringbould, M. & Ingham, P., 2018, *South Pacific Air War Volume 2: The Struggle for Moresby, March–April 1942*, Avonmore Books, South Australia

Collie, C. & Marutani, H., 2009, *The Path of Infinite Sorrow: The Japanese on the Kokoda Track*, Allen & Unwin, Sydney

Cooper, A., 2014, *Kokoda Air Strikes: Allied Air Forces in New Guinea, 1942*, New South Books, Sydney

Dawson, J., 2003, *Kokoda Survivor*, self-published

Day, D., 2003, *The Politics of War: Australia at War, 1939–45: From Churchill to MacArthur*, HarperCollins Publishers, Sydney

Dornan, P., 1999, *The Silent Men: Syria to Kokoda and to Gona*, Allen & Unwin, Sydney

Drea, E.J., 2017, 'Making Japanese Soldiers', in James, K. (ed.), *Kokoda: Beyond the legend*, Cambridge University Press, Melbourne, pp. 188–205

FitzSimons, P., 2004, *Kokoda*, Hodder, Sydney

Frank, R.B., 1990, *Guadalcanal: The definitive account of the landmark battle*, Penguin Books, USA

Friedman, K.I., 2007, *Morning of the Rising Sun: The heroic story of the battle for Guadalcanal*, Friedman, USA

Gailey, H., 2000, *MacArthur Strikes Back: Decision at Buna: New Guinea, 1942–43*, Presidio, USA

Gallaway, J., 2000, *The Odd Couple: Blamey and MacArthur at War*, University of Queensland Press, Brisbane

Gamble, B., 2006, *Darkest Hour: The True Story of Lark Force at Rabaul—Australia's Worst Military Disaster of World War II*, Zenith Press, USA

Gamble, B., 2018, *Kangaroo Squadron: American Courage in the Darkest Days of World War II*, Da Capo Press, New York

Garland, A., undated, 'At Kokoda with B Company, OC 10m Platoon, B Company', reproduced in Johnson, C., 2006, *Mud Over Blood: The 39th Infantry Battalion 1941–43—Kokoda to Gona*, History House, Victoria

Geddes, M., 2004, *Blood, sweat and tears: Australia's WWII remembered by the men and women who lived it*, Penguin Books, Melbourne

Hall, T., 1981, *New Guinea, 1942–44*, Methuen, Australia

Ham, P., 2004, *Kokoda*, HarperCollins, Sydney

Happell, C., 2008, *The Bone Man of Kokoda: The extraordinary story of Kokichi Nishimura and the Kokoda Track*, Pan Macmillan, Australia

Hawthorne, S., 2003, *The Kokoda Trail: A history*, Central Queensland University Press

Hayashi, S. & Coox, A.D., 1959, *KŌGUN: The Japanese Army in the Pacific War*, The Marine Corps Association, Quantico, USA

Henderson, J., 1992, *Onward Boy Soldiers: The Battle for Milne Bay, 1942*, University of Western Australia Press, Perth

Hooper, A.E., 1994, *Love, War & Letters: PNG 1940–45*, Robert Brown & Associates (QLD) Pty Ltd

Horner, D.M., 1978, *Crisis of Command: Australian Generalship and the Japanese Threat, 1941–1943*, Australian National University Press, Canberra

Horner, D.M., 1996, *Inside the War Cabinet: Directing Australia's War Effort 1939–45*, Allen & Unwin, Sydney

Horner, D.M., 1998, *Blamey: Commander-in-Chief*, Allen & Unwin, Sydney

Hull, W., 1995, *Salvos with the Forces: Red Shield Services during World War Two*, The Salvation Army, Mont Albert, Victoria

Isom, D.W., 2007, *Midway Inquest: Why the Japanese Lost the Battle of Midway*, Bloomington and Indianapolis, United States

James, B., 2008, *Field Guide to the Kokoda Track: An historical guide to the lost battlefields*, Tower Books, Sydney

James, C., 1999, *ANGAU One Man Law*, Australian Military History Press, Riverwood, NSW

Johnson, C., 2006, *Mud Over Blood: The 39th Infantry Battalion 1941–43—Kokoda to Gona*, History House, Victoria

Johnston, G.H., 1944, *New Guinea Diary*, Angus & Robertson, Sydney

Johnston, M., 1996, *At the Frontline: Experiences of Australian soldiers in World War II*, Cambridge University Press, UK

Johnston, M., 2000, *Fighting the Enemy: Australian soldiers and their adversaries in World War II*, Cambridge University Press, UK

Johnston, M & Stanley, P., 2002, *Alamein: The Australian Story*, Oxford University Press, Melbourne

Keogh, E.G., 1965, *South West Pacific 1941–45*, Grayflower Productions, Melbourne

Kienzle, R., 2011, *The Architect of Kokoda: Bert Kienzle—The man who made the Kokoda Trail*, Hachette Australia, Sydney

Kienzle, R., 2017, 'On the Trail of an Extraordinary Man', in James, K. (ed.) *Kokoda: Beyond the legend*, Cambridge University Press, Melbourne, pp. 238–251

Likeman, R., 2012, *From the Tropics to the Desert: German New Guinea, Egypt & Palestine 1914–1921—The Australian Doctors at War Series, Volume 2*, Rosenberg Publishing, Australia

McAulay, L., 1991, *Blood and Iron: The battle for Kokoda 1942*, Hutchinson Australia

McDonald, N., 2004, *Chester Wilmot Reports: Broadcasts that Shaped World War II*, ABC Books, Sydney

McKernan, M., 2006, *The Strength of a Nation: Six years of Australians fighting for the nation and defending the homefront in WWII*, Allen & Unwin, Sydney

McLeod, J., 2019, *Shadows on the Track: Australia's Medical War in Papua 1942–43 (Kokoda—Milne Bay—The Beachhead Battles)*, Big Sky Publishing, Sydney

Mayo, L., 1975, *Bloody Buna: The campaign that halted the Japanese invasion of Australia*, Australian National University Press, Canberra

Paull, R., 1958, *Retreat from Kokoda*, Heinemann, Melbourne

Phelan, K., undated, 'The Advance of C Company, 1 Platoon, HQ Co', reproduced in Johnson, C., 2006, *Mud Over Blood: The 39th Infantry Battalion 1941–43—Kokoda to Gona*, History House, Victoria

Phelan, K., undated, 'At Kokoda with A Company 1 Platoon, HQ Co', reproduced in Johnson, C., 2006, *Mud Over Blood: The 39th Infantry Battalion 1941–43—Kokoda to Gona*, History House, Victoria

Pratten, G., 2009, *Australian Battalion Commanders in the Second World War*, Cambridge University Press, Melbourne

Ramsay Silver, L., 2004, *The Bridge at Parit Sulong: An investigation of mass murder Malaya 1942*, The Watermark Press, Sydney

Reading, G., 1946, *Papuan Story*, Angus & Robertson, Sydney

Redlich, P., 2012, *My Brother Vivian . . . and the Christian Martyrs of Papua New Guinea*, self-published, NSW, Australia

Robertson, J., 1981, *Australia at War 1939–1945*, William Heinemann, Melbourne

Rowell, S.F., 1974, *Full Circle*, Melbourne University Press

Russell, L., 1958, *The Knights of Bushido: A Short History of Japanese War Crime*, Cassell, London

Shaw, W.I., 2012, *On Radji Beach: The Story of the Australian Nurses after the Fall of Singapore*, Pan Macmillan, Sydney

Smith, M.S., 2000, *Bloody Ridge: The battle that saved Guadalcanal*, Presidio Press, USA

Sublett, F., 2000, *Kokoda to the Sea: A history of the 1942 campaign in Papua*, Slouch Hat Publications, McCrae, Australia

Tanaka, K., 1980, *Operations of the Imperial Japanese Armed Forces in the Papua New Guinea Theatre during World War II*, Japan Papua New Guinea Goodwill Society, Japan

Thompson, P., 2008, *Pacific Fury: How Australia and her Allies defeated the Japanese scourge*, William Heinemann, Sydney

Thomson, J., 2000, *Winning with Intelligence: A Biography of Brigadier John David Rogers, CBE, MC 1895–1978*, Australian Military History Press, Loftus, NSW

Tomkins, D. & Hughes, T., 1969, *The Road from Gona*, Angus and Robertson, Sydney

Tracey, R., 2017, 'Command Failures on the Kokoda Trail', in James K. (ed.), *Kokoda: Beyond the legend*, Cambridge University Press, Melbourne, pp. 112–31

Wakeling, A., 2018, *Stern Justice: The Forgotten Story of Australia, Japan and the Pacific War Crimes Trials*, Viking/ Penguin, Australia

Wilkinson, J., undated, 'Eight days on the Kokoda Track towards Kokoda: Diary of WO11 Jack Wilkinson, PX 11 attached to B Company', reproduced in Johnson, C., 2006, *Mud Over Blood: the 39th Infantry Battalion 1941–43—Kokoda to Gona*, History House, Victoria

Wilkinson, J., undated, 'Memories of a Medic', reproduced in Johnson, C., 2006, *Mud Over Blood: The 39th Infantry Battalion 1941–43—Kokoda to Gona*, History House, Victoria

Williams, P., 2012, *The Kokoda Campaign, 1942: Myth and Reality*, Cambridge University Press, Melbourne

Williams, P., 2017, 'Against overwhelming odds? Opposing strengths on the Kokoda Trail', in James, K. (ed.), *Kokoda: Beyond the legend*, Cambridge University Press, Melbourne, pp. 222–35

Zobel, J.W., 2017, 'Victory at all costs: Douglas MacArthur's Papuan Campaign of 1942–43', in James, K. (ed.), *Kokoda: Beyond the legend*, Cambridge University Press, Melbourne, pp. 92–111

Journals/Manuscripts/Newspapers

Brett, G., 1947, 'The MacArthur I knew', *True Magazine* (October)

Coulthart, R., 2010, 'Kokoda mystery solved', *The Australian*, 24 April

Grahamslaw, T., 1971, 'Missionaries Slaughtered in Grim Advance on Moresby', *Pacific Island Monthly*, April 42(4): 71–75 & 117–23

Grahamslaw, T., (unpublished), 'Recollections of ANGAU', https://pngaa.org/site/blog/2015/09/16/recollections-of-angau-tom-grahamslaw/

Gridneff, I., 2010, 'Keeping track of the Bone Man's memories', *The Canberra Times*, 30 January

Howell, D., 39th Battalion Association, personal communication with author

Matthews, T., 2003, 'Missionary Martyrs', *Wartime: Official Magazine of the Australian War Memorial*, 21:13–15.

Parkinson, M., 1943, 'Epic Letter before Death', *Queensland Times*, 5 May

Philippart, J.D., 2004, 'The Expeditionary Airfield as a Center of Gravity—Henderson Field during the Guadalcanal Campaign (August 1942–February 1943)', USAF Air Command and Staff College Wright Flyer Paper No. 19, Air University Press, Maxwell Air Force Base, Alabama

Ramsay, D., 2006, 'The forgotten indigenous Papuan and New Guinean soldiers of the New Guinea Campaigns 1942–45', Conference Paper, United Service, 57(2) June

Robinson, N.K., 1979, 'Villagers at War: Some Papua New Guinea Experiences in World War II', Pacific Research Monograph No. 2, Australian National University Press, Canberra

Vernon, G., 1943, 'A War Diary: The Owen Stanley Campaign July–November 1942' (the personal diary of Captain Geoffrey Hampden 'Doc' Vernon MCD—AAMC), published by the 39th Battalion Association, Victoria

Waiko, J., 1988, 'Damp Soil My Bed, Rotten Log My Pillow: A Villager's Experience of the Japanese Invasion', *'O'O: A Journal of Solomon Island Studies*, No. 4:45–59

Waiko, J., 1991, 'Oral History and the War: The View from Papua New Guinea', in Geoffrey White (ed.) Remembering the Pacific War, Occasional Paper 36 Center for Pacific Island Studies, School of Hawaiian, Asian & Pacific Studies, University of Hawai'i at Mānoa Honolulu, pp. 3–16

Endnotes

Prologue
1 Quote from McCarthy, 1959, p. 115.

Chapter 1
1 McCarthy, 1959.
2 Alpin, 1980; Gamble, 2006, McCarthy, 1959; Pratten, 2009.
3 Alpin, 1980; Claringbould, M. & Ingham, P., 2018; Downs, 1999; Gamble, 2006; Happell, 2008; McCarthy, 1959; Pratten, 2009.
4 AWM 54 607/9/1.
5 AWM 54 607/9/1.
6 AWM 54 607/9/1.
7 AWM 54 607/9/1.
8 AWM 54 607/9/1.
9 AWM 54 607/9/1.
10 AWM 54 607/9/1.
11 AWM 54 607/9/1; AWM PR90/053; Bradley, 2012; Gamble, 2006.
12 AWM 54, 607/9/1.
13 Cameron, 2007; Cameron, 2014; Cameron, 2018a; Cameron, 2018b.
14 AWM 54, 607/9/1.
15 Quote from Gamble, 2006, pp. 150–51.
16 Alpin, 1980; Bradley, 2012; Gamble, 2006; McCarthy, 1959.
17 Quote from Downs, 1999, p. 106.
18 Quote from Gamble, 2006, p. 149.
19 Downs, 1999; Gamble, 2006.
20 Alpin, 1980; Gamble, 2006; Wakeling, 2018.
21 Alpin, 1980; Gamble, 2006; Johnson, 2006.

Chapter 2
1 Bergerud, 1996; Braga, 2004; Horner, 1978; Tanaka, 1980.
2 Borneman, 2016; Day, 2003; Gallaway, 2000; Horner, 1978.
3 Borneman, 2016, p. 208.
4 Thomson, 2000, p. 141.

5 Budden, 1987; Cooper, 2014; Harwood, 1979; Hayashi & Cox, 1959; Horner, 1978; Keogh, 1965; McCarthy, 1959; Gillison, 1962.
6 Quote from Horner, 1998, p. 268.
7 Quotes from Campbell, 2007, p. 17.
8 Day, 2003; Gallaway, 2000; Horner, 1978; Robertson, 1981.
9 Brett, 1947, p. 20.
10 McCarthy, 1959; Milner, 1955.
11 Quotes from Austin, 2007, p. 12 and p. 55.
12 Budden, 1987; McCarthy, 1959.
13 Budden, 1987; Harwood, 1979; Horner, 1978; McCarthy, 1959; McKernan, 2006.
14 Quote from Austin, 2007, p. 10.
15 Quote from Pratten, 2009, p. 169.
16 Quote from Horner, 1978, p. 82.
17 Brune, 1991; Brune, 2003; Dornan, 1999; Horner, 1978; McAulay, 1991; McKernan, 2006.
18 James, 1999, p. 3.
19 Brune, 1991, 2003; Dornan, 1999; James, 1999; McAulay, 1991.
20 James, 1999, p. 5.
21 Quote from McAulay, 1990, p. 12.
22 Braga, 2004; Horner, 1978; Johnston & Stanley, 2002; McCarthy, 1959; Williams, 2012.
23 Isom, 2007; Tanaka, 1980.

Chapter 3
1 Quote from Milner, 1955, p. 43.
2 Quotes from Campbell, 2007, p. 46.
3 Blake, 2019; Bradley, 2008; Bradley, 2012.
4 Gailey, 2000.
5 See Blake, 2019. Copy of the document kindly supplied to the author by Dr Gregory Blake.
6 McCarthy, 1959; Williams, 2008; Williams, 2012.
7 Braga, 2004; Horner, 1978; McCarthy, 1959; Pratten, 2009.
8 Quote from Pratten, 2009, p. 169.
9 AWM PR00527.
10 Braga, 2004; Horner, 1978; McCarthy, 1959; Pratten, 2009.
11 Quote from Johnston, 1996, p. 181.
12 Borneman, 2016; Gamble, 2018; Gailey, 2000; Horner, 1978; Milner, 1955.
13 McCarthy, 1959.
14 Quote from Austin, 2007, p. 37.
15 Bradley, 2008; Bradley, 2010; Bullard, 2007; Hayashi & Cox, 1959; Keogh, 1965; McCarthy, 1959; Smith, 2000; Tanaka, 1980; Williams, 2012.
16 Barter, 1994; Pratten, 2009.
17 Bergerud, 1996, p. 54.
18 Quote from Johnston, 2000, p. 77.
19 Quote from McAulay, 1991, p. 19.

20 Johnston, 2000; Ramsay Silver, 2004.
21 Shaw, 2012.
22 Johnston, 2000, p. 89.

Chapter 4

1 Alpin, 1980; Gamble, 2006; McCarthy, 1959; Pratten, 2009.
2 Brune, 1991, 2003; Byrnes, 1989; McAulay, 1991.
3 Tracey, 2017, pp. 112–31.
4 Quote from McAulay, 1991, p. 33.
5 UNSW AWFA 235.
6 AWM MSS 0768.
7 AWM MSS 0768; Bride, (undated); Tomkins & Hughes, 1969.
8 Quote from Redlich, 2012, pp. 38–39.
9 AWM MSS 0768; Bride, undated.
10 Byrnes, 1989; Hawthorne, 2003; Sinclair, 1990.
11 Austin, 2007; David Howell, 39th Battalion Association, personal
   communication with author.
12 Quote from Austin, 2007, p. 78.
13 Johnson, 2006; Howell, personal communication.
14 Quote from Brune, 1991, p. 39.
15 Quote from Brune, 1991, p. 39.
16 Quote from Barrett, 1987, p. 207.
17 Hawthorne, 2003; James, 2008; Kienzle, 2011.
18 Keogh, 1965; McCarthy, 1959; McKernan, 2006; Powell, 2003.
19 Bergerud, 1996; McCarthy, 1959; Powell, 2003; Robinson, 1979.
20 AMW 52 1/10/1 002 ANGAU Headquarters War Diary: May to June 1942.
21 Quote from Robinson, 1979, p. 15.
22 Quote from Robinson, 1979, p. 15.

Chapter 5

1 Brune, 1991
2 Kienzle, 2011.
3 Kienzle, 2011; Oakes, 2002.
4 Kienzle, 2011, p. 105.
5 Kienzle, 2011, p. 109.
6 Quote from Brune, 1991, p. 33.
7 Quotes from Brune, 1991, pp. 33–34.
8 AWM 52 1/10/1 004.
9 AWM 52 1/10/1 004.
10 AWM 52 1/10/1 004.
11 Quote Kienzle, 2017, p. 244 and quote from Brune, 1991, p. 34.
12 Austin, 2007; Brune, 1991; Keogh, 1965; McCarthy, 1959; McKernan, 2006;
   Paull, 1958; Walker, 1957.
13 UNSW AWFA 1592.
14 Quotes from Horner, 1978, pp. 126–27.
15 AWM 55 No. 28.

16 McCarthy, 1959; Paull, 1958.

17 Bradley, 2008.

18 Bullard, 2007; Williams, 2012.

19 AWM 54 253/5/8.

20 Quote from Likeman, 2012, pp. 170–71.

21 Cameron, 2017; Likeman, 2012.

22 Vernon, 1943, p. 1.

23 AWM PR00787 (original of AWM 54 253/5/8).

24 Quote from Hooper, 1994, p. 105.

Chapter 6

1   Austin, 2007; Johnson, 2006.

2   UNSW AWFA 230.

3   UNSW AWFA 230.

4   Quote in Geddes, 2004, pp. 197–98.

5   UNSW AWFA 742.

6   AWM 52 8/2/30; Austin, 2007; McCarthy, 1959.

7   AWM PR00787.

8   Vernon, 1943, p. 2.

9   Wilkinson, undated, in Johnson, 2006, p. 79.

10 Wilkinson, undated, in Johnson, 2006, p. 79.

11 Quote from Walker, 1957, pp. 15–16.

12 AWM PR89/087.

13 UNSW AWFA 1592.

14 FitzSimons, 2004, p. 161.

15 Austin, 2007; Brune, 1991; James, 2008; McCarthy, 1959; Paull, 1958.

16 Quote from Brune, 1991, p. 34.

17 Austin, 2007; Johnson, 2006; Powell, 2003.

18 Wilkinson, undated, in Johnson, 2006, p. 62.

19 AWM PR89/087.

20 AWM 52 1/10/1 004.

21 Wilkinson, undated, in Johnson, 2006, pp. 62–63.

22 AWM PR89/087.

23 Wilkinson, undated, in Johnson, 2006, p. 63.

24 AWM PR89/087.

25 Wilkinson, undated, in Johnson, 2006, p. 63.

26 AWM 52 1/10/1 004.

27 AWM PR89/087.

28 Dawson, 2003, pp. 27–28.

29 Paull, 1958, p. 41.

30 Wilkinson, undated, in Johnson, 2006, p. 62.

31 Wilkinson, undated, in Johnson, 2006, pp. 62–63.

32 AWM PR89/087.

33 Garland, undated, in Johnson, 2006, p. 64.

Chapter 7
1 AWM 52 8/3/78.
2 Quote from Kienzle, 2011, p. 128.
3 Quote from Brune, 1991, pp. 35–36.
4 AWM 52 1/10/1 004.
5 AWM 52 1/10/1 004.
6 Garland, undated, in Johnson, 2006, p. 64.
7 Dawson, 2003, pp. 28–9.
8 Vernon, 1943, pp. 1–2.
9 Vernon, 1943, p. 2.
10 Vernon, 1943, p. 2.
11 AWM PR00787.
12 Vernon, 1943, pp. 3–4.
13 Hawthorne, 2003; James, 2008.
14 Hull, 1995.
15 Vernon, 1943, p. 4.
16 AWM PR00787.

Chapter 8
1 Grahamslaw, 1971, pp. 71–75 and 117–23; Kienzle, 2011.
2 Grahamslaw, unpublished manuscript.
3 McCarthy, 1959; McAulay, 1991; Perrin, 1990.
4 AWM 52 1/10/1 003.
5 Gamble, 2018.
6 Perrin, 1990.
7 AWM 52 1/10/1 003.
8 Benson, 1957; Hall, 1981; McCarthy, 1959.
9 Redlich, 2012; Tomkins & Hughes, 1969.
10 AWM MSS 0768.
11 Redlich, 2012.
12 AWM 3DRL/5092.
13 AWM 3DRL/5092.

Chapter 9
1 Benson, 1958, p. 20.
2 Benson, 1958, p. 20; Collie & Marutani, 2009; Williams, 2012.
3 AWM MSS 0768.
4 AWM 3DRL 15092; Thompson, 2008.
5 Quote from Sinclair, 1990, p. 138.
6 AWM MSS 0768.
7 AWM 3DRL/5092.
8 Parkinson, 1943.
9 Benson, 1957, p. 22.
10 AWM MSS 0768.
11 Benson, 1957; Byrnes, 1989; Perrin, 1999.
12 Parkinson, 1943.

13 AWM 52 1/10/1 003.

14 Quote from Perrin, 1990, p. 68.

15 AWM 52 1/10/1 003.

16 Tomkins & Hughes, 1969, p. 50.

17 Tomkins & Hughes, 1969, p. 52.

18 Redlich, 2012.

Chapter 10

1 Cooper, 2014; Ham, 2004; McCarthy, 1959; Paull, 1958.

2 Collie & Marutani, 2009.

3 Quote from Collie & Marutani, 2009, p. 63.

4 Quote from Collie & Marutani, 2009, p. 64.

5 McAulay, 1991; Williams, 2012.

6 AWM 55 Enemy Publication No. 27.

7 Benson, 1957, p. 22.

8 Benson, 1957, p. 22.

9 AWM 52 1/10/1 003.

10 Tomkins & Hughes, 1969.

11 Waiko, 1988, pp. 45–46.

12 Quotes from Collie & Marutani, 2009, p. 65.

13 Collie & Marutani, 2009; Mayo, 1975.

14 Paull, 1958, p. 42.

15 Grahamslaw, unpublished manuscript; see also Grahamslaw, 1971.

16 Perrin, 1990.

17 Austin, 2007; Benson, 1957; James, 2008; McAulay, 1991; Matthews, 2003; Paull, 1958; Powell, 2003.

18 Garland, undated, in Johnson, 2006, pp. 64–66.

19 AWM 52 8/3/78; Johnson, 2006; McAulay, 1991; McCarthy, 1959; Paull, 1958.

20 AWM 3DRL/5092.

21 Quote from Tomkins & Hughes, 1969, pp. 35–36.

22 AWM MSS 0768.

23 AWM MSS 0768.

24 Quote from Hooper, 1994, p. 105.

25 AWM MSS 0768.

26 Grahamslaw, 1971, p. 72.

27 Brune, 2003; Bride, undated; Tomkins & Hughes, 1969.

Chapter 11

1 Gailey, 2000.

2 Cooper, 2014; Gailey, 2000; Gamble, 2018; Gillison, 1962; McAulay, 1991.

3 Cooper, 2014; Gillison, 1962; McAulay, 1991.

4 Quote from Sinclair, 1990, pp. 137–38.

5 Quote from Sinclair, 1990, p. 138.

6 Collie & Marutani, 2009; Williams, 2008, 2012; Williams, 2017, in James, pp. 222–35.

7 Quote from Paull, 1958, p. 44.

8   Collie & Marutani, 2009; Johnson, 2006; Paull, 1958; Williams, 2012, 2017.
9   Drea, 2017, in James, pp. 188–205.
10 Collie & Marutani, 2009; Paull, 1958; Williams, 2008, 2012, 2017.
11 Collie & Marutani, 2009; Paull, 1958; Williams, 2008, 2012, 2017; Austin, 2007.
12 Paull, 1958, p. 26.
13 Bradley, 2012; Paull, 1958; Williams, 2012.
14 Bradley, 2012; Paull, 1958; Williams, 2012; Downs, 1999.
15 Bradley, 2012; Paull, 1958; Williams, 2012; Downs, 1999.
16 Quote from Ham, 2004, p. 9.
17 McAulay, 1991; McCarthy, 1959; Williams, 2012.
18 Grahamslaw, unpublished manuscript.
19 AWM 52 1/10/1 003.
20 Bradley, 2012; Byrnes, 1989; Downs, 1999; McCarthy, 1959; Powell, 2003.
21 AWM 52 1/10/1 003.
22 Quote from Sinclair, 1990, pp. 138–39.
23 AWM MSS 0768.
24 AWM 3DRL/5092.
25 AWM MSS 0768.
26 Parkinson, 1943.
27 AWM MSS 0768.
28 AWM MSS 0768.
29 AWM 3DRL/5092.
30 Paull, 1958, pp. 47–48.
31 Benson, 1957, p. 24.
32 AWM 3DRL/5092.
33 Redlich, 2012.

Chapter 12
1   Downs, 1999; Horner, 1978, 1996, 1998; Keogh, 1965; McCarthy, 1959; Powell, 2003; Wigmore, 1957.
2   Cooper, 2014; Gillison, 1962; Milner, 1955.
3   Cooper, 2014; Paull, 1958.
4   Cooper, 2014, p. 295.
5   Cooper, 2014, p. 295; Gamble, 2018; Gillison, 1962.
6   AWM 55 Enemy Publication No. 27.
7   McAulay, 1991.
8   Cooper, 2014; Gillison, 1962; Paull, 1958.
9   Cooper, 2014; Gillison, 1962; Paull, 1958.
10 AWM 55 Enemy Publication No. 27.
11 Cooper, 2014.
12 Cooper, 2014; Gillison, 1962.
13 Cooper, 2014; McAulay, 1991.
14 Cooper, 2014; McAulay, 1991.
15 AWM 3DRL/5092.
16 AWM MSS 0768.

Chapter 13

1   Brune, 1991; McCarthy, 1959.
2   AWM 52 1/10/1 003.
3   Grahamslaw, 1971, p. 72.
4   AWM 52 1/10/1 003.
5   Grahamslaw, unpublished manuscript; see also Grahamslaw 1971, pp. 72–73.
6   AWM 52 1/10/1 003.
7   Grahamslaw, unpublished manuscript; see also Grahamslaw 1971, pp. 72–73.
8   Quote from Sinclair, 1990, p. 138.
9   Quote from Sinclair, 1990, p. 138.
10 Quote from Byrnes, 1989, p. 206.
11 Quote from Sinclair, 1990, p. 138.
12 Byrnes, 1989.
13 Quote from Byrnes, 1989, p. 206.
14 Tomkins & Hughes, 1969.
15 McCarthy, 1959.
16 Byrnes, 1989; McCarthy, 1959; Sinclair, 1990.
17 Quote from Byrnes, 1989, p. 206.
18 Vernon, 1943, p. 7.
19 Johnston, 1944, p. 129.

Chapter 14

1   Quote from Byrnes, 1989, p. 206.
2   Quote from Sinclair, 1990, p. 139.
3   Quote from Bradley, 2012, p. 46.
4   Reading, 1946, pp. 21–22.
5   AWM 52 1/10/1 005; Bradley, 2012; Byrnes, 1989; McAulay, 1991; Sinclair, 1990; Tracey, 2017.
6   Claringbould & Ingham, 2018; Cooper, 2014.
7   Quote from Sinclair, 1990, p. 140.
8   Quote from Ramsay, 2006, p. 2.
9   Quote from Sinclair, 1990, p. 138.
10 Bradley, 2012, p. 46.
11 AWM 52 8/3/78; McCarthy, 1959; Bradley, 2012.
12 Quote from Johnson, 2006, p. 76.
13 AWM 55 Enemy Publication No. 27.
14 Williams, 2008, 2012.

Chapter 15

1   Grahamslaw, unpublished manuscript.
2   AWM 3DRL/5092.
3   Parkinson, 1943.
4   AWM 3DRL/5092.
5   Hooper, 1994, p. 114.
6   Quote from Mayo, 1975, p. 16.
7   Quote from Waiko, 1991, p. 6.

8 Vernon, 1943.
9 Quote from McDonald, 2004, pp. 276–78.

Chapter 16

1 Quote from McCarthy, 1959, p. 125.
2 UNSW AWFA 1592.
3 Dawson, 2003, p. 30.
4 Quotes from Sinclair, 1990, p. 138.
5 Dawson, 2003, p. 30.
6 UNSW AWFA 1592.
7 Dawson, 2003, pp. 30–31.
8 AWM 52 8/3/78; McCarthy, 1959.
9 Quote from Ham, 2004, p. 46.
10 Collie & Marutani, 2009, p. 70.
11 AWM 52 1/10/1 003; see also Grahamslaw unpublished manuscript.
12 AWM 52 1/10/1 003; see also Grahamslaw unpublished manuscript;
   McCarthy, 1959; Perrin, 1990; Sublett, 2000.
13 Quote from Perrin, 1990, pp. 71–72.
14 Austin, 2007; Johnson, 2006; McCarthy, 1959.
15 Wilkinson, undated, in Johnson, 2006, p. 68 and Wilkinson, undated, in
   Johnson, 2006, p. 84.
16 Cooper, 2014.
17 Grahamslaw unpublished manuscript.
18 AWM 52 1/10/1 003.
19 AWM 3DRL/5092.
20 Parkinson, 1943.
21 AWM 52 1/10/1 004.

Chapter 17

1 Austin, 2007; Sinclair, 1990.
2 Byrnes, 1989; Williams, 2012.
3 Quote from Austin, 2007, pp. 88–89.
4 AWM 52 8/3/78.
5 UNSW AWFA 1592.
6 Dawson, 2003, pp. 31–32.
7 AWM 52 8/3/78.
8 AWM 55 Enemy Publication No. 27.
9 AWM 52 8/3/78.
10 Quote from Perrin, 1990, p. 70.
11 Phelan, undated, in Johnson, 2006, p. 87.
12 Quotes from McAulay, 1991, pp. 46 and 60.
13 AWM 52 1/10/1 003.
14 Quote from Austin, 2007, p. 89.
15 Cooper, 2014.
16 Bullard, 2007; Cooper, 2014; Gillison, 1962.
17 AWM 3DRL/5092

18 Redlich, 2012.
19 AWM 3DRL/5092.
20 Parkinson, 1943.
21 AWM 52 1/10/1 002.
22 Grahamslaw unpublished manuscript.
23 AWM 52 1/10/1 003.
24 Grahamslaw unpublished manuscript.
25 Quote from Redlich, 2012, pp. 46–47.

Chapter 18
1 Quote from Bradley, 2012, p. 45.
2 Quote from Barrett, 1987, p. 161.
3 Brune, 1991; McCarthy, 1959.
4 Quote from Austin, 2007, pp. 89–90.
5 Quote from Brune, 1991, p. 54.
6 Quote from Austin, 2007, p. 90.
7 Quote from Paull, 1958, p. 54.
8 McCarthy, 1959; Paull, 1958.
9 Anderson, 2014; Brune, 1991; Johnson, 2006; McCarthy, 1959; Paull, 1958; Williams, 2012.
10 Paull, 1958, p. 54.
11 UNSW AWFA 235.
12 Anderson, 2014; Brune, 1991; Johnson, 2006; McCarthy, 1959; Paull, 1958.
13 Anderson, 2014.
14 Quote from Austin, 2007, pp. 90–91.
15 Redlich, 2012.
16 Redlich, 2012, p. 47.
17 Redlich, 2012, p. 48.

Chapter 19
1 AWM 52 8/3/78.
2 UNSW AWFA 235.
3 Anderson, 2014; Paull, 1958; Williams, 2012.
4 McCarthy, 1959; Paull, 1958.
5 Quote from Brune, 1991.
6 McCarthy, 1959; Paull, 1958.
7 Quote from Johnson, 2006, p. 76.
8 Quote from Brune, 1991, p. 42.
9 Quote from Coulthart, 2010.
10 Coulthart, 2010; McCarthy, 1959; Paull, 1958.
11 Quotes from Johnson, 2006, p. 76.
12 Johnson, 2006; McCarthy, 1959; Paull, 1958; Williams, 2012.
13 AWM 52 8/3/78.
14 Brune, 1991; McCarthy, 1959; Paull, 1958.
15 Dawson, 2003, p. 32.
16 Austin, 2007; Johnson, 2006; McCarthy, 1959.

17 Quote from Johnson, 2006, p. 77.
18 Quote from Byrnes, 1989, p. 207.
19 Quote from Byrnes, 1989, p. 207.
20 Dawson, 2003, pp. 32–33.
21 UNSW AWFA 235.
22 Quotes from McCarthy, 1959, p. 127.
23 Dawson, 2003, p. 32–33.
24 Dawson, 2003, p. 33.
25 Quote from Byrnes, 1989, p. 207.
26 Quote from Paull, 1958, p. 55.
27 Quote from Byrnes, 1989, p. 207.
28 Quote from Brune, 1991, p. 42.
29 UNSW AWFA 574 .
30 Dawson, 2003, p. 33.
31 Dawson, 2003, p. 33.
32 Quote from Brune, 1991, p. 42.
33 Quote from Austin, 2007, p. 95.
34 Quote from Collie & Marutani, 2006, p. 69.
35 Quote from Austin, 2007, p. 92.
36 Wilkinson, undated, in Johnson, 2006, p. 84.
37 AWM 52 1/10/1 003.
38 AWM 52 1/10/1 003.
39 Grahamslaw unpublished manuscript.
40 Collie & Marutani, 2006; Coulthart, 2010; Gridneff, 2010.

Chapter 20
1 McCarthy, 1959.
2 Quote from Austin, 2007, pp. 93–95.
3 McCarthy, 1959.
4 AWM 52 1/10/1 003.
5 AWM 52 1/10/1 003; Grahamslaw unpublished manuscript.
6 Redlich, 2012, p. 48.
7 Redlich, 2012, p. 101
8 Redlich, 2012, p. 101
9 McAulay, 1991; National Archives Australia (NAA), J1889, BL43895/13.
10 Bullard, 2008; Hayashi & Coox, 1959; McAulay, 1991; Tanaka, 1980; Zobel, 2017, in James, pp. 92–111.
11 Quote from Tanaka, 1980, p. 15.
12 Anderson, 2018; Brune, 2003; Bullard, 2008; Hayashi & Coox, 1959; Henderson, 1992; McAulay, 1991; Miller, 1955; Tanaka, 1980; Zobel, 2017.
13 Bergerud, 1996, pp. 81–82.
14 Anderson, 2018; Bergerud, 1996; Borneman, 2016; Brune, 2003; Keogh, 1965; McAulay, 1991; Henderson, 1992; Tanaka, 1980; Williams, 2008, 2012.
15 Budden, 1987; Harwood, 1979; Horner, 1978.
16 Quote from Horner, 1978, p. 104.
17 Quote from Horner, 1978, p. 102.

18 Robertson, 1981, p. 117.
19 Quote from Horner, 1996, p. 133.

Chapter 21

1   Quote from Brune, 1991, p. 33.
2   AWM 52 1/10/1 003.
3   Reading, 1946, p. 68.
4   Vernon, 1943, p. 4.
5   Vernon, 1943, pp. 4–5.
6   Vernon, 1943, p. 5.
7   AWM PR00787.
8   AWM PR00787.
9   Quote from Paull, 1958, p. 44.
10 Vernon, 1943, p. 6.
11 Vernon, 1943, p. 8.
12 Walker, 1957, p. 18.
13 Vernon, 1943, p. 8.
14 Quote from Brune, 1991, p. 43.

Chapter 22

1   Quote from Austin, 2007, p. 95.
2   Austin, 2007; Brune, 1991, 2003; McCarthy, 1959.
3   Dawson, 2003, p. 34.
4   Quote from Austin, 2007, pp. 95–96.
5   Quote from Paull, 1958, p. 57.
6   Quote from Bradley, 2012, p. 47.
7   Quote from Austin, 2007, pp. 95–96.
8   Austin, 2007; Brune, 1991, 2003; McCarthy, 1959; Williams, 2012.
9   Quote from McDonald, 2004, pp. 278–80.

Chapter 23

1   McCarthy, 1959; Williams, 2012.
2   Vernon, 1943, p. 9.
3   Byrnes, 1989; McCarthy, 1959.
4   Garland, undated, in Johnson, 2006, p. 66.
5   AWM PR89/087.
6   Dawson, 2003, p. 34.
7   Vernon, 1943, p. 9.
8   Quote from Anderson, 2014, p. 34.
9   McAulay, 1991.
10 Quote from Austin, 2007, p. 96.
11 Quote from Brune, 1991, p. 45.
12 UNSW AWFA 1407.
13 Quote from Brune, 1991, pp. 45–47.
14 Garland, undated, in Johnson, 2006, p. 66.
15 AWM PR89/087.

16 Dawson, 2003, p. 34.
17 McCarthy, 1959.
18 Quote from Ham, 2004, p. 49.
19 AWM 52 1/10/1 003; Grahamslaw unpublished manuscript.
20 Grahamslaw unpublished manuscript.

Chapter 24
1 AWM PR89/087.
2 AWM PR89/087.
3 UNSW AWFA 704.
4 UNSW AWFA 1592.
5 Dawson, 2003, p. 34.
6 Quote from Collie & Marutani, 2009, p. 73.
7 Collie & Marutani, 2009.
8 AWM 55 Current Translation 3/2 No. 266.
9 UNSW AWFA 458.
10 Dawson, 2003, pp. 34–35.
11 Sinclair, 1990.
12 Quote from Johnson, 2006, p. 77.
13 UNSW AWFA 574.
14 Vernon, 1943, pp. 9–10.
15 Wilkinson, undated, in Johnson, 2006, p. 69.
16 Byrnes, 1989; McCarthy, 1959.
17 Wilkinson, undated, in Johnson, 2006, p. 69.
18 Vernon, 1943, p. 10.
19 Quote from Perrin, 1990, pp. 72–73.
20 Perrin, 1990.

Chapter 25
1 McCarthy, 1959.
2 Quote from Austin, 2007, p. 98.
3 Vernon, 1943, p. 10.
4 UNSW AWFA 458.
5 Garland, undated, in Johnson, 2006, p. 67.
6 UNSW AWFA 1592.
7 Wilkinson, undated, in Johnson, 2006, p. 69.
8 Quote from Austin, 2007, p. 98.
9 Vernon, 1943, pp. 10–11.
10 AWM 52 1/10/1 003
11 Quotes from McCarthy, 1959, p. 129.
12 McCarthy, 1959; Paull, 1958.
13 Vernon, 1943, p. 11.
14 Vernon, 1943, p. 13.
15 Dawson, 2003, p. 35.
16 Byrnes, 1989; Sinclair, 1990.

17 AWM 52 8/3/78.
18 Quote from Austin, 2007, p. 98.
19 Wilkinson, undated, in Johnson, 2006, p. 69.
20 McCarthy, 1959, p. 130.
21 AWM 55 Current Translation 3/2 No. 87.
22 AWM ATIS 3 August 1942.
23 Anderson, 2014; Williams, 2012.
24 AWM 54 577/7/26 Notebook no. 32.
25 AWM 54 577/7/26 Notebook no. 32.

Chapter 26
1 Quotes from Paull, 1958, p. 65.
2 AWM 52 1/10/1 003.
3 Quote from Brune, 1991, p. 49.
4 AWM 52 1/10/1 010.
5 Wilkinson, undated, in Johnson, 2006, pp. 68–69.
6 AWM PR89/087.
7 AWM PR89/087.
8 AWM PR89/087.
9 AWM 52 8/3/78.
10 Quote from Austin, 2007, p. 99.
11 Quote from Austin, 2007, p. 100.
12 AWM 52 1/10/1 004.
13 Quote from Kienzle, 2011, p. 135.
14 AWM 52 1/10/1 003.
15 Quote from Robinson, 1979, p. 20.
16 McAulay, 1991.
17 AWM 55 No. 28 Intelligence Reports Issued by Yazawa Butai HQ; Bullard, 2008; Collie & Marutani, 2009; McAulay, 1991; Zobel, 2017.
18 McAulay, 1991; McCarthy, 1959.

Chapter 27
1 Cooper, 2014; Hooper, 1994; McAulay, 1991; McCarthy, 1959.
2 Cooper, 2014; Hooper, 1994; McAulay, 1991; McCarthy, 1959; Byrnes, 1989.
3 AWM 55 Enemy Publication No. 27; McAulay, 1991.
4 McAulay, 1991; McCarthy, 1959.
5 Quote from Bullard, 2007, p. 128.
6 Vernon, 1943, pp. 12–13.
7 Vernon, 1943, p. 15.
8 Grahamslaw, 1971, p. 75.
9 Grahamslaw, 1971, pp. 75 and 117.
10 Grahamslaw, 1971, p. 117.

Chapter 28
1 Johnson, 2006.
2 AWM 52 8/3/78.

3 Quote from Austin, 2007, p. 101.
4 AWM 52 8/3/78.
5 UNSW AWFA 1287.
6 McCarthy, 1959; McLeod, 2019; Walker, 1957.
7 Wilkinson, undated, in Johnson, 2006, pp. 69–70.
8 AWM 52 1/10/1 010.
9 Vernon, 1943, p. 13.
10 AWM 52 8/3/78.
11 AWM PR89/087.
12 Quote from McAulay, 1991, pp. 61–62.
13 McAulay, 1991, pp. 58, 61–62 and 64.
14 Phelan, undated, in Johnson, 2006, p. 88.
15 UNSW AWFA 509.
16 UNSW AWFA 509.
17 AWM 52 1/10/1 004.
18 AWM 52 1/10/1 004.
19 AWM 52 1/10/1 010.
20 AWM 55 Current Translation 3/2 No. 218.
21 Quote from Brune, 1991, p. 52.
22 AWM 52 8/3/78.
23 Geddes, 2004, p. 189.
24 AWM 52 8/3/78.
25 Vernon, 1943, p.14.

Chapter 29

1 AWM 52 8/3/78.
2 AWM 55 Current Translation 3/2 No. 266.
3 AWM 52 8/3/78; Johnson, 2006.
4 AWM 52 8/3/78; Johnson, 2006.
5 AWM 52 8/3/78.
6 UNSW AWFA 230.
7 Quotes Paull, 1958, p. 68.
8 AWM 52 1/10/1 004.
9 AWM 52 8/3/78.
10 AWM 52 8/3/78.
11 AWM 52 8/3/78.
12 AWM 52 8/3/78.
13 AWM 52 1/10/1 004.
14 Kienzle, 2011.
15 UNSW AWFA 1234.
16 Cooper, 2014; Gamble, 2018; Gillison, 1962; McAulay, 1991.
17 AWM 55 Current Translation 3/2 No. 87.
18 Johnston, 1944, pp. 133–34.

Chapter 30

1   AWM 52 8/3/78.
2   Quote from Austin, 2007, p. 101.
3   AWM PR89/087.
4   Brune, 1991, 2003; Horner, 1978; Johnson, 2006.
5   AWM 52 8/3/78; Austin, 2007; Johnson, 2006; McCarthy, 1959.
6   UNSW AWFA 1592.
7   Kienzle, 2011.
8   AWM 52 1/10/1 004.
9   James, 2008.
10 UNSW AWFA 574.
11 AWM 52 8/3/78.
12 UNSW AWFA 509.
13 UNSW AWFA 509.
14 UNSW AWFA 193.
15 AWM 3DRL/5092; Bride, undated; Redlich, 2012.
16 McLeod, 2019; Vernon, 1943; Walker, 1957.
17 Vernon, 1943, pp. 14–15.
18 Quote from Austin, 2007, p. 125.
19 Grahamslaw unpublished manuscript.
20 Kienzle, 2011.
21 Grahamslaw, 1971, p. 117.
22 Grahamslaw, 1971.

Chapter 31

1   AWM 52 8/3/78; Anderson, 2014; Johnson, 2006.
2   McCarthy, 1959.
3   Quote from Austin, 2007, p. 103.
4   AWM 52 8/3/78; Johnson, 2006.
5   AWM 52 8/3/78; Johnson, 2006.
6   AWM 52 8/3/78; Johnson, 2006.
7   AWM 52 8/3/78; Johnson, 2006.
8   AWM 52 8/3/78.
9   AWM 52 1/10/1 003.
10 AWM 52 1/10/1 004.
11 Brune, 1991, 2003; McCarthy, 1959.
12 Quote from McCarthy, 1959, p. 140.
13 AWM 52 8/3/78.
14 Brune, 1991, 2003; McCarthy, 1959.
15 Brune, 1991, 2003; McCarthy, 1959.
16 Reading, 1946, p. 97.
17 Quote from Bergerud, 1996, pp. 342–43.
18 Hooper, 1994, p. 117.

Chapter 32

1 AWM 52 8/3/78.
2 Austin, 2007; Keogh, 1965; McCarthy, 1959; Williams, 2012, 2017.
3 Quote from Austin, 2007, p. 99.
4 McAulay, 1991.
5 Austin, 2007; Brune, 1991; Johnson, 2006; Keogh, 1965; McCarthy, 1959; Paull, 1958; Williams, 2012, 2017.
6 Quote from Brune, 1991, p. 59.
7 Quote from Brune, 1991, p. 57.
8 Austin, 2007; Johnson, 2006; Keogh, 1965; McCarthy, 1959; Paull, 1958; Williams, 2012, 2017.
9 Vernon, 1943, pp. 15–16.
10 Vernon, 1943, p. 16.
11 AWM 52 1/10/1 004.
12 McAulay, 1991; McCarthy, 1959; Milner, 1955.
13 Quote from Bullard, 2007, p. 132.
14 Bergerud, 1996; Frank, 1990; Friedman, 2007; Philippart, 2004; Smith, 2000.
15 Bergerud, 1996; Frank, 1990; Friedman, 2007; Philippart, 2004; Smith, 2000.

Chapter 33

1 AWM 52 8/3/78; AWM 52 1/10/1 003; Brune, 1991; Johnson, 2006; McCarthy, 1959.
2 Quote from Austin, 2007, p. 103.
3 AWM 52 8/3/78.
4 Johnson, 2006.
5 Paull, 1958, p. 70.
6 Quote from Brune, 1991, pp. 52–53.
7 AWM 52 1/10/1 004.
8 Vernon, 1943, p. 16.
9 Vernon, 1943, p. 16.
10 Anderson, 2014; Austin, 2007; Johnson, 2006; McCarthy, 1959; McAulay, 1991.
11 McAulay, 1991.
12 Paull, 1958.
13 AWM 55 Current Translation 3/2 No. 266.
14 Quote from Redlich, 2012, p. 52.
15 Redlich, 2012.

Chapter 34

1 Austin, 2007; Johnson, 2006; McCarthy, 1959.
2 Quote from Johnson, 2006, pp. 93–94.
3 Quote from Austin, 2007, pp. 103–104.
4 Quote from Austin, 2007, p. 104.
5 Wilkinson, undated, in Johnson, 2006, p. 95.
6 UNSW AWFA 1805.
7 Quote from Austin, 2007, pp. 105–106.
8 Johnson, 2006; McCarthy, 1959; Williams, 2012.

9   Quote from Paull, 1958, p. 73.

10 Johnson, 2006; McCarthy, 1959; Paull, 1958.

11 UNSW AWFA 1407.

12 Quote from Johnson, 2006, p. 95.

13 Wilkinson, undated, in Johnson, 2006, p. 95.

14 AWM 52 8/3/78.

15 Phelan, undated, in Johnson, 2006, p. 95.

16 Johnson, 2006; McCarthy, 1959.

17 Quote from Austin, 2007, pp. 107–108.

18 Austin, 2007.

Chapter 35

1   UNSW AWFA 588.

2   McAulay, 1991.

3   UNSW AWFA 588.

4   AWM 52 8/3/78; Johnson, 2006.

5   UNSW AWFA 230.

6   Quote from Geddes, 2004, p. 200.

7   Phelan, undated, in Johnson, 2006, p. 100.

8   Quote from Austin, 2007, p. 107; see also McAulay, 1991, p. 76.

9   Quote from Geddes, 2004, p. 201.

10 Johnson, 2006.

Chapter 36

1   AWM 52 8/3/78.

2   Austin, 2007; Johnson, 2006; McAulay, 1991; McCarthy, 1959.

3   AWM 52 8/3/78.

4   Paull, 1958, p. 72.

5   Quote from McAulay, 1991, p. 75.

6   AWM 52 8/3/78.

7   AWM 52 8/3/78.

8   McCarthy, 1959, p. 134.

9   McCarthy, 1959, p. 134.

10 Johnson, 2006; McCarthy, 1959.

11 UNSW AWFA 742.

12 Quote from Brune, 1991, p. 61.

13 UNSW AWFA 1324.

14 AWM 52 8/3/78.

15 AWM 55 Current Translation 3/2 No. 218.

16 AWM 55 Current Translation 3/2 No. 266.

17 Anderson, 204; Johnson, 2006; McCarthy, 1959.

18 UNSW AWFA 1287.

19 AWM 52 8/3/78.

20 McLeod, 2019; Walker, 1957.

21 AWM 52 1/10/1 004.

22 Quote from Kienzle, 2011, p. 143.

Chapter 37

1 AWM 52 8/3/78.
2 Austin, 2007.
3 UNSW AWFA 1407.
4 Austin, 2007.
5 Austin, 2007, p. 108.
6 Johnson, 2006.
7 Quote from Austin, 2007, p. 108
8 Austin, 2007, p. 109.
9 AWM 52 8/3/78; Johnson, 2006; McCarthy, 1959.
10 AWM 52 8/3/78; Johnson, 2006; McCarthy, 1959; Byrnes, 1989; Sinclair, 1990.
11 Quote from Austin, 2007, pp. 109–10.
12 Austin, 2007, p. 109.
13 Austin, 2007; Johnson, 2006; McCarthy, 1959.

Chapter 38

1 Quote from Austin, 2007, p. 110.
2 AWM 52 8/3/78; Austin, 2007; Johnson, 2006; McCarthy, 1959.
3 UNSW AWFA 1238.
4 Quote from Austin, 2007, p. 110.
5 AWM 52 8/3/78; Austin, 2007; Johnson, 2006.
6 Quote from Austin, 2007, p. 111.
7 Austin, 2007; Johnson, 2006; McCarthy, 1959.
8 UNSW AWFA 1238.
9 Quote from Austin, 2007, p. 112.
10 UNSW AWFA 588.
11 UNSW AWFA 230.
12 AWM 55 Current Translation 3/2 No. 218.
13 Austin, 2007; Johnson, 2006; McCarthy, 1959.
14 Quote from Austin, 2007, p. 111.
15 AWM 52 8/3/78; Austin, 2007; Johnson, 2006.
16 Austin, 2007; Johnson, 2006.
17 McCarthy, 1959, p. 135.
18 AWM 55 Current Translation 3/2 No. 218.
19 AWM 55 Current Translation 3/2 No. 218.
20 AWM 52 8/3/78.
21 McAulay, 1991.
22 Quote from Waiko, 1991, p. 8.
23 Quote from Bergerud, 1996, p. 109.
24 Bergerud, 1996.
25 McAulay, 1991.
26 AWM 3DRL/5092.
27 AWM 52 1/10/1 004.
28 Vernon, 1943, p. 17.

Chapter 39

1 Quote from Austin, 2007, p. 115.
2 AWM 52 8/3/78; Johnson, 2006.
3 Austin, 2007; Johnson, 2006.
4 Quote from Geddes, 2004, p. 202
5 Quote from Austin, 2007, p. 112.
6 Austin, 2007; Johnson, 2006.
7 Quotes from Austin, 2007, p. 112.
8 Quote from Austin, 2007, p. 112.
9 AWM 55 Current Translation 3/2 No. 87.
10 McAulay, 1991.
11 McAulay, 1991, p. 84.
12 AWM 55 Current Translation 3/2 No. 218.
13 AWM 55 Current Translation 3/2 No. 218.
14 Quote from Austin, 2007, p. 113.
15 Paull, 1958, p. 77.
16 Austin, 2007; Johnson, 2006.
17 Quotes from Austin, 2007, p. 113.
18 AWM 55 Current Translation 3/2 No. 218.
19 Anderson, 2011.
20 Johnson, 2006.
21 McCarthy, 1959, p. 136.
22 Quote from Austin, 2007, p. 113.
23 UNSW AWFA 588.
24 UNSW AWFA 588.
25 Quote from Austin, 2007, p. 114.
26 AWM 52 8/3/78.
27 AWM 52 1/10/1 004.
28 Vernon, 1943, pp. 17–18.
29 Vernon, 1943, p. 18.

Chapter 40

1 AWM 52 8/3/78.
2 Quote from Austin, 2007, pp. 117–18.
3 UNSW AWFA 230.
4 Quote from Paull, 1958, p. 81.
5 Quote from Austin, 2007, pp. 114–15.
6 Quote from Austin, 2007, p.115.
7 UNSW AWFA 1238.
8 Quotes from Austin, 2007, p. 115.
9 AWM 55 Current Translation 3/2 No. 218.
10 Austin, 2007; Johnson, 2006.
11 UNSW AWFA 1407.
12 Quote from Smith, 2000, p. 27.
13 Quote from Bullard, 2007, p. 151.
14 Parkinson, 1943.

15 AWM 3DRL/5092.
16 Quote from Horner, 1998, pp. 134–35.

Chapter 41

1   UNSW AWFA 588.
2   UNSW AWFA 588.
3   UNSW AWFA 588.
4   Quote from Austin, 2007, p. 119; see also Geddes, 2004, p. 203.
5   Quote from Austin, 2007, pp. 119–20.
6   McAulay, 1991; McCarthy, 1959.
7   Quote from Austin, 2007, pp. 120–21.
8   Quote from Austin, 2007, p. 121.
9   AWM 52 8/3/78; Johnson, 2006; McCarthy, 1959.
10 AWM52 1/10/1 010.
11 Rowell, 1974, p. 111.

Chapter 42

1   AWM MSS 0768.
2   AWM MSS 0768.
3   Benson, 1957; Hooper, 1994.
4   AWM MSS 0768.
5   AWM MSS 0768.
6   Hooper, 1994; McAulay, 1991.
7   Benson, 1957, p. 34.
8   AWM MSS 0768; Benson, 1957.
9   Benson, 1957, p. 35.
10 Benson, 1957, p. 36.
11 Benson, 1957, p. 37.
12 Benson, 1957.
13 Benson, 1957, pp. 38–39.
14 Benson, 1957, pp. 42–43.
15 AWM MSS 0768; Benson, 1957.

Chapter 43

1   AWM 52 1/10/1 005; Hall, 1981.
2   AWM 52 1/10/1 005.
3   Quote from Redlich, 2012, p. 80.
4   Hall, 1981.
5   Hall, 1981; NAA, J1889, BL43895/13.
6   NAA, J1889, BL43895/13; Hall, 1981; James, 2008; Johnson, 2006.
7   NAA, J1889, BL43895/13; Grahamslaw, 1971; Hall, 1981.
8   Hall, p. 98.
9   NAA, J1889, BL43895/13; Grahamslaw, 1971; Hall, 1981; Matthews, 2003; Vernon, 1943.
10 NAA, J1889, BL43895/13; Grahamslaw, 1971; Hall, 1981.
11 Quote from Hill, 1981, p. 96.

12 NAA, J1889, BL43895/13; Hall, 1981.

Chapter 44

1 Quote from Redlich, 2012, p. 52.
2 Redlich, 2012; Tomkins & Hughes, 1969.
3 Redlich, 2012; Tomkins & Hughes, 1969.
4 Redlich, 2012; Tomkins & Hughes, 1969; NAA, J1889, BL43895/13; Bride, undated; Redlich, 2012.
5 Tomkins & Hughes, 1969; NAA, J1889, BL43895/13; Bride, undated; Redlich, 2012.
6 NAA, J1889, BL43895/13.
7 NAA, J1889, BL43895/13.
8 Quote from Redlich, 2012, p. 53.
9 Redlich, 2012.
10 Quote from Gamble, 2018, p. 294.

Chapter 45

1 AWM 55 Current Translation 3/2 No. 218.
2 AWM 55 Current Translation 3/2 No. 266.
3 AWM52 1/10/1 004.
4 Quote from Kienzle, 2011, p. 143.
5 AWM 52 8/3/78; Byrnes, 1989; Johnson, 2006.
6 Ibid; Austin, 2007; McCarthy, 1959; Sinclair, 1990.
7 AWM 52 8/3/78.
8 Quote from Austin, 2007, pp. 121–22.
9 Austin, 2007, p. 122.
10 Quote from Paull, 1958, p. 82.
11 Quote from Austin, 2007, p. 122.
12 Austin, 2007, p. 123.
13 Austin, 2007, p. 122.
14 AWM52 1/10/1 003.
15 Johnston 1944, p. 135.
16 UNSW AWFA 588.
17 AWM 52 8/3/78; Brune, 2007; Horner, 1978; Pratten, 2009.
18 Keogh, 1965, p. 182.
19 Quote from Kienzle, 2011, p. 144.

Epilogue

1 Quote from Wakeling, 2018, p. 69.
2 Wakeling, 2018, p. 72.
3 James, 2008; Russell, 1958; Sissons, 2006; Wakeling, 2018.
4 Sissons, 2006.
5 Quote from James, 2008, p. 411.
6 AWM 3DRL/5092.
7 Quote from James, 2008, p. 413.
8 James, 2008, p. 412.

9   James, 2008.
10 AWM MSS 0768.
11 Benson, 1957, p. 189.
12 Byrnes, 1989.
13 James, 2008.
14 Grahamslaw, unpublished manuscript.
15 Grahamslaw, unpublished manuscript.
16 Grahamslaw, unpublished manuscript.
17 NAA B2455—V50190.

Index

Note: Ranks and titles are ignored in filing.
An 'n' after a page number indicates a reference to a footnote.

David W. Cameron is a Canberra-based author. He graduated from the University of Sydney in Prehistoric Archaeology (First Class Honours) in 1989 and completed his PhD in Palaeoanthropology at the School of Archaeology, Australian National University, in 1995. He has written several books on primate evolutionary biology and Australian military history as well as over 70 internationally peer-reviewed papers for various academic journals and book chapters. He is a former Australian Research Council academic at the Australian National University's School of Archaeology and the University of Sydney's Department of Anatomy and Histology. David has conducted numerous research and fieldwork projects in Europe, the United States, the Middle East and Asia.